LEARNING TO LIVE IN THE KNOWLEDGE SOCIETY

T0180655

IFIP – The International Federation for Information Processing

IFIP was founded in 1960 under the auspices of UNESCO, following the First World Computer Congress held in Paris the previous year. An umbrella organization for societies working in information processing, IFIP's aim is two-fold: to support information processing within its member countries and to encourage technology transfer to developing nations. As its mission statement clearly states,

> *IFIP's mission is to be the leading, truly international, apolitical organization which encourages and assists in the development, exploitation and application of information technology for the benefit of all people.*

IFIP is a non-profitmaking organization, run almost solely by 2500 volunteers. It operates through a number of technical committees, which organize events and publications. IFIP's events range from an international congress to local seminars, but the most important are:

• The IFIP World Computer Congress, held every second year;
• Open conferences;
• Working conferences.

The flagship event is the IFIP World Computer Congress, at which both invited and contributed papers are presented. Contributed papers are rigorously refereed and the rejection rate is high.

As with the Congress, participation in the open conferences is open to all and papers may be invited or submitted. Again, submitted papers are stringently refereed.

The working conferences are structured differently. They are usually run by a working group and attendance is small and by invitation only. Their purpose is to create an atmosphere conducive to innovation and development. Refereeing is less rigorous and papers are subjected to extensive group discussion.

Publications arising from IFIP events vary. The papers presented at the IFIP World Computer Congress and at open conferences are published as conference proceedings, while the results of the working conferences are often published as collections of selected and edited papers.

Any national society whose primary activity is in information may apply to become a full member of IFIP, although full membership is restricted to one society per country. Full members are entitled to vote at the annual General Assembly, National societies preferring a less committed involvement may apply for associate or corresponding membership. Associate members enjoy the same benefits as full members, but without voting rights. Corresponding members are not represented in IFIP bodies. Affiliated membership is open to non-national societies, and individual and honorary membership schemes are also offered.

LEARNING TO LIVE IN THE KNOWLEDGE SOCIETY

IFIP 20th World Computer Congress,
IFIP TC 3 ED-L2L Conference
September 7-10, 2008, Milano, Italy

Edited by

Michael Kendall
East Midlands Broadband Community
United Kingdom

Brian Samways
Fellow of British Computer Society
United Kingdom

 Springer

Learning to live in the Knowledge Society
Edited by Michael Kendall and Brian Samways

p. cm. (IFIP International Federation for Information Processing, a Springer Series in Computer Science)

ISSN: 1571-5736 / 1861-2288 (Internet)

ISBN: 978-1-4419-3525-0   eISBN: 978-0-387-09729-9

Printed on acid-free paper

9 8 7 6 5 4 3 2 1

springer.com

IFIP 2008 World Computer Congress (WCC'08)

Message from the Chairs

Every two years, the International Federation for Information Processing hosts a major event which showcases the scientific endeavours of its over one hundred Technical Committees and Working Groups. 2008 sees the 20th World Computer Congress (WCC 2008) take place for the first time in Italy, in Milan from 7-10 September 2008, at the MIC - Milano Convention Centre. The Congress is hosted by the Italian Computer Society, AICA, under the chairmanship of Giulio Occhini.

The Congress runs as a federation of co-located conferences offered by the different IFIP bodies, under the chairmanship of the scientific chair, Judith Bishop. For this Congress, we have a larger than usual number of thirteen conferences, ranging from Theoretical Computer Science, to Open Source Systems, to Entertainment Computing. Some of these are established conferences that run each year and some represent new, breaking areas of computing. Each conference had a call for papers, an International Programme Committee of experts and a thorough peer reviewed process. The Congress received 661 papers for the thirteen conferences, and selected 375 from those representing an acceptance rate of 56% (averaged over all conferences).

An innovative feature of WCC 2008 is the setting aside of two hours each day for cross-sessions relating to the integration of business and research, featuring the use of IT in Italian industry, sport, fashion and so on. This part is organized by Ivo De Lotto. The Congress will be opened by representatives from government bodies and Societies associated with IT in Italy.

This volume is one of fourteen volumes associated with the scientific conferences and the industry sessions. Each covers a specific topic and separately or together they form a valuable record of the state of computing research in the world in 2008. Each volume was prepared for publication in the Springer IFIP Series by the conference's volume editors. The overall Chair for all the volumes published for the Congress is John Impagliazzo.

For full details on the Congress, refer to the webpage http://www.wcc2008.org.

Judith Bishop, South Africa, Co-Chair, International Program Committee
Ivo De Lotto, Italy, Co-Chair, International Program Committee
Giulio Occhini, Italy, Chair, Organizing Committee
John Impagliazzo, United States, Publications Chair

WCC 2008 Scientific Conferences

TC12	AI	Artificial Intelligence 2008
TC10	BICC	Biologically Inspired Cooperative Computing
WG 5.4	CAI	Computer-Aided Innovation (Topical Session)
WG 10.2	DIPES	Distributed and Parallel Embedded Systems
TC14	ECS	Entertainment Computing Symposium
TC3	ED_L2L	Learning to Live in the Knowledge Society
WG 9.7 TC3	HCE3	History of Computing and Education 3
TC13	HCI	Human Computer Interaction
TC8	ISREP	Information Systems Research, Education and Practice
WG 12.6	KMIA	Knowledge Management in Action
TC2 WG 2.13	OSS	Open Source Systems
TC11	IFIP SEC	Information Security Conference
TC1	TCS	Theoretical Computer Science

IFIP
- is the leading multinational, apolitical organization in Information and Communications Technologies and Sciences
- is recognized by United Nations and other world bodies
- represents IT Societies from 56 countries or regions, covering all 5 continents with a total membership of over half a million
- links more than 3500 scientists from Academia and Industry, organized in more than 101 Working Groups reporting to 13 Technical Committees
- sponsors 100 conferences yearly providing unparalleled coverage from theoretical informatics to the relationship between informatics and society including hardware and software technologies, and networked information systems

Details of the IFIP Technical Committees and Working Groups can be found on the website at http://www.ifip.org.

IFIP and TC3

IFIP is a non-governmental, non-profit umbrella organisation for national societies in the field of information processing. It was established in 1960 under the auspices of UNESCO as the aftermath of the first World Computer Congress held in Paris in 1959. IFIP's mission is to be the leading, truly international, a political organisation which encourages and assists in the development, exploitation and application of information technology (IT) for the benefit of all people.

TC3 is the Technical Committee for ICT and Education, and its aims are:
1. To provide an international forum for educators to discuss research and practice in
   a. teaching informatics
   b. educational uses of communication and information technologies (ICT)
2. To establish models for informatics curricula, training programs, and teaching methodologies
3. To consider the relationship of informatics in other curriculum areas
4. To promote the ongoing education of ICT professionals and those in the workforce whose employment involves the use of information and communication technologies
5. To examine the impact of information and communication technologies on the whole educational environment
   a. teaching and learning
   b. administration and management of the educational enterprise
   c. local, national and regional policy-making and collaboration.

The work of TC3 is carried out through its Working Groups (WG) and Special Interest Groups (SIG).
WG 3.1 Informatics and ICT in Secondary Education
WG 3.2 Informatics and ICT in Higher Education
WG 3.3 Research on Education Applications of Information Technologies
WG 3.4 IT Professional and Vocational Education in Information Technology
WG 3.5 Informatics in Elementary Education
WG 3.6 Distance Learning
WG 3.7 Information Technology in Educational Management
SIG 3.8 Lifelong Learning
SIG 3.9 Digital Literacy

To find out more about the work and people of the TC3 community you find information and links on the web site at http://www.ifip-tc3.net/

Jan Wibe
Chair
Technical Committee 3

Foreword

ED-L2L, Learning to Live in the Knowledge Society, is one of the co-located conferences of the 20th World Computer Congress (WCC2008). The event is organized under the auspices of IFIP (International Federation for Information Processing) and is to be held in Milan from 7th to 10th September 2008.

ED-L2L is devoted to themes related to ICT for education in the knowledge society. It provides an international forum for professionals from all continents to discuss research and practice in ICT and education. The event brings together educators, researchers, policy makers, curriculum designers, teacher educators, members of academia, teachers and content producers.

ED-L2L is organised by the IFIP Technical Committee 3, Education, with the support of the Institute for Educational Technology, part of the National Research Council of Italy. The Institute is devoted to the study of educational innovation brought about through the use of ICT.

Submissions to ED-L2L are published in this conference book. The published papers are devoted to the published conference themes:

- Developing digital literacy for the knowledge society: information problem solving, creating, capturing and transferring knowledge, commitment to lifelong learning
- Teaching and learning in the knowledge society, playful and fun learning at home and in the school
- New models, processes and systems for formal and informal learning environments and organisations
- Developing a collective intelligence, learning together and sharing knowledge
- ICT issues in education - ethics, equality, inclusion and parental role
- Educating ICT professionals for the global knowledge society
- Managing the transition to the knowledge society

The published papers clearly show the major interests of our community and conference are related to innovative learning environments for teaching and learning in the knowledge society and related issues with the majority of papers refer to these themes. Digital literacy and themes related to digital inclusion are included as strong conference themes.

To ensure contributions are of the highest quality, all conference presentations have been selected following a refereeing process carried out by an international panel of 32 members, the International Programme Committee and Editors, all of whom belong to IFIP TC3 working groups. All papers have been peer reviewed by at least 3 international experts in Education and ICT.

The International Programme Committee selected four different formats for the proceedings: eight-page papers, four-page papers, four page workshop proposals and poster summaries. The high quality of the contributions, along with the importance of the themes addressed, ensures that the conference will further understanding of the nature of education processes and systems required for the transition to the knowledge society.

Vittorio Midoro
Chair
International Programme Committee

International Programme Committee ED-L2L

Vittorio Midoro (IT) IPC Chair
Michael Kendall (UK) Editor
Brian Samways (UK) Co-Editor
Jan Wibe (NO) TC3 Chair
Rosa Maria Bottino (IT)
Sindre Røsvik (NO)
Francesca Puddu (IT)

IPC Reviewers

Bernard Cornu (FR)
Ernesto Cuadros-Vargas (PE)
Monique Grandbastien (FR)
Ivan Kalas (SL)
Willis King (US)
Carlos Delgado Kloos (ES)
Anton Knierzinger (AT)
Jari Koivisto (FN)
John Impagliazzo (US)
Zdena Lustigova (CZ)
Raymond Morel (CH)
Wolfgang Muller (DE)
Bob Munro (UK)
Eleni Ntrenogianni (GR)
Lena Olsson (SE)
Fernando Ramos (PT)
Ian Selwood (UK)
Alain Senteni (MU)
Sigrid Shubert (DE)
Elizabeth Stacey (AU)
Arthur Tatnall (AU)
Barrie Thompson (UK)
Marta Turcsanyi-Szabo (HU)
Joe Turner (US)
Raul Wazlawick (BR)
Peter Waker (ZA)

Contents

Chapter 1

Digital Literacy for the Knowledge Society 1

An approach to digital literacy for adults: the EuNIC proposal..................3
Manuela Delfino, Maria Ferraris, Donatella Persico and Francesca Pozzi

Digital literacy as a challenge for Teacher Education: Implications
for educational frameworks and learning environments..........................11
Lena Olsson and Eva Edman-Stålbrant

The Use of Interactive Whiteboards to Support the Creation, Capture
and Sharing of Knowledge in South African Schools............................19
Hannah Slay, Ingrid Siebörger and Cheryl Hodgkinson-Williams

Chapter 2

Planning and Modelling for Teaching and Learning

Scenario planning and learning technologies: The foundation
of lifelong learning..29
Bent B. Andresen

Supporting the Design of Pilot Learning Activities with the Pedagogical
Plan Manager...37
*Rosa Maria Bottino, Jeffrey Earp, Giorgio Olimpo, Michela Ott, Francesca
Pozzi and Mauro Tavella*

Groups can do IT: A Model for Cooperative
Work in Information Technology...45
Leila Goosen and Elsa Mentz

Chapter 3

ICT for Inclusion

A general and flexible model for the pedagogical description
of learning objects..55
Serena Alvino, Paola Forcheri, Maria Grazia Ierardi and Luigi Sarti

Using ICT to Improve the Education of Students with Learning Disabilities 63
   Tas Adam and Arthur Tatnall

Ethics, Equality and Inclusion for Students with a Chronic Health Condition 71
   Tony Potas and Anthony Jones

AudioGene: Mobile Learning Genetics through Audio by Blind Learners 79
   Jaime Sánchez and Fernando Aguayo

Chapter 4

Innovative Learning Environments 1

Design and implementation of a user friendly environment
for Learning Objects creation 89
   Giovanni Adorni, Diego Brondo and Mauro Coccoli

Exploring Touching Learning Environments 93
   *Gustavo Ramírez González, Mario Muñoz Organero
   and Carlos Delgado Kloos*

Adaptation of Impulsive and Reflective Learning Behavior
in a Game-Based Environment 97
   Franziska Spring-Keller

Learning with Smart Multipurpose Interactive Learning Environment 101
   *Mária Bieliková, Marko Divéky, Peter Jurnečka, Rudolf Kajan
   and Ľuboš Omelina*

Eeney, Meeney, Miney, Mo? Selecting a First Programming Language 105
   Leila Goosen, Elsa Mentz and Hercules Nieuwoudt

Chapter 5

Exploiting ICT for Teaching and Learning

Preparing the stage for using emerging technologies in science education 111
   Christine Redman

Promoting Thinking Skills within the Secondary Classroom Using
Digital Media 119
   Maree A. Skillen

Practice makes perfect: Role-play – because our students deserve it! 127
   Anders Tveit

Gearing up for Robotics: An investigation into the acquisition of the concepts
associated with gears by teachers in a constructionist robotics environment 135
   Debora E. Lipson, John Murnane and Anne McDougall

Chapter 6

Online Distance Learning

Approaching TEL in university teaching: the faculty training need 145
Guglielmo Trentin, Jane Klobas and Stefano Renzi

Merger of Knowledge Network and Users Support for Lifelong
Learning Services 149
Christian-Andreas Schumann, Claudia Tittmann and Sabine Tittmann

Development of Instruments for Evaluation of Quality of Distance Studies.......... 153
Lina Tankeleviciene

Knowledge Network Internetworking 157
Kirstin Schwidrowski

Chapter 7

ICT Issues in Education

Virtual Learning Communities: a learning object integrated
into e-learning platform 163
*Patricia Alejandra Behar, Ana Paula Frozi de Castro e Souza and Maira
Bernardi*

The development of ICT networks for South African schools:
Two pilot studies in disadvantaged areas 167
Ingrid Siebörger, Alfredo Terzoli and Cheryl Hodgkinson-Williams

Supporting Teachers to Plan Culturally Contextualized Learning Activities 171
*Ap. Fabiano Pinatti de Carvalho, Junia C. Anacleto
and Vania P. de Almeida Neris*

The Web as a Learning Environment: Focus on Contents vs. Focus
on the Search Process 175
Francesco Caviglia and Maria Ferraris

How to favour know-how transfer from experienced teachers to novices? 179
Thierry Condamines

Chapter 8

Educating ICT Professionals

Where Will Professional Software Engineering Education Go Next? 185
Bill Davey and Arthur Tatnall

Maintaining Industrial Competence: The Challenges for Continuous
Professional Development and the Role for Universities.................................... 193
J. Barrie Thompson and Helen M. Edwards

EUCIP in Italian Universities 201
   C.R. Alfonsi, E. Breno, M. Calzarossa, P. Ciancarini, P. Maresca,
   L. Mich, F. Sala and N. Scarabottolo

Competence Based Tutoring Online: A Proposal for Linking Global
and Specific E-learning Models 209
   Monica Banzato and Gustavo Daniel Constantino

Chapter 9

Innovative Learning Environments 2

An Ontology-Based Modeling Approach for Developing
a Competencies-Oriented Collective Intelligence 219
   Mihaela Brut, Florence Sedes, Toader Jucan, Romulus Grigoras
   and Vincent Charvillat,

Maintenance of Learner's Characteristics by Spreading a Change.........................223
   Michal Šimún, Anton Andrejko and Mária Bieliková

Future Learning Strategy and ePortfolios in Education 227
   Christian Dorninger and Christian Schrack

"What is it?": A Culture Sensitive Educational Game...231
   Eliane Pereira, Junia Anacleto, Alexandre Ferreira,
   Aparecido Carvalho and Izaura Carelli

Chapter 10

Knowledge and Technology

The Contribution of Computer Science Education in a Creative Society 237
   Ralf Romeike

The Medium And The Message: Building an Online Learning
Community to Implement Curriculum Planning and Assessment
in Primary Schools, New South Wales, Australia..245
   Vicki Lowery

Accessing knowledge through narrative context..253
   Giuliana Dettori and Francesca Morselli

Design of Exercises and Test Items for Internetworking Based
on a Framework of Exercise Classes 261
   Stefan Freischlad

Chapter 11

Digital Literacy for a Knowledge Society 2

Transitions towards a Knowledge Society: Aspectual Pre-evaluation
of a Culture-Sensitive Implementation Framework 271
Mamello Thinyane, Alfredo Terzoli and Peter Clayton

Social networking and the third age: Significance and impact of targeted
learning initiatives based on web communities of third agers 279
Manuela Repetto and Guglielmo Trentin

The role of indigenous knowledge in computer education in Africa 287
Lorenzo Dalvit, Sarah Murray and Alfredo Terzoli

Designing knowledge-rich curricula 295
Marijke Hezemans and Magda Ritzen

Chapter 12

Innovative Learning Environments 3

Knowledge Creation Through Engagement in a Personal
Learning Environment 305
Mary P. Welsh

KidSmart: an essential tool for mathematical education in nursery schools 313
Annarosa Serpe

Learning with Interactive Stories 321
Sebastian A. Weiß and Wolfgang Müller

From e-learning to "co-learning": the role of virtual communities 329
Luigi Colazzo, Andrea Molinari and Nicola Villa

Chapter 13

Workshops

Workshop: A Creative Introduction to Programming with Scratch 341
Ralf Romeike

Using Alnuset to construct the notions of equivalence
and equality in algebra 345
Giampaolo Chiappini, Bettina Pedemonte and Elisabetta Robotti

PITO: A Children-Friendly Interface for Security Tools 349
Luigi Catuogno

Chapter 14

Posters

WAPE: a system for distance learning of programming......................................355
  Victor Kasyanov and Elena Kasyanova

Topic Maps for Learning Design..357
  Giovanni Andorni, Mauro Coccoli, Gianni Vercelli and Giuliano Vivanet

Systematic Exploration of Informatics Systems..359
  Peer Stechert

Development of E-Learning Design Criteria with Secure
Realization Concepts 361
  Christian J. Eibl and Sigrid E. Schubert

New e-learning environments for teaching and learning Science............................363
  Zdena Lustigova and Frantisek Lustig

Building Virtual Communities and Virtual Teams of Science teachers:
the case of Telmae 365
  Zdena Lustigova

Data Communications Laboratory as a Core Element for Modern Education.........367
  Tomáš Zeman, Jaromír Hrad, Jakub Slíva and Jiří Hájek

Towards an intelligent tool based on Concept Maps for an Automated
Meaningful Learning 369
  *Lorenzo Moreno, Evelio J. González, Beatrice Popescu, José D. Piñeiro
  and Claudia L. Oliveira Groenwald*

Multilanguage e-Learning Course for Industrial Automation................................371
  Jaromír Hrad, Tomáš Zeman and Jiří Hájek,

Chapter 1

Digital Literacy for the Knowledge Society 1

An approach to digital literacy for adults: the EuNIC proposal

Manuela Delfino, Maria Ferraris, Donatella Persico and Francesca Pozzi
CNR, Institute for Educational Technology – Via de Marini, 6 - 16149
Genova, Italy {delfino, ferraris, persico, pozzi}@itd.cnr.it,
WWW home page: http://www.itd.cnr.it/

Abstract. Recent surveys point to the need to enhance digital literacy competences among adults. Still, digital literacy courses addressing adults usually face a number of problems due to the lack of common backgrounds and purposes among learners. This paper illustrates NIC (Nucleo Informatico Concettuale - Conceptual Informatics Nucleus), an approach to adult digital literacy that focuses on few key concepts and skills and adopts a problem-based approach. NIC, which was developed and widely tested in Italy, has been recently transferred to a European context by the EuNIC project. The main results of this process are reported together with some reflections about strong points and weaknesses of the suggested approach and, more in general, about critical aspects of adult digital literacy actions.

1 Introduction

Although digital literacy is considered one of the key competences that all individuals need for fully participating in the information society [1], a large part of the European population still seems to lack even the most basic skills which underpin that competence. The 2005 Eurostat survey, which focused on what they call "e-skills" or "computer skills" of Europeans, was carried out on a sample of 200.000 people aged 17 to 74 and showed that 37% of the sample had no computer skills at all, 15% had a low level of competence, 26% a medium level and 22% declared to be familiar with a wide range of computer uses [2]. These values vary remarkably according to the country of origin, level of education and age. In young people the lack of e-skills drops to 10% and to 4% in students; in the latter group all countries report the highest level of e-skills (i.e., an average of 43% versus 22% in the whole sample). This survey only supplies information on basic e-skills, whose mastery is only a prerequisite of digital literacy. Nonetheless, the Eurostat data clearly show that social groups of people outside education and training circuits and in the

Please use the following format when citing this chapter:

Delfino, M., Ferraris, M., Persico, D. and Pozzi, F., 2008, in IFIP International Federation for Information Processing, Volume 281; *Learning to Live in the Knowledge Society*; Michael Kendall and Brian Samways; (Boston: Springer), pp. 3–10.

working age, are more likely to be "excluded" by the "digital world" – 46% of people aged between 24 and 55 has either a very low level of e-skills or none.

Hence there's a need to close this gap that can be addressed by increasing ICT access opportunities and by promoting initiatives aimed at the development of digital literacy in this age range.

Unlike school education, adult training often takes place over a short period of time, outside a real context, and involves people with very different backgrounds and motivations. With these constraints, an introductory course is unlikely to change a neophyte into an experienced and fluent ICT user. Being "fluent" requires substantial training, experience based on solving authentic problems and a number of non-technological prerequisites [3]. Moreover, as technology tends to change in a very fast way, what we mean by "competency in a technological environment" constantly evolves [4: 55]. In other words, digital literacy cannot be intended as a well defined set of competences acquired once and for all, indeed, it entails a continuous learning process. As a consequence, a major aim of the initial training should be to put the beginners in the line to become digital literates, by fostering their capability to learn something new in an autonomous way. To this purpose, the approach adopted in the various courses based on the ECDL syllabus [5] does not seem to be the most suitable since it provides a step by step and largely rote acquisition of different skills in the use of computers and their applications. Typically, after courses based on how-to-do approaches, it is quite common to notice that participants find it hard to face unknown situations and cannot transfer ways of working from a familiar situation to an unknown one. A plausible hypothesis is that, no matter how continuous the evolution of digital literacy is, there is a conceptual and operative basic core to be mastered which is crucial to acquire new knowledge. If this is true, too much emphasis on computer technicalities may even prevent the acknowledgement of this basic core of concepts and skills.

Moreover, this approach, as Eisenberg and Johnson write, "addresses the "how" of computer use, but rarely the "when" or "why." Participants may learn isolated skills and tool uses, yet many will lack an understanding of how those various skills fit together to solve problems and complete tasks" [6]. This suggests that, in a digital literacy action, problems and tasks should drive the learning process instead of being used just as examples of how to operate with the computer.

All these considerations are at the basis of NIC, an approach to adult digital literacy which was recently transferred to other European contexts within an EC project. In the following, the description of the approach, the transfer strategy at European level, and the outcomes of pilot courses in various countries are discussed.

2   NIC: an approach to adult digital literacy

NIC, the acronym of "Nucleo Informatico Concettuale" (Conceptual Informatics Nucleus), is a face to face course for adults designed in 2001 by the Institute for Educational Technology of the Italian National Research Council (ITD) and used in the local training system of the Provincia of Genova (District of Genova).

The aim of NIC is to train a "wise beginner user", i.e. a user who is able to interact with the computer to carry out simple tasks (write a text, send an e-mail, search and browse web pages, etc.); who understands how technology works and has an idea of its limits and potential. Most importantly, wise beginners can improve their computer competence in an autonomous way (e.g., by find out and learn how to use new functions of an application).

The NIC approach is not "technology oriented", but rather "concept and problem oriented". Instead of teaching how to use specific environments and developing skills that may turn out to be fragile, superficial and technology-dependent, this approach is based on training to master a set of conceptual and operative tools underlying all digital environments and use them to solve meaningful problems.

For this reason, an important feature of the NIC approach is its focus on a small nucleus of basic concepts and skills, which are considered essential to interact with the computer and to underpin new, autonomous learning. This nucleus was distilled during the design phase of the course by refining the definition of wise beginner user, by analyzing naives' difficulties and by involving experts in the multiple revision of a draft inventory of conceptual, terminological and operative knowledge.

A second essential feature of the NIC approach is the use of a problem-based method in order to make students transparently learn "why", "when" and "how" to use the main computer functions and applications to solve real or realistic problems. Consistently with this approach, a large portion of the NIC course is devoted to the development of a project that requires participants to face a number of different tasks in a complex situation usually chosen by the teacher according to the competences, interests and professional background of the group of learners involved.

Another key point in the NIC methodology lies in the attention devoted to the promotion of habits and attitudes that play a key role in beginner's autonomy (e.g., using "trial and error" strategies, reading and understanding computer messages, using the online help, working out procedures rather than trying to memorize them). These behaviours cannot certainly be taught, but can be encouraged and solicited through activities and teaching strategies aimed at stimulating or inducing them.

2.1   NIC contents and structure

According to the above features, the NIC course is organized into three stages:

1) the *Central core* that, in a short period of time, aims to the acquisition of fundamental skills (e.g., how to use mouse and keyboard, access files and folders, manipulate windows) and the introduction of core concepts, mostly essentials about the way computers work and the interplay of their main hardware and software components. This is a crucial stage, as it concerns concepts and skills that are prerequisite for further learning.

2) the *Immersion*, that entails the development of a project requiring the integrated use of different applications (word-processor, web-browser, e-mail, data-base, spreadsheet, multimedia presentation). The aim is not to provide detailed and exhaustive competences on the use of these programs, but to consolidate the core concepts introduced in the first phase, to demonstrate recurrent patterns common to different applications and to develop awareness of the types of problems that can be solved with each application. The project that drives this stage is chosen by the NIC teacher, according to the learners' interests and backgrounds, provided that all the above mentioned applications are used. During the first edition of the NIC course, in

2001, the project concerned the introduction of the new currency, a topical issue at that time. This is how the problem was posed: *"In a few months we will change our currency, from Lira to Euro. You all work in a bank. Your director asks you to conduct a survey to find out clients' opinions and knowledge about Euro. You should prepare a questionnaire, distribute it, collect the results, analyze them and present a final report"*. This problem required learners to use a word processor to draw up a questionnaire; to use e-mail to distribute it; to use Internet in order to retrieve information (texts, images, etc.); to design and populate a data-base with the answers to the questionnaires; to transfer data from a data-base to a spreadsheet for analysing them and creating charts; to prepare a presentation and illustrate the survey results.

3) the *Emersion* stage, aiming to support informed choices of future training initiatives and to widen the course horizons, by setting computing in an historical framework and giving practical suggestions to foster an autonomous computer use.

2.2   NIC teaching strategy and instructional materials

The way in which contents and activities of the course are presented to students is crucial for the success of the initiative. The NIC approach includes some specific teaching strategies: (1) a very gradual approach to new concepts and operative skills to foster the development of stable learning and avoid cognitive overload; (2) frequent switches from explanations to practice, to reify new concepts through hands-on activities or use practical tasks to introduce new concepts; (3) strong emphasis on stable concepts and skills rather than on technology-dependent aspects; this can be obtained by avoiding unneeded technical terms, discouraging rote learning, stressing the importance of giving priority to the problem and its definition before focusing on the technical ways to solve it; (4) students' engagement in activities that promote motivation and good habits.

To support the learning process, the NIC course provides three kinds of materials: (a) a set of interactive tutorials aiming to help the development of basic skills (e.g., the use of the mouse) or to support the comprehension of some key concepts (e.g., files organisation in folders); (b) the student worksheets, a collection of printed learning materials provided to students at the end of each lesson; (c) a set of files to be used by students for carrying out exercises and activities.

After a first tuning in 2001, the course was run in Liguria (Italy) in more than 160 editions, funded by the European Social Fund or by the Provincia di Genova, and involved more than 1700 participants. The good results obtained and the exportability demonstrated by the approach encouraged its further dissemination.

3   Transferring NIC at European level: the EuNIC experience

The EuNIC project, run from January 2006 to June 2007, aimed at turning the NIC principles and practice into a European approach to digital literacy for adults [7] thanks to the cooperation of five countries (Italy, Portugal, Greece, Latvia, Bulgaria).

The transfer occurred by collaboratively adapting and tuning the approach to the partners' needs, and subsequently testing it in each partner country through pilot courses. These courses were meant to be managed by pioneer teachers who would become the experts in their country for the EuNIC approach. All partners addressed the EuNIC pilot courses to adults, aged between 21 and 65, both unemployed and employed, with different professional backgrounds (e.g., housewives, farmers, teachers). This was compatible with the NIC approach, which was originally designed for adults with little or no computer skills and was independent of their profession and experience. The EuNIC transfer experiments involved 13 teachers and 60 participants across the four target countries. In the following, the actions undertaken by the consortium are described and the project results are discussed.

3.1 Adapting materials and training teachers

In order to transfer the NIC approach, the original materials underwent a revision which included an evaluation of the core concepts to verify their validity after five years from their formulation and the updating of technology-dependent aspects.

In particular, some Italian teachers experienced with the NIC approach carried out an analysis of the materials, with the aim to identify weaknesses. Furthermore, the original materials – based on Windows ME - were updated according to new software versions and to new devices available (Windows XP was chosen). Finally, aspects peculiar to the Italian culture were modified and adapted to a European audience: after their translation into English, all materials were translated into the national language and customized to local needs by each partner.

The teachers, selected on the basis of the local contexts and affordances, played a key role in the process of methodological transfer because they were in charge of running the EuNIC courses, tuning the approach according to the context and collecting the data needed to evaluate the experiment [8]. In case of success, dissemination of the approach at national level would have to rely on these teachers for the training of more EuNIC teachers. To help them acquire a deep understanding of the methodology and the learning materials, particular attention was devoted to the development of a *Teacher's guide* containing guidelines on how to organize each lesson, how to handle each kind of activity, what material to use, and so on.

The approach was presented to the pioneer teachers in an online course, during which they were required to perform individual study and collaborative activities.

3.2 The EuNIC evaluation model

The EuNIC evaluation model was conceived as an integral part of the approach itself and was aimed to provide the EuNIC partners with methods and tools to monitor and evaluate the pilot courses. It intended to gather data about the participants to pilot courses, to assess course quality as perceived by students and teachers, and to evaluate the course effectiveness in terms of learning achievements. The evaluation model focuses on three elements: the context, the teachers and the students.

The first group of indicators, the *Contextual indicators*, is aimed at investigating the level of flexibility of the approach. In other words, these indicators are intended to answer the question whether and to what extent it is possible to apply the same course structure and schedule in other countries. They were identified throughout the project development and during a conclusive workshop, by discussing the critical aspects of the project and how they could be faced with project partners and teachers. The second group, the *Teacher centred indicators*, aims to understand what EuNIC teachers thought about the materials and the friendliness and transferability of the approach. The third group, the *Student centred indicators*, is aimed at gathering data about the students' impressions on the course and the level of learning achievements. The second and third type of indicators were estimated through a set of tools aimed at gathering qualitative and quantitative information from all pilot courses in a systematic and consistent way. These tools included pre-course and end-of-course questionnaires for both teachers and students, a teacher logbook, a final student assessment test and teacher guidelines on how to deliver and mark the final test. In accordance with the approach, the final assessment test consisted in practical tasks entailing the acquisition of the basic concepts and skills.

While acknowledging the exploratory nature of the EuNIC project, the following section reports the major outcomes obtained by the application of the evaluation model to the pilot courses [9]. They are the basis for a reflection on the effectiveness of the transfer process and provide suggestions for further improvement and dissemination of the approach.

4   Project results

4.1   Learning outcomes

The learning outcomes of the pilot courses turned out to be very satisfactory. In a range from 1 to 3, students from all the partners countries obtained a mean test rate of 2.86 (SD=0.34). Even in those tasks that required students a high degree of autonomy (e.g., find out a way to carry out a given task), the mean test rate was definitely high (M=2.8, SD=0.4). No major variations seemed to occur when studying the distribution according to the country, the age, or the educational qualification. Quite interestingly, students who had initially declared to be totally unskilled with computers, obtained very good results too (M=2.88, SD=0.38). One more favourable element emerging from the final assessment results is that students' evaluation of their confidence in carrying out each task is positively correlated to test results for those tasks (2-tailed Pearson correlation .63; P<0.01). This suggests that students were aware of their ability, which is an important component of learning autonomy, a major aim of the course.

Students' perceptions of their achievements was also quite high, as testified by the answers to the following questions of the final questionnaire: "To what extent do you feel you are now an autonomous computer user?" (M=3.83, SD=0.84, range from 0 to 5) and "Have you learnt something useful?" (M=4.43; SD=0.80).

4.2 Course acceptance and materials transferability

Since the very beginning of the project, there was also a very positive acceptance of the NIC approach on the side of the project partners. The partner delegates who participated in this first meeting showed great appreciation for the approach and they all underlined the fact that, in their countries, the need for such a non-technical approach was very strongly felt and that their institution had joined the project in order to break with a past of unsuccessful, technology-oriented digital literacy courses. Consistently with this initial attitude of the partners, both students' and teachers' perception about the course, as it emerged from the end-of-course questionnaires, show a positive overall evaluation of the learning materials.

In particular, in a range from 0 to 5, students assigned a mean of 4.31 to overall course quality, 3.98 to learning material quality and 3.92 to balance/coherence of contents. No particular variations were registered according to the students countries.

In a range from 0 to 3, teachers mean ratings of the effectiveness of the EuNIC approach was 2.67 for the Central core, 3 for the Immersion and 2.83 for the Emersion stage (SD=0.40; 0.0; 0.41 respectively). Teachers' opinions on the EuNIC materials were also very comforting: the mean ratings of the students' worksheets and of the teacher guide were 2.91 (SD=0.30), while the mean rating of the tutorials was 2.92 (SD=0.33). Other data from the teachers final questionnaires support a good degree of transferability of the materials to different contexts. First of all, teachers rated quite low the difficulties in understanding the NIC approach (M=0.5, SD=0.84 for the Central core phase; M=1.17, SD=0.75 for the Immersion phase; M=1.0, SD=0.63 for the Emersion). Furthermore, their understanding of the approach was confirmed during the teacher training course, when they were asked to devise a problem relevant for their target population. In Bulgaria the target population was composed of teachers and so the proposal concerned the evaluation of teachers' achievements. In Greece the target population consisted of housewives and farmers: they proposed to carry out a survey on the ecological habits of Greek families and an investigation on how farmers may access European funding. Overall the EuNIC teachers showed the ability to choose topics motivating students and well suited to the course purposes, thus demonstrating their understanding of the key features of the method and of the approach flexibility.

5 Conclusions

The EuNIC project intended to probe the transferability of the NIC approach through a number of pilot courses in order to come out with some indications laying the foundations for further work in the area. Even though the exploratory nature of the EuNIC project doesn't allow to say a final word about the transferability of the NIC approach, the process of adaptation, updating and localization of materials, and the training of teachers, suggested some considerations on the approach validity.

Transferring the approach required a revision on two axes: the axe of *space,* in order to extend the use of the NIC approach from a local context to different European countries, and the axe of *time,* in order to update the materials according to technological developments occurred in the five years after its first design.

During the revision, while the materials related to the applications needed to be updated on both the axes, none of the experts – researchers and teachers – felt the need to alter the problem-based approach, the core of key skills and concepts or the teaching strategy. In other words, the essence of the NIC approach remained unaltered. Probably, due to technological developments, future revisions will need to have greater impact, especially on the choice of applications to be introduced in the course. For example, while so far the MS Office suite has been the classical set of applications taught in courses for beginners, it is likely that other types of tools (e.g., multimedia and communication applications) will deserve more attention in future.

A final consideration concerns the fact that digital literacy involves non-technological key competences too. For instance, in order to effectively retrieve information from the web, just knowing how to use a search engine is not enough, since other abilities are required (e.g., to be able to select adequate key words, to discriminate between low and high quality information). Indeed, courses addressing adults with different backgrounds often face problems when participants lack some of the necessary non digital knowledge (e.g., linguistic, mathematical, logical thinking). On one hand, this strengthens the idea that courses for beginners should focus not only on few concepts and problems selected according to the participants' previous competences, but also on the above-mentioned non technological skills. More generally, this points to the need that in the field of adult lifelong learning, technology introductory courses should be integrated with actions concerning other kinds of *literacies*, recognizing the idea that there is only one literacy where digital and non digital competences are intertwined.

References

[1] European Parliament and Council, Recommendation of the European Parliament and of the Council, of 18 December 2006, on key competences for lifelong learning Official Journal of the European Union L.394/5, 2006.

[2] Eurostat, How skilled are Europeans in using computers and the Internet?. *Collection Statistic in focus*, 17, 2006.

[3] K. Williams, Literacy and computer literacy: Analyzing the NRC's being fluent with information technology. *The Journal of Literacy and Technology*, 3(1) (2003).

[4] U. Bunz, Growing from computer literacy towards computer mediated communication competence: evolution of a field and evaluation of new measurement instrument. *Information Technology, Education and Society*, 4(2), 53-84 (2003).

[5] European Computer Driving Licence, (Apr. 6, 2008); http://www.ecdl.com/.

[6] M.B. Eisenberg, and D. Johnson. Learning and Teaching Information Technology - Computer Skills in Context, *ERIC Digest*, ED465377 (2002; updated version in 2006).

[7] CNR-ITD, *Report 2:EuNIC:towards the definition of a European approach to digital literacy*.T.R.01/07 [http://www.eu-nic-project.eu/pdf/EuNIC%202Report.pdf]

[8] CNR-ITD, *Report 3:Supporting the EuNIC teachers*. T.R.02/07 [http://www.eu-nic-project.eu/pdf/EuNIC_Report3.pdf]

[9] CNR-ITD, *Report 4:EuNIC transferability strategy*. T.R. 03/07 [http://www.eu-nic-project.eu/pdf/EUNIC%204Report.pdf]

Digital literacy as a challenge for Teacher Education

Implications for educational frameworks and learning environments

Lena Olsson and Eva Edman-Stålbrant
Lärum, Learning Resource Centre/Stockholm University
Konradsbergsgatan 5, 100 26 Stockholm, Sweden WWW home page:
http://www.larum.su.se

Abstract. Relationships between technological development and learning are described and the development of cultural tools and external memories are pointed out. The processes of how learning integrates with ICT are viewed from socio-cultural as well as constructionist theoretical perspectives. The concept of digital literacy is understood to be closely related to learning processes as social practices. Examples of how digital literacies can be introduced and performed in courses and educational programs within teacher education are given. Learning environments which can support development of digital literacies are presented with examples from Stockholm Institute of Education/Stockholm University.

1 Introduction

Technology transforms learning and the conditions for learning. The challenge to teacher education is to translate ICT into learning possibilities. The use of ICT has inspired a modernized literacy idea, digital literacy, which has become a collective concept for traditional literacies such as reading and writing as well as information and media literacy concepts. UNESCO defines literacy as the ability to identify, understand, interpret, create, communicate and compute, using printed and written materials associated with varying contexts. Literacy involves a continuum of learning to enable an individual to achieve his or her goals, to develop his or her knowledge and potential and to participate fully in the wider society.

Digital literacy has become an important issue within the EU. The objective within EU is to support development of digital competencies as well as digital repositories to raise the level of knowledge and employment in European countries. The political dimension brings discussion, new research and new definitions of digital literacy concepts. Digital literacies are often understood as various kinds of

Please use the following format when citing this chapter:

Olsson, L. and Edman-Stålbrant, E., 2008, in IFIP International Federation for Information Processing, Volume 281; *Learning to Live in the Knowledge Society*; Michael Kendall and Brian Samways; (Boston: Springer), pp. 11–18.

skills which can be learned in order to master technology. In this paper digital literacies are viewed from a socio-cultural viewpoint which highlights the interplay between technology and learning as social practice.

2 Technological developments and its relation to learning

What is involved in learning with technology and how may this have a bearing on how we understand digital literacies?

The relationships between learning and material culture (technologies) are pointed out by Säljö: "all human knowing is at some stage dependent on materiality and the coordination between minds, communication and artefacts; what we call learning changes over time and thus is a moving target" [1,2]. Through history we can see how minds and cognition, learning and knowledge have been shaped by which kinds of means of communication and resources were available. A key process in knowledge development is the development of cultural tools where our experiences and insights get externalised and in-scripted into material objects. Those externalisations are according to Säljö physical and intellectual at the same time. Cultural tools - from the making of images as rock paintings via book printing to digital technology - rely on materiality. Our intellectual artefacts, concepts, formulas, classification systems, social languages interplay with material artefacts such as instruments, documents, databases etc. These cultural tools will, due to what social and discursive qualities, assumptions and functions are embedded within them, influence our learning processes. [2,3]

In what way have learning processes changed with technological development? How do people and tool shape each other? We can view the functioning of technology as a black box. Tools/ machine are accepted as solid and its functions and processes are accepted without questioning (i.e. the example of the calculator. We can perform complex tasks even if we don't know the steps or the processes. Knowledge structures are inherent in technological systems and tools and we learn the procedure to get the relevant knowledge, rather than trying to understand the structure or system. The development of external memories and storage systems, books, libraries, databases and other archival systems means that the information storage issues are solved. Furthermore it has had massive implications for learning. There are now reliable, public, accessible repositories of data etc which can be used endlessly. [4,5]

Midoro has further clarified the characteristics of scripts as texts and multimedia and the potentials of digital technology. The hyper-mediality of digital documents gives further possibility to handle parts of documents which implies a new way of handling content [6].

Thus a lot of information and potential knowledge such as text, audiovisual etc is organized in external memory systems and can be retrieved and translated into new knowledge by someone who knows how [7] Knowing how, i.e. to search information in databases or work with a communication and learning platform involves meta-communication and meta-cognition of how to do a search or develop a model. This means that we now deal with concepts rather than hierarchal organized knowledge. Studies of information searching processes show how people develop new behaviour which is conceptually oriented rather than hierarchal organized [3,8].

Individual and mobile storage devices such as mobile phones, i-pods mean that we can retrieve and manipulate information from external systems and databases and communicate, produce and present new material instantly without physical boundaries.

2.1 Digital literacy – a matter of learning as social practice

The close relationship between technology and learning implies that digital literacy can be recognized as a "compound and complex concept that changes with the development of digital media"[9]. Digital literacies can be sorted into various dimensions, which can be useful when trying to set up programs for development of courses and educational programs. Information literacy can be described as the ability to collect, organize, evaluate information and form valid opinions on what is learned. Technology literacy can be described as the ability to use technology, use and access new media and the internet and communicate information. Media literacy is how to use new media in a creative way, produce, communicate and present contents to a wider audience. Global literacy is to understand the global complexity and interact and communicate accordingly. Literacy of responsibility is to consider social consequences and use and communicate information safely from privacy and other social issues. [10]

Our understanding of and the conditions for digital literacy have to do with how we build representations of knowledge into digital collective memory banks; how we master and communicate these representations, and how we reconvert them into new knowledge [2] Other fundamentals are the social contexts where we learn and use digital tools/environments individually or as part of a group or community. Focus should be on learning in practice rather than acquiring specific skills to master technology. Digital literacies are here understood as social practices closely related to the use of technology.

Socio-cultural perspectives on learning and knowledge originate from social constructivism and cultural history theories. Socio-cultural theory is often used to create frameworks of teacher education. To explain digital literacies as social practices the following aspects of socio-cultural theory are helpful: learning is situated; learning is social; learning is dependent on mediation and learning has to do with participation in communities of practice.

Learning is situated. This idea, which is well represented in many areas of research is that thinking as well as learning and production of knowledge is always embedded or situated in a context. This implies that learning as it normally occurs is a function of the activity, context and culture in which it happens. This contrasts with most classroom learning activities which involve knowledge which is abstract and out of context. The principles are that knowledge needs to be presented in an authentic context, i.e., settings and applications that would normally involve that knowledge. This implies that if we wish to design or understand the learning processes teacher education students engage in we have to comprehend the contexts or environments where they take place [11].

Learning is social. Social interaction plays a fundamental role in the development of cognition. Vygotsky claimed that cognitive activities/ learning always takes place on two levels: first, on the social level, and later, on the individual level; first, between people and then inside the individual. This applies equally to voluntary attention, to logical memory, and to the formation of concepts. All the higher functions originate as actual relationships between individuals.[12]. Learning as a social phenomenon is understood by looking at the learner as situated in a context which he interrelates to. It involves our experience of participation. Learning thus requires social interaction and collaboration.

Learning can be interpreted as participation in communities of practice. A community according to Wenger is characterized by mutual engagement, joint enterprise and shared repertoires. The concept of practice has a connotation of doing but it is not just doing in itself. It is doing in a social context that constitutes social practice. The concept of practice includes both the practical and theoretical, ideals and reality, talking and doing [7]. Communities of practice have been a very useful concept in explaining learning within networked communities and the conditions for e-learning, and on-line learning, i.e. working with portfolios on a learning platform where shared ideas and behavior are vital elements.Learning is according to Wenger above all the ability to negotiate new meaning to earlier experience. [7]

3 Learning environments and educational frameworks

A challenge Teacher Education in Sweden has to face is how to reach the quantitative targets concerning proficiency and ability which is: "For teaching qualification the student will show ability to use ICT in teaching activities and realize the role of multimedia". Further more "During the time of education the student will continuously use ICT as a support for his/her studies". [13]

3.1 Learning environments

At Stockholm Institute of Education the ICT issue has to a large extent been managed with the help of the Learning Resource Centre (LRC), Lärum. The objectives are to provide tools and spaces for learning and teaching and develop the competencies of future teachers as well as having an initiating, coordinating, and developing role concerning ICT and its use in education and research.

The LRC is organized into three functional units: the University College Library with information services, user education and physical/virtual learning spaces; the Media Production department with a media laboratory with facilities for text, images, video production and services for computer- and video-conferencing; the Educational ICT-department with the task to build collaborative projects with teachers, students, school projects, support distance education and provide competence development. The staff includes professional librarians, media producers, ICT-teachers, technicians, web designer, and project managers from various disciplines. This means that different competencies can be taken into account in order to produce learning and teaching spaces and tools.

The LRC provides hybrid learning environments with digital systems and physical repositories such as the library collections and video-archives. Tools for analysis, production, mediating and presenting new knowledge are supplied such as the self-managed diagnostic web tool for basic ICT proficiency and the e-archive where students' can write their thesis's. A guiding idea is that people learn best when they are participating in design or creative activities and that the learner should be given better opportunities to construct together with their peers. The library and the media laboratory with computer work areas are open, lively spaces for individual and group work social interaction and students' communication patterns.

To serve the purpose of exploring new working methods which can be used in schools the LRC together with three companies (Hewlett Packard, Luxo and Kinnarps) developed the Classroom of the Future. The latest technology can be used in a truly flexible hybrid environment such as tools to design learning objects, engage in games and robots.

In the socio-cultural perspective the artefact is central. Students' thinking is thought to be intimate connected to the artefacts they are using shown in the interaction between student and artefact where the student often can manage complicated actions without being able to verbalize them. Säljö means that it is useless trying to understand what goes on in one student's head – instead we try to understand learning in the interaction between students, teachers and artefacts. [1]

When learning is shaped by the social environment every person has a larger extent of potential for learning than the definite capacity of the individual when learning is facilitated just by someone with larger knowledge.[12] This range of a person's potential is called the zone of proximal development and is essential according to Vygotsky's ideas. Learning in the zone of proximal development is a combined activity in which the teacher simultaneously keeps an eye on the goals of course and on what the student with assistance is capable to do. [15] Scaffolding is a strategy that teachers use to move learning forward in the zone of proximal development. It is a collaborative process. It involves negotiation of meaning between the teacher and the student about expectations and how to improve the learning process in the best way. Examples of scaffolding are when the teacher provides the student with support such as e.g. hints encouragement, cognitive structures and reminders during the learning process through the course [16].

Due to this theoretical view of knowledge one of the main tasks of the LRC, is to provide students and teachers with learning environments in their actual work situations where they are able to learn in social interaction and a variety of artefacts. Another task is to create and support with relevant scaffolds so learning can take place in the zone of proximal development whether it is students or teachers who are the learners.

3.2 Educational frameworks

In order to improve the quality of students' scientific understanding and theoretical basis a general course was designed 2005 with the objectives to develop general abilities and competencies progressively throughout the teacher programme. The level 2 course objectives were to:

- Distinguish and use theoretical perspectives on human development and socialization, learning and education and special education issues
- Read and work with scientific texts
- Analyse texts and pedagogical case studies from different perspectives

Another goal was to develop and establish digital literacy competencies within the course work. A team of teachers and LRC staff described the abilities and literacies in the form of a general matrix. To get the students on the same proficiency level of digital literacy a self-managed diagnostic web tool for basic ICT proficiency was developed and introduced at the LRC.

The idea is that the development of digital literacies takes its starting point in the basic learning practices students engage in by using adequate tools/artefacts. The use of tools becomes an active part of the tasks and students' individual and group practices and repertoires. Learning is here seen as an individual and social process of experience, construction and negotiation with ICT artefacts in a context.

Communicative abilities	Manage and perform a group seminar on course content	Use digital work methods individually /group LMS blogs
	Present surveys and investigations	Advanced digital presentation, movie, audio, scanned pictures
Evaluative abilities	Assess owns own learning process reflection on meta learning	Use digital assessment tools i.e. portfolio in a Learning Management system
Ability to apply a scientific perspective on course contents	Distinguish between method, theory knowledge theoretical concepts	Use advanced search technology on internet, database searching source management, quality assessment

Table 1. [Examples of general base course]

3.2.1 A case study on teacher trainers

The issue of digital literacy for students has put special demands on teacher trainers. The LRC ICT teacher's task is to develop the competence of teacher educators. A teacher trainer should have the ability to:

- decide what kind of digital tools are appropriate for their course content and be able to present their course on line
- determine what kind of digital tools and work methods which support, develop or increase the quality of their course
- realize the affordances with different digital examinations so they can choose the best form of examination according to the aims and guideline
- clarify and highlight teaching and learning issues, for the students, according to chosen digital tools and methods

In June, 2007, the LRC ICT teachers met with a group of teacher trainers who wanted to increase the quality of their course by being tutored by the LRC. They performed a distance course during two semesters, the second year in the general field of the teacher programme. The LRC team treated this as pilot-work which could be evaluated and further developed. Teacher trainers and the LRC team met 4 times to thoroughly go through the course objectives and the former assignments according to the objectives. The LRC team developed the course with new tools and new ways of using tools, which had positive consequences for the teachers' as well as the students' development of digital literacies (including communication competence). Another outcome was a revision of some of the assignments so that they got to be more firmly connected both to the course's objectives and the qualitative targets. Parts of the course were developed in software called Compendium, which is a mind mapping tool which enables you to provide hyperlinks between different parts of the diagram.

The course is still an ongoing project. A second group of teacher trainers were showed the documentation as a point of departure for transforming a campus course into a distance course. This second group was not as highly motivated as the original group, they had not planned for digital competence development and their digital literacy level was much lower. Nevertheless they felt highly motivated when they saw the structure and they understood the digital literacy target and its role in relation to the development of student abilities and towards the course objectives. The result was that the documentation of the first course content and digital components constituted a design support tool for creating new learning activities and a new understanding of digital competence according to course objectives and qualitative targets.

The success with the second teacher group occurred because the documentation served as a scaffolding artefact and highlighted how digital tools are related to a course context which was familiar to them, in accordance with the socio-cultural perspective. Another outcome was the importance of taking a point of departure in the content in order to get teacher trainers motivated. Another factor was the transparent progression of digital abilities aiming for digital competence both for students and teachers. As a transparent progression it served well as a planning tool for other learning activities as well as an evaluating tool. A result from the original course team was that they considered that the digital tools increased the course quality. When the students were supported by digital tools such as a web course on information literacy, they could exercise at home and were better prepared in class. The teachers could then start the next lesson on a higher level than before. When effectiveness of this kind becomes obvious to the teacher trainers they have no difficulties to find motivation.

4 Conclusions

To get a deeper understanding of what we mean by digital literacies it is fruitful to engage in a discussion of learning processes and technological development. Learning processes have been conditioned by technological development insofar that knowledge structures, culture and human experience get in-scripted into material objects. Digital artefacts or cultural tools with intellectual and technical/material resources can be mediated, distributed and used in ways which influence learning processes profoundly. We mean that learning should be viewed as social practices and that learning is dependent of context, social interaction and shared repertoires.

The implication of how we can comprehend digital literacy then is firstly that the concept changes with the development of digital technology and digital artefacts/media. Secondly , to develop digital literacies within educational programs the students' use of tools should be determined by and integrated in the learning practices directed towards the learning of course content and achieving of course objectives. To further inspire digital literacy development, learning environments should be designed with the complexity of learning processes and social nature in mind. Scaffolding is proposed as an important tool for introduction of digital literacies.

References

1. Säljö, R., *Lärande och kulturella redskap: om lärprocesser och det kollektiva minnet.* (Stockholm: Norsteds akademiska förlag 2005).
2. Säljö, R, Technologies and the transformations on learning. (Kaleidoscope conference, Berlin Dec 26-27, 2007)
3. Olsson, L., Att söka och använda information i en encyklopedi. (Arbetsrapport, Vinnova 1998)(in Swedish)
4. Gärdenfors, P., *Fängslande information.* (Stockholm: Natur och Kultur 1996) (in Swedish)
5. Olsson, L., *The computerized library – machine dreams of the 70's* (Diss..Linköping: Linköping Studies of Arts and Science 121. 1995)
6. Midoro,V. Literacy for the knowledge society. (EDEN Classroom Conference, Oct. 26-28, Stockholm 2007)
7. Wenger, E. *Communities of practice. Learning, Meaning, and Identity.* (Cambridge: Cambridge University Press, 1998)
8. Kerka, S. Extending Information Literacy in Electronic Environments ((2000)
9. Söby, M, Editorial. Digital kompetanse, Nordic Journal of Digital Literacy (Special issue 2007. Oslo: Universitetsforlaget).
10. Varis,T., New literacies and e-Learning comptencies. http://elearningeuropa.info/directory/index (2005)
11.Lave, J., & Wenger, E. *Situated Learning: Legitimate Peripheral Participation.* (Cambridge, UK: Cambridge University Press1990).
12.Vygotsky, L.S. *Mind in Society.* Ed. by M. Cole, V. John-Steiner, S. Scribner E. Souberman. (Cambridge, Ma/London: Harvard University Press 1978)pp 57-60
13.Swedish National Agency for Higher Education   SFS 2006:173, 1 kap, 8 §
14.Wertsch, J.V. *Voices of the mind: A sociocultural approach to mediated action.* (Cambridge, MA : Harvard University Press 1991)
15.Wood, D.; Bruner, J.S.; Ross, G. The role of tutoring problem solving. Journal of *Child Psychology and Psychiatry*, 17(2), pp. 89-100 (1976).
16.Shephard, L-A. Linking Formative Assessment to scaffolding. *Educational leadership* November (2005).

The Use of Interactive Whiteboards to Support the Creation, Capture and Sharing of Knowledge in South African Schools

Hannah Slay[1], Ingrid Siebörger[1] and Cheryl Hodgkinson-Williams[2]
[1] Computer Science Department, Rhodes University
Grahamstown. South Africa, 6139 [h.slay,i.sieborger]@ru.ac.za
WWW home page: http://www.cs.ru.ac.za
[2] Education Department, Rhodes University
Grahamstown. South Africa, 6139 chodgkinsonwilliams@gmail.com

Abstract. This paper illustrates how interactive whiteboards (IWBs) have been used to support the dynamic creation, capture and sharing of knowledge in primary and secondary schools in South Africa. It reports on the findings of a feasibility study undertaken by the Eastern Cape Department of Education to determine the perceived benefits and drawbacks of teachers and learners of using IWBs in the classroom. The research highlights how both teachers and learners can critically engage with multiple sources of information to construct their own knowledge, aiding learners in the learning process and helping teachers to scaffold that learning process. The study illustrates that IWBs have the potential to be beneficial in the South Africa classroom by affording teachers and learners a new medium through which they can create, capture and share knowledge.

1. Introduction

Don Tapscott [1], notes that today's generation of children have a fundamental preference for interactive media (the Internet, video games) rather than broadcast media (television, radio). Tapscott explains this preference, citing the hierarchical nature of broadcast media as compared to the shared power of interactive media. Applying this viewpoint of interactivity to an educational context, he calls for a shift in pedagogy from traditional "broadcast learning" (for example chalk-and-talk) to more interactive learning styles.

Aware of some of the on-going debates about the potential value of IWBs in schools and their potential value in realizing interactive learning styles, the Eastern Cape Department of Education (ECDoE) requested a team of researchers in the Computer Science and Education Departments at Rhodes University undertake one of a number of feasibility studies to investigate teachers' and learners' perceptions of the potential benefits and drawbacks of using IWBs - specifically the eBeam technology [2], a cheaper IWB technology that makes use of a radio transmitter attached to an ordinary non-interactive whiteboard - in schools in order to encourage evidence-based policy [3] and evidence-based practice [4].

This paper reports on the findings of a feasibility study undertaken in the Eastern Cape from August to December 2006, to determine the perceived benefits and drawbacks of teachers and learners of using IWBs in the classroom. In particular, it illustrates how IWBs

Please use the following format when citing this chapter:

Slay, H., Siebörger, I. and Hodgkinson-Williams, C., 2008, in IFIP International Federation for Information Processing, Volume 281; *Learning to Live in the Knowledge Society*; Michael Kendall and Brian Samways; (Boston: Springer), pp. 19–26.

have been used to support the dynamic creation, capture and sharing of knowledge in primary and secondary schools in South Africa.

2. Related Work

Before we can describe how learners create, capture and share knowledge using IWBs, we must first define what we understand knowledge to mean. Throughout this paper, we draw from Davenport and Prusak's definition of knowledge as "a fluid mix of framed experience, contextual information, values and expert insight that provides a framework for evaluating and incorporating new experiences and information" [5: 5]. Note that this definition has two components: firstly there is information that has been processed and internalized; and secondly, the purpose of knowledge is to evaluate new experiences. With this definition, we can now examine existing work in the field.

Previous research into interactive whiteboard use in the classroom elicited a number of positive and negative sentiments from learners. However, on the whole, learners seemed to enjoy the use of IWBs in the classroom [6, 7, 8] and found them easy to use [6]. Learners also commented that they enjoyed the multimedia content that could be presented using the IWB, finding these lessons more interesting than traditional content [9]. Learners commented that the visual aspect of the IWB together with the verbal comments from their teachers complimented each other and helped them to better understand the content taught to them [6, 10]. Learners felt that the IWB helped the teacher to explain concepts more effectively which allowed them to better understand and learn the new concepts [10, 11].

Linked to the visual aspect of the IWB, learners also discussed how the ability for the teacher to go back and forth over lesson content, easily repeating sections that learners might have struggled with also helped them to understand new concepts better and made for effective learning [9].

There is ongoing debate as to the reason behind the popularity of multimedia content on IWBs [12]. From a purely technical viewpoint, some refer to the IWBs ability to present information in vibrant colours, and the ability to move, manipulate, and zoom in on information as enhancing the learning process [13, 14]. Others link its popularity with its ability to display a wide variety of information so concepts become more tangible and therefore easier to grasp [8]. Finally it is also argued that an IWB supports a wider range of learning styles, since teachers are able to draw on a variety of different resources to suit the learners' needs [9]. It is interesting to note the different theories underpinning the popularity of multimedia content for IWBs. We see most of these as a conflation of the attributes of a laptop-projector combination to an IWB, as the ability to display, manipulate (zoom, navigate), and adapt to different learning styles are all characteristics of a display rather than an interaction device (i.e. touch sensitive surface).

According to [15] the impact of using IWBs is seen in the interactivity of teaching and the associated participation of the learners. IWBs afford teachers the ability to either prepare content or materials in advance or during the lesson in front of the class. In addition, teachers are also able to quickly retrieve materials during lessons as needed for display to the whole class and are able to manipulate items directly on the display as one would with a standard computer interface [15]. This ability to create, capture and share knowledge using IWBs in the classroom was one of a number of affordances that were investigated during the course of this study.

3. User Study

The main research question that the team sought to address was how and why do IWBs using "intelligent" or "smart" pens enable or constrain teaching and learning in South African primary and secondary schools. This paper analyses the results of this study, illustrating how IWBs are used to support the dynamic creation, capture and sharing of knowledge in South African primary and secondary schools.

In order to undertake the investigation, the ECDoE supplied eBeam projection systems, for two secondary schools and one primary school in Grahamstown. As the ECDoE was contemplating purchasing only one eBeam per school, we needed to explore not only how teachers could use IWBs in their individual classrooms, but what logistical issues might enable or constrain the optimal use of eBeam technology across at least three classrooms. One teacher, Teacher A, participated from the primary school and one teacher, Teacher B, participated from one of the secondary schools. In the other secondary school, three teachers, Teachers C, D, and E, were involved in order to enable an investigation into the advantages and disadvantages of the mobility of the eBeam unit.

Teacher A is a Grade 5, 6 and 7 English first additional language teacher, who teaches a range of learners who mostly speak English as their second or third language. We observed her Grade 6 English first additional language class, with 29 learners. Teacher B, teaches English and Life Orientation. We observed his grade 11 English class, where the average age of the learners was 17 years old. This class had the largest class size out of all involved in the study. At its peak, there were 54 learners in the one small classroom. Teacher C is an Economics, Business Economics and Business Studies teacher. Throughout the duration of the study, we observed her grade 11 Business Economics class, with an average age of 17 years, and a total of 34 learners in the class. Teacher D is an English, History and Life Orientation teacher. During the course of the study we observed her Grade 9 English class, which consisted of 30 learners who were about 15 years old. The last teacher from School 3 is Teacher E, a mathematics and science teacher. We observed this teacher's grade 11 Mathematics class, where there were 22 learners enrolled in the class.

The three schools were chosen according to the key criteria that emerged from the literature and from other studies that were recently conducted in the same geographical area [16]. The Grahamstown area was chosen as it is close to Rhodes University where the research team is based, and because recent studies by the research team had enabled us to establish the necessary relationships with the school principals and teachers to be able to conduct a study of this nature. All schools involved in the study are equipped with ICT facilities, and are connected to the Internet. All teachers involved in the study have prior ICT experience (whether through formal or informal training) necessary to use ICTs in a classroom environment.

To ensure that teachers were provided with adequate training, four 2-hour training sessions were held. The first session was held at a local independent school that had recently purchased an IWB and a teacher, familiar with IWBs, demonstrated its use to the group of teachers, their school principals and the researchers. We assumed that it would be useful for teachers to observe how IWBs are used in a classroom situation. In subsequent training sessions, teachers: learned how to assemble, calibrate, and disassemble equipment; were given basic instructions on presenting lessons with the hardware; and presented a lesson they had prepared in front of the other participants and researchers; respectively. Throughout the training, researchers observed teachers' ICT skills and attempted to provide additional support to those who were less familiar with ICTs. Prior to the first, and on completion of the last observation, each teacher was interviewed to elicit their opinion on their experiences with the IWB. As we were also interested in the learners' perceptions, 10 learners from each of the teacher's classes were selected to participate in post-observation focus group interviews. The learners were selected according to their availability and willingness to participate in the focus group [17]. We chose the focus group approach to encourage discussion amongst the learners as some of them may have felt too shy to comment on a one-to-one basis.

4. Findings and Discussion

The findings in this section will discuss the two aspects of creating and capturing knowledge, and sharing knowledge separately.

4.1.   Create and Capture Knowledge

This section describes the creation and capture of knowledge on the part of the learners and teachers separately, presenting comments from both teachers and learner experiences during the user study.

4.1.1.   Learners

When describing the use of ICTs in class, Teacher B explained how in outcomes based education learners are encouraged to be the producers of knowledge and to understand how knowledge is constructed from various information sources. He commented, saying *"And it actually works really well because they [the learners] are so much more in charge of getting the information and that's an important part of outcomes based curriculum that they must find the information. That they become aware of the producers of information and knowledge and they become aware of the how information is used and how they can use it and shape what they want to say"*.

Teacher B also discussed how the use of the IWB in the classroom allowed him to retrieve content and materials quickly and with ease, a benefit also discussed in [15]. He commented saying *"They [the learners] benefited from the fact that firstly whatever resources we were using was much easier to get a hold of and to get into and then secondly there was a lot less hassle with having to write answers and clean the board and that whole repetitive schlep thing"*.

Teacher A's learners commented that the IWB supported creation and capture of knowledge as they could learn collaboratively: *"It was much easier for us because we could see everything together, we didn't have to wait until our group got a chance to go and see the information on the computer"*. Extending this, Teacher B's learners commented that when using an IWB, their teacher could *"pay more attention to us than writing on the board"*. Therefore IWBs in the classroom afforded learners the opportunity to be creators of knowledge, to have easy access to different sources of information and work collaboratively with each other and their teacher to produce and capture knowledge.

4.1.2.   Teachers

Teacher B discussed in great detail how the use of the IWB allowed him to have easy access to different content and materials during his lessons. This meant that he was easily able to pull in extra material that he had not necessarily intended to use to support the learners understanding of concepts. This allowed him to respond to the changing dynamics of the learners and support their understanding of concepts as he taught them. This was a benefit also highlighted by researchers in [15]. He commented as follows:

Beforehand if I were to just use the laptop and projector I would have to pretty much make sure that I know where everything is stored and that you would have to set up beforehand on the hard-drive, you know, where everything is, but it is so much easier to navigate around the laptop or the hard-drive and find data sources and things like that. So you don't always have to have all the definitions already sorted out or already put on a slide or whatever and then that becomes part of the lesson, looking things up [...] Not only navigating around what data you have to teach but then also finding alternative sources and just basically being able to have all the sources at hand and being able to manipulate the data much more easily than having to come to the laptop and look for things, you can just do it right there.

From these comments we can clearly see that the IWB afforded Teacher B the opportunity to dynamically create and capture new knowledge in order to scaffold learning in his classroom. Teacher A made use of the IWB during her teaching to capture the knowledge of her learners. The IWB affords the teacher the ability to capture the pen strokes that the learners write on the IWB. This meant that when learners presented their collective group knowledge to the rest of the class by writing their brainstormed ideas on the IWB, Teacher A was able to capture the content, which was saved for later use by the learners and herself.

4.2. Sharing Knowledge

Throughout the teaching and learning environments involved in this study, we observed the process of sharing knowledge as consisting of three types of communication, which together resulted in the generation of a larger body of knowledge. In the first type of communication, teachers shared knowledge to the learners in the form of the prepared course material. Secondly, the learners may be involved in a collaborative discussion amongst themselves, sharing knowledge between learners and collectively creating knowledge. The third type of communication shared knowledge from the learners to the teacher. This section will illustrate these three types of communication separately, with reference to our observations from the user study.

4.2.1. Teacher to Learner

The ability to incorporate multimedia content into the teaching environment using the eBeam was a benefit that was highlighted by both learners and teachers during the course of this study. Throughout the study, teachers integrated numerous multimedia sources in their teaching, including: static images; Microsoft Encarta; Online sources such as governmental websites; Flash-based story books; PowerPoint Presentations; Microsoft Excel; and Geometer's Sketchpad. These findings are similar to those suggested by Hall and Higgins [7], who found this to be one of the major advantages of IWBs in learning environments cited by primary school students. Wall, Higgins and Smith quote a student saying "the pictures help you to understand what the teacher is talking about" [7: 860]. An example of this was when Teacher A used the IWB to display an image of the Southern Cross constellation to the learners: '*I remember when one of the other researchers from America was telling the children about the Southern Cross and they'd never heard of this. So I could go to the computer and show them – all forty students were around me, so I just set up the eBeam and everyone could see it on the large screen*', aiding the learners in understanding what the American researcher was talking about.

In addition, we found that learners often referred to the fun and thought-provoking content when using the eBeam in the classroom. The primary school learners in Teacher A's class, and Teacher A herself commented on the effectiveness of using Flash-based story books in class.

Four of the five focus groups commented that it was the ability to see or visualize what the teacher was talking about that helped them learn and understand new concepts; sharing knowledge from the teacher to the learner. The mathematics learners from School 3 were the most vocal about how this visualization helped them: *"It's that we could see the things. You see, in a function in algebra you have the standard formula which is $ax^2 + bx + c$. ... So we could actually see what effect 'a' had on the graph and what effect 'b' has on the graph immediately. [...] You can imagine that when you sketch a single graph by hand it takes a long time and then if you want to change the value of 'a' you have to draw again to see the differences. So we could learn more things in a single period than what we would learn over like a week".* The mathematics teacher at School 3 also commented on advantages of the visual nature of the IWB saying that it makes it easier for the learners to learn and for him to teach them complicated abstract concepts in mathematics: *'... because they can visualize them and see the effect that it has on changing the parameters. Shifting axes, moving sideway It becomes very interesting. But when you teach without anything that would make them see, it becomes very difficult.'* These findings are similar to previous research work where it was reported that the visual aspects of the IWB helped learners to understand content, making the teacher's explanations more effective [6, 7, 9, 10, 11]. Learners "most commonly associated the IWB with visual ways of learning. The majority commented on how the visual and verbal elements complemented each other and promoted effective learning..." [18: 860] and consequently knowledge sharing.

4.2.2. Learner to Learner

During the course of this study the researchers noticed how the learners were able to make use of the IWB and other related ICT resources to help construct their knowledge within particular topics. The IWB and other related resources formed part of the collection of resources that learners employed to research about topics under discussion in the classroom. Learners were observed sharing knowledge amongst one another in two different contexts: when working in groups; and when reporting their findings to classmates from the front of the classroom (using the eBeam).

Working in groups, learners would discuss and compare their various sources, constructing their own knowledge with the materials available to them. Teacher E described how his learners worked collaboratively during his class, saying *'I ask groups to do different work. And then the groups come together and they share what they have learnt. They share that knowledge together'.* Group work has often been acknowledged in related work as an associated benefit of the use of IWBs in teaching and learning environments. Levy [8] found that as IWBs allowed the teacher to present work more efficiently, more time was used for activity-based, interactive learning in groups. Pupils in this study found that sharing ideas with other classmates helped them to learn to explain and articulate their ideas.

As well as increased learner to learner participation in group contexts, Teacher C noted that her learners were more willing to participant when the IWB was used in class, saying *'... [the learners] are more willing to advise the child who is writing [on the IWB] what next step to do. So the class is active'.* These findings mirror those described by Levy [8], where she describes a shift in the roles of learners when using IWB, from a passive learning environment to more active participation where learners ask and answer questions that can be explored immediately on the IWB.

4.2.3.   Learner to Teacher

One of the major advantages claimed in existing work of using IWBs in classes is that learners appear to be more motivated to participate in their lessons when using an IWB. A study by BECTA suggest this motivation is due to "the high level of interaction – students enjoy interacting physically with the board, manipulating text and images" [19: 3]. During the course of this study the researches noticed that there was a definite enthusiasm amongst the learners when teachers were using the IWB in the classroom. During one of the classroom observations Teacher A commented to the researchers that learners in her class, particularly the weaker learners, were participating more eagerly than they had previously. When teachers asked questions in class there was generally a flurry of hands of learners wanting to answer, while excitement appeared even more pronounced when learners were presented with an opportunity to interact with the IWB directly.

As described in the previous section, across most classes that we observed, learners were encouraged to work together in groups. During these classes, teachers would then allow for time during which each of the groups would present their knowledge and understanding of the topic to the rest of the class. During this period the other learners and the teachers would discuss the topic in detail clarifying, correcting and confirming the knowledge constructed by each group. When not working in groups the learners were also encouraged to come and present some of their ideas and understandings on the IWB to the rest of the class which could then be discussed in detail by all the learners and their teacher. Teacher A described this enthusiasm to learn and participate that she had noticed in her weaker students, saying *"But what I found is ... those learners are very much involved. ... I think its something new for everyone, and they felt that they could be part of the process too you know... I could see that they were trying to read along with the story. And afterwards when I tested them to see if they could read a line at least, I could see that they had improved".*

Teacher D also described how learners seemed more willing to participate and contribute to the learning process when the teacher was teaching using an IWB, saying *"The moment they see something new, they are more interested in using it. The moment you say the class will be held in the principal's classroom, they know we are going to be using the eBeam so they'll all rush in. And even if someone doesn't know the answer they always want to write on the board".*

5. Conclusion

This paper has described how IWBs have been used in South African primary and secondary schools in the Eastern Cape Province to support the creation, capture and sharing of knowledge between teachers and learners. It has highlighted how both teachers and learners are afforded the opportunity to be creators and of knowledge through access to multiple digital resources. This process highlights how both teachers and learners can critically engage with multiple sources of information to construct their own knowledge, aiding learners in the learning process and helping teachers to scaffold that learning process. In addition, the visual nature of the IWB allowed teachers "to show" or learners "to see" or visualize the new content and concepts that they were learning about. The IWB also allowed both the teachers and the learners to capture the new knowledge that they were creating through various methods, such as saving brainstorming content from the learners as vector diagrams.

Finally, the IWB also afforded the teachers and learners the opportunity to share knowledge through group work and collaboration. This process corrected and solidified the knowledge that each participant was constructing. From this study it would appear that IWBs have the potential to be beneficial in the South Africa classroom by affording teachers and learners a new medium through which they can create, capture and share knowledge.

References

1. Tapscott, D. (2000) *Growing Up Digital: The Rise of the Net Generation*. New York, USA: McGraw-Hill.
2. Luidia Systems (2007) *eBeam Interactive Whiteboard Technology*.   [cited 21 May 2007]; Available from: http://www.e-beam.com.
3. Pawson, R. (2004) *Evidence-based policy: A realist perspective*, in *Making realism work: Realist social theory and empirical research.*, Carter, B. and New, C., Editors. Routledge: London.
4. Cordingley, P. (2004) *Teachers using evidence: using what we know about teaching and learning to reconceptualize evidence-based practice*, in *Evidence-based practice in education*, Thomas, G. and Pring, R., Editors. Open University Press: Maidenhead, Berkshire.
5. Davenport, T. and Prusak, L. (1998) *Working Knowledge*. Boston, USA: Harvard Business School Press.
6. Goodison, T. (2003) *Integrating ICT in the classroom: a case study of two contrasting lessons*. British Journal of Education Technology. **34**: p. 549–567.
7. Hall, I. and Higgins, S. (2005) *Primary school students' perception of interactive whiteboards*. Journal of Computer Assisted Learning. **21**(2): p. 102-117.
8. Levy, P. (2002) *Interactive Whiteboards in learning and teaching in two Sheffield schools: a developmental study*. Report by Department of Information Studies, University of Sheffield. Last accessed 21 May 2007. (Online http://dis.shef.ac.uk/eirg/projects/wboards.htm
9. Glover, D. and Miller, D. (2001) *Running with technology: the pedagogic impact of the large scale introduction of interactive whiteboards in one secondary school*. Technology, Pedagogy and Education. **10**(3): p. 257-278.
10. Wall, K., Higgins, S., and Smith, H.J. (2005) *"The visual helps me understand the complicated things": pupil views of teaching and learning with interactive whiteboards*. British Journal of Education Technology. **36**(5): p. 851-867.
11. McCallum, B., Hargreaves, E., and Gipps, C. (2000) *Learning: the pupil's voice*. Cambridge Journal of Education. **30**(2): p. 275-289.
12. Smith, H.J., Higgins, S., Wall, K., and Miller, J. (2005) *Interactive whiteboards: boon or bandwagon? A critical review of the literature*. Journal of Computer Assisted Learning. **21**: p. 91-101.
13. Damcott, D., Landato, J., Marsh, C., and Rainey, W. (2002) *Report on the use of the smart board interactive whiteboard in physical science*. Report by Smarter Kids Foundation. Last accessed 21 May 2007. (Online http://smarterkids.org/research/paper3.asp
14. Edwards, J., Hartnell, M., and Martin, R. (2002) *Interactive whiteboards: some lessons from the classroom*. Micro Math. **18**: p. 30-33.
15. Kennewell, S., Tanner, H., Jones, S., and Beauchamp, G. (2007) *Analysing the use of interactive technology to implement interactive teaching*. Journal of Computer Assisted Learning.
16. Brandt, I. (2006) *Models of Internet connectivity for secondary schools in the Grahamstown Circuit*, in *Computer Science Department*. Rhodes Univeristy: Grahamstown, South Afirca
17. Cohen, L., Manion, L., and Morrison, K. (2000) *Research methods in education*. London: Routledge.
18. Morgan, C. and Morris, G. (1998) *Good teaching and learning : pupils and teachers speak*. Philadelphia, USA: Open University Press.
19. Becta (2004) *What the research says about interactive whiteboards*. Report by BECTA. Last accessed 25 March 2008. (Online Report BEC1-15006) http://publications.teachernet.gov.uk/eOrderingDownload/15006MIG2793.pdf

Chapter 2

Planning and Modelling for Teaching and Learning

Scenario planning and learning technologies
The foundation of lifelong learning

Bent B. Andresen, Ph. D.
Danish School of Education, University of Aarhus
Tuborgvej 164, 2400 Copenhagen NV, Denmark
www.dpu.dk/om/bba

Abstract. In this paper, the author reports findings from research concerning the planning of learning scenarios in education. The purpose of the research is to explore the value of this scenario planning and reflection-on-action. In particular, the research objective is to explore how this innovative method can guide the adoption of ICT in education and cultivate competencies for lifelong and lifewide learning.

1. Introduction

Lifelong and lifewide learning can be considered a guiding principle for provision and participation across the full continuum of learning contexts. The implementation of this vision into formal education is currently a challenge. A crucial component is the pedagogical approaches of teachers – from preschool to university and adult education. This paper deals with research concerning a complex of problems related to the foundation of this challenge: the planning of learning events. The main question is: How to design innovative learning scenarios that fosters lifewide and lifelong learning?

1.1 Why learning scenarios?

Proponents of scenario planning make it clear that scenarios are not predictions of the future [1]. Rather, they aim to perceive futures in the present and foster innovation. The results may lead to better thinking and reflection on current trends and developments and an ongoing strategic conversation about the future [2].

During the past few decades, scenario planning has emerged in various fields and for various purposes. Scenarios represent a natural bridge between mind and world. The notion of scenario itself can be defined as a brief narrative that describe possible futures and find paths towards realization, based on plausible hypotheses and assumptions grounded in the present [1].

Please use the following format when citing this chapter:

Andresen, B.B., 2008, in IFIP International Federation for Information Processing, Volume 281; *Learning to Live in the Knowledge Society;* Michael Kendall and Brian Samways; (Boston: Springer), pp. 29–36.

Scenario thinking has become a kind of literacy. At an early age, everybody has to be able to make up scenarios, whose potentials, problems, and pace of work can then be considered and appreciated [1]. It implies the use of meta-cognitive skills and is an underlying part of lifelong and lifewide learning [3].

What matters is reflective thinking about learning for practical improvement. Thinking reflectively requires the subject of a thought process to become its object. For example, having applied themselves to mastering a particular mental technique, reflection-on-action allows individuals to then think about this technique, assimilate it, relate it to other aspects of their experiences, and to change or adapt it. Individuals who are reflective also follow up such thought processes with practice or action [3].

Progress is often based on increased simplicity. Consequently, the scenarios may be relatively simple. Moreover, they do not have to be new in an objective sense of the word. According to a theory of innovation, what matters is the perceived newness [4]. If some teachers, for example, perceive a learning scenario to be new and manage to realize it because it is not too complex, then their practice can be considered innovative even if some of their colleagues adopted the same approach last year or before.

The scenarios may address specific factors that maintain difficulties for the learners [5]. In this manner, scenario planning is a way to address current barriers to lifelong and lifewide learning and professional development.

2. Reflection-on-action

Scenario planning promotes reflective competencies and facilitates conversation about what is going on and what might occur in future education [6]. It is about re-perceiving the learning environment and promoting differentiated, flexible, proactive stances toward the pedagogical practice of the future. In particular, it is designed to identify and focus on important 'what if'-questions, which provide fresh ideas that challenge practice which relies on habits more than on evidence [7].

This approach is different from that traditionally employed, which involves general models of 'best practice'. Rather than attempting to apply general models to practical situations, the aim is to make better decisions about what to do or avoid doing.

The teachers' planning process may rely on their conscious thinking and modification while on the job. This reflection-in-action typically includes iterative loops running though: observation, reflection, decision, and acting. On ordinary days, however, the four activities may not accurately reflect standard practice, because teachers may lack opportunity and time. Their workload often works against regular and systematic reflection-in-action.

Some teachers may also consider reflection-in-action an academic pursuit, i.e., not associate it with working as a teacher at all (Hatton and Smith, 1994). Therefore, reflection-in-action may be extraordinary, but not rare.

In-service education and innovative projects and initiatives, on the other hand, often promote reflection [9] [10]. At such events, the teachers frequently reflect on their practice, thinking back on what they have done and how their knowledge may have contributed to the outcome.

In addition, the teaching, supervision, and mentoring provided at these events often inspire the participant's considerations regarding recognized and unrecognized conflicts between institutional ideals and workplace practice. Teachers may, for instance, reflect on future practice, thinking ahead without a direct connection to present action [8].

To begin with, the teachers may articulate and clarify their beliefs and experiences. This preliminary articulation then provides a useful basis for reflection on arrangement of environments where the learners can interact, learn, and learn to learn [11].

Thereafter, the teachers may give voice to their ideas and write their scenarios down. Hereby, they can frame the often complex situations and ambiguous problems they are facing, analyze possible approaches, and plan to modify their actions as a result [12]. In short, the single loop of planning is extended to a double loop that will allow the teachers to 'stop-and-think' [8] and lead to genuine reflection and innovation (fig. 1).

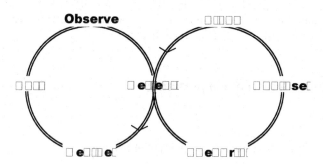

Fig. 1. Scenario planning

3. Learning modalities of the information society

In the knowledge society, the learning environment is changing since both the learners and teachers make frequent use of the intranet and mobile and stationary digital devices. Consequently, a purpose of scenario planning is to deploy and actually use ICT to support learning. In particular, it deals with the frequent use of this technology in educational settings including access to after-hours ICT facilities.

The scenarios developed by the teachers are decisive, since a crucial component is the teachers' pedagogical approaches [13]. In essence, education is communication, and the teachers may focus on innovative ways of communication to foster the changes called learning. Their longer-term planning may also address fundamental questions like: "Is ICT changing education and what might schools become?" [14]?

The shorter-term planning may consider the 'symbiotic' relationship between learning and ICT, reflecting the way in which learners actually make use of the technology. In particular, teachers may consider future communication and arrangement of environments. Their planning may thereby reflect questions like: "Under which circumstances do the learners make use of ICT and does it make a difference?"

Together, a group of teachers may design visionary scenarios concerning when and how to communicate in or out of schools by means of ICT. The process may be initiated through a joint discussion of the curriculum objectives and the potential role of digital technology in fulfilling the desired learning outcomes in a collegial model of scenario planning. It may then be followed by collaborative scenario planning exploring the possible implementation of ICT and all the issues that may need to be taken into account [15].

During this process, the collegial team may draw on the different types of knowledge and skills of each member of the team in order for all to be able to develop professionally through the mutual interaction [15]. The notions of 'apprentice' and 'master' may represent teachers with relatively little ICT-experience and teachers, knowing how to use ICT effectively to teach their subject and to support their wider professional role. By engaging in scenario thinking both 'apprentice' and 'master' can, almost as a by-product, develop greater levels of confidence and apply ICT more effectively than before.

4. Case studies on scenario planning

4.1. Impact of reflection-on action - preschool teachers

The impact of scenario building can be examined by researching innovative development projects. This section contains results from at study regarding a Danish municipality, which allocates time to these processes [16]. According to a vision of the local authority of Vordingborg, reflection-on-action constitutes an important element in lifelong learning. Since lifelong learning has become the guiding principle for provision and participation across the full continuum of learning contexts, the staffs of educational institutions have got time to practice what they teach.

Consequently, the local authority has allocated 25 pct. of the planning time to reflection-of-action. This includes the staffs of all educational institutions (0-16 years). My research, currently in progress, investigates the reception among the staff of two kinds of day nurseries (0-3 and 3-6 years) and primary and secondary schools (grade 0-10).

Findings from the first case study indicate that the staffs are very much in line with the local authority [16]. The staffs emphasize that that the initiative develops their community of practice. In particular, they get time:

- To study their educational practice in depth;
- To develop mutual understanding;

- To inspire each other;
- To experience individual strengths and potentials;
- To increase consciousness of pedagogical practice;
- To get access to models to develop this practice;
- To be innovative and creative together;
- To combine theory and practice;
- To be updated;
- To develop common visions;
- To develop their pedagogical practice;
- To develop relationships between children and adults;
- To debate and develop the curriculum;
- To foster collaboration and team based learning;
- To read together;
- To develop common notions and language;
- To consider notions like learning and learning environment;
- To create;
- To document;
- To learn from each other at the institutions;
- To foster cooperation between institutions;
- To foster cooperation in the municipality.

In particular, the reflection-on-action is aimed at scenario planning that strengthen the relationships between the children and the staffs or foster learning from various activities. The research findings document that the time allocated to reflection-on-action represents an important first step towards learning communities of practice and lifelong and lifewide learning. Almost all the participants declared that they greatly appreciated the following activities:

- Rewarding reflection-on-action together with their colleagues
- Substantial contribution to the description of innovative learning scenarios
- Intense dialogue concerning these innovate scenarios.

4.2. Impact of scenario writing - teachers in primary and secondary education

The impact of scenario building can also be observed by researching courses for teachers, in which it is considered a key activity. What matters is not whether the courses studied are aimed at a certain degree or are short-term courses (non-award bearing), but that they give priority to reflection-on-action. The following paragraphs present results from at study regarding the Danish ICT Driving License in which scenario planning is considered the main collaborative activity.

The objective of these in-service courses for teachers is to foster the application of ICT into the classrooms by means of scenario planning. Eight different courses has been developed and offered to teachers of schools (grades 0-12) and teacher education institutions. During each course, which last 4-9 months, the participants typically produce multi-faceted scenarios specifying the objectives, expected learning outcomes and products, and main roles of teachers and learners at various stages.

Narratives about imagined goal-oriented sequences of learning activities often address some or all of these topics:

1. Clarification and articulation of learner learning outcomes (construction, rather than reproduction of knowledge; value beyond school);
2. Brief description of content (topics, concepts, and working methods)
3. Main roles of teachers and learners (who does what?)
4. Overview of organization (duration; subject or cross-curricular; plenum and/or small group work; support of learners with special needs);
5. Methods of evaluation (continuously and summarizing);
6. Take-off activities (learners' previous experiences and qualifications; method of introduction);
7. Learner productions.

So far, three out of four Danish teachers at grade 1-10 have been engaged in the scenario-based collaborative e-learning event. The scenarios produced by the teachers encompass a broad spectrum of learning activities concerning:

- Collaborative learning with digital portfolios and learner logs;
- Knowledge processing activities with creative writing;
- Information retrieval as part of self-directed learning;
- Real (not 'as if') communication aimed at various target groups and with various layouts and graphical designs;
- Compensational use of digital technology.

Even though some teams of teachers have not been through this kind of process before, they benefit from writing down their scenarios. Participants with a nodding acquaintance with the use of the digital technology in education may prefer using headwords or bullets. They benefit, however, more from using their pedagogical imagination in scenario telling. The proses, among other things, allow them to give the grounds for their choices between various pedagogical approaches.

To be approved, each scenario must describe a well grounded and innovative application of ICT into the schools. Every team of teachers has to present their exact arguments. Consequently, the provision of feedback is tailored to the reflections and scenario planning of each team.

The first real course based on a scenario-model was tested and evaluated in 1999/2000 with 7.000 teachers. 88% of these participants considered the course content to be highly relevant and 90% appreciated the teamwork in this period [17]. It helped them focus their learning and increased the quality of their scenario planning. A later study [18] provided similar results, and the research findings are considered evident, since they are generally documented over a longer period.

Another later study addressed the question of the value of the scenario planning in the long run. Data was collected one year after the completion of the course. In particular, the further study addressed the crucial question: "Did the teachers consider the scenario planning useful afterwards?" The participants, who completed the course, reported a positive impact. For example, 86% acknowledged that the course was useful in promoting the use of the Internet in their classes [18]. The participants reported that they are planning scenarios with learners making use of the internet more often than before. In addition, they acknowledged that the course had high impact on their own use of E-mail and Learning Management Systems, the Internet, and word processing (fig. 2).

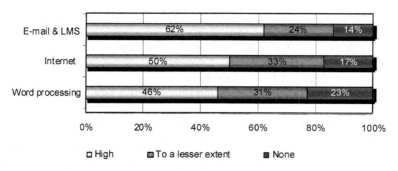

Fig. 2. Impact on teaching

5. Conclusion

In the first part of the paper, the author argues that learning scenarios may be a generic technique to stimulate thinking about innovative teaching and learning events. The scenarios produced at these occasions may aim to perceive innovative practice in the present practice. Teachers – from preschool to university – may promote a capacity to plan learning scenarios, and to choose among potential candidate scenarios while on the job (reflecting-in-action).

Moreover, in-service education, and international, national or local developments, projects and initiatives may foster reflecting-on-action. Supervision and mentoring provided at these events may also support the teacher's scenario planning.

In the last part of the paper, the author reports positive research findings regarding such events. They support the teachers imagining the steps taken by the learners with various objectives and paces. In conclusion, the scenario planning is a useful tool for teachers who adopt digital technology and new learning standards in education.

Acknowledgements

The EU has sponsored the work described in this paper through the projects Agent DYSL and PEDACTICE. UNESCO has sponsored the work through the project Multimedia in Education. The Danish Ministry of Education has sponsored the work through the projects KVIS and Skole-IT.

References

1. Lankshear, C. & Knobel, M. (2006). New literacies. Everyday practices and classroom learning. Second edition. Berkshire: Open University Press. McGraw-Hill Education.

2. Snoek, M. (2003). The Use and Methodology of Scenario Making. European Journal of Teacher Education, Vol. 26, No. 1.
3. OECD (2006). The definition and selection of key competencies. Executive Summary. (DeSeCo   project).   Available   from: www.oecd.org/dataoecd/47/61/35070367.pdf
4. Rogers, E. M. (2003). Diffusion of Innovations. Fifth Edition. New York: Free Press.
5. Nordahl, T. (2005). *Læringsmiljø og pedagogisk analyse. En beskrivelse og evaluering av LP-modellen.* Rapport 19/05. Oslo: NOVA.
6. Cautreels, P. (2003). A Personal Reflection on Scenario Writing as a Powerful Tool to Become a More Professional Teacher Teacher. European Journal of Teacher Education, Vol. 13, No. 2.
7. Berger, P. L. & Luckmann, T. (1966). The social construction of reality. New York: Doubleday.
8. Schön, D. A. (1983). The reflective practitioner. How professionals think in action. New York: Basic Books.
9. Hansen, O. (2000). SocraTESS ODL Network. Final Report. Hinnerup: Pædagogisk, Psykologisk Rådgivning.
10. Scrimshaw, P. (2004). Enabling teachers to make successful use of ICT. London: BECTA.
11. Dewey, J. (1916). Democracy and Education. New York. Macmillan.
12. Hatton, N. & Smith, D. (2006). Reflection in teacher education: Towards definition and implementation. Sydney: The University of Sydney: School of Teaching and Curriculum Studies.
13. Cox, M. et al. (2003). ICT and pedagogy. A review of the research literature. London: DfES.
14. Abbott, C. (2001). ICT – changing Education. London: RoutledgeFalmer.
15. Mutton, T. et al. (2006). Mentor skills in a new context: working with trainee teachers to develop the use of information and communications technology in their subject teaching. Technology, Pedagogy and Education. Vol. 15, No. 3.
16. Andresen, B. B. (2007). Mangfoldighed og pædagogisk forandringsledelse – et 2½-årigt udviklingsprojekt i Vordingborg Kommune. Første delrapport. Vordingborg: Fagsekretariat for Pædagogik.
17. Andresen, B. B. (2000). Det første år med det pædagogiske IT-kørekort. Århus: UNI-C. Available from:
18. Styregruppen for Skole-IT (2002). Effektundersøgelse 2 af Skole-IT. København: Rambøll Management.

Supporting the Design of Pilot Learning Activities with the Pedagogical Plan Manager

Rosa Maria Bottino, Jeffrey Earp, Giorgio Olimpo, Michela Ott,
Francesca Pozzi and Mauro Tavella
Istituto per le Tecnologie Didattiche, Consiglio Nazionale delle Ricerche,
Via De Marini 6, 16149 Genova, Italy. bottino@itd.cnr.it,
WWW home page: http://www.itd.cnr.it

Abstract. Pilot actions for introducing ICT-based innovation in school education generally involve a multitude of elements and a range of different actors. Accounting for and grasping this complexity calls for systematic pedagogical planning efforts that provide a solid basis for accommodating the different perspectives, for analysing the factors at play and also for casting light on the initial assumptions and theoretical framework adopted. These are the issues currently being addressed in a European project called ReMath, in which the authors are developing and testing a prototype ICT-based tool called the Pedagogical Plan Manager (PPM). The system supports the construction and sharing of pedagogical plans within a community of different actors operating in different contexts with different visions. This paper briefly describes some of the requirements that have shaped the PPM and outlines the conceptual model on which it is based. The system is described in the light of two vital characteristics it presents for the design of learning activities, namely expressiveness and flexibility.

1 Introduction

Pilot actions aimed at bringing innovation to school education through ICT are potentially complex endeavours involving a multitude of elements and a range of different actors such as teachers, researchers, pedagogical experts, designers, etc. So when it comes to the design of experimental learning activities, adequate account needs to be taken of the various factors and perspectives involved. A well articulated pedagogical plan can provide a solid basis for pilot analysis and help in gaining understanding of the dynamics at play. In addition, such a plan can cast light on the

Please use the following format when citing this chapter:

Bottino, R.M., Earp, J., Olimpo, G., Ott, M., Pozzi, F. and Tavella, M., 2008, in IFIP International Federation for Information Processing, Volume 281; _Learning to Live in the Knowledge Society_; Michael Kendall and Brian Samways; (Boston: Springer), pp. 37–44.

conceptual framework of the pilot action and on the assumptions underpinning the design of learning activities, areas that have a strong bearing on the outcome and can thus prove critical in the eventual take-up of the innovation in question.

In recent times, pedagogical questions involved in ICT-based educational actions have been attracting increasing interest. In the field of learning design, much attention is currently being focused on how different pedagogical visions can be accommodated and expressed in the authoring of learning actions, invoking pedagogical planning of some kind [1,2]. This is the direction of the work reported in this paper, which is based on the conviction that, as well as supporting the preparation of "units of learning" (UoL) [3] and suchlike, ICT can also be a support for critical reflection, helping to clarify, crystallize and capture pedagogical aspects which often remain implicit or hidden in the design process.

These concerns are an integral part of the authors' present activities within the EC ReMath project[1], where a strong need exists to address the specific requirements of researchers in the design of pedagogical plans. The project involves cross-experimentation of innovative ICT-based learning activities at European level and entails collective exploration of design issues, pilot activities and comparison of results in the light of multiple approaches and contexts. This has led to the definition of the "pedagogical scenario", seen as a description of aspects deemed relevant for the design of innovative ICT-based learning activities. The conceptual model of the pedagogical scenario has provided the basis for the development of a web-based tool called the Pedagogical Plan Manager (PPM). This tool is designed for the production and sharing of instantiated pedagogical scenarios, henceforth called "pedagogical plans". As reported in the following sections, the PPM's specific mission is to support reflective and documented pedagogical design in experimental piloting. The authors believe, however, that the approach and solutions adopted are applicable to the wider educational context, and they do not exclude future integration of capabilities for enacting learner-oriented activities online.

2 The Context and Specific Requirements

The ReMath project has the aim of building an integrated theoretical and operative framework for mathematics learning through ICT-based representation of mathematical meanings. In efforts towards achieving and demonstrating this integration, research teams based in different European countries have each developed a digital maths learning tool that reifies the particular theoretical framework/s inspiring their work. These teams are carrying out cross-experimentation to compare and relate the theoretical frameworks adopted in the development of the tools. As the project's basic assumptions stress the importance of the learning process, exploration does not occur at tool level, but rather is based on exchange among researchers about the learning processes mediated by the use of the developed tools. Furthermore, collaboration involves both researchers specialized in the mathematics domain as well as those in the field of education technology, so as

---

[1] ReMath: Representing Mathematics with digital technologies (IST4-26751).

to enhance dialogue not only on a content and epistemological level, but also at a pedagogical and didactical level.

In this context, the authors identified a number of key project requirements that were deemed important for the development of both the pedagogical scenario model and the prototype tool which was to concretize that model. The main requirements identified were to:

- help researchers make explicit the theoretical assumptions that are implicit in their educational software tool and in the learning activities based on the different software;
- give teams in different countries and settings the means to express their particular design ideas for pilots without forcing them to conform to a preset structural format reflecting a single (external) cultural vision of teaching/learning;
- support cross-experimentation of innovative mathematics software in order to explore how a team (a) approaches the design of learning activities based on a tool that it has not itself developed, and (b) how it adapts these to its specific pedagogical aims, research objectives and experimental context;
- support reflection, discussion and comparison within the ReMath community, whose mission is to explore the basis for integrating disparate theoretical frameworks.

Meeting such requirements and accounting for the diverse perspectives and concerns that the project brings together clearly called for a design solution offering considerable expressiveness and a high degree of structural flexibility. These two fundamental characteristics of the Pedagogical Plan Manager are described in greater detail in the following section.

3 Expressiveness and Flexibility of the Pedagogical Plan Manager

As mentioned above, the Pedagogical Plan Manager is based on a pedagogical scenario model. The model is seen as a dynamic, flexible and modular basis for the production of pedagogical plans. While the pedagogical scenario does share some characteristics with other learning design artefacts such as the "unit of learning", it differs from these in several important ways, one of which is the explicit and concerted effort to accommodate the perspective of the researcher. Accordingly, the model features a number of attributes for expressing (among other things) the reason why an educational action is proposed, the theoretical and didactical framework in which it is positioned, the innovation it is intended to introduce and the way it is to be implemented. The aim is to bring to light key (often submerged) issues involved in the designing process and in the resulting design artefact, as well as to foster reflection on the adopted solutions. [2,4]

The attributes of the pedagogical scenario are organized in a schema of descriptors which, when instantiated with data (open text and multimedia), form a pedagogical plan. These descriptors are grouped into four major categories - Identity, Target, Rationale, Specifications - each of which is further refined into more detailed descriptor sets and single descriptors, as follows.

- IDENTITY - identifies and classifies a plan , also for storing and retrieving it in the PPM system;
- TARGET - indicates the population addressed, the context in which that population is embedded, the educational goals to be achieved;
- RATIONALE - expresses plan rationale and the theoretical framework that has informed the design process;
- SPECIFICATIONS – indicates the tools and resources to be used by students, how these are be used, and a work plan.

The nature and organization of this descriptor schema are key factors in ensuring that the pedagogical scenario instance, the pedagogical plan, is capable of a high degree of expressiveness. The adopted model supports and enhances this capability by treating the pedagogical scenario as a tree-like hierarchical structure whose different levels are to be instantiated using the same descriptor schema, populated at appropriate degrees of abstraction. This not only allows authors to express and explore their concerns at considerable depth, it is also crucial for encouraging them to consider and reflect on how they articulate their pedagogical ideas through(out) the design, from high-level "vision statement" to the operational details of learning activities. As Beetham [5] puts it, "(authors') priorities may only emerge as they reflect on the (design) decisions they have taken". To foster this emergence, in the PPM it is the authors themselves who determine the exact organization and granularity they wish to adopt when expressing their design ideas, rather than having to conform to a fixed structure and/or adopt predetermined entities (*activity, lesson, unit, module,* etc.) that reflect a single, possibly unfamiliar cultural/pedagogical vision. The need for such flexibility emerged in previous ITD experiences [6] in pedagogical planning and is considered essential in experimental piloting contexts like ReMath, which foresees cross-experimentation and collaborative development of plans. For example, various degrees of adaptation will be required in order to permit a comprehensive, instantiated plan (one proposing detailed experimental activities for meeting certain goals within a certain context) to be reused in a variety of different settings. Likewise, when building plans in a collaborative framework, authors need to have the means to capture and exchange nascent ideas, possibly expressed at a fairly high level of abstraction, which are then fleshed out with the particulars of the learning context, its specific requirements and restraints. An instance of such "germination" might be a description of an interesting educational "affordance" of a software program considered useful for tackling a problematic area of learning, or perhaps, at a more abstract level, a proposal for the adoption of a specific theoretical approach to subject teaching.

As with expressiveness, the quality of flexibility is firmly rooted in the conceptual model underpinning the PPM, whereby the pedagogical plan is treated as a tree-like hierarchical structure comprising multiple levels of abstraction (see Fig.1. below). This approach offers a number of advantages. It makes it easier to manage the potential complexity of plans by allowing top-down *representation*, which is helpful irrespective of how the authoring *process* is actually carried out: top-down, bottom-up, middle-out, or zigzag fashion. Each node of the hierarchy is a complete pedagogical scenario in itself, populated with data at an appropriate level of abstraction using the same descriptor schema (though not all fields will necessarily need populating at all levels). Top-down representation acts as a stimulus for recognizing and making explicit structural aspects of the plan that are conceptually meaningful but often "hidden" or overlooked in the design. In addition, it allows those in experimental contexts to express and investigate research concerns at different degrees of granularity. It facilitates collaborative development by allowing authors to decide in what direction, and how far, to take the refinement. It supports reuse through modularity, i.e. by proposing a set of loosely coupled elementary components that have strong internal (conceptual) coherence.

Top-down representation is implemented in the PPM by introducing the notions of the Hierarchical Pedagogical Plan (HIPP) and the Single Node Pedagogical Plan, or SNiPP. The HIPP and SNiPP are the fundamental entities that users work with in the PPM for shaping pedagogical plans and displaying their contents. As Fig.1 shows, the HIPP is a structure comprising a set of one or more SNiPPs which, as stated above, are complete pedagogical scenarios in themselves; so potentially each entity may be interpreted - as required - either as an individual node (SNiPP) or as a tree/sub-tree with that node as its root (HIPP).

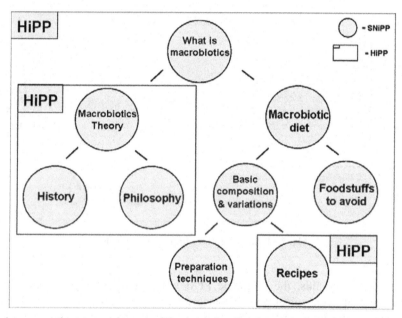

Fig. 1. an example structure (organised by topic) showing the two main entities represented in the PPM: HiPP and SNiPP

4 Prototype of the Pedagogical Plan Manager

The prototype version of the PPM (http://ppm.itd.cnr.it/) that the authors have developed is currently being used in the ReMath project for collaborative creation, sharing and reuse of pedagogical plans. As already mentioned, the basic idea underpinning the PPM is to represent pedagogical plans as hierarchical entities which can be built and read at different levels of detail. This structure should support both "authors" (providing them with the possibility to work with a top-down structure) and "readers", who in top-down organization have a facilitating factor for understanding complex plans, i.e. grasping the general structure, relating rationales with concrete details, etc.

The PPM interface has been designed so as to allow both authors and readers to deal easily and naturally with the hierarchical structure, to navigate from the general to the particular and vice versa, and to explicitly select the fields they want to focus on.

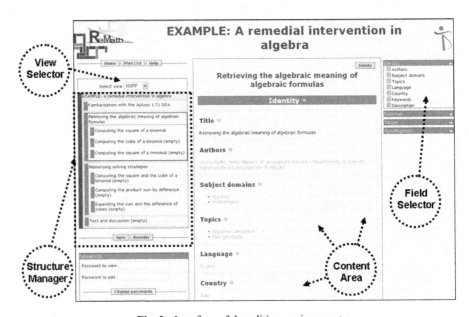

Fig. 2 - Interface of the editing environment

In order to do this, the prototype PPM provides three basic functionalities: management of pedagogical plans (Manager); building/modifying plans (Editor); and viewing/navigating existing plans (Viewer). The Manager is a simple repository for browsing and selecting from the list of existing plans. The Editor and the Viewer share a set of common facilities (see Fig.2), including: a *Structure Manager*, an interactive map of the plan hierarchy for viewing and shaping plan structure; a *View Selector*, which allows the user to work either with SNiPPs or with HiPPs, switching from one to the other as required; and a *Field Selector*, for selecting exactly the type and number of descriptors the user wishes to work with at any given moment.

Using the Field Selector in conjunction with the View Selector, the user can input/display on a single web page the data for a single descriptor (e.g. curriculum goals) or to a set thereof (e.g. goals) at different levels of the hierarchy. In this way both authors and readers can "drill down" through a plan as desired [4], a possibility which helps in reaping the aforementioned benefits of top-down representation.

To further facilitate plan construction via top-down representation, authors can populate a given field in a given SNiPP automatically by electing to inherit the data that is contained in the corresponding field within the immediate parent SNiPP.

The descriptive fields in the content area can be completed with data of various kind (free text, images, hyperlinks, html code), and it is also possible to upload attached files: guidance for completing each field is available in a pop-up. As well as inserting data for identification and description purposes, authors can include links to any web-based tools to be used in learning activities and can also integrate any digital learning resources to be used in enactment. In the PPM, the term "resources" refers both to: (1) "input" artefacts needed *a priori* for carrying out activities with students (worksheets to fill out, web sites to visit, etc.); and (2) runtime-generated artefacts that result from enacted activities, whether these be elaborations of a given "input" resource (a completed worksheet, a filled-out table) or something produced from scratch, like student reports. So a plan can include a resource, in the form of either a concrete instance or a description, which is to be progressively elaborated across a sequence of learning activities.

In response to the demands of the ReMath project, the PPM has been designed as a wholly web-based tool accessible via standard web browser. This, combined with real-time online editing via Ajax permits collaborative development of plans online, an essential function in experimental piloting of learning activities, which almost invariably involve a team design effort. To further support collaboration, fields in the PPM Editor feature a "Comment" window for appending remarks in the plan authoring process. This is currently being used in ReMath as a space for exchange and collaboration about plan contents, and has been earmarked for further development in the next version of the tool.

5 Conclusions

This paper has presented a conceptual model and related ICT-based tool that were conceived and developed to support the pedagogical design of experimental learning initiatives engaging different actors, contexts and visions. Particular attention has been devoted to key criteria that have guided the development of the Pedagogical Plan Manager, namely expressiveness and flexibility. These are supported and enhanced by the adoption of top-down representation of pedagogical plans, which helps in mastering the potential complexity of a plan design (and of plan designing) and in recognizing and making explicit significant structural aspects.

While the authors are keen to explore this potential, they are also keenly aware of possible drawbacks. With top-down representation, particular care is required to ensure manageability (especially in terms of interface design) and to avoid the attendant risk of information overload [4]. Likewise, the benefits derived from a high degree of flexibility need to be considered in the light of the increased effort and engagement that may be required of both authors and readers.

In order to strike a suitable balance between these factors, it is necessary to have a clear idea of how effectively the PPM has actually satisfied different users' needs in the ReMath project. To this purpose the authors have developed and implemented an evaluation strategy intended to verify the soundness of the "pedagogical scenario" both as a conceptual model and as a concrete entity implemented via the PPM tool. Preliminary results from pedagogical plan authors indicate that they appreciate the PPM's qualities of expressiveness and flexibility; useful feedback has also been collected for determining areas of priority for further development. As the evaluation effort continues over the remaining stages of the ReMath project, it is expected that other valuable indications will emerge.

REFERENCES

1. R. van Es, R. Koper, Testing the pedagogical expressiveness of IMS-LD *Educational Technology & Society*. Volume 9 (1), 2006, pp. 229-249. http://hdl.handle.net/1820/305

2. Britain S. Learning design systems: current and future developments, in *Rethinking Pedagogy for a Digital Age - Designing and Delivering E-Learning* H. Beetham; R.Sharpe (eds). 2007. Routledge, UK. pp. 103-114

3. Koper, R., and Olivier, B. 2004. Representing the learning design of units of learning. *Educational Technology & Society* 7(3): pp. 97-111 http://www.ifets.info/journals/7_3/10.pdf

4. Falconer, H. Beetham, R. Oliver, L. Lockyer, A. Littlejohn, Mod4L Final Report: Representing Learning Designs. Joint Information Systems Committee (JISC), 2007. http://mod4l.com/tiki-download_file.php?fileId=7

5. Beetham H. An Approach to Learning Activity Design, in *Rethinking Pedagogy for a Digital Age - Designing and Delivering E-Learning* H. Beetham; R.Sharpe (eds). 2007. Routledge, UK. pp. 26-40

6. J. Earp, F. Pozzi, Fostering reflection in ICT-based pedagogical Planning in:, *Proceedings of the First International LAMS Conference 2006: Designing the Future of Learning*. R. Philip, A Voerman & J. Dalziel (Eds). Sydney, LAMS Foundation, 2006. pp35-44 http://lamsfoundation.org/lams2006/papers.htm

Groups can do IT
A Model for Cooperative Work in Information Technology

Leila Goosen [1] and Elsa Mentz [2]
1 Department of Science, Mathematics and Technology Education,
Groenkloof Campus, University of Pretoria, 0001 South Africa
lgoosen@gk.up.ac.za
2 Department of Computer Science Education,
Potchefstroom Campus, North-West University, 2520 South Africa
snsem@puknet.puk.ac.za

Abstract. As the Information Technology (IT) professionals of the future, learners of programming need to master skills with regard to learning together and sharing knowledge. The research question that will serve to focus this paper is: "How can we integrate cooperative group work meaningfully into the teaching and learning of programming skills?" In answer, this paper presents a new model for cooperative learning environments in IT classrooms that emphasizes the importance of structuring cooperative groups for effectiveness. Learning from the past, we base the model on literature and previous research done by the authors. Appropriate implementation of the model requires the basic elements of positive interdependence, individual accountability, promotive interaction, interpersonal and small-group skills, and group processing.

1. Introduction

These days, programming projects are growing in size and complexity [1]. Large groups of programmers therefore need to work together to solve problems and develop solutions. Most companies are increasingly requiring members of their work force to be well equipped with essential cooperative and communication skills [2].

In order for Information Technology (IT) learners to be responsive to these changing requirements of the workplace, while learning programming, they must also develop the necessary social skills. "Cooperative learning techniques have been applied with a wide variety of subject matter and a broad spectrum of populations" to teach introductory computer programming [3]. These educational techniques produce increases in learning skills, improve learner motivation and have significant positive effects on learner performance and attitudes towards instructional content [4]. [3]

Please use the following format when citing this chapter:

Goosen, L. and Mentz, E., 2008, in IFIP International Federation for Information Processing, Volume 281; *Learning to Live in the Knowledge Society*; Michael Kendall and Brian Samways; (Boston: Springer), pp. 45–52.

also refer to evidence accumulated from existing educational research that "suggests that cooperative learning results in higher student achievement, more positive attitudes toward the subject, (and) improved student retention". Many of these advantages are also transferable skills that influence both the ways in which learners learn cooperatively, and when they learn individually.

Cooperative work contributes to conceptual learning and the knowledge construction process when they consider alternative viewpoints on problem solution, thus creating possibilities for the re-construction of their own perceptions and answers [5] [1] believe that during the process of actively thinking and working together to construct problem solutions, cooperative projects provide learners with opportunities to share and explore ideas, learn new concepts, expose different points of view, and experience the satisfaction and challenges of working with others. Working cooperatively not only nurtures and develops these skills, "but also promotes deep learning through interaction, problem solving and dialogue" [6]. Exposure to these kinds of opportunities encourages cooperation between learners, considered one of the attributes of good teaching practice.

It is, however, crucial to understand that teachers' contributions are of key importance in making cooperative learning encounters constructive for all learners. Teachers need to promote interactions between learners during cooperative work that lead to the type of thinking and problem solving that is necessary to involve them in the learning process [4]. Another review of research by [7] "demonstrates that the benefits of cooperative learning are enhanced when … teachers have been trained in how to implement this pedagogical strategy." Such training not only adds to the advantages of this instructional approach, but also empowers teachers to help their learners in the IT classroom to utilize cooperative skills effectively. The research question that will therefore serve to focus this paper is: "How can we integrate cooperative group work meaningfully into the teaching and learning of programming skills?"

2. Key Elements of Effective Cooperative Action

Those experienced in the use of cooperative groups know that promoting successful cooperative learning "does not just happen" [6] - you cannot simply put learners in a group and hope that they will work together well [7]. Literature [see e.g. 9] emphasizes the importance of structuring cooperative work for effectiveness, by ensuring that the following key elements are evident:

1. Positive interdependence: Link group members so that they believe that they cannot individually succeed unless they all do,
2. Individual accountability: Expect each group member to be responsible for making their own personal contributions to the group and learning,
3. Interpersonal and social skills: Group members are expected to use interpersonal and small-group skills that would facilitate learning when helping each other as they work on their task, such as assuming a leadership role and effective communication ,
4. Face-to-face interaction ought be exhibited, and

5. Group processing: The group needs to reflect about how it is functioning).

3. Model for Group Work

3.1 Positive Independence

According to [7], "(e)xplicitly structuring positive... interdependence in groups... appears to be critical for successful cooperative learning." Interdependent group members realize that they cannot achieve success unless all the members of the group achieve success. Teachers need to establish mutuality in terms of common goals and "benefits from achieving goals" [9]. Having the completion of the project as a common goal should serve as one of the main factors in uniting group members in a joint effort. This mutual goal should be relevant and convincing enough to overcome learners' possible competing agendas and any conflict that might arise within the group. Because the learners in these projects are in high school, peer pressure plays an important role in encouraging good work ethics and commitment to the project.

Benefits received from achieving the common goal (in this case marks for the project) are usually distributed equally among group members, as this highlights the common fate of group members. Results in a study by [11] confirm that the majority of respondents preferred a division of the majority of marks equally among group members, with only a small portion allocated based on individual contributions. Teachers can also strengthen positive interdependence in a group by ensuring that each group member is able to complete a part of the total project [9].

3.2 Individual Accountability

[12] stress the importance of assessing for individual accountability, to ensure that all group members participate. Individual accountability is important for group success, since some members tend to dominate and some to withdraw, unless mechanisms are in place forcing everyone to participate. Individual accountability is established when each group member understands that she/he is required in each cyclic meeting to briefly report what she/he has been working on and what progress has been made [7,2]. In this way, the meetings also motivate learners to make meaningful progress, so that they have something significant to report. By requiring groups to keep a record of their decisions at meetings, each group member can be held accountable for those parts of the project that the group had agreed was her/his responsibility. All group members are individually responsible for demonstrating their own knowledge and skills with regard to programming by applying these to their parts of the project [10]. Learners also write their class tests and examinations with regard to their programming knowledge and skills individually [13].

3.3   Interpersonal and Small Group Skills

It is necessary to train learners in the interpersonal and small-group skills that facilitate learning [7]. Learners need to be taught how to communicate with each other [2], incorporating the concepts of compromise, participation, interaction and cooperation. It is also important to teach group members how to "avoid negative comments, and to present their critiques in a positive light" [14].

During the first period allocated to the project, learners receive training in small group processes by participating in various activities and games. One of these illustrate the elements of good group organization, including having a clear purpose, how to define group goals, and planning the project well [15]. The actual "planning meeting" takes place in the second period allocated to the project. Teachers need to make sure that the time allocated for planning the group work (at least one period) is spent in appropriate discussion and thorough planning, as this planning is important in order for everyone to know exactly what they will be doing. Each group should provide an account of how they had planned their work, with details written down of things such as the division of tasks between various members. If they do not plan carefully, a group might take very long to really get started, and spend too long changing their minds about what to do. As a result, they might not have enough time to complete their projects to the extent that they would have preferred. During the planning meeting, learners are responsible themselves for developing appropriate ground rules through discussion within the group [7,13].

3.4   Face to Face Interactions

Face-to-face interaction is supposed to take place each time the groups meet. When they sit together in their groups while carrying on with their cyclic meetings, learners should communicate efficiently with each another, and cooperate in order to make orderly progress. They need to provide explanations and elaboration to help other group members understand key principles and concepts related to their responsibilities within the project. Teachers need to create a situation where learners realize that effective learning is a shared responsibility, and where they share their resources, provide mutual support and encourage each other to achieve success [12].

3.5   Group Processing

Teachers should structure group tasks to ensure that learners learn to work together and get the opportunity to assume more of the organization and management of their groups [15]. During group processing learners' mastery and application of group skills are monitored regularly through teacher observation, as well as by having learners submit detailed self and peer assessment reports, in a rubric format, at the end of each cycle [2]. The assessment instrument consists of items specifying positive contributions from different group members towards the project, possible weak spots displayed, and an indication of the global contribution level for each group member. Teachers then use these assessments to provide timely and appropriate feedback to learners reflecting "observations from their peers and the teacher about how they are doing as group members" [2].

Disruptive group members could at times appear to be bored and do not always interact well with their groups. Sometimes their effort and interest are minimal in comparison to other group members. Now and then, it could be difficult to get and then hold their attention. They might benefit from realizing that it is important for the good functioning of the group to be willing to listen to the other people in the group and find out what their ideas are. This kind of behavior reminds us that teachers should not only be trained in how to handle 'trouble-makers' in groups, but also how to teach their learners how to handle such group members themselves.

If the results of group processing show some group members acting disrespectfully or uncooperatively, it is important that teachers take swift action to correct such situations. Persistently disrespectful or uncooperative learners could eventually be required to work alone, or among themselves, "rather than be an undue burden to other learners' group experiences" [2]. We are convinced that we train teachers well in ensuring that they implement these elements successfully in their learners' groups, many of the problems experienced in IT classes when implementing groups, could disappear [8]. The presence of the basic elements of group work should enable groups to work effectively to bring in the required group projects according to specifications and initial planning. In order to maximize all learners' involvement in the project, it is important that the pitch of the project is just right: On the one hand, some of the tasks should provide a challenge to learners, while other tasks require the use of skills that they feel comfortably capable of using [10].

3.6   Allocating Specific Roles in the Group

Learners need to experience that they need to effectively implement several member roles in order to successfully maximize their group's interaction and accomplishments. The main aim of these roles is the assignment of different responsibilities to group members and determining how group members are to act and/or function with-in the group [1]. In this way "poor drivers" can be avoided - they usually have domineering personalities, leading to them not knowing how to delegate responsibilities, but instead want to do everything themselves. The opposite would be learners who become "free riders", avoiding responsibility and/or contributing by letting others handle all the work [5]. As the only role that teachers often assign to group members when working in groups is that of group leader [8], learners are exposed to some of the common pitfalls that could occur when leading groups and how to take up responsibility. Since teachers generally do not know other different roles that can be assigned to learners when working in groups [8], this aspect needs specific attention during training workshops.

Learners are required to rotate between different roles what can be assumed within the group, and to record this information as part of their cyclic meeting, e.g. who the leader, scribe etc. was for a specific cycle [2]. The scribe/recorder/secretary is responsible for documenting the group conversation and providing the group consensus solution for the problem. Other positions in a group are the speaker/presenter, who presents the group's answer to the class, and the facilitator, in charge of encouraging everyone to participate. The role of a planner, to outline where and how the group is proceeding through the assignment can be added.

3.7   Assessment in Group Context

Many arguments put forward why teachers do not often use groups when teaching IT centre on perceptions that assessment in group context and the administration of group work is difficult [8,12]. Teachers need access to techniques that they can implement in order to obtain information for the assessment of individual learners in the group project situation. One of the queries most often encountered with regard to group work (that teachers need to be trained in extensively) is the issue of assessing individuals' involvement when the product of the group work is a single project [11]. This aspect is intricately tied into the elements of positive interdependence and individual accountability mentioned in previous sections. A final cumulative peer assessment instrument is used that explicitly asks "each student to rate each group member on" [2] group skills such as communication and cooperation. A principle suggested by [14] is used when marking group projects: All group members start with the same grade, but that grade is then adjusted for each member, in accordance with their individual contributions as reflected in their peer assessments [4].

We now implement and test this model for cooperative groups in South African IT classes, by piloting it in selected schools, to determine the effectiveness of the model when teaching programming, as well as to identify possible shortcomings.

4. Piloting the Model

4.1   Training Workshops

In order to pilot the model, we train selected teachers in the effective use of group strategies for implementation in the teaching and learning of programming skills in the IT class. This training is in accordance with the model as described in the previous section of this paper, and takes place in a workshop setting. We follow a pre-test - post-test approach, with teachers involved completing a questionnaire before the training workshop to determine their base knowledge, skills, attitudes and perceptions of group teaching and learning in the IT class. After the training workshop, teachers again complete a questionnaire in order to determine the impact of the training on the same. Due to the small number of participants, mainly descriptive statistical analysis is used.

Workshops consist of a solid theoretical framework for using group learning in computer programming, as well as clear practical applications of knowledge and skills gained. Theoretical and practical work are intertwined in the workshop to ensure that the necessary knowledge, skills and attitudes are acquired in such a way that teachers are able to implement it effectively in their own IT classrooms. Responses in a study by [8] indicated that current IT teachers lack theoretical knowledge of group work. Not only were teachers uninformed, but they did not seem to appreciate the dynamics of group work and the contribution that group work could make to effective learning and teaching in the IT class. Ignorance of the possible advantages of group learning strategies could be one of the important reasons why teachers generally do not use it for teaching programming skills. If such teachers were to undergo training, one needs to query them to establish whether this is in fact the case; if so, we need to make them aware of this potential.

4.2   Teaching the Model

The selected teachers then proceed to teach programming skills in accordance with their training in cooperative strategies. During this implementation of the model in their classrooms, we ask teachers to complete a short journal entry for each implementation opportunity, detailing their experiences of cooperative teaching and learning. These provide rich qualitative information towards evaluation of the model. Researchers visit teachers on a regular basis to determine problems that they might be experiencing. During these visits, the journals form the basis for semi-structured interviews. The researchers also provide teachers with advice, information and emotional support to help teachers keep up their spirits and efforts. At the conclusion of the pilot study in schools, teachers complete a final questionnaire. We hold a focus group discussion as a debriefing session for teachers, to gain assistance from teachers to interpret results and provide a versatile, dynamic source of data directly from participants [13] - we analyze this qualitatively.

5. Conclusion

Learners need to master the basic knowledge and skills regarding group work, assume various roles within the group, resolve conflict constructively when it arises, and should be able to put these into practice successfully while working together in a group. In light of the scenario as described in the introduction to this paper, empowering learners in this way represents a valuable investment in each of these learners' futures. We are convinced that this model should enable teachers to understand the dynamics of group work and the contribution that group work could make to effective learning and teaching in the IT class.

Acknowledgements

We based this paper on work financially supported by the National Research Foundation (NRF). Any opinions, conclusions or recommendations expressed in this paper are those of the authors and the NRF does not accept liability in regard thereto.

References

1.   D. Smarkusky, R. Dempsey, J. Ludka, and F. de Quillettes, Enhanching team knowledge: Instruction vs. experience, in: Proceedings *of the 36ᵗʰ SIGCSE Technical Symposium on Computer Science Education* (ACM Press, New York, 2005), pp. 460-464.

2. D. McKinney and L.F. Denton, Affective Assessment of Team Skills in Agile CS1 Labs: The Good, the Bad, and the Ugly, in: Proceedings of the 36ᵗʰ SIGCSE Technical Symposium on Computer Science Education (ACM Press, New York, 2005), pp. 465-469.
3. L.L. Beck, A.W. Chizhik, and A.C. McElroy, Cooperative learning techniques in CS1: Design and experimental evaluation, in: Proceedings of the 36ᵗʰ SIGCSE Technical Symposium on Computer Science Education (ACM Press, New York, 2005), pp. 470-474.
4. R.M. Gillies, Teachers' and students' verbal behaviours during cooperative and small-group learning, British Journal of Educational Psychology, 76, 271-287 (2006).
5. E. Nuutila, S. Törmä, and L. Malmi, PBL and Computer Programming - The Seven Steps Method with Adaptations, Computer Science Education, 15(2), 123-142 (2005).
6. F. Sudweeks, Promoting Cooperation and Collaboration in a Web-based Learning Environment, in: Proceedings of the Informing Science and Information Technology Education Joint Conference, pp. 1439-1446, (March 30, 2007) http://proceedings.informingscience.org/IS2003Proceedings/docs/193Sudwe.pdf
7. R.M. Gillies, Structuring cooperative group work in classrooms, International Journal of Educational Research, 3(1-2), 35-49 (2003).
8. E. Mentz and L. Goosen, Are groups working in the Information Technology class? South African Journal of Education, 27(2), 329-343 (2007).
9. D.W. Johnson and R.T. Johnson, Essential Components of Peace Education, Theory into Practice, 44(4), 280-292 (2005).
10. S.E. Peterson and J.A. Miller, Comparing the Quality of Students' Experiences during Cooperative Learning and Large-Group Instruction, Journal of Educational Research, 97(3), 123-133 (2004).
11. O. Hazzan, Computer Science Students' Conception of the Relationship between Reward (Grade) and Cooperation, in: Proceedings of the 8th annual Conference on Innovation and Technology in Computer Science Education (ACM Press, New York, 2003), pp. 178-182.
12. S. Veenman, N. Van Benthum, D. Bootsma, J. Van Dieren, and N. Van Der Kemp, Cooperative learning and teacher education, Teaching and Teacher Education 18, 87-103 (2002).
13. S.N. Mitchell, R. Reilly, F.G. Bramwell, F. Lilly, and A. Solnosky, Friendship and Choosing Groupmates: Preferences for Teacher-Selected vs. Student-Selected Groupings in High School Science Classes, Journal of Instructional Psychology, 31(1), 20-32 (2004).
14. L. Pollock and M. Jochen, Making Parallel Programming Accessible to Inexperienced Programmers through Cooperative Learning, in: Proceedings of the 32nd SIGCSE Technical Symposium on Computer Science Education (ACM Press, New York, 2001), pp. 224-228.
15. K. McWhaw, H. Schnackenberg, J. Sclater, and P.C. Abrami, From co-operation to collaboration: Helping students become collaborative learners, In: Co-operative Learning: The social and intellectual outcomes of learning in groups, edited by R.M. Gillies (Routledge Falmer, London, 2003), pp. 69-84.

Chapter 3

ICT for Inclusion

A general and flexible model for the pedagogical description of learning objects

Serena Alvino[1], Paola Forcheri[2], Maria Grazia Ierardi[2] and Luigi Sarti[1]
[1] CNR, Istituto per le Tecnologie Didattiche
Via De Marini 6, 16149 Genova, Italy
{alvino,sarti}@itd.cnr.it
WWW home page: http://www.itd.cnr.it
[2] CNR, Istituto Di Matematica Applicata e Tecnologie Informatiche
Via De Marini 6, Genova, Italy
{forcheri,marygz}@ge.imati.cnr.it
WWW home page: http://www.ge.imati.cnr.it

Abstract. We illustrate a pedagogical metadata model (IMATI-ITD pedagogical metadata model) that captures didactic features of LOs according to the view of the education world. This model allows to describe a variety of contexts and can be effectively instantiated in many specific educational situations, thus combining generality with flexibility features.

1 Introduction

Learning object (LO) technology still struggles to gain momentum and acceptance in the communities of teachers and instructional designers; in fact, the considerable effort needed for realising easily reusable material and for integrating others' products in a specific pedagogical plan makes the sharing of didactical material a difficult task [1]. To support users' motivation to invest their time and efforts in this activity, notable efforts are devoted to turning repositories of LOs (LORs) into a basis for building learning communities of teachers and trainers [2]. A recent example is the SLOOP project (http://www.sloopproject.eu/): it fosters the development of such communities by integrating in a LOR functionalities aimed at supporting the enrichment of pre-existing material. Another proposal is LODE, an open source collaborative environment built around a LOR and based on an interactive model of the reuse activity [3].

The work carried out produced very valuable results. However, its effective application in the education realm requires LO producers to provide users with a clear pedagogical picture of the material [4]. As a matter of fact, it is generally recognised that present metadata standards, like IEEE LOM [4], have a limited capacity to offer

Please use the following format when citing this chapter:

Alvino, S., Forcheri, P., Ierardi, M.G. and Sarti, L., 2008, in IFIP International Federation for Information Processing, Volume 281; *Learning to Live in the Knowledge Society*; Michael Kendall and Brian Samways; (Boston: Springer), pp. 55–62.

this picture according to the view of the education world [6]. To overcome this problem, several studies analyse the problem from the perspective of the education practice: some suggest methods for defining pedagogical metadata based on the analysis of the prospective users (e.g., [7]); others propose application profiles including descriptors that are selected according to the orientation and objectives of specific communities of users (e.g.: GEM http://thegateway.org/, EDNA http://www.edna.edu.au/). These studies show the complexity of devising a pedagogical metadata model apt at being successfully employed by a variety of user communities, as these are usually characterised by different languages, backgrounds, motivations and objectives. The solution of this problem requires, in our view, a model that combines generality with flexibility, so to be sharable among different communities and, at the same time, adaptable to the specificity of each of them.

Our work gives a contribution in this direction. Starting from an initial proposal, we adopted an iterative approach to the evaluation of its adherence to the needs of a number of communities. We then elaborated an extensible model for pedagogical metadata (IMATI-ITD pedagogical metadata model), that includes: 1) a set of descriptors, generally sharable among communities, that constitutes the common framework for capturing LO features; 2) for each community and each descriptor, a vocabulary of possible values that represent (as names and meanings) the conception of the descriptor within that specific community.

Metadata provide the underpinnings of our model. For each metadata element the set of possible values represents the union of the conceptions of the various communities. To make the proposal effectively applicable, moreover, the model is integrated with a set of tools that allow users, in both the indexing and the retrieval phases, to obtain a personalized view of the model, representing its adaptation to the community at hand. Adaptable glossaries are also provided.

The model and the approach we followed in devising it are presented in this paper. We observe, preliminarily, that the model, focusing on the pedagogical aspects, is not intended to describe content-related aspects, for which we refer to international standard schemata.

2   Describing LOs' pedagogical dimension

2.1   Conceptual approach

The conceptual design of our pedagogical model (see **Fig. 1**) is based on the observation that teachers, in their work, make use not only of material to be employed directly with students, but also of schemata, scripts, meta-models that support them in developing educational proposals. Material of this type, oriented to plan activities such as for example a web-based discussion between peers, or a collaborative project, is a very valuable reusable educational resource, as it constitutes a sort of guide to carry out innovative classroom activities.

Pedagogical metadata, as a consequence, should help the teacher to efficiently select LOs that are representative of two kinds of materials: resources, oriented to students, aimed at being used directly in the education practice; and resources, oriented to teachers, aimed at organising it (see **Fig. 1**).

Depending on the type of help offered to teachers, on the level of abstraction from the context and on the level of formalization, teacher-oriented resources are of various nature: 1) *Units of Learning (UoL)*, representing such resources as lessons, modules or entire courses described with formal languages (EML – Educational Modelling Languages; see for instance the IMS Learning Design specification: http://www.imsglobal.org/learningdesign/index.cfm); 2) *Pedagogical patterns and the like*, representing resources that model specific strategies or techniques to solve classes of educational problems, thus making good practices transferable [8]; 3) *Lesson plans*, representing resources that illustrate teaching proposals, instantiated in a specific knowledge domain, in terms of objectives, strategies, supporting tools, resources, possible uses and so on; they are formulated in plain natural language and no constraints are imposed on their structure.

As we already discussed in [9], learner-oriented resources, in turn, can be classified depending on the role they are intended to play in the learning process. In particular, we consider educational module, endowed with well-identified educational objectives and pedagogical approaches, so we call them *Structured LO*. We also include auxiliary materials (report forms, FAQs, bibliographies, etc.), which have a general-purpose or context-related function: we call them *Functional LOs*.

From the point of view of the pedagogical structure, *Structured LOs* and *Teacher oriented LOs* are endowed with (or suggest, in case of *Teacher oriented LOs*) an articulated pedagogical architecture; moreover, they are inspired by precise assumptions on learning and implement (or offer a model for realising) a specific learning strategy. *Functional LOs*, on the contrary, feature limited pedagogical orientation (for example, a bibliography comprises references suitable to the learner level and background, but it does not include an explicit pedagogical strategy). The pedagogical description of *Functional LOs*, thus, partly differs from that of the other kinds of LOs.

2.2   Realisation

The IMATI-ITD pedagogical metadata model realises the above illustrated view by integrating descriptors from the main international metadata standards with new ones aimed at identifying the context of use, the educational features, the structure and the learning approach of the resource. More precisely, our proposal is organized in five categories of metadata: *Pedagogical Model, General, Audience, Educational Features, Annotation* (see **Fig. 1**).

The category *Pedagogical Model* constitutes the characteristic feature of our proposal. It includes a descriptor, *Type*, that differentiates LOs according to the ideas discussed in Section 2.1. This element is mandatory and for any given LO it can assume one and only one of the values of its vocabulary. Moreover, the descriptor *Type* acts as a selector of the other descriptors in the *Pedagogical Model* category:

- *Functional LOs* are described on the basis of the typology of the resource *(ResourceType);* the values for this descriptor include, for instance, *FAQ list, game, movie, computer simulation* etc.

- *Structured LOs* are described on the basis of the pedagogical orientation, the didactic strategy, the type of activity proposed and the (self)-assessment material, if any. The element aimed at describing the pedagogical orientation *(SubType)* relies on a single-choice set of values: *Guided*, if the educational resource aims to introduce the student into a new topic under a planned guidance; *Problem*, if it proposes a problem situation to be explored autonomously by the student; *Mixed*, if it integrates the two approaches [9]. A vocabulary of thirteen multiple-choice values is provided for the element describing the didactic strategy.
- *Teacher-oriented LOs* are described similarly to *Structured LOs*. In this case, however, descriptors refer to activities, lessons, didactic units or modules that the LO proposes.

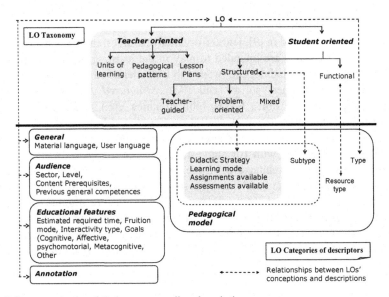

Fig. 1. LO conceptions and their corresponding descriptions.

The category *General* includes two descriptors analogous to the LOM descriptors 1.3 *General.Language* and 5.11 *Educational.Language* respectively [4].

The category *Audience* describes the characteristics of the intended user of a LO (in case of teacher-oriented LOs this is the final user, i.e. the learner). It includes elements, similar in their meanings to analogous descriptors of other proposals, to describe the sector and level of the intended student. Differently from other proposals, this category also comprises elements to describe prerequisites that refer not only to the content domain but also to the general competences that should be mastered to successfully deal with the LO.

The category *Educational Features* describes features such as the time estimated necessary for the fruition of the LO (by means of a descriptor with the same meaning and values as the LOM 5.9 *Typical learning time* element) and the fruition mode (*presence, distance* or *blended*). Other elements in this category describe the nature of the interaction that is to be activated by the LO and the physical environment (for example *lab, museum, classroom* ...) that is more suitable to foster its effective fruition. We also include in this category the educational goals. Differently from other proposals, we consider not only the cognitive domain of Bloom's taxonomy [10], but also the psychomotor and affective ones. We also add descriptors for meta-cognitive goals and for specific school goals (for example those connected with the relationship with the parents of 6 to 11 years old students in the context of Italian primary schools).

The category *Annotation* corresponds to the LOM *Annotation* category.

For the technical details of the IMATI-ITD model we refer to [11].

3 The validation process

We intended to develop a pedagogical metadata model that would meet as much as possible the needs of a variety of teachers communities. To this aim, we designed a preliminary version based on both our previous experience and on widespread LO metadata specifications, such as the *Learning Object Metadata* (LOM) schema [4], the *Gateway to Educational Materials* (GEM, http://thegateway.org) project proposal and the one formulated by the *Education Network Australia* (EdNA, http://www.edna.edu.au/).

We then carried out a validation process of the effectiveness of our choices with four groups of prospective users, each group belonging to a different educational realm. The user groups we considered were: 1) *practitioners* in the academic field, represented by instructional designers, e-learning experts and faculty members (14 persons); 2) *pre-service teachers and trainers*, represented by M. S. students, attending a basic course in "E-learning and knowledge management" (20 persons), and student teachers attending the postgraduate Specialisation School for Teaching in Secondary Schools (80 persons); 3) *vocational instructors*, represented by professionals working in a large European insurance company (8 persons); 4) *primary school teachers*, represented by schoolmistresses involved in a project aimed at developing a repository of animation-based LO for 6 to 11 years old children (34 persons).

The validation process was carried out iteratively. Each step provided us with feedbacks and suggestions from the specific group of users involved; on this basis, we refined and enriched the model. We gathered heterogeneous hints, since we integrated two different validation strategies:

• An experimental approach. By using a web-based tool that was designed and implemented to this purpose, participants had to index some LOs and to write down notes about the critical aspects that emerged. Validation focused on the elements, specific of our proposal, whose values are listed in a closed vocabulary. After indexing the LOs, each participant was individually interviewed. The results of the interviews were used as a basis to progressively modify the model.

A participatory approach [12] was used in the case of primary school teachers. It allowed us to set a validation context fostering the negotiation of meanings and the sharing of different points of view. The process was developed as a distant cooperation supported by frequent audio-conferencing meetings, interspersed with local group meetings. This work started with an initial step of "grounding", aimed at setting the workspace, sharing specific objectives and defining a shared language to talk about the problem. Teachers participated actively into decision making and helpfully contributed to adapt the model to the requirements of their activity and situation, still taking into account the general purpose of the model.

The validation strategy was very effective in negotiating a shared view on the elements of the model, which the teachers accepted and actively contributed to improve. We refer to [13] for a discussion of the results. For the sake of space, here we limit ourselves to summarise (see **Table 1**) the appreciation for the model, resulting from the overall validation process, shown by 80 prospective teachers.

Table 1. Appreciation of the general features of the model (% of respondents). Respondents: 80 prospective teachers.

		YES	NO	no answer
Model	Does the model capture the LO educational features ?	95,00	3,75	1,25
IMATI-ITD	Are metadata names clearly understandable?	77,50	22,50	0,00
Metadata	Would you add other metadata?	13,75	85,00	1,25
	Would you remove some metadata?	15,00	83,75	1,25
	Are metadata useful for searching for LOs?	88,75	10,00	1,25
The metadata *Pedagogical Model.Type*	Does its values represent, from a methodological point of view, all possible types of LOs?	95.00	5,00	0,00
	Is it effective the mandatory choice of one and only one value for describing a LO?	80,50	19,50	0,00
Vocabularies	Are vocabularies clear?	78,75	20,00	1,25
	Would you add values in any vocabulary?	11,25	87,50	1,25
	Would you eliminate values in any vocabulary?	10,00	88,75	1,25

4   Discussing the model and the validation process

Some results of the validation process summarized in **Table 1** seem to indicate that our proposal is quite a valuable attempt to describe the pedagogical aspects of LOs. However, some critical elements emerged that regard the usability of the model. Sometimes users find it difficult to univocally interpret specific terms of the model. For instance, when dealing with the element *Type* of the category *Pedagogical Model,* users belonging to different communities interpret differently the meaning of the *structured* vs. *functional* distinction. Regardless of the web-based tool's functionalities aimed at supporting the user's choices (e.g., a glossary or an on-line help), ambiguities arise because of differences in specific community sub-cultures and jargons. For instance the same LO can be regarded as a *simulation* by some, or as a *case study* by others. Of course, there is also a linguistic problem related to the translation of most of the terms used in the model into the user's native language.

Another critical aspect is the level of detail captured by some vocabularies: if, on one side, it reflects the expressiveness of the model, on the other side, it often needs to be tuned to specific user needs. This is particularly evident with the *Audience.level* element: primary school teachers, for instance, need to distinguish between two-year periods in the curriculum, whereas practitioners in adult and lifelong learning are not concerned with such fine-grain distinctions, which are regarded as noise. Similarly, the

Audience.sector element calls for quite a refined vocabulary in the university context, and for a more limited one in primary school. Furthermore, both these elements heavily depend on social, cultural and national systems: even at the same university level curricula are likely to differ depending on the nations, thus requiring adaptations of the *Audience.sector* vocabulary.

The above considerations highlight the need of adapting both element names and vocabularies to the requirements of specific communities of users. Accordingly, a two-layer architecture has been identified.

The abstract metadata model is defined as a namespace schema [14] that acts as a foundation for a number of application profile schemata, each one tailored and optimized for a specific user community. The application profiles can use elements from the complete model, refine the definitions and narrow down vocabularies, but they cannot create new elements nor extend the original vocabularies.

In our approach an application profile is defined on the basis of the full metadata model through the following steps: 1) the subset of descriptor elements that suits the expressive needs of the target community is identified (care must be paid to maintain the structural consistency of the resulting (sub)schema); 2) if necessary, the names of the identified elements are translated into the community's native language; 3) for each vocabulary, a subset of items is identified similarly to point 1 above and, if required, translated into the target language. This process is not free from hindrances and pitfalls, and requires the involvement of representatives of the user communities in a participative effort.

5 Future perspectives

According to the Dublin Core Metadata Initiative (DCMI) Glossary http://dublincore.org/documents/usageguide/glossary.shtml), "an application profile is not complete without documentation that defines the policies and best practices appropriate to the application". Such a documentation can only be built upon an extensive set of experimental, situated activities aimed at validating the model in as many and various contexts as possible, with the direct involvement of users: this will be the direction of our future research task.

The experiments described above relied on hand-coded user interfaces; extending the scope of the validation will call for a better articulation of the supporting tools. A formal representation of the model is the next step: by developing an XML schema for the abstract model it will be possible to automate, to some extent, the task of generating the repository structure, the user interface software and the representation of the new application profile. Suitable software modules will support the selection of elements and vocabulary items that constitute the application profile, and they will automatically produce its formal representation, the logical schema of the database hosting the LO repository, and the skeleton of the interface applications that support users in loading and querying the repository. One possible evolution path would involve the extension of the architecture outlined in section 4 with a third layer, namely the interface one. As a matter of fact, some minor adaptation issues could be dealt with by the user interface, thus limiting the uncontrolled proliferation of slightly differing application schemata. On the other hand, encapsulating the model specialization into a formally defined application schema can improve reusability and interchange among different repositories.

"The limits of my language indicate the limits of my world" ([15], prop. 5.6). Language supports thinking, and even such a confined linguistic tool as a metadata description model can influence the way people look at educational material, enhancing their ability to capture and represent meaning and refining their selection skills.

Acknowledgments

This work was supported in part by the Italian Ministry of University and Research, Project VICE (Virtual Communities for Learning). The authors are grateful to all the people who contributed to the model validation process for their precious suggestions.

References

1. T. Hand, Learning Objects: User Perspectives on the Conditions Surrounding Their Use. In L. Cantoni & C. McLoughlin (Eds.), *Proc. of World Conference on Educational Multimedia*, Hypermedia and Telecommunications 2004. Chesapeake, VA: AACE, 66-72.
2. O. Liber, Learning objects: conditions for viability, *J. Comp. Assisted Learning*, **21**(5), 366-373, 2005.
3. G. Dettori, P. Forcheri, and M.G. Ierardi, Endowing LOs with a social dimension. In ICWL 2006, Wenyin Liu, Qing Li, Rynson W. H. Lau, LNCS, Springer 2006, 189-202.
4. A. Littlejohn, *Reusing online resources*, Kogan Page, London. 2004.
5. IEEE Learning Technology Standards Committee, Learning Object Metadata, Final Draft Standard, IEEE 1484.12.1-2002. Available in: http://ltsc.ieee.org/wg12, 2002.
6. J. Griffith, G. Stubbs, and M. Watkins, From course notes to granules: A guide to deriving Learning Object components, in Computers in Human Behavior, **23**(6), 2007, 2696-2720.
7. B. Simon, and J. Quemada, A Reflection of Metadata Standards Based on Reference Scenarios", in *Proc. der GMW,* Tagung 2002, 2002.
8. P. McAndrew, P. Goodyear, and J. Dalziel, Patterns, designs and activities: unifying descriptions of learning structures, *I. J. of Learning Technology*, **2**(2-3), 2006, 216-242.
9. E. Busetti, G. Dettori, P. Forcheri, and M.G. Ierardi, A pedagogical approach to the design of learning objects for complex domains, *I. J. Distant Educ. Technologies*, **5**(2), 2007, 1-17.
10. B.S. Bloom,Taxonomy of Educational Objectives. The Classification of Educational Goals, in Handbook I, Cognitive Domain. B. S. Bloom, Ed. New York: Longman, 1956.
11. S. Alvino, P. Forcheri, M.G. Ierardi, and L. Sarti, Un modello per la descrizione pedagogica di learning objects, Progetto MIUR-VICE, Deliverable 2007.
12. T. Winograd, *Bringing design to software* (Addison-Wesley, Boston, MA, 1996).
13. S. Alvino, P. Forcheri, M.G. Ierardi, and L. Sarti, Describing learning features of reusable resources: a proposal, *International Journal of Social Sciences* 2 (3), 2007, 156-162.
14. J. Mason, and H. Galatis, Theory and practice of application profile development in Australian education and training, *Proc. Int'l Conf. on Dublin Core and Metadata Applications*, 2007.
15. Wittgenstein, L., Logisch-Philosophische Abhandlung, Annalen der Naturphilosophie, 14, 1921. Trad. It.: Conte A.G. (a cura di) Tractatus logico-philosophicus e Quaderni 1914-1916, Einaudi, Torino, 1964.

Using ICT to Improve the Education of Students with Learning Disabilities

Tas Adam and Arthur Tatnall
1 School of Information Systems,
Victoria University, Melbourne, Australia
Tas.Adam@vu.edu.au
2 Centre for International Corporate Governance Research
Victoria University, Melbourne, Australia
Arthur.Tatnall@vu.edu.au

Abstract. The potential of Information and Communications Technology in all forms of education has been well demonstrated. In this paper we examine how ICT can improve the education of students with learning disabilities (LD). We will begin by examining the nature of learning disabilities and discussing the different approaches to schooling for students with LD. Learning models have evolved over recent years in response to many factors including the advent of technology in education. This is particularly important in this arena where technology can make a significant difference to educating these students, but only if it is used appropriately. The paper then looks at a case study of use of ICT in a school catering for students with LD.

1 Children with Learning Disabilities

The term *Learning Disability* (LD) is used to refer to any retardation, disorder, or delayed development in one or more of the processes of speech, language, reading, writing, arithmetic, or other school subjects resulting from a psychological handicap caused by a possible cerebral dysfunction and/or emotional or behavioural disturbances [1-3]. Learning disabilities are not the result of mental retardation, sensory deprivation, or cultural and instructional factors [4]. Sometimes the alternative term *Special Needs* is used in regard to education of children, but this term can, however, refer to many different things spanning both physical and mental needs. In this paper we will refer to children with the particular type of special need resulting from learning disabilities.

Over the years a number of LD definitions have been proposed, but none has emerged as an unequivocal favourite [5]. Presently, the two definitions enjoying the greatest support are the legislative definition found in the Individuals with

Please use the following format when citing this chapter:

Adam, T. and Tatnall, A., 2008, in IFIP International Federation for Information Processing, Volume 281; *Learning to Live in the Knowledge Society;* Michael Kendall and Brian Samways; (Boston: Springer), pp. 63–70.

Disabilities Education Act [6] and the one proposed by the National Joint Committee on Learning Disabilities [7], which is a consortium of representatives from organisations interested in LD. A more recent definition comes from the Learning Disabilities Association of Canada [8] who define Learning Disabilities as: "a number of disorders which may affect the acquisition, organization, retention, understanding or use of verbal or nonverbal information. These disorders affect learning in individuals who otherwise demonstrate at least average abilities essential for thinking and/or reasoning. As such, learning disabilities are distinct from global intellectual deficiency." The Association suggests that learning disabilities result from impairments in one or more processes related to perceiving, thinking, learning or remembering, and include language processing; phonological processing; visual spatial processing; processing speed; memory and attention; and executive functions [3]. They go on to note that LD varies in severity and may interfere with the acquisition and use of oral language, reading, written language and mathematics [8].

The prevalence of LD in Australia is around 10-15% of students at the primary levels, and is still significant at the secondary level at 5-10% [9-11]. These figures show a similar rate to the USA and other countries [7].

A significant issue that has concerned many education authorities around the world is whether students with learning disabilities should receive their education in mainstream classrooms or in some form of special schools. A number of researchers support the view that students with LD require an alternative approach to their learning, while others claim that it is best to integrate these students with mainstream classes [12]. While many integration and remedial programs have proved ineffective for this group of students [1]. The literature shows that in some selected fields, such as mathematics and social studies, specialist instruction has had little success [13-15]. Overall however, there is considerable evidence to support the view that of separate schools should exist for students with learning disabilities [16].

2   ICT and Education of Students with Learning Disabilities

Many studies over the last 30 years have shown that technology can play a significant role in any work with specific disadvantaged groups such as the blind and those with movement disabilities. It can do so in the provision of media to facilitate communication and education [17], but also in other learning. Studies have also investigated how information and communications technologies (ICT) can influence the education of students with LD and have shown that this technology can play an important and useful role [18, 19].

Over the last few years the Victorian government has begun to place considerable emphasis on the importance and availability of ICT for students with LD [2]. At a seminar in 2005 the Minister reiterated a major policy to support Victoria schools in various ways so that students would enhance their learning and employability position prospects. This was also to apply to students with LD [20]. Also in recognition of the potential role of ICT the Australian Commonwealth Government has recently announced a plan to equip every senior school student with a laptop computer.

Schunck and Nielsson [21] outline three stages in the use of technology in education. This stage (Figure 1) is the paradigm of the verbal tradition (what Schunck and Nielsson call the paradigm of the past), that is characterised by a verbal flow of information streaming from the teacher directly to the students [2].

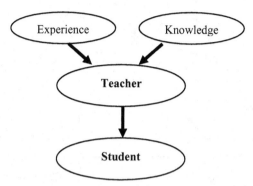

Figure 1: Paradigm of the verbal tradition

In the second paradigm that Schunck and Nielsson call the paradigm of today, communication is two way and students also communicate amongst themselves, but the teacher is really still at the centre. It is a paradigm where both teacher and student share responsibility, but the teacher remains the main source of information.

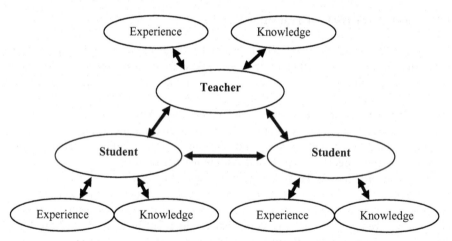

Figure 2: Paradigm of the teacher-centred classroom

The third paradigm (Figure 3 below) – what Schunck and Nielsson call the e-learning paradigm, differs in placement of a knowledge base at its centre. It gives both students and teachers important roles where the teacher acts as a consultant for students on where information can be obtained and communicates knowledge and experience to the students. This is a technology-based paradigm in which students make extensive use of ICT to obtain information and experiences. The learning responsibilities of the students here are for 'searching', rather than 'receiving' [2].

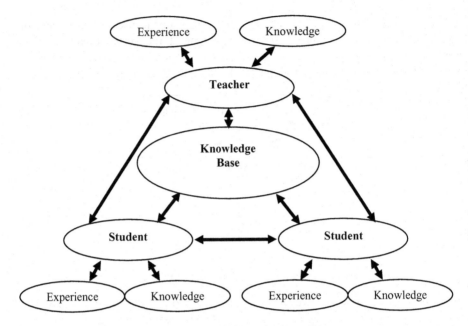

Figure 3: The e-learning paradigm

2.1   The Concord School Transition Centre

Concord is a specialist school which caters for students with mild to moderate intellectual disability. The students come from diverse socio-economic backgrounds and are between the ages of 5 and 18 years. The school has 86 teaching and ancillary staff and an enrolment of 270 students [22]. Enrolment is dependent on eligibility criteria that have been determined by the Victorian Department of Education and Training. Concord supports integration into or from mainstream schools and offers support services to parent, careers and students. These include social workers, guidance officers, speech therapists and visiting teacher services [22].

The Concord School Transition Centre caters for approximately 60 students from Years 10-12. Three learning programs are delivered here offering an *applied learning* curriculum. In Year 10, students complete a pre-transition learning program designed to prepare them for post-compulsory schooling. In Years 11, 12 are four groups each of approximately twelve students. Students in three groups complete their VCAL (Victorian Certificate of Applied Learning) award over two years. The fourth class has a Special Needs Learning Framework (SLNF) learning program [22], also over two years, developed by Concord Transition Centre staff to meet the needs of the high support students. An interesting ICT initiative is the One-to-One (121) program that will require the school to invest in a computer (lap-top or desk-top) for each of these students, as well as other accompanying software and hardware. The 121 ICT project offers opportunities for students to use technology that will improve their literacy output, access and exposure to technology as well as increasing engagement [2]. VCAL students have demonstrated that they experience learning success and engagement when given access to technology, and lack of ongoing access to such technology that is the primary area of concern. Observations of student behaviour and students' expressed learning preferences over the past twelve months have significantly raised awareness regarding need to access ICT [23].

Presently the VCAL students at Concord School develop electronic portfolios, and it is hoped that access to 121 ICT will further support the students' skills and abilities in this area. The implementation of 121 ICT classroom environments will also require development of a new shared curriculum and a new pedagogical focus [24] and necessitate moving away from autonomous teaching practices and incorporating new approaches to teaching [25], including a teacher commitment to personalised learning for students and where learning experiences are student directed – Schunck and Nielsson's e-learning paradigm. Sustained transformation will require that staff commit to undertaking the necessary professional development required in order to prepare for these changes [25].

2.2   ICT and Collaborative Learning at Concord School

In moving towards Schunck and Nielsson's e-learning paradigm, the School hopes to empower its students by using student directed collaborative tools to enable them to find content and pursue personal interests using the Internet. By introducing these Web 2.0 tools and teaching students to use them the School is aiming to give them a voice so that they can make choices and create an online presence through content creation [26]. It is expected that the students will create and publish content and also respond to the content creation of others. Created content can be aggregated to show progress and richness and depth of learning and students can respond to the work of others, provide feedback, and learn through their interactions with others online. Not only are students learning but they are also learning how to be independent learners.

For the last two years Concord School has trialled use of social software (Lumil, WordPressMU, ccHost, Urdit, Gregarius and Scuttle), networked learning activities and practices. These tools and technologies are complimentary and are used concurrently as much of the power of social software is its interoperability.

The move towards web based collaborative practices and activities has resulted in a change in teaching practice. Students have begun using these services for leisure activities and free time, due to their ease of use and breadth of content. Priorities and activities of networked learning and social software are a good fit with Concord's curriculum focus of Personal Learning, and Concord's enthusiastic teaching staff is no doubt the key to the acceptance of these technologies and practices [26].

Selection of software and student activities is framed by how it can be shared on the web, and as small elements sp that students can build on the work of others. Given the breadth of curriculum innovation that has occurred, and the sense of success that has accompanied these changes, many teachers have found renewed energy and excitement to try new ideas and approaches in their use of ICT [26]. Professional discussions are no longer bound by a commitment to previous practices and commitments but are focussed on increasing student learning outcomes. In additional to changes to the curriculum, Concord has begun implementing a web-based approach to student assessment and knowledge management.

3 Methodology

Our research has involved examining how several schools that cater for students
with LD have made use of ICT in their curricula. This has involved participant
observation, interviews, surveys and discussions as well as an examination of the
technology that might potentially be useful here. In an area like this that depends on
both human and non-human actors, actor-network theory (ANT) [27] can provide a
useful framework. ANT considers equally contributions of human and non-human
actors, reacting against the idea that characteristics of humans and social
organisations distinguish their actions from the inanimate behaviour of technological
objects. It offers a socio-technical approach in which neither social nor technical
positions are privileged, denying purely social or technical relations are possible.

The actors involved in this technology-based learner interface include: students,
parents, teachers, the Web, computers, Education Department policies, technology
policy, school and classroom environments, learning approaches and paradigms,
methods of instruction, engagement methods, thinking processes, technology
infrastructure-bandwidth, curriculum, Web curriculum, Internet resources, digital
libraries [1]. Figure 4 shows some of the main actors and interactions involved.

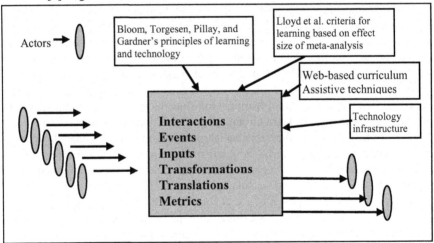

Figure 4: Actors, networks and interactions

In an ANT framework, actors are seen to contest and negotiate with each other
in an attempt to influence the final outcome in a direction of their own liking. The
Education Department, for example, might want ensure that all schools offer a
similar level of service to students and to ensure their accountability. The parents of
a student with LD, on the other hand, would want the best for their own child
regardless of what was going on in other schools. The technology (both hardware
and software) itself acts in the way it was designed, both intentionally and
unintentionally, to act. In utilising an ANT approach, this study involved interviews
and discussion with the actors or, in the case of the technology, with those who
speak for them. The main advice on method suggested by Latour [28] is to 'follow
the actors' and to let them set the framework and limits of the study themselves.

4 Conclusion

For educational purposes, much of the power of the Internet lies in is its ability to foster virtual learning communities, and LD students are no exception to this. The difference this technology can make to these students in many ways is remarkable. ICT certainly offers students the capacity to construct their own learning experiences, and our investigations suggest that this applies also to students with Learning Difficulties. One of the problems that this group face, however, is not being a big enough political lobby to be able to obtain the funding and support that they deserve and that could make a huge difference to their education.

References

1. Adam, T. and A. Tatnall. *Using Web-Based Technologies to Enhance the Learning of Students with Learning Disabilities who Live in Regional Areas.* in *IT in Regional Areas (ITiRA-2002).* 2002. Rockhampton, Australia: CQU.
2. Adam, T., A. Rigoni, and A. Tatnall, *Designing and Implementing Curriculum for Students with Special Needs: A Case Study of a Thinking Curriculum.* Journal of Business Systems, Governance and Ethics, 2006. **1**(1): p. 49-63.
3. Adam, T. and A. Tatnall. *Building a Virtual Knowledge Community of Schools for Children with Special Needs.* in *Information Technologies for Education and Training (iTET).* 2007. Charles University, Prague: ETIC Prague.
4. Kirk, S.A., *Educating exceptional children.* 1962, Boston: Houghton Mifflin.
5. Tucker, J., L.J. Stevens, and J.E. Ysseldyke, *Learning Disabilities: the Experts Speak Out.* Journal of Learning Disabilities, 1983(16): p. 6-14.
6. IDEA, *Individuals with Disabilities Education Act.* 1997, United States.
7. NJCLD, *Learning disabilities: Issues on definition revised,* in *Collective Perspectives on Issues Affecting Learning Disabilities.* 1994, PRO-ED: Austin, TX. p. 61-66.
8. Learning Disabilities Association of Canada. *Official Definition of Learning Disabilities.* 2002 [cited May 2007]; Available from: http://www.ldac-taac.ca/Defined/defined_new-e.asp.
9. ABS, *Commercial Training Providers, Australia - 1994.* 1996, Australian Bureau of Statistics: Canberra. p. Catalogue No. 6352.0.
10. ABS, *Education and Training Experience Australia.* 1997, Australian Bureau of Statistics: Canberra. p. Catalogue No. 6278.0.
11. Ministerial Council on Education; Employment; Training and Youth Affairs, *National Schools Statistics Collection 1989-97.* 1997, Australian Bureau of Statistics: Canberra.
12. Bulgren, J., *Effectiveness of a concept teaching routine in enhancing the performance of LD students in secondary-level mainstream classes.* Learning Disability Quarterly, 1998. **11**.

13. Swanson, L., *Cognitive processing Deficits in poor readers with symptoms of reading disabilities: More alike than different.* Journal of Educational Psychology, 1999. **91**(2.): p. 321-333.

14. Klinger, J.K., *Outcomes for Students With and Without Learning Disabilities in Inclusive Classrooms.* Learning Disabilities Research & Practice, 1998. **13**(3): p. 153-161.

15. Johnson, G., R. Gersten, and D. Carmine, *Effects of Instructional Design Variables on Vocabulary acquisition of LD students: A Study of computer-assisted Instruction.* Journal of Learning Disabilities, 1998. **20**(4).

16. Adam, T. and A. Tatnall. *Using Information and Communication Technologies to Enhance the Learning Outcomes of a Virtual Community of Students with Learning Disabilities.* in *ACIS 2003.* 2003. Perth: ACIS.

17. Poon, P. and P. Head. *Computers Assisting People.* in *1st Pan Pacific Computer Conference.* 1985. Melbourne: Australian Computer Society.

18. Quinn, C.N., *Designing an Instructional Game: Reflections for Quest on Independence.* Journal of Education and Information Technologies., 1996. **1**(1): p. 251-269.

19. Pillay, H., *Cognition and Recreational Computer Games: Implications for Educational Technology.* Journal of Research on Computing in Education, 2000. **32**(1): p. 32-41.

20. Adam, T., A. Rigoni, and A. Tatnall. *The Application of ICT in the Development of a Thinking Curriculum: a Pilot Project for Students with Special Needs.* in *1st Victoria University Business Research Conference.* 2005.

21. Schunck, L.G. and L. Nielsson. *Varying Learning Paradigms.* [Web publication] 2001 [cited June 2003]; Available from: www.fcfu.dk/artikel/paradigm.htm.

22. Concord School. *School Profile.* 2007 [cited November 2007]; Available from: http://www.concordsch.vic.edu.au/web/.

23. Caldwell, B. *Global Transformations.* 2005 [cited November 2005]; Available from: http://www.educationaltransformations.com.au/publications.php.

24. Davies, B. and B.J. Davies, *Strategic Leadership, in The Essentials Of School Leadership.* 2005, London: Paul Chapman Publishing and Corwin Press.

25. Southworth, G., *Learning-Centred Leadership, in The Essentials Of School Leadership.* 2005, London: Paul Chapman Publishing and Corwin Press.

26. Adam, T., A. Tatnall, and R. Olsen. *Catching Students and Teachers in the Web.* in *We-B 2007.* 2007. Melbourne: Victoria University.

27. Latour, B., *The Powers of Association, in Power, Action and Belief. A New Sociology of Knowledge? Sociological Review monograph 32,* J. Law, Editor. 1986, Routledge & Kegan Paul: London. p. 264-280.

28. Latour, B., *Aramis or the Love of Technology.* 1996, Cambridge, Ma: Harvard University Press.

Ethics, Equality and Inclusion for Students with a Chronic Health Condition

Tony Potas[1] and Anthony Jones[2]
1 Royal Children's Hospital Education Institute, Melbourne, Australia
tony.potas@rch.org.au,
WWW home page: http://www.rch.org.au/edinst/
2 ICT in Education and Research, Faculty of Education,University of
Melbourne, Australia
a.jones@unimelb.edu.au,
WWW home page: http://www.edfac.unimelb.edu.au/cgi-
bin/public/staff_profile.cgi?id=7001

Abstract. Students with a chronic disease are often overlooked by education systems. The World Health Organization (WHO) characterizes chronic diseases conditions that "are permanent, leave residual disability, are caused by nonreversible pathological alteration, require special training of the patient for rehabilitation or may require a long period of supervision, observation and care" [1]. Research data indicates that in many cases these students are at risk of dropping out of school. In order to redress the imbalance of access and equity for students with a chronic health condition, the Royal Children's Hospital Education Institute in Melbourne, Australia, has developed programs that based on an educational model designed to empower schools to support this cohort of students. In this paper the implementation and evaluation of two projects developed in response educational needs of students who are absent from school for extended periods because of chronic illness are presented. While both projects have been successfully implemented, a new research component in the second project has only recently commenced.

1 Introduction

The Royal Children's Hospital Education Institute (the Institute) was founded in 1998 replacing the previous Special School that was regulated by the Victorian state Department of Education and Early Childhood Development (DEECD). Historically teachers within the Special School setting at hospitals provided small-group and face- to-face bedside teaching for students admitted as inpatients.

Please use the following format when citing this chapter:

Potas, T. and Jones, A., 2008, in IFIP International Federation for Information Processing, Volume 281; *Learning to Live in the Knowledge Society*; Michael Kendall and Brian Samways; (Boston: Springer), pp. 71–78.

The need for in-house teachers was seen as critical to students' academic progress as their stay in hospital could be lengthy. Over the past decade the length of stay in hospital for children and young people has reduced [1] due in part to medical technology, community based health support systems and home care. In 2007 the Institute's database indicated that 1528 students required educational support, with 1146 (75%) spending less than 3 weeks in hospital.

These briefer stays in hospital caused the Institute to redefine its support role, employing teachers and health professionals as Education Advisors to liaise with the student's school to ensure educational and social continuity. This empowering of schools involved providing teachers, school coordinators, students and their peers with relevant information, communications tools, and pathways that promoted ongoing teaching and learning despite student isolation and medical needs. This approach enables schools to comply with state and federal anti-discrimination and equity legislation.

Historically the Education Institute has used a range of ICTs to support the connection between students and their schools, for example trialing Blackberries, and video phones, setting up a student portal, accessing the Technical and Further Education virtual campus, setting up a web server using Manhattan as open source virtual classroom environment, and recently purchasing and installing Adobe Connect video conferencing software. But the sustainability of the majority of these communications systems has been problematic. Cost is always a factor in determining which system provides the best outcomes for students and schools.

Schools are slow to embrace this type of technology, due in part to the range of communications systems used by schools all having different interfaces and functionality requirements. Security is always an issue, with firewalls configured to block connections with services outside the school domain. The lack of school staff with the expertise to maximize the potential of new and emerging technologies and the take-up is further exacerbated by lack of training programs at the school level.

In supporting the need for effective ongoing communications with key stakeholders, the Institute uses new and emerging ICT and related research to inform best practice in the development of models that assist schools minimize the disconnection of students with chronic health conditions. Using such technologies is part of the Institute's accountability framework, and two projects that make different uses of ICT to support students who are absent from school are reported here.

2 Education Advisory Service (EAS)

The EAS is in its ninth year of operation. Funding for the service is provided by DEECD through the provision of a strategic contract with the Student Wellbeing branch. The EAS brings together and disseminates education and health knowledge to provide the best possible outcomes for students with a chronic health condition. To achieve this purpose the service is designed to empower schools by enhancing or building their capacity to support this cohort of students.

Information and communications technologies are one of many empowerment tools used by the service to connect students to their curriculum and peer-group.

Research reported by the Commonwealth Department of Education, Science and Training [2] about the capacity of ICT to improve learning and teaching shows that it can play a key role in the complex task of better engaging students in their learning process. There is ample literature indicating that the use of on-line web-based virtual classrooms has surged ahead in the last ten years. This type of technology is utilized by the service to connect students to their school's curriculum and their peer group.

In 2006 an evaluation of the service was conducted by The University of Melbourne, Centre for Program Evaluation. The evaluation report [3] included feedback from the following stakeholder domains; the home, the school and the hospital. A section of the report noted that *the use of information and communications technologies to maintain real time contact with students with chronic health conditions seems, at this stage, to be under-utilised by schools. ICT such as video conferencing and the RCH Education Institute's virtual classroom have not been widely taken up by schools, as options for supporting students with chronic health conditions in maintaining connections with their school activities and peers during periods of absence* [3].

2.1 Participants

Students referred to the service are patients of the RCH, and enrolled in primary or secondary level at a government, Catholic or independent school, and have a health condition that will have or is having a significant impact on their education. Education Advisors assigned to the service attend multidisciplinary team meetings for a wide range of diagnostic groups at RCH that refer to the service. Working with health professionals in this context assists the Education Advisor to establish the education and social implications associated with the student's medical treatment.

Both education and health systems place the student/patient and the family at the centre of care, a model that embraces collaboration, empowerment and education. This supports the principles of inclusion and individualized education for all students as referred to in the Blueprint for government schools [4].

The key contact person at the student's school depends in part on the student's level of schooling, primary or secondary. In a primary setting the classroom teacher is generally the key contact with additional support from an Assistant Principal usually assigned a welfare role in the school. In a secondary setting the key contact may be a Year Level Coordinator or a Welfare Coordinator or an Integration Coordinator.

2.2 Method

One part of the evaluation report [3] was a literature review whose initial focus was to identify best practice models that support the educational and social needs of students with a chronic health condition. It was found that documented examples of such models in Australian or international literature was limited. However, the review indicated that a large number of studies articulate stakeholder concerns about the educational and social support for students with a chronic health.

Part of the review highlighted the following theme. **Information and Communications Technologies (ICTs) may Enhance the Coordination of Health, Educational and Social Support** – *The literature indicates that the use of emerging communications technologies may assist students with chronic health conditions to keep in touch with their schools and peers and may also assist the flow of information between education and health professionals working to support students and their families* [3].

The evaluation of the service involved an action research approach to review the service framework and processes. A qualitative research method used to evaluate the service had two data collection phases. Phase One involved focus group meetings with the EAS team (internal stakeholders). Phase Two involved semi-structured interviews with a sample of external key stakeholder groups.

Phase One involved seven meetings with the EAS team. Discussions focused on identifying each stage of service, and identifying the challenges that face the service, and identifying staff responses to those challenges.

Phase Two primary focus involved data collection from the schools accessing the service. Twenty one students with chronic health conditions, their families and their schools and eight health professionals from RCH were approached to participate in the evaluation.

2.3 Outcomes

A total of six recommendations were included in the evaluation report 'Finding a way forward'. Two have significance within the context of this paper. **Recommendation 1**-That the RCH Education Institute develop a new database to improve reporting and data collection processes; **Recommendation 2** -That the RCH Education Institute develop a framework of processes and procedures to support ongoing improvement in the service.

The final draft of the operational framework has been endorsed by the Board of Directors. Within the framework there are three stages of service, the initial stage, the empowerment stage and the review and close stage. Implementation of the operational framework commenced in March 2008.

Records of school and student contact are stored in a third party database with little flexibility to extract reports. The RCH Education Institute has worked with the RCH Information Technology Department to customize IBA (patient administration system) to address the needs of the service.

An Education Needs Assessment form, (part of the initial stage of service), provides Education Advisors with a formal reporting mechanism that enables the determination of appropriate adjustments to the school's curriculum and environment to support the student's needs. This form is interfaced through the new database system.

Completion of the initial stage of service informs the empowerment stage of service. Education Advisors identify activities used to empower schools. Capacity to clearly identify ICT supports in the previous database system was problematic. The new system clearly identifies ICT supports including laptop provision, virtual classroom usage, online tutoring and video conferencing.

The review and close stage includes a built in evaluation form for schools. The form is designed to ascertain the quality of service provided, the schools preferred communications method and to identify areas of service improvement.

Implementing new systems of support for students with a chronic health condition and their schools using a project management methodology may improve outcomes for all stakeholders.

3 Back on Track program (BoT)

Funded by the Bone Marrow Donor Institute and launched in 2005, the *Back on Track* program aimed to assist students who are experiencing prolonged absence from school following a diagnosis of cancer and are either in transition from primary to secondary school, or are at upper secondary level. A report to the Bone Marrow Donor Institute and the Institute noted that because it relies on *new and emerging technologies for learning exchange and communication, the Program requires a shift in thinking and working for many teachers and clinical staff. Such cultural shifts may be considerable in some settings and changes of this nature take time* [5].

Some University of Melbourne pre-service teacher education students began working online with BoT students in 2006. The first online tutors were preparing to become secondary school Information Technology teachers, and they provided online support to BoT students in the subject areas they were qualified in.

In July 2007 researchers from the university and the Institute commenced a three year research project funded by a grant from the Australian Research Council. This project aims to extend the work done in previous years, focusing on perceptions of the students about learning in an online mode, and on the needs of their teachers. The focus in this paper will be on teachers and continuing ICT professional development.

3.1 Participants

Student participants in the *Back on Track* program are at secondary school and are likely to have lengthy absences following diagnosis and treatment for cancer. Teacher participants are teachers from the school of the student. When a student enters the BoT program educational advisors from the Institute meet with teachers from the school and the student's parents to form a student support group. The aim is to clarify the role of the Institute as a conduit for enhancing digital communication between student and teacher, and to explain some of the possible effects a chronic health condition might have on the student's study habits. Other participants are the BoT education program coordinators, one of whom will be the "case manager" for the student, and online tutors who are volunteer pre-service teachers.

3.2 Method

BoT students have access to a laptop computer so they can email, chat online or video conference with Institute advisors, teachers and friends. This process commences while the students are receiving treatment in hospital, and continues while they are part of BoT. The duration of any student's involvement depends on their health. Students leave the program when they complete their convalescence or rehabilitation and return to school. A conceptual illustration of the lines of communication is given in Fig.1. All electronic communication passes through a server at the Institute. In Fig.1 the broken lines indicate types of communication that will not be part of the project. Not all data that is generated by participants and automatically recorded on the VLE will be used by the research team. In particular, student communications with either their family or peers will be excluded. All the electronic communication aspects of BoT and other Institute projects are moderated by education advisors in accordance with RCH protocols.

Each BoT student's school is contacted in order to ascertain the infrastructure and support needed by the student from both the Institute and the school. The student's learning needs are discussed with the student and one or more teachers. Data for the research is being collected through the traditional ethnographic formats of recording conversations and describing the setting and activities that are part of the project. Some data is collected electronically as the system automatically records users, frequency and length of connection.

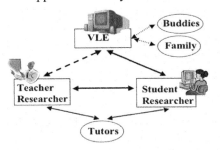

Fig. 1. Conceptual view of communications.

This model requires well planned initial and on-going professional development with teacher participants. Reasonable levels of ICT competence and confidence are necessary before a person is employed as an education program coordinator, and the Institute has developed processes for ensuring all staff are involved in on-going refinement of their ICT knowledge and skills that relate to the hardware and software the use as part of their work.

The term "Teacher Researcher" in Fig.1 refers to the classroom teachers who taught the student. Generally secondary students have several teachers they maintain contact with. As students can come from anywhere within a radius of approximately 400 kilometres from Melbourne, the education program coordinators often have to travel long distances to make contact with some teachers and families. Technically the communications model used for this project requires little more than Internet access, and this has reduced the need for advisors and technicians to make multiple visits to schools and student's homes to install equipment.

While many of technical problems have been overcome following the introduction of the new communications model, there remain many problems related to the levels of knowledge and experience that teachers have about using ICT for teaching and learning. Many teachers do not use ICT as an integral component of their everyday classroom practice. Several attempts have been made to conceptualise the connections and interaction between the subject knowledge of teachers, the approach to teaching they apply in the classroom, and the use of ICT. In Fig.2 a model based on Schulman's [6] pedagogical content knowledge of teachers is presented. This conceptual configuration of technological pedagogical content knowledge (TPCK) [7] is being used within the research project. The components of the Mishra & Koehler model [7] content, pedagogy, technology, and all intersection areas, will be investigated in relation to the perceptions of participating teachers. Teachers will be asked about their previous and current experiences with teaching and learning with ICT in general, and with online teaching in particular. Both staff from the Institute and the researchers are aware of the burden that communicating with a single student who has a chronic illness and no longer attends normal classes can become to teachers not trained in the techniques of online teaching.

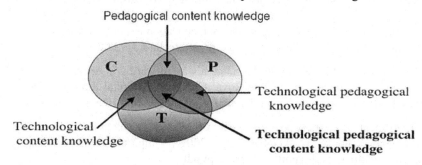

Fig. 2. Technological pedagogical content knowledge (Mishra & Koehler, 2006).

Both practice and methodology in this project are informed by recent research, conducted in local primary and secondary schools, into classroom uses of ICT for teaching and learning [8, 9]. A major difference is that in this project students will be asked about their experiences and perceptions of online communication with peers and teachers, especially for learning.

Conclusion

Although not referred to overtly in this paper, in Australia there is legislation at both federal and state levels that makes it illegal for teachers and schools to discriminate against students who encounter an impediment to their learning. Students with a chronic illness who can be absent from school for months are an example of a group who confront an impediment to their learning. The Education Institute aims to encourage schools to accept their responsibility for students with a chronic health condition through being proactive, and meeting as soon as possible with teachers and administrators from schools of students referred to the Institute.

Making use of the communications affordances of ICT, the Institute has been looking for effective methods, both in terms of education and cost, to connect students who are absent from school as a result of a chronic health condition with their teachers and peers. The projects described in this paper have supplied some answers, but are not in themselves a complete solution. However it is important that bodies such as the Institute continue to seek funding to enable new developments in communications technology to be evaluated to help disconnected students re-engage with their education.

References

1. World Health Organization, WHO 2005 Health topics: Chronic disease. (July 5, 2005); http://www.who.int/topics/chronic_disease/en

2. Department of Education, Science and Training, Information and Communications Technology for Teaching and Learning. Schooling Issues Digest No 2. (July 14, 2007); http://www.dest.gov.au/sectors/school_education/publications_resources/schooling_issues_digest/schooling_issues_digest_technology.htm

3. L. Campbell, and P. St Ledger, "Finding a way forward…" An evaluation of the Education Advisory Service for the Royal Children's Hospital Education Institute. (Centre for Program Development, University of Melbourne, 2006).

4. Department of Education and Early Childhood Development, Blueprint for government schools (November 28, 2007); http://www.eduweb.vic.gov.au/edulibrary/public/govrel/reports/blueprint-rpt.pdf

5. L. Campbell, and P. St Leger, On the right track: An evaluation of the Back on Track Pilot program on behalf of the Royal Children's Hospital Education Institute. (Centre for Program Development, University of Melbourne, 2006).

6. L. Schulman, Knowledge and teacher: foundations of the new reform. *Harvard Educational Review* **56**, 1-22 (1987)

7. P. Mishra, and M. Koehler, Technological pedagogical content knowledge: A framework for teacher knowledge. *Teachers College Record* **108**(6), 1017-1054 (2006).

8. A. McDougall, and A. Jones, Theory and history, questions and methodology: current and future issues in research into ICT in education. *Technology, Pedagogy and Education.* **15** (3): 353-360 (2006).

9 A. Jones, and J. Martin, Monitoring classroom use of ICT in order to improve implementation. In D. Watson, and D. Benzie (eds), *Imaging the Future for ICT and Education: IFIP WG 3.1, 3.3 & 3.5 Joint Conference - CD Proceedings.* 176-186. Alesund, Norway: Hogskolen i Alesund/Alesund University College (2006).

Audiogene: Mobile Learning Genetics through Audio by Blind Learners

Jaime Sánchez and Fernando Aguayo
Department of Computer Science, University of Chile

Abstract. Science learning is a complex task for children at school age, especially for blind children. The purpose of this study was to develop and evaluate *AudioGene*, a game that uses mobile and audio-based technology to assist the interaction between blind and sighted children, and help them to learn biology and become more socially integrated. *AudioGene* was designed considering the communalities and specific particularities of the mental model of both blind and sighted users. The goals of this virtual environment were to integrate blind and sighted users, learn genetics concepts, and create ways of collaboration between them through the use of mobile devices. The software usability was evaluated and the results show that audio-based technology accompanied with ad-hoc methodology can play a role in the school integration of blind users. Relevant gains in this task as we expect from the initial results of this pilot study could reveal that mobile gaming can be a powerful tool for science learning of both blind and sighted students in school integrated learning settings.

1 Introduction

Science teaching and learning and particularly the concepts related to genetics are difficult to learn by the students due to the abstraction associated to the concepts involved and the impossibility of doing direct observation of phenomena and performing experiments to recreate similar environments.

The use of mobile devices eliminates the barriers imposed by the interaction in a reduced space (and not always available) such as a laboratory and allows a more fluid communication between the participants.

Diverse authors have analyzed the impact of games on problem solving. Some of them state that games can promote higher order learning skills, such as increased meaningful dialogues among learners [1]. Other studies also describe positive effects of games on social skills [2].

School integration and social inclusion are very important issues nowadays in

Please use the following format when citing this chapter:

Sánchez, J. and Aguayo, F., 2008, in IFIP International Federation for Information Processing, Volume 281; *Learning to Live in the Knowledge Society*; Michael Kendall and Brian Samways; (Boston: Springer), pp. 79–86.

society and education. Several studies [3] to determine the role that technology can play in the school integration of users with disabilities into current classroom have been carried out.

Some studies have used interactive games for assisting blind people for learning and cognition purposes. AudioChile and AudioVida [4] are audio-based virtual environments oriented to enhance problem solving, navigation and orientation skills in users with visual disabilities.

Eriksson & Gärdenfors [5] propose web-based games for children with different visual impairments. They suggest two kinds of games: image-based games for children with partial sight and sound-based games for completely blind children.

Danesh et al. propose GeneyTM [6], a collaborative application for problem solving using genetics content through the use of PDAs oriented to sighted children and covering similar content of this study.

In the work exposed by de Freitas y Levene [7] a complete analysis of the development of mobile devices for education is presented. Emphasis is made on a way of using these devices for helping users with disabilities. As a result, they mention the benefits of new technologies in tasks such as locating places, help for mobility, and cognitive assistance for orientation in real environments.

In this study we propose and evaluate *AudioGene*, a mobile sound-based virtual environment for science learning and school integration of legally blind children with sighted children.

2 *AudioGene*

The metaphor of *AudioGene* was defined as a virtual gaming world including certain genetics concepts such as DNA, mutation, genotype, phenotype and gene. The contents were taken from the science school syllabus for 7th to 10th grade. The game was designed for mobile devices, in particular pocketPC devices, but allowing the possibility of be mapped by other mobile devices that have Windows as operating system.

The game contains different interaction zones for the characters controlled by students, such as lava, water, mountain and earth (see Figure 1). The game presents a story that consists in a tree of life that has certain characteristics and is dying so the goal is to replace the tree by another one with the same characteristics using a combination of seeds that will result in a similar tree.

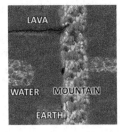

Fig. 1. Virtual world of *AudioGene* displaying different interaction zones for the characters controlled by students, such as lava, water, mountain and earth.

In order to achieve the goal of the game the user has to evolve the character chosen into superior entities. This allows the players to use the new acquired skills through the game in order to find the seeds that are spread throughout the virtual world. All new skills are gained during the acquisition of genetic knowledge through three ways: 1.The player travels through the world in a free way and interacts with the characters encountered; 2. The player solves a specific mission of the game, and 3. The player, in conjunction with his or her partners, solves the mission. The difference with the previous missions is that the other ones could be accomplished without the help of partners.

The fact of working with a pocketPC device restricts the design of the graphic interface due to its size. To accomplish this, we avoided the use of buttons and status information. Computer controlled characters also teach the users about contents concerning genetics through dialogs that are triggered as the user approaches them.

The audio interface is composed by two types of sounds. The first one is used for spatial orientation and consists in using sound clues. The second one is for learning contents about genetics using pre-recorded sentences.

These sounds may correspond to the area where the user is located. As an example, when the user is over the water, an associated sound to water is played.

In relation to the audio system, it is known that headsets only allow the use of 2 sound sources (A and B in Figure 2, left) which offer the option of 3 spatial combinations. The first two combinations correspond to only one of the sources being used (identified as left or right) and the other source match the use of both sources (which is intuitively identified as front) (see Figure 2, left). The proposed system consists in adding a new variable (C) to the sound system, which allows three new combinations and extend the spatial system to six combinations. When adding a rear sound to the user (C) we obtain a system like the one shown in Figure 2, right.

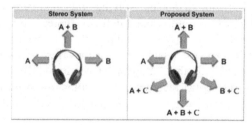

Fig. 2. Audio system proposed for *AudioGene* using an audio mask in comparison with the stereo system.

3 Research Methodology

The methodology to evaluate the *AudioGene* consisted of two stages. In the first stage, the usability was evaluated with end users. All blind children that participated in the study were legally blind; this implies totally blind and children with residual vision. In the second stage, the work dynamics in the classroom was analyzed, considering aspects such as the motivation and the commitment of the students with this new way to learn (around a mobile game), the changes in the conditions of learning (interaction inside the classroom), and the results obtained in the cognitive development and specific learning. In addition, we studied the impact of using the game in the school integration of blind children with their sighted classmates.

3.1   Usability Evaluation

Three different groups that interacted with *AudioGene* were formed. Each group was consisted of 1 legally blind child and 3 sighted children forming a sample of 3 users with visual disabilities and 9 sighted users. The legally blind users were composed by 2 totally blind users and 1 user with residual vision with ages ranging from 8 to 12 years old. None of them had associated deficits. The sighted users had ages ranging from 8 to 14 years old. All blind users participated in the specific integration program. Two facilitators administered the tests to the children. The facilitators aside from orienting and helping children in the tasks also observed the behavior of the users when playing *AudioGene*.

Two usability instruments were used during testing: (1) End-User Questionnaire [8], and (2) Open questionnaire. The End User Usability test was administered to the participants of the study. This was applied at the end of the usability sessions. It is basically a software acceptance test and consists of 18 sentences with an answered scale of 10 points (minimum of 1 and maximum of 10). The Open Questionnaire consisted of 5 open questions that helped to identify the level of integration the game can achieve.

A facilitator provided a PocketPC to each user and gave them instructions for the task to be accomplished by playing the game as teamwork. Each team played during a session of 30 minutes with AudioGene solving collaborative tasks. In order to do this they had to coordinate themselves and define a strategy to attain the objective. Once the strategy was defined, students could play with *AudioGene*.

After the end of the experience end user questionnaires were administered. Each usability testing consisted of the following steps: introduction to the software, software interaction, anecdotic recording, application of evaluation instruments, session recording, session protocol reports, and software design and redesign.

3.1.1 Results

In general, the game was highly accepted in all categories for blind users (Satisfaction; 8.4 (out of 10); Control and Use: 9.2; Sound: 8.9) and sighted users (Satisfaction; 8.3; Control and Use: 8.8; Sound: 8.6; Image: 9.3). There were not critical differences between sighted users (see Figure 3) and blind users

From the "Game Satisfaction" category the assertions that obtained the highest scores in both blind and sighted users corresponded to "I would play again with the software" (9.3 and 9.7 respectively) and "The software is entertaining" (10 and 9.8 respectively). The asseveration "The software has different levels of difficulty" obtained the lowest score, 5.7 for blind users and 6.3 for sighted users, which reveals that this was the task with increasing level of difficulty while users solved tasks. In the "Game Control and Usage" category, the assertion that obtained the highest score in both type of users was "The software is easy to use" (10 for blind users and 9.4 for sighted users). This result denotes the easiness of use achieved by the proposed interface of *AudioGene*.

The assertion "The sounds used in the software conveys me information" obtained the highest score from blind children, 9.7, and 7.3 for sighted users. This reveals the adequate selection of sound made for the game because they were useful for them to solve the tasks assigned.

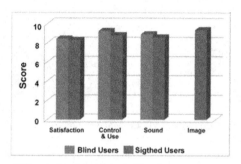

Fig. 3. Results of the usability evaluation of *AudioGene*.

Learners commented that sounds were identifiable, high-quality and clear. They emphasized the fact that *AudioGene* let them work together, fully interact, and solve tasks collaboratively between blind and sighted children. They showed a high interest in the fact that characters were able to win skills and solve tasks in connection with these skills. A sighted student value the game because "*It made me work together with my blind partners*".

In general, the answers obtained support the goal of the game for learning (the game is useful "*to interact with my friends and learn*"), and in some specific cases science learning (the game is useful "*to learn things about science*").

The users were motivated in the fact that by using the new skills provided by *AudioGene* they can solve different group tasks. For the question, what did you like in the software? A sighted child answered: "*it is entertaining, interactive and we can learn more. I was very entertained because I had a mission with my partners*" Another child said: "*I liked to obtain powers (skills) because the questions were difficult and it was like a challenge*". A blind child commented: "*I liked the lava because all of my partners entered to it and we all together could cross it*"

3.2 Learning and Social Integration Evaluation

The sample consisted of 5 legally blind children and 3 sighted children. These 8 students were distributed in two groups of 4 children each. Each of these groups was conformed by one blind user and 3 sighted users.

From the blind children, 2 were totally blind and 3 had residual vision. Four of the children assist to the "*La Maisonette*" school that currently implement an integration program and the other four children assist to the "*Escuela de Ciegos Santa Lucía*", school specialized in blind students (see Figure 4). Both schools are located in Santiago de Chile. Two facilitators participated in the evaluations; both of them were special education teachers specialized in vision disabilities.

In order to know what do children thought about the whole experience working with *AudioGene*, a short open questionnaire was used. This questionnaire consisted of questions such as, "How do you regularly play with your partners?", "What do you think about *AudioGene*?", "What do you think about this new way of learning?", and "Would you like to have more games like this one?"

Fig. 4. Children playing *AudioGene*. (A) "La Maissonette" school students (B) "Escuela de Ciegos Santa Lucía" students.

We wanted to know the novelty that a serious game like *AudioGene* can provide to children interaction and integration. The other questions focused on finding answers in the field of social integration and learning.

With the purpose of carrying out this research the following stages were followed: 1. Introduction to the game; 2. Collaborative gaming with *AudioGene* during a session of 30 minutes; and 3. Application of the open questionnaire. All evaluations were carried out in the schools.

3.2.1 Results

Some interesting answers from the children describe how they regularly play with other children. For example, when playing soccer, they put the ball inside plastic bags in order to hear sounds when the ball is moving. Thanks to these particular sounds children with visual disabilities are able to follow the ball movements and play soccer without problems. Most of them mentioned that they do not have common games to play between sighted and blind children.

All of them found that *AudioGene* was entertaining and motivating. They focused mainly in the possibility of accomplishing tasks in conjunction with their partners. Sighted children liked to be able to play with their blind partners. For blind children the fact of being able to work in conjunction with sighted children through the use of technology was a very good experience and they liked to be one of the participants of the teamwork.

For the question, did you like to play with your friend? All teams agreed that to play all together was a very good experience. All of them could participate and achieve the proposed objective as a team and also having individual tasks and responsibilities.

Children found that learning with a mobile game was more entertaining than reading books and also more motivating. Even a blind girl added "*I am going to propose it to the Madame...(her teacher)*".

They pointed that one of the advantages of *AudioGene* was that they can be all together in teams interacting, playing and learning. An integrated blind girl states: "(I found it) *good, because all of us can be there and is entertaining to play with it. In the way that it teaches that all the people in the world are different; there is no person similar to another. Some can cross the lava, another one can cross the water but the ones that can cross the lava cannot cross the water...*" The idea behind this answer is that the metaphor used in the game teaches her that all people are different with different skills and virtues. One of the children supports the idea of creating and having more games for school integration and concludes "*... we cannot live in a world where all is made for the people that are sighted or in a world where the sighted are separated from the blind*"

About the question, would you play again *AudioGene*? All the children answered affirmatively to this question.

All of these answers inject motivation and ideas to continue working with this gaming tool and test its capabilities for learning biology concepts more fully in the near future.

4 Discussion

The purpose of this study was to develop and evaluate *AudioGene*, a game that uses mobile technology to promote interaction between blind and sighted children, social integration and in doing so, to learn science. We think that it is important to generate school spots where blind children feel motivated for learning and constructing knowledge. In this direction, new technologies can help immensely especially for communication and collaboration between sighted and blind children.

This new way of learning around a mobile game specially tailored to blind children, helps to improve the accessibility of all users to technology-based learning materials and thus improve their learning. Applications such as *AudioGene* open the possibility of creating more inclusive learning contexts where sighted users and users with visual disabilities can work together collaboratively and achieve common objectives.

The experience presented by Freitas y Levene [7] can be complemented with the results presented in this work. The use of mobile devices not only can assist the learning of legally blind users, but also by embedding applications such as *AudioGene*, can become powerful tools for school integration and social inclusion.

The positive effects of games on social skills mentioned by Pellegrini et al. [2] is corroborated in this work because the use of *AudioGene* allowed blind children to be socially integrated with their sighted partners, participating actively in social activities, and showing high interest and motivation for learning by using mobile gaming. From the comments made by the children we highlight the fact that the use of the game allowed legally blind children to work integrated with sighted classmates, feeling themselves as taking advantage of the school life. This result is very relevant to achieve a more complete learning beyond contents.

The fact that *AudioGene* is a mobile application allows the children to play inside and outside of their classrooms and learn more naturally in other nit fully explored learning contexts with the assistance of technology.

The remaining work in this study is to identify whether the biological concepts embedded in the game are fully learned by the students, both by constructing new knowledge and complementing the knowledge learned in their regular classes. In addition, we should identify whether the virtual world provided by the game has to be extended to generate more degrees of difficulty in the learning tasks to be accomplished. We have to identify in a deeper way the degree of students' integration that can be achieved with *AudioGene*. Finally, testing the use of *AudioGene* in environments outside the classroom, like a museum, could be a challenging task in searching for innovative ways learning science.

Acknowledgements

This report was funded by the Chilean National Fund of Science and Technology, Fondecyt, Project 1060797.

References

1.   K. McDonald and R. Hannafin, Using web-based computer games to meet the demands of today's high stakes testing: A mixed method inquiry. Journal of Research on Technology in Education, 2003, 55(4), pp. 459–472
2.   A. Pellegrini, P. Blatchford and B. Kentaro, A Short-term Longitudinal Study of Children's Playground Games in Primary School: Implications for Adjustment to School and Social Adjustment in the USA and the UK. Social Development, 2004 13(1), pp. 107–123
3.   E. Feyerer, K. Miesenberger and D. Wohlhart, ICT and Assistive Technology in Teachers Education and Training. Computer Helping People with Special Needs: Proceedings of 8th International Conference, ICCHP 2002, Linz, Austria, July 15-20, 2002, pp. 297-334
4.   J. Sánchez, and M. Sáenz, 3D sound interactive environments for blind children problem solving skills. Behaviour & Information Technology, Vol. 25, No. 4, July – August 2006, pp. 367 – 378.
5.   Y. Eriksson and D. Gärdenfors, Computer games for children with visual impairments. Proceedings of the 5th International conference on Disability, Virtual Reality and Associated Technologies, 20-22 September, 2004, New College, Oxford, UK, pp. 79-86.
6.   A. Danesh and K.M. Inkpen, F. Lau, K. Shu and K.S. Booth, GeneyTM: designing a collaborative activity for the palm handheld computer. In Proceedings of the Conference on Human Factors in Computing Systems (CHI 2001), Seattle, USA, pp. 388–395.
7.   S. de Freitas and M. Levene, Evaluating the development of wearable devices, personal data assistants and the use of other mobile devices in further and higher education institutions. JISC Technol. and Stand. Watch Report: Wearable Technology, 2003, TSW 03-05, pp. 1-21
8.   J. Sánchez, End-user and facilitator questionnaire for Software Usability. Usability evaluation test. University of Chile, 2003.

Chapter 4

Innovative Learning Environments 1

Design and implementation of a user friendly environment for Learning Objects creation

Giovanni Adorni, Diego Brondo and Mauro Coccoli
University of Genoa, Department of Communication,
Computer, and Systems Science
E-Learning & Knowledge Management Laboratory
Viale Causa, 13 - 16145 Genova, Italy
{adorni, diego.brondo, mauro.coccoli}@unige.it
WWW home page: http://elkm.unige.it

Abstract. The aim of this paper is describing the SCOMaker, a user friendly authoring tool for the automated production of SCOs, mainly oriented to distance learning and learning object design. It is a freely available open source application to assist teachers and academics in the publishing of web content without the need to become proficient in HTML, XML markup or any other language. SCOMaker can export content as self-contained web pages or as SCORM 2004 packages usable on a LMS server or designed for a database SCO repository. This project has been developed by ELKM (E-Learning & Knowledge Management) and led by the University of Genoa.

1 Introduction

The progress of Information and Communication Technologies (ICT) is changing in depth production, management, and exchange of knowledge: methodologies and tools for communication, investigation, and information research are rapidly changing too [1]. Several years of experience in developing e-learning projects at the University of Genoa [2], have pointed out a scenario of increasing managerial complexity, due to the existence of heterogeneous technologies. In an open and heterogeneous environment, the interaction among different tools and platforms, and legacy systems can only be obtained by means of seamless integration and communication, and the use of standards. Another key point is the usability: researchers, teachers, and anyone else having to develop learning objects, has to cope with complex technologies, programming language and elaborate software. Hence the objective of the project is to develop an easy-to-use [3] tool enabling authors of educational materials to produce and deliver sharable objects and documents

Please use the following format when citing this chapter:

Adorni, G., Brondo, D. and Coccoli, M., 2008, in IFIP International Federation for Information Processing, Volume 281; *Learning to Live in the Knowledge Society*; Michael Kendall and Brian Samways; (Boston: Springer), pp. 89–92.

(compliant to international standards, ADL SCORM [4] in primis) in a short time and with a little effort. In this respect, a specific tool has been designed, which we called "the SCOMaker". Furthermore the SCOMaker is thought as a part of a comprehensive pipeline of software tools that cover the whole process of course design, from concept map indexing to publication or storage passing through the creation of learning objects [5]. SCOMaker can be adapted to several application scenarios and learning backgrounds (school, university, primary school, business). On account of this and on the different skill proficiency of potential users, it was of primary relevance to develop a system respecting two main concepts: being accessible and easy-to-use.

2   Software architecture

The first step, in building educational materials, is to create a concept map, a logical and well-formed diagram showing the relationships between concepts of the topics of the lesson. This diagram is a good way for encoding knowledge and

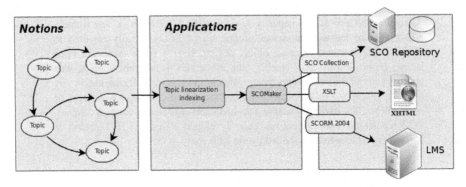

Fig. 1. Learning object production line

connecting this encoded knowledge to relevant information resources. In the notions schema, shown in Figure 1, topics represent the subjects of discourse and arrows are the associations, representing relationships between the subjects.

Following topics association it is possible to glean a linear sequence of topic obtaining a well ordered index (chapters, sections, subsection, etc.). The concept map represents in all respects the index of the e-learning course and, due to its intrinsically hierarchical nature, it can be easily turned into a XML tree following the priority rules. The XML file index can be imported into the SCOMaker creating the framework of the project. The second step is the creation of the content based on the above logical structure and this can be obtained in two different ways. First way writing from the scratch and importing documents and multimedia contents. Second way importing and adding content to an empty framework solution obtained with the topic linearization. Any topic can be linked by author to one or more occurrences, which connect the subjects to pertinent information resources (i.e. PDF documents, images, multimedia files, etc). Such contents are organized in the XML file and from this point on it can be re-edited or rendered in different shapes. Moreover users can modify the framework freely.

3   Implementation

We developed a web application written in PHP, a reflective programming language, and used XHTML, a markup language that has the same depth of expression as HTML but with a syntax that conforms to XML syntax, for the web interface [6]. This guarantees documents to be well-formed and a better accessibility.

A significant advantage of building web applications to support standard browser features is that they should perform as specified regardless of the operating system or OS version installed on a given client. Additionally, the ability of users to customize many of the display settings of their browser (such as selecting different font sizes, colors, and typefaces) can give an advance to the web application accessibility [7]. SCOMaker was developed taking into account an user-centered design [8], with its intended users in mind at all times. The web interface was designed to be as easy as possible, just like an internet page and all the complex operation for contents and outputs manipulation are completely transparent. So that teachers, instructors or business managers have to focus their attention only on the contents of the lesson .

3.1   Content management

Contents could be of different type: text, images, HTML pages, WiKi, multimedia files imported into SCOMaker with the use of an URI to the remote resource, or embedded ones written directly with the SCOMaker editor.

Each asset (text field, image, multimedia content, etc.) is handled by a specific PHP class. These classes handle both the module interface providing a suitable editor for each content type and the object manipulation methods (PHP functions). This way of project makes possible to developers to easily add new features, fulfilling new educational purposes, just making new modules for handling different type of contents. This modular approach guarantees flexibility and adaptiveness to different pedagogical methodologies and a further extension of SCOMaker features or new standards to come.

Once obtained a structure complying to own intents, the only thing left is the users to save the entire project. Thanks to a set of plugins the customers can choose among different output formats. Using a module rather than another, the learning structure will be converted into different formats for different purposes.

3.2   SCOMaker outputs

Users can create XML output of the course they are creating for a later time modification; or trough a SCORM 2004 standard converter can create a Sharable Content Object portable on any LMS platform SCORM compliant. Moreover they can send the output to a database with the purpose of adding their work into a learning objects repository. Finally they can create a web version of the lesson in XHTML pages readable on-line through suited XML/XSL-Transformations. This modular approach gives robustness to the standard changes, or database repository changes.

4   Conclusion

Much web publishing applications for authoring such as Frontpage and Dreamweaver provides a set of powerful and complex tools whose use implies a somewhat computer knowledge and a fairly steep learning curve. Moreover too generic software doesn't give appropriate e-learning solutions [9]. With SCOMaker we tried to identify the elements of a learning resource and offer them in an easy and user friendly way. Users in out-and-out learning building, can use SCOMaker features with extreme ease and often without the need for data conversion, thus saving on potential data losses and incompatibilities.

Bibliography

1. W. Horton, Evaluating E-learning (ASTD 2001)
2. G. Adorni, M. Coccoli and G. Vercelli, Integrated Management of Courses in a Distance Learning Environment, In Proc. of the Twelfth International Conference on Distributed Multimedia Systems, Bridging the gap between communication and intelligence. vol. 1, pp. 222-227 (2006)
3. Butow, User Interface Design for Mere Mortals (Addison-Wesley 2007)
4. ADL Initiative, SCORM 2004 2nd Edition Overview in ADL (Advanced Distributed Learning) (2004)
5. G. Adorni, M. Coccoli and G. Vercelli, EifFE-L: e-learning Experiences with the Platform of the University of Genova, Journal of E-Learning and knowledge society vol. 1, No. 3 (2005)
6. T. Felke-Morris, Web Development & Design Foundations With XHTML (Addison-Wesley 2007)
7. J. Slatin and S. Rush, Maximum Accessibility: Making Your Web Site More Usable for Everyone (Addison-Wesley 2003)
8. J. Lazar, Web Usability: A User-Centered Design Approach (Addison-Wesley 2006)
9. G. Bonaiuti, E-Learning 2.0 Il futuro dell'apprendimento in rete, tra formale e informale (Erickson 2006)

Exploring Touching Learning Environments

Gustavo Ramírez González, Mario Muñoz Organero and Carlos Delgado Kloos
Carlos III University of Madrid, Leganes Campus, Madrid, Spain.
{gramirez@inv.it.uc3m.es, munozm@it.uc3m.es, cdk@it.uc3m.es}

Abstract. There are several ways for learning, but in actual society, the proliferation of technology alternatives enables multiple learning scenarios and environments. Part of the most important technologies for this, are associated to mobile phones. Classically, the mobile were expected to deliver content, but they were not specifically designed for interacting with real objects and context. This paper proposes the concept of Touching Learning Environments as part of the evolution of M-learning and Ubiquitous Computing, enabling touching technologies in mobile devices; this technology is known as Near Field Communication NFC.

1. Introduction

The actual deployment and evolution of ubiquitous computing is possible due the progress and widespread dissemination of some enabler technologies such as RFID, Bluetooth and NFC. The use of these technologies combined with the extensive market penetration of mobile phones and their powerful options for personalization and mobility, offer an unprecedented atmosphere for the creation of new learning environments.

This new learning environment consists basically in the interaction of a person with the context, basically by touching things, this things will give information and it could be part of learning activities. The long term vision is a place where people can get information and learning experience by "talking" or manipulating objects. The goal of this paper is to definite this concept and show some possible scenarios. To facilitate the reading, most of technical details will eliminate, but a basic explanation of technologies involved will be included.

The structure of the paper is as follows. First some background about related technology will be exposed in section 2. Then a set of generic touching learning

Please use the following format when citing this chapter:

González, G.R., Organero, M.M. and Kloos, C.D., 2008, in IFIP International Federation for Information Processing, Volume 281; *Learning to Live in the Knowledge Society*; Michael Kendall and Brian Samways; (Boston: Springer), pp. 93–96.

scenarios are exposed in section 3. Finally some conclusions and future work are presented at the end of the paper.

2. Enabling technologies for Touching Learning

2.1 RFID Radio Frequency Identification

RFID [1] is probably the most relevant technology in the building of the ubiquitous computing. It basically began as a promise to eliminate many business problems especially in the logistics of units, material handling and inventory in general for the supply chain and the retail sector. Furthermore, other applications [2] such as access control, luggage tracking, electronic payment systems, homeland security, livestock history, library tracking of books and receiving assistance. On the other hand there are some interesting experiences motivated by the every day activities of people or explore the concept of smart products.

2.2 NFC Near Field Communication

Near Field Communication (NFC) is one of the latest wireless networking technologies based on RFID. As a short-range wireless connectivity technology, NFC provides intuitive, simple, and safe communication between electronic devices. NFC [3] is distinguished by its intuitive interface. Different trials of this technology have successfully illustrated how people carrying mobile phones can make purchases, get directions, exchange information, and buy transportation tickets simply by bringing them close to NFC-enabled devices embedded in information kiosks, retail, advertising, vending machines, and other devices. Formed in 2004, the NFC Forum [4] envisions a world where people can access content and services in an intuitive way, leading to secure universal commerce and connectivity. The Forum believes that NFC technology makes business sense for transportation and content providers, device manufacturers, financial services organizations, and more. An ABI Research forecasts that by 2012, some 292 million handsets (over 20 percent of the global mobile handset market) will ship with built in NFC capabilities [5].

3. Generic Touching Learning Scenarios

At this stage, "Touching Learning" or "Learning by Touching" can be defined as: the used services and applications in a learning environment where the learning actor can interact with environment resources for learning purposes or for communication, only by touching.

NFC, as technological enabler can be used in several ways. A set of generic learning touching scenarios are presented. These scenarios are expected to be as generic as possible to be applied in any specific instances. The first one describes the basic function of "Touching for searching". The second presents a "Personal

Physical Context", this is the relationship established between a person and several objects. The third one shows the action of direct interaction and control from the mobile user to the surrounding "intelligent" objects. Some implementations of this touching learning scenarios can be found in [6].

3.1 Touching to Search in the Physical Context

The Web is a huge repository of information that must be organized in order to be able to find useful things for the final user. Nowadays there is a well known series of search engines. Due to their friendly web based interfaces it is easy to find information in the Web. In general, there are various mechanisms to do that, but the most popular is based on references and indexation. By introducing these mechanisms, the concept of searching can define. The main difference between the information in the Web and the information in the Physical context is that the information is associated and lives attached to a particular object, describing it and providing some times the access mechanisms for its remote control and adaptation. In Figure 1 show an application of this scenario in a lab, where student look for the content of the cabinet touching the tag and it display a set of codes or names related with the content.

Figure 1. Scenario of Touching to Search.

3.2 Touching in Personal Physical Context

Touching in personal Physical Context is the relationship established between a person and several objects that personalizes the behavior of the objects according to the mobile user preferences. Mobile users with an NFC enabled mobile device can personalize the behavior of their local environment simply by touching the objects, exchanging profiles and taking the appropriate actions. A person in its daily routine interacts with diverse physical objects. This interaction in an NFC enable scenario is produced by the contact of mobile devices with physical objects with different purposes. Due to this relation, the information obtained by the physical contact with objects can be stored, analyzed and processed in the mobile device or can be shared and synchronized with other personal devices or with external computers depending on the information in the user profile.

3.3 Touching to Adapt Physical Context

This third scenario establishes an association between a user and the surrounding objects which is by itself active. The physical environment of the user, adapt to the user not only in an automatic process which is the result of the exchange and processing of user and object profiles, but in a proactive way which can be controlled by the user by means of a peer to peer communication process. Using NFC P2P capabilities allows us to implement real scenarios implementing this idea. As an example we can find a classroom containing some devices such as an overhead projector, a bookshelf and some other devices which can be controlled by the professor or the students in some different ways depending on their profiles.

4. Conclusions and future work

This paper proposes the concept of Touching Learning Scenarios using NFC as technology to enable mobility and interaction with physical spaces. It also proposes three generic scenarios. Mobile Phone is one of the best candidates to enable transparency in learning systems. This basic technology combined with others as NFC, increases the possibilities of adoption. As part of our future work, more scenarios are expected specially using other characteristics of NFC more than basic tagging. The design of experiences linking the Touching Learning concept with formal and informal learning is expected.

Acknowledgments

This work was supported by the Spanish "Programa Nacional de Tecnologías de la Sociedad de la Información" through the projects TSI2005-08225-C07-01 and -02. Gustavo Ramirez is funded by the EU Programme Alban, scholarship No. E06D101768CO and by University of Cauca.

References

1. P. Sweeney, RFID For Dummies, Wiley Publishing, 2005.
2. RFID Journal web site; http://www.rfidjournal.com/
3. NFC Forum. White Paper, The Keys to Truly Interoperable Communications. 2006.
4. NFC Forum http://www.nfc-forum.org
5. ABI Research Press Release, Twenty Percent of Mobile Handsets Will Include Near Field Communication by 2012.
6. G. Ramírez, M. Muñoz and C. Delgado, IOT early possibilities in learning scenarios, Workshop on Designing the Internet of Things for Workplace Realities: Social and Cultural Aspects in Design and Organization (Social-IoT), Zurich, Switzerland, March 26, 2008.

Adaptation of Impulsive and Reflective Learning Behavior in a Game-Based Environment

Franziska Spring-Keller
University of Zurich, Department of Informatics, Educational Engineering
Lab, Switzerland, spring@ifi.uzh.ch

Abstract. This research deals with learning in digital environments. Adaptive game-based learning considers learners' preferred learning behavior and adapts the game system accordingly. In order to analyze learning behavior, the focus lies on a specific cognitive style, impulsive and reflective (I/R), which describe behaviors in problem-solving and decision-making environments. Impulsive people tend to react much faster than reflective ones but make more mistakes in their choices. Since impulsive behavior in learning is considered as rather weak behavior, this research of game-based learning environments wants to encourage impulsive learners and not particularly force a change in learning behavior. This approach is illustrated on the strategy and simulation game "Hortus".

1 Introduction

Every person has a different preference and approach of how to learn something new. Some people prefer to indulge in theoretical information while others rather like to learn from hands on experience.

There are also different research approaches to analyzing and supporting learner preferences. The analysis of these preferences is either based on a theoretical learner model or is implicitly collected (data mining) from user behavior during the use of a learning unit without a model from learning theory. Learner models mostly provide instructions of how to support a learner. Unfortunately, many studies of learning behavior are not based on recognized theories or could not deliver clear results of learning improvement [1, 2].

This paper focuses on a mixed approach that takes a specific learner attribute, cognitive style, and analyzes this behavior implicitly during the use of a learning unit. The cognitive style – impulsive and reflective – provides the most convenient conditions to implicitly analyze user behavior.

Please use the following format when citing this chapter:

Spring-Keller, F., 2008, in IFIP International Federation for Information Processing, Volume 281; *Learning to Live in the Knowledge Society*; Michael Kendall and Brian Samways; (Boston: Springer), pp. 97–100.

1.1 Cognitive style – impulsive and reflective (I/R)

In problem-solving environments, there are a lot of situations where learners have to make decisions under great uncertainty. Some people rather solve few problems in order to avoid a high error rate. This group is defined as reflective. Other people rush over the whole situation and their goal is more to solve as many problems as possible in the given amount of time. These people are called impulsive [3]. Impulsive and reflective (I/R) behavior is measured using the so-called Matching Familiar Figures Test (MFFT) by Kagan et al. [4] and a revised and digitized version by Van Merrienboer and Jelsma [5].

In classic learning environments, impulsive learners are trained to re-think and change their behavior into a more reflective approach since the impulsive behavior is considered a weak behavior. This type of training is not the preferable and efficient way from the point of view of an impulsive learner. Therefore this trait will be investigated in greater detail in the game-based environment described below. Game-based learning environments train problem-solving skills and most of the game designs tolerate "making mistakes". This crucial aspect is mostly not tolerated in classic learning environments [6].

1.2 Learning in Games

This research looks at a very particular kind of game-based learning environment. It includes simulation and strategy games such as Civilization or Sim City. These games are very popular and are often used for educational purposes [7, 8]. Students learn how to deal with restricted resources or experience historical events from an active perspective. Learning in these kinds of games is integrated into the game system and is not separated from the game context. Students learn by doing in a situated context [9]. The better they play the game, the better they understand the rules and the learning content, respectively. Information and background knowledge is provided on demand when players need it. These aspects support situated learning in the respective context.

Commercial games like Sim City are too complex and too big to use for learner analysis and adaptation. Therefore, in this research a separate game, "Hortus", is developed that is based on the same learning concept as Sim City or Civilization.

2   An adaptive learning game to support I/R behavior

2.1   Analysis of I/R behavior

Recent studies have used the MFFT or have transferred its dimensions to multiple choice systems [10]. This is much easier because there is a restricted amount of choices that can be either right or wrong. However, a choice does not necessarily have to be right or wrong according to the definition of I/R. In authentic problem-solving environments there is rarely a right and a wrong choice. In a game like Hortus, there are several possiblities of how to solve a problem. The game has five ascending goals. Each goal has vast possibilities of how to achieve them. However, the closer the player gets to the goal, the more countable the number of possible solutions becomes. There is a dynamic calculation and creation of a graph showing possible paths to the next sub-goal. Each single path is weighted depending on the quality of the choice.

The weights of each path are based on several criteria. For instance, one criterion is how economical players use their resources. Additional user behavior is collected to provide an accurate result for I/R. This is click frequency, time until a decision was made etc.

2.2   Instructions for I/R

Once the learners' profiles reveal whether they are impulsive or reflective, the game system reacts accordingly. This can occur on two levels: the information-based layer and content-based layer [11]. The first layer does not affect the game system. Instead, it mainly analyses past behavior, anticipates possible future steps or strategic decisions for the user. The other layer affects the game system.

For further research, content-based adaptation is of main interest. Changing some elements in a game system is much more challenging than changing the appearance of learning content in an e-learning unit. The goal is to create a personal learning experience for learners without changing the overall learning goal. An example would be adding or removing a resource in the game. By adding a single resource, the game could become strategically challenging for reflective learners who prefer to make strategies and plan ahead. Another possibility is to add more action elements for impulsive learners.

3   Conclusion

The state of the art in impulsive and reflective learning behavior is to measure it either with the Matching Familiar Figures Test (MFFT) or with multiple choice tasks. In this paper, a concept is introduced where I/R is measured in an authentic environment with several possible solutions to a specific problem. A game-based environment provides this kind of environment. Since impulsive learners like to avoid direct questions because they are afraid to seem incompetent [12], a game for learning could help them by not getting them into this awkward situation.

Depending on the definition of an expert player/learner, impulsive people do not necessarily have to be forced into reflective behavior. Learning success might not only depend on how good and how fast someone solves a problem, but also on how someone deals with resources in the game or what kind of mistakes the player made. Therefore it has to be empirically tested if impulsive behavior has to be changed or can be enforced. The goal is to leave learners in their preferred area to the extent possible and not to force them to learn other styles that are preset by the designer or creator of the learning environment.

References

1.D.H. Jonassen and B.L. Grabowski, *Handbook of Individual Differences in Learnin, and Instruction* (Hillsdale, NJ: Lawrence Erlbaum Associates, 1993).
2.F. Coffield, D. Moseley, E. Hall and K. Ecclestone, Should we be using learning styles? What research has to say to practice. Learning and Skills Research Centre (London: Cromwell Press Ltd, 2004).
3.R.J. Sternberg, and L.-F. Zhang, *Perspectives on Thinking, Learning, and Cognitive Styles* (New Jersey: Lawrence Erlbaum Associates, 2001).
4.J. Kagan, B.L. Rosman, D. Day, J. Albert and W. Philips, (1964). Information processing in the child: Significance of analytic and reflective attitude. *Psychological Monographs*. Ed. 78, Vol. 1, Whole No. 578, 1964.
5.J.J.G. Van Merriënboer and O. Jelsma, The Matching Familiar Figure Test: Computer or Experimenter Controlled Administration. *Educational and Psychological Measurement* 48, pp. 161-164, 1988.
6. J.P. Gee, *What Video Games Have To Teach Us About Learning And Literacy* (Palgrave Macmillan, New York, 2003).
7. K.D. Squire, (2003) Video Games in Education. *International Journal of Intelligent Simulations and Gaming*, (2)1, pp. 49-62, 2003
8. K. Squire, Possibility spaces. In Katie Salen (Ed). *The ecology of games*. In the MacArthur Foundation Series on Digital Media Literacies (Chicago: MacArthur Foundation, in press).
9. J.P. Gee, What would a state-of-the-art instructional video game look like? *Innovate* 1 (6), (2005).
10. H.H. Mammar and F.T. Bernard, Incorporating cognitive styles into adaptive multimodal interfaces. CogSci , George Mason University, Fairfax, VA, August 8-10, 2002.
11. D. Burgos, C. Tattersall and R. Koper. Representing adaptive eLearning strategies in IMS Learning Design. Paper presented at the TENCompetence Conference, Sofia, Bulgaria, March 2006.
12. J. Kagan and N. Kogan, In Weiner, A.S. and Adams, W.V. (1974) The Effect of Failure and Frustration on Reflective and Impulsive Children. *Journal of Experimental Child Psychology*, 17, pp. 353-359, 1970.

Learning with Smart Multipurpose Interactive Learning Environment

Mária Bieliková, Marko Divéky, Peter Jurnečka,
Rudolf Kajan and Ľuboš Omelina
Institution of Informatics and Software Engineering, Faculty of Informatics
and Information Technologies, Slovak University of Technology,
Ilkovičova 3, 842 16 Bratislava, Slovakia, bielik@fiit.stuba.sk,
WWW home page: http://www.fiit.stuba.sk/~bielik

Abstract. In this paper, we describe an innovative concept of three-dimensional interactive educational games that combine the excitement and looks of popular computer games with the educational potential of electronic study materials and its realization by a system called S.M.I.L.E. – Smart Multipurpose Interactive Learning Environment. One of its key features is the consideration of various learners' abilities. In this paper, we concentrate on the description of features that enable different users (including handicapped) to learn effectively by playing educational games. We follow the idea that everyone needs access to quality education and are convinced that by enabling cooperative education not just among learners, but also between handicapped and able-bodied ones, we bring the humane dimension into education.

1 Introduction

Education has significantly evolved for the last decade, thanks to modern information technologies. Learners not only have access to a countless number of diverse educational materials, but also can educate interactively and share their ideas and knowledge with each other – even if they are miles apart. However, only a few of them are adaptive and therefore provide better support for individual learners [1].

Many learners lack motivation into studying. Educational games (i.e. serious games) are a new element that evolves rapidly [2]. Computer games not only offer enjoyment and fun, both of which play a crucial role in effective learning [3], but also do a great job in motivating. However, the most popular ones are currently far away from being educational and, on the other hand, educational games often lack the thrill of their popular counterparts and have a fixed plot that cannot be altered.

Another problem that needs to be addressed is the fact that learners with a handicap are often ignored and forgotten. Handicapped learners have absolutely no options to play today's modern educational computer games. We propose an

Please use the following format when citing this chapter:

Bieliková, M., Divéky, M., Jurnečka, P., Kajan, R. and Omelina, L., 2008, in IFIP International Federation for Information Processing, Volume 281; *Learning to Live in the Knowledge Society*; Michael Kendall and Brian Samways; (Boston: Springer), pp. 101–104.

innovative concept that forms a unique solution for the above mentioned problems. It combines the advantages from both interactive educational materials and popular computer games by giving teachers (i.e. authors of educational materials) the ability to transform study materials into exciting educational games that can be played even by handicapped (e.g., visually impaired or deaf) learners.

2 Educational Games Model and its Realization

Our model of educational games is based on today's most popular genre of computer games – Role Playing Games (RPGs). We focused on three-dimensional games, since their two-dimensional counterparts have been overcome by today's modern games. Moreover, 3D games support the development and training of spatial memory, what is important for everyone, but especially for vision-impaired users.

Games based on the RPG genre take place in a realistic world set in a specific time or in an imaginary world that is or is not close to reality. Players are represented by and control an avatar and solve various quests throughout the game. These require the player to find certain objects that he needs to correctly use or combine in order to solve a particular problem, and/or require the player to choose a correct answer to a certain question. Quests are assigned to players by Non-player Characters (NPCs) that cannot be controlled by players and interact with them through dialogs.

Our educational games model consists of two *environments* that encourage learners to first train and educate themselves and afterwards to test their newly gained knowledge and skills. The *learning environment* intended for self-training and raising the players' level of knowledge, presents a persistent virtual world that is made of quests based on all available educational materials. It practically resembles one vast game that contains all possible educational quests.

The second environment consists of *teacher-created games*. It presents a practical and enjoyable form of evaluating the players' level of knowledge and skills from a desired field. Games are specified by teachers either *visually* (by defining their concept) or *automatically generated* according to parameters set by the teacher. The visual approach to game creation makes our solution innovative, since nearly all current games do not offer mechanisms for creating games and their environments suitable for teachers who are not IT professionals. However, it is the automatic game generation based on teachers' preferences that makes our approach distinctive. The automatic generation of educational games consists of two separate phases: the *Quest Generation* and *Game Generation* phases that utilize artificial intelligence-based algorithms for solving particular tasks (e.g., simulated annealing to find appropriate landmarks during the landscape generation process, or depth search strategy with backtracking for quest generation). This process is described in more detail in [4].

3 Considering Different Learners

Having handicapped learners in mind, we chose to provide interfaces for all, and thus we designed the educational games with the possibility to be fully controlled via voice recognition and with peripherals for the handicapped, such as Braille keyboards. A mobile phone's keypad or PDA can also be used as an input device.

Diversity in Vision. Games can be played by means of voice-activated commands using a version of the Game Client specialized for blind and vision-impaired users. To other players, a blind player looks just like any other player, with the exception that he moves according to waypoints automatically placed when the game is created. Players with minor vision impairment can customize the visual appearance of important in-game elements, such as NPCs.

Diversity in Hearing. The default used interface is purely visual, and so the design does not need to be altered in order to provide support for deaf learners. The only exception to this rule is the playback of videos in knowledge materials. Nevertheless, hearing-impaired learners can choose to have subtitles shown below all played videos. On the other hand, all created educational games utilize environmental and character sounds in their otherwise visual interfaces. Deaf players, and also players with a hearing impairment use interfaces that contain extended graphical effects instead of sounds of any kind. In case a sound should be played, such players are shown a graphical image associated to the particular sound.

Diversity in Levels of Knowledge. Thanks to the fact that we can estimate the level of knowledge of each subject for every player and the fact that each quest is classified according to subjects it is related to, all educational games are adapted individually to every player's (estimated) level of knowledge and skills. Players are dynamically navigated into solving quests (e.g., by pointing players at map locations of the in-game NPCs that assign them) most suitable for their estimated knowledge level. Additionally, while solving quests, options of the appropriate difficulty are chosen for players to solve.

By utilizing the Item Response Theory [5], we are able to predict how will players react to both tasks and questions they are given while solving quests, and thus to measure their level of forgetfulness by testing them on tasks and questions they have previously successfully completed and answered.

Diversity in Skills. We let each and every player choose how he interacts with the educational games. For example, players who wish to interact with a standard keyboard have the option to specify their own controls. Naturally, players can also choose from a number of predefined control schemes and are able to further customize these schemes according to their liking.

Diversity in Styles. In the virtual world, every player is represented by an avatar – a virtual character according to which other players notice his presence. The option to personalize every player's avatar plays a crucial role in getting the players immersed into the gameplay and accepting the avatar as the player's own in-game identity. A player chooses a specific geometry model that can be further customized, e.g. players can specify its height by scaling the desired model.

Naturally, creating and importing a custom geometry model is rather difficult and cumbersome. Therefore, we have enabled players to assign different textures to various parts of their avatar's model, what proved as an effective and amusing method in differentiating players' avatars. Each geometry model, representing the body of an avatar, has distinct zones representing various body parts, e.g. a head, torso, hands and feet and players have the option to assign a desired texture (clothing) to each zone. A great advantage of this approach is the fact that the number of possible different avatars created grows exponentially according to the number of available geometry models and textures.

Additionally, a unique feature of our S.M.I.L.E. system is the possibility of players to give their avatars their own faces via textures created from the players' photographs (specified in a special format that allows automatic mapping of significant face elements). This feature is especially important and useful for educational purposes (as in opposite it may not be desirable in many cases for standard computer games where players usually do not want to present their identity).

4 Conclusions

The main contribution of the presented work is in devising a novel concept of three-dimensional educational computer games that can be adapted to different learners and to various abilities of a particular learner. A unique feature is the proposal of methods that allow teachers themselves to define educational games based on the stored educational materials without requiring *any* knowledge of programming. Three-dimensional educational games (including the persistent virtual world) are dynamically generated based on teachers' preferences. User interfaces are designed as adaptable in such a way that they support handicapped learners.

In order to validate the presented concept, we have developed a system called S.M.I.L.E. that encapsulates and combines the advantages of two distinct worlds – interactive educational materials and popular computer games. It also enables handicapped learners to educate together with their non-disabled colleagues. Such concept has not yet been realized to our knowledge in any of the existing applications. We have had positive feedback on the adaptability and adaptivity features from both teachers and students at elementary and secondary schools for handicapped children, where we demonstrated the S.M.I.L.E. system.

Acknowledgement. This work was partially supported by the Cultural and Educational Grant Agency of the Slovak Republic, grant No. KEGA 3/5187/07.

References

1. P. Brusilovsky and C. Peylo, Adaptive and intelligent Web-based educational systems, *Int. Journal of Artificial Int. in Education* 13(2-4), 59-172 (2003).
2. M. Zyda, Creating a Science of Games, *Comm. of the ACM*, 50(7) 27-29 (2007).
3. G. Dryden and J. Vos, *The Learning Revolution* (Jalmar Press, Austin, 1999).
4. M. Divéky, P. Jurnečka, R. Kajan, L. Omelina, and M. Bieliková, Adaptive Educational Gameplay within Smart Multipurpose Interactive Learning Environment, in: Semantic Media Adaptation and Personalization, edited by P. Mylonas, M. Wallace, M. Angelides (IEEE CS, Los Alamitos, CA, USA, 2007), pp. 165-170.
5. F. Baker, The Basics of Item Response Theory, ERIC Clearinghouse on Assessment and Evaluation (University of Maryland, College Park, MD, 2001).

Eeney, Meeney, Miney, Mo?
Selecting a First Programming Language

Leila Goosen [1], Elsa Mentz [2] and Hercules Nieuwoudt [2]
1 Faculty of Education, University of Pretoria, 0001 South Africa
lgoosen@gk.up.ac.za
2 Faculty of Education Sciences, North-West University, 2520
South Africa {snsem,nsohdn}@puknet.puk.ac.za

Abstract. This study established a list of criteria to select a first programming language. We used a literature study to create criteria for developing thinking and programming skills, student appropriate programming learning environments, new tendencies in programming, practical programming issues, affordability, training and resources, and general-purpose programming. An empirical study verified the validity of selection criteria identified.

1 Introduction

With so many languages available for teaching programming at an introductory level [1], choices remain controversial [2]. Computer technology and languages develop at an alarming rate [3], and programmers cover more languages in their lifetime than ever before. While learning practical programming skills in a particular language, it is even more important for novice programmers to develop a sound theoretical understanding of programming, to prepare for later learning future languages and environments. Rapid technology and language changes also mean that selecting the wrong implementation could mean that both its use and its teaching will be outdated shortly. Even if ignoring limitations regarding support, costs, training etc., one needs to select a programming language for use in a first course using different criteria [1].

2 Results

We used a literature study to develop criteria for selecting a first programming language. Further details regarding the research method and the instrument used can be accessed via [4]. Access to complete results, including access to quotes from respondents in the comments sections of the survey, and additional discussion of results, are also provided.

Please use the following format when citing this chapter:

Goosen, L., Mentz, E. and Nieuwoudt, H., 2008, in IFIP International Federation for Information Processing, Volume 281; *Learning to Live in the Knowledge Society*; Michael Kendall and Brian Samways; (Boston: Springer), pp. 105–108.

2.1   Relevance of Selection Criteria

Three items in the questionnaire regarding the relevance of selection criteria received averages for importance that places them in the lowest quarter of results. In terms of application, the items place in the lower half of results. According to the respondents in the empirical study, the relevance of selection criteria comprised some of the least important issues and was not applied largely. Use of selection criteria established in this study in situations other than the South African context applicable to this study, might make it necessary to reconsider some of them. Many aspects contemplated within the South African context, such as financial considerations would probably remain valid for most situations. Other criteria, e.g. regarding general-purpose programming, or training for industry, would depend on the applicable context. Finally, the relevance of new tendencies in programming would depend on the amount of time that has elapsed since the completion of this study.

2.2   Develop Thinking and Programming Skills

Respondents agree that the selected language should provide an instructional environment that promotes the development of problem solving skills, as the averages for this item distinguish it as both the most important and most applied item. An item with regard to providing students with a firm foundation in good programming practices was applied second most and is the fifth most important. The adequate matching of the adopted programming language to the abilities of students of IT with regard to both level and nature is one of the least important items. Its average for application, however, places it in the top half of items. The latter agrees with literature that the needs, knowledge and abilities of novice users are meaningfully different from those of experienced programmers. Items regarding the development of higher order and critical thinking skills, as well as encouraging a self-regulated approach to solving problems, achieved averages placing them around the top third of items for importance and application. The average for an item that refers to the development of these abilities places it in the middle relative to other criteria with regard to both importance and application. Encouraging programming principles such as programming abstractions [5] and promoting top-down design [6] with step-wise refinement are some of the least important items, but were applied much more, with the latter placing in the top quarter of averages for application.

2.3   Requirements of Appropriate Programming Learning Environments

The item with the third highest average for application refers to providing students with a safe, stable, structured and controlled programming environment [see e.g. 6]. Items with regard to supplying students with understandable error messages, and offering effective debugging tools [1] obtained the fourth and fifth highest averages for application. These items also received averages for importance placing them within the top third of results. Items regarding the programming environment suiting the needs of novice programmers in that it is easy to learn [7], offer relative simplicity of commands [1], and not frustrate students with features for professional programmers [5,6], have averages placing them in the lower half of results. However, these items were applied more than would be expected, with application averages placing them in or close to the top third of results.

2.4   New Tendencies in Programming

The selected programming language offering possibilities for OO design [8] received averages for importance and application placing it in the top quarter of results in both these categories. However, both [2] and [5] point to problems that can occur when using OOP and the difficulties students face when learning to program in an OO style. Using visual languages [1] could offset some of the difficulties with regard to OOP mentioned - this item received averages for importance and application placing this item just inside the lower half of results. Respondents considered the concepts of encapsulation, inheritance and polymorphism some of the least important, with averages placing them in the lowest quarter of results. These items obtained application averages placing them in the lower half of results.

2.5   Issues Influencing Programming Used in Practice

The item regarding the language having reasonable prospects for continued support from its developers [7] has an average that places it as the sixth most important selection criteria, while its average for application is in the higher half of results. Whether or not the language has sufficient capacity for database connectivity also places in the higher half of results for both importance and application. The international standardization of, and trends with regard to, programming languages used [7], place in the lower half of results for importance and in the lowest quarter for application. Considering the popularity and/or demand for specific languages in industry [2] received similar results for importance and application. The language being suitable and having capabilities for the Internet [3] is the least important selection criteria and was also applied second least.

2.6   Affordability, Training and Resources

Respondents considered the affordability of the language to be the second most important item of all. However, the affordability of a selected programming language was applied so little that it places in the lowest quarter of results. The availability of affordable, sufficient in-service teacher training, and having learning and teaching support materials and other resources for the language available to teachers, were considered the third and fourth most important items, but inversely, these items obtained the third and fourth lowest application averages! Similarly, possibilities for training of pre-service teachers [7], and having particularly textbooks available, received averages that place them as the eleventh and seventh most important items. However, application averages for these items are well inside the lowest quarter of results. Although having resources for an OBE approach to teaching the subject [8] has an average placing it in the middle of results, it was in fact applied the least.

2.7   Programming for Various Purposes

Using a general-purpose programming language [7] to support programming for various purposes received averages for both importance and application placing it inside the lower half of results. The same goes for the average for the importance of being able to use the language with academic tools. The average for the application of the latter, as well as the application average for being able to use the language with commercial tools, places these in the lowest quarter of results, while being able to use the language with commercial tools is the fourth least important item.

3   Conclusions

Results in this study arranged selection criteria as being more important relative to others for those with the highest averages, and less important for those obtaining lower averages. During the selection process of a first programming language for high schools, decision makers could pay closer attention to those criteria identified as most important. They could also save time and effort by assigning less importance to criteria with lower averages. Also consider perspectives from literature, especially in cases where these differ from the importance as assigned in this study.

References

1. A.I. Ali and F. Kohun, Suggested Topics for an IS Introductory Course in Java, in: Proceedings of the Informing Science and Information Technology Education Joint Conference (Flagstaff, Arizona, USA, June 2005), pp.33-49, (April 25, 2007); http://proceedings.informingscience.org/InSITE2005/I19f28Ali.pdf

2. Joint Task Force on Computing Curricula, *Chapter 7 Introductory courses.* CC2001 Computer Science volume, Final Report (December 15, 2001); (April 2, 2003); http://www.acm.org/sigcse/cc2001/index.html.

3. J. Barrow, J.H. Gelderblom, and M.G. Miller, *Introducing Delphi programming: theory through practice* (Oxford University Press, Cape Town, 2002).

4. L. Goosen, *Criteria and guidelines for the selection and implementation of a first programming language in high schools* PhD thesis, North-West University (Potchefstroom Campus) (2004); http:// www.puk.ac.za/biblioteek/proefskrifte/2004/goosen_l.pdf

5. N. Mehic and Y. Hasan, Challenges in Teaching Java Technology, in: Proceedings of the 2003 Informing Science Conference (Cracow, Poland, June 2003), pp.301-309, (April 25, 2007); http://proceedings.informing science.org/IS2001Proceedings/pdf/MehicEBKChall.pdf

6. D.B. Palumbo, Programming language/problem-solving research: a review of relevant issues, *Review of educational research* **60**(1), 65-89 (1990).

7. Department of Education, *National Curriculum Statement Grades 10 – 12 (General): Information Technology* (Government Printer, Pretoria, 2003).

8. Department of Education, *National curriculum statement Grades 10-12 (Schools): Guidelines for the development of learning programmes Information Technology* (Extracted from IT.ZIP, August 19, 2003); http://wced.wcape.gov.za/ncs_fet

Chapter 5

Exploiting ICT for Teaching and Learning

Preparing the stage for using emerging technologies in science education

Dr Christine Redman
The University of Melbourne, Graduate School of Education, Melbourne,
3010, Victoria, Australia, redmanc@unimelb.edu.au
http://www.edfac.unimelb.edu.au/sme/about/redman.html

Abstract. This paper reviews a sequence of learning experiences that were embedded into a university subject that sought, in part, to support the purposeful uptake of 'emerging technologies'. The assumption that university students use technology regularly does not take account that only certain types of technologies are utilized, and more for immediate social purposes. This paper explains how and why different technologies were selected for use in a university subject. The decisions were informed by a sound pedagogical approach designed to deepen the teaching and learning experiences with the science concepts. The technologies were potentially those that could contribute to more effective classroom teaching of science education. Enriching dialogical and social learning communities formed progressively during student participation with, and use of a range of technologies and engagement with science conceptual challenges. These communities had sharply focused and targeted science learning outcomes, yet used a creative and discursive centered approach for extending and sharing their new and refined understandings.

1 Background to the Study

This paper describes an approach to staging the learning experiences in science education using a pedagogical informed approach that inculcated technology tools in a university level subject. The approach was, in part, designed as a response to a preliminary 2006 report conducted by research teams from the Biomedical Multimedia unit and the Centre for the Study of Higher Education at The University of Melbourne [1]. The Melbourne University study (MUS) reported that first-year students were regular users of a variety of technologies, and indicated students used 'emerging technologies' but not in the ways expected. In this study 'emerging technologies' refers to blogging and video-podcasting. They were chosen as they were the less familiar technologies, and yet had sound pedagogical potential for

Please use the following format when citing this chapter:

Redman, C., 2008, in IFIP International Federation for Information Processing, Volume 281; *Learning to Live in the Knowledge Society;* Michael Kendall and Brian Samways; (Boston: Springer), pp. 111–118.

classrooms. A 2007 Curtin University study found 'few students (7.3%) were frequent users of blogs' [2] and subsequently recommended that 'university teacher(s) ... challenge them (students) to go beyond their use purely for social ends, and use them to be participative constructors of knowledge in engaging learning experiences'[2]. The two University studies identified blogging and video-podcasting, as learning experiences provided for a 4-year, pre-service primary teacher degree subject.

The science learning experiences incorporated pedagogically useful tools for personal learning, and these were embedded into the sequential science informed way of immersing these emerging technologies into a pre-service teacher (PST) subject. The sequencing and use of the technologies emanated from a social-constructivist learning theory approach [3], which informed the choice of pedagogical strategies. These strategies aimed to provide PSTs with insights into more effective approaches for using Information Communication Technology (ICT) for enhancing learning opportunities while enhancing their own science teaching and learning experiences.

The MUS had sought to understand what being a 2006 Digital Native meant and had reviewed which ICT tools first-year students had used in the previous 12 months. Two thousand first-year students were surveyed and it was found they had unrestricted access to a mobile phone (96%), desktop computer (90%), digital camera (76%), MP3 player (69%), lap top computer (63%). The most common uses were; sending or receiving email (94%), creating documents (88%), playing digital music files (84%), searching for information (83%), communicating via instant messaging (80%). The MUS indicated that certain technology tools were more frequently utilised. Two ICT tools frequently used were the social communication tools of emailing and short messaging service (SMS). Both support instant sharing of ideas while still allowing opportunity for the careful crafting of a written message.

1.1 Introduction to the Study

This paper examines the result of a creating a learning journey and how that meta-cognitive approach used a sequence of ICT tools to create rich dialogical learning opportunities. Blogging and video-podcasting were selected as they could utilise and refine their literacy skills of speaking, listening, reading and writing, provide opportunities to re-visit and share their science learning experiences, support reviews of and reflecting on their science experiences and encourage progressively more informed discussions about the science concepts.

Blogging and video-podcasting were incorporated to enhance the meaningful and empowered use of ICT, for quality learning outcomes in science education. The sequence sought to promote the effective development of an understanding about key events in lunar phases. The tools that were used early in the sequence were chosen as they were already part of PST's daily-lived experiences. Emailing and SMS were their more familiar communication devices in their social world [4]. Blogging and video-podcasting were introduced later as the less familiar tools. In the initial survey only 6 out of the 148 PSTs had accessed Podcasts. The use of more familiar technologies engendered feelings of confidence as all PST's had mobile phones, and only 10 did not have a built in camera phone.

148 third-year students in the Faculty of Education in a large Australian University were enrolled in this year-long science and technology subject. Prior to this study they had participated in a semester-long ICT-in-Education subject that provided ICT experiences suitable for the primary classroom. The PST's reflected on how their use of ICT tools to enhance and disseminate their science ideas.

In small groups, PST's communicated initially via email and SMS. These ICT tools supported the development of a shared focus in a community of practice, which could later transform into a community of inquiry, [5] as understandings of the science concept developed. The tasks became progressively more technically challenging, as the PST's collaborated to resolve technical difficulties, and they shared their science discoveries in their 'virtual' community of inquiry [6]. The emphasis was not on mastering the technology but rather on working co-operatively to refine and deepen their understanding of a challenging science understanding [7] through engagement with the 'social technology' tools. The imperative of their known needs created a need to turn to others and they found others were resources to help them develop their technological practices and science understandings. This process encouraged their active reflection on their personal learning about the science concepts and importantly ways to utilize ICT to make these science ideas more explicit and available to share [8]. As the PSTs advanced in their science understandings, the ICT tools changed to support their development, sharing, investigation and communication of their science reasoning.

1.2 Literature Review

The MUS showed that first-year students in higher education settings had regular Internet access and as 'Digital Natives' accessed a changing range of ICT tools. The term Digital Natives captures the sense of being born into a community, and as the first born growing up with technological practices as 'habits of mind'. They have developed approaches to deal with new ICT tools through their prior practices. Bourdieu called this habitus [9]. Prensky [10] states that Digital Natives have 'spent their entire lives surrounded by and using computers, using video games, digital music players, video cams, cell phones, and all the other toys and tools of the digital age' (p 1). Yet this use of ICT can be closely tied to personal needs and this can impact on their confidence to try new things, or not [11]. ICT may afford [12] people different opportunities based on their prior experiences and needs. Using ICT to enhance your educational opportunity was provided through discussion, sharing and deepening of understandings. This study sought to see if conversational and social opportunities to reflect on learning could be increased and deepened by including use of the 'social technologies' into the courses.

In this study the integral tasks drew first on the everyday technologies of the mobile phone and email. As the PSTs experienced something new they could instantly share it, using SMS or email. This capitalised on the properties of familiar technology, supporting immediate connection to others, and shared the moment and excitement of learning. Dewey [13] states that learning is part of the social lived world and he considered learning experiences to be dynamic. The social elements of ICT support contact at anytime and the immediate sharing of new revelations.

2 Staging the Learning Experience

2.1 Creating and establishing a learning environment that valued learning

Early in the year the PSTs participated in activities designed to enhance their science knowledge base. The activities sought to extend their understanding of everyday science topics and required them to highlight their new understandings. The PSTs articulated their understandings in twice weekly written responses.

Several activities modeled to PSTs that the development and refinement of knowledge was valued. They were encouraged to enjoy learning new things, to become aware of what it is like to be a learner and to experience curiosity, wonder and discovery. This subject flagged that they did not know 'everything', but that they were actively engaged in an effective learning process and that it was more important to discover 'what they did not know' and to find ways to better understand it.

2.2 Reflection and Review of one's personal existing understandings

At the beginning of lectures PSTs probed and recorded their current understandings of science concepts. This exploration of prior knowledge [14] supports learners to examine their *current* understandings and to explore, probe and test these understanding. Learners are not use to articulating their science understandings, and therefore, may not have the words 'ready at hand' to express what their thoughts. So, when pressed to explain a science concept, they can not always explain it, nor are they able to state *all* that they know. While discussing their tentative explanations, PST"S state 'oh, yes and...' as they recollect connected ideas.

In lectures, after pondering their understanding, PSTs were sometimes asked to draw their explanation. When labeling their drawing PSTs realised their explanation may not be correct and how well they understand it, and become aware of what need to know to be able to explain it. *'I am curious about the angle to which the moon changes shape .... Sorry if i'm not making any sense, i'm finding it hard to verbalise!'* PSTs need to comprehensively understand and be able to articulate science concepts to explain them in classrooms and also to become aware that 'others' may have alternative understandings for many science concepts.

Lunar phases are widely recognised as a conceptually challenging [15-17] and were selected to represent and model aspects of what makes science education difficult to teach [16]. People may have alternative understandings to, or lack awareness of, the scientifically accurate explanation. The PSTs were engaged in understanding a science concept acknowledged to be difficult to reconcile, taking active responsibility for their learning in a progressively meta-cognitive way.

People may hold alternative conceptions such as, 'the earth's shadow causes the moon's shape to change', and are frustrated when they find out this is incorrect. A PST recorded in a lecture, *'I'm not really sure ... We did learn this (before) but I was a little confused then 2'*. Another asked, *'Where does the new moon go??'* Another stated, *'I can't specifically remember how the moon looks at each position, but I have an idea of how it works?'* Once PSTs are aware what they do not specifically understand or can not articulate, they are more likely to want to resolve it. A PST recorded in a lecture that, *if the earth is a spherical shape ... why does its shadow cause a concave shape? This is most puzzling for me. I will aim to find the answer to this over the next few weeks of classes.'* The second component of this process required the PSTs to explain in words their current understanding of lunar phases, draw their explanation and label their drawing to elucidate and explore their understandings of key events.

Some PSTs became aware that their written explanation did not make sense when transferred into a labeled drawing, but this had highlighted their specific learning needs. It had served to focus them on refining their understanding, language or ability to communicate the ideas. When drawing another PST stated, *'I am not completely sure, but I think it involves the moon rotating on it's axis...'*

The PSTs had explored their understanding of lunar phases privately, and perhaps socially and publicly, with friends after the lecture. After these exploratory activities they were aware of their current understandings.

2.3 Introducing and incorporating Blogging as a learning event

Blogging provides an effective communication tool for classroom use. Literacy is highly valued in the primary classroom and in science education for communication, reviewing and sharing of ideas. The blogging experience capitalized on the PST's propensity to communicate using email and SMS, and informal language, in their social forms of communication, and may have supported the development and active engagement in the 'virtual conversations'. Blogging was an assessable component of their subject to concede that there was a significant amount of time required and to ensure that all group members participated. The assessment was individually graded and the assessment rubric preferenced the individual's experience, with a component that attended to their shared group journey.

Guidelines for the blogging discussions encouraged curiosity and an open-ended problem-solving approach. The blogging groups were provided with this focus to sustain their conversations. Over the weeks, it guided them through different ways of engaging with the moon. The blog site was available in the first ten weeks but could be accessed all year. After the year ended PSTs were still posting, and reflecting on what and how they had learnt. *'This blogging experience has unquestionably refined my understandings of the moon and its relationship with the sun and the earth. By beginning with observing the moon it gave me a chance to approach science in a completely different light...The process allowed me to let my guard down, ...*

In lectures, aspects of blogging were examined, focusing on how it could contribute to classroom learning. It was concluded that blogs supported the active sharing of ideas and the asking of questions. Drawings and pictures could be scanned in and they could share sound files with each other. Many searched the Internet while blogging, as they attempted to resolve questions, and shared websites. *'Hey I was so into this website it has so muich (sic) information on everything that you would need to know as a teacher and it is fantastic!!! The site is run by...'* And another, *'hey guys, here is a calendar showing phases of the moon this year, just thought it was interesting to see if our observations were accurate. (I hope i can upload it properly!)* The response was ... *Yes you did upload the moon calendar correctly! Thanks so much for that! It was really interesting ....*

The formal assessment of the blog took account of the PST's personal learning and growth in science knowledge and the development of their professional awareness of blogging as a tool for teaching and learning in the classroom. *'hahahaha I see what you are saying but I think that the moon would continue to orbit the way it but then again hypothetically what if the earth ... i don't know i think i am confusing myself'*

2.4 Sharing the learning experience through Video-podcasting

PSTs were introduced to four Podcasts, three were science focused and came from the United Kingdom, United States and Australian universities. They presented recent science research and interviews with scientists, adding a richer human account to the research journey. The fourth podcast focused on a father and his eight-year-old son talking about their daily lives. PSTs enjoyed this podcast immensely.

PSTs created a video-podcast that shared their group's deliberations on blogging as a tool explaining how it had supported their learning about lunar phases. They included their lunar photos, drawings and photos of their dynamic lunar models and they demonstrated the ideas they needed to understand lunar phases, based on their experiences as learners and teachers, *'I feel like the podcast process has really extended my understandings. At the end of the first assignment, I was only in tune with the ideas and concepts that I had just discovered, and the implications for learning based on my experiences as a learner. ... I now feel like I have a deeper level of understanding.'* From another PST *'So I am looking at how our blogging ... has helped my understandings. When I look back at my original drawings I can see that I wasn't very aware of where the light was in my pictures... This was a really important part in my learning journey and where I really started to make connections and answer my own questions.'*

3 Behind the scenes –

3.1 Weaknesses/Difficulties

It took many meetings in the previous year to set up blogging. Choices included:
1. run it in a university site or in an Education Faculty site
2. have it open to the world, or only to the blogging group
3. software packages that were free or need to be purchased
4. with or without images and sound files

A team took time to create the structure to work with multiple blog groups. This took more time than anticipated, but was stable. Getting groups formed was time-consuming. Students could not always log in, or post a blog or lost their passwords. Some groups commented regularly on each other's posts and uploaded images. Some groups had 'lurkers' who took awhile to get involved. Many PSTs learnt new skills and celebrated, *'sorry about the ... i have had to combat all sorts of technological difficulties to post our photos from our modelling session. but i have finally conquered all my technological demons, triumph is mine! here they are so enjoy...'*

3.2 Strengths/Successes

The technical advice and support was terrific. Without this structure the project would never have happened. Students gave technical assistance to others and shared their hints with groups. Late in 2008 interviews will be conducted to ascertain the stability of their science understandings and their reflections on the use of blogging and video-podcasting. Initial forays indicate that the experience was positive.

4 Conclusion

The ICT tools appeared to be 'a natural' fit into the PSTs' lifestyle. Emailing and SMS were successful. Blogging seems to have been effective, perhaps as it was relatively easy, quick to do and supported their sense as primary teachers who prioritize development of student's literacy skills. Video podcasting created an audience, a reason to reflect on, communicate and celebrate their achievements. The sharing of their lived experiences was felt to be enhanced due to the deliberate slow staging and establishing of a virtual learning community who felt comfortable exploring and developing their science understandings together. It appears that they have transformed their understandings through shared and lived experiences rather than reproducing knowledge from books [18]. In the scaffolding of their experiences and sense of a shared purpose in a virtual community of inquiry, they were focused on a joint project [6] and a desire to better understand lunar phases. The ICT tools appeared to have served them well. It supported them as they developed new practices and ways to interact with and make sense of the material world [4, 9, 20].

References

1. G. Kennedy, K.-L. Krause, T. Judd, A. Churchward, and K. Gray, *First year students' experiences with technology: Are they really digital natives?* Melbourne, Australia: Biomedical Multimedia Unit, University of Melbourne. [November 9, 2007] http://www.bmu.unimelb.edu.au/research/munatives/natives_report2006.pdf
2. B. Oliver, and V. Goerke, Australian undergraduates' use and ownership of emerging technologies; Implications and opportunities for creating engaging learning experiences for the Net Generation, *Australasian Journal of Educational Technology.* **23**(2), 171-186 (2007).
3. K. R. Skamp, *Teaching primary science constructively* (Thomson Learning, Melbourne, 2007).
4. R. Harré, Material objects in social worlds, *Theory, Culture & Society.* **19** (5-6), 23-33 (2002).

5. J.B. Pena-Shaff and C. Nicholls, Analyzing student interactions and meaning construction in computer bulletin board discussions, *Computers & Education.* **42**(3), 243-265 (2004).
6. T. Schatzki, *Social Practices: A Wittgensteinian approach to human activity and the social* (Cambridge University Press, Cambridge, 1996).
7. C. Redman and R. Fawns, Discursive positioning and effecting change in a community of practice. (2004) (November 9, 2007); www.aare.edu.au/04pap/red04632.pdf
8. J. Dewey, *Experience and nature* (Dover Publications, New York, 1925).
9. P. Bourdieu, *Outline of a Theory of Practice* (Cambridge University Press, Cambridge, 1977).
10. M. Prensky, Digital Natives, Digital Immigrants, On the horizon. (accessed November 9, 2007); http://www.marcprensky.com/writing/Prensky%20-%20Digital%20Natives,%20Digital%20Immigrants%20-%20Part1.pdf
11. C. Redman, Towards a dialogical perspective on agency in student learning. (2007) (November 9, 2007); http://www.aare.edu.au/07pap/red07364.pdf
12. J. Gibson, *The ecological approach to visual perception* (Houghton Mifflin, Boston, 1979).
13. J. Dewey, *The public and its problems* (Ohio University Press, Athens, 1927).
14. R. Driver, H. Asoko, J. Leach, E. Mortimer, and P. Scott, Constructing scientific knowledge in the classroom, *Educational Researcher.* 23(7), 5-12 (1994).
15. V. A. Atwood and R.K. Atwood, Preservice elementary teachers' conceptions of what causes day and night, *School Science and Mathematics* 95, 290-294 (1995).
16. C. Redman, Moon rise, Moon set, *Investigating* **1**(17), 22-7 (2001).
17. K. C. Trundle, R.K. Atwood, and J.E. Christopher, Preservice elementary teachers' conceptions of moon phases before and after instruction, *Journal of Research in Science Teaching* **39**(7), 633-658 (2002).
18. R.A. Bhaskar, *Reflections On Meta-Reality: A Philosophy for the Present* (Sage, New Delhi, 2002).
19. C. Linehan and J. McCarthy, Positioning in practice: Understanding participation in the social world, *Journal for the Theory of Social Behaviour*, 30, 435-453 (2000).
20. P. Sullivan and J. McCarthy, Toward a dialogical perspective on agency, *Journal for the Theory of Social Behaviour*, 34, 291-309 (2004).

Promoting Thinking Skills within the Secondary Classroom Using Digital Media

Maree A. Skillen
Arden Anglican School 50 Oxford Street, Epping, Australia
m.skillen@arden.nsw.edu.au

Abstract. One of the recurring themes concerning the integration of ICT into secondary education relates to opportunities for moving classroom-based activities for learners towards higher levels of thinking and learning. The research described in this paper involved an investigation of the implementation of digital media into a New South Wales Year 9/10 IST (Information and Software Technology) elective course. It concentrated on the subsequent assessment and impact that the software has had on creating an inquiry-based situation to promote higher-order thinking skills of students within a secondary classroom completing digital media projects for the web. The case study of a composite class of fifteen Year 9 and 10 students utilised a mixed methodology involving both qualitative and quantitative procedures. Results from the study suggested that technology allowed learning and motivation of students to be enhanced and that there was a willingness exhibited by individuals to engage in tasks and discussions. It is argued that teaching and learning can be enriched as the technological tools and pedagogical processes are brought together in appropriate ways. By referring to the integration of technology as being a meaningful tool that will transform the culture of schools but requires attention to the habits of mind; newly defined thinking tasks such as problem solving, and the necessary cognitive operations such as analysing, inferring and evaluating are possible.

1 Introduction

This study emerged from an interest and experience of multimedia in the secondary classroom. The research described focused particularly on an interest in how technology is used as a tool in the teaching and learning process with particular emphasis on the concept of constructivism and the emphasis that a constructivist perspective has on students' evolving knowledge, the critical role social negotiation

Please use the following format when citing this chapter:

Skillen, M.A., 2008, in IFIP International Federation for Information Processing, Volume 281; *Learning to Live in the Knowledge Society*; Michael Kendall and Brian Samways; (Boston: Springer), pp. 119–126.

plays in helping students interpret their experiences and the promotion of thinking skills when using technology. Further, it is identified that the primary responsibility of the instructional expert is to create and maintain a collaborative problem-solving environment. Hackbarth [7] supports this view by referring to constructivism as having become a dominant force in education. The essential principle of this revolutionary theory is that each of us assembles the bits and pieces of our experience in ways that, in many respects, are unique. Drawing upon prior conceptions and feelings, we actively interact with our surroundings in an ongoing effort to make the diversity of our experiences all sensible and coherent. The essential challenge of constructivism has been in its shifting the locus of control over learning from the teacher to the student. Educational technologists, with their roots in behavioural psychology, have long sought to design programs in such a way that students would be enticed to achieve pre-specified objectives. Constructivists have claimed that this violates both what we now know about the nature of learning (situated, interactive) and about the nature of knowledge (perspectival, conventional, tentative, evolutionary). They have maintained that objectives should be negotiated with students based on their felt needs, that planned activities should emerge from within the contexts of their lived worlds; that students should collaborate with peers in the social construction of personally significant meaning, and that evaluation should be a personalised, ongoing, shared analysis of progress.

The influences of constructivism on educational technology can be seen in many areas. Models of communication can portray the process as interactive, with the message as much determined by the selective perception of the recipient as by the style of the author. Mediated programs are seen now more in terms of providing students with opportunities to expand their horizons. Interactive multimedia presentations are seen to provide students with insights into the thinking of experts, and the "scaffolding" needed to enable their own uniquely coloured construction of disciplined knowledge. Romiszowski [14] defines interactive instruction as a process in which the learner is involved in overtly responding to material by making selections or giving answers to questions. He continues by commenting that interactivity in the instructional process operates by setting tasks for the learner to deal with but its value and its nature are best described by the "depth of processing" or the quality of thinking that is demanded from the student. Interactive multimedia (IMM) comes in various forms and has the potential to enhance education though there has been little opportunity for educators to gain experience in how to effectively use and critically evaluate this new media [15]. IMM products have the capacity to shift the locus of 'ownership' and 'control' in learning. Whereas learning has traditionally been 'controlled' by the teacher, the instructor or the computer-based instructional system, the end-users of IMM courseware can be empowered to own and control their own learning [9]. IMM is a particularly effective medium for providing such search-through-problem environments. The other central issue in IMM instructional design is the design philosophy of increasing learner control over the 'what' and the 'how' of learning. It is important for designers of IMM products to provide the end-user with 'a handful of simple ways to travel from one object to another (by keyword, object search, text type or random choice) which lets people create many paths through a rich territory without getting lost or hitting a dead-end'.

2 Aims of the Study

The goals of the study involved the amalgamation of two aims, namely, an investigation into the evaluation and implementation of digital media which includes multimedia and web-based solutions, and an examination of their effect on and contribution to the learning environment in relation to the promotion of thinking skills among students. These may be expressed in terms of the following objectives: (1) To evaluate the educational value of a variety of digital media; (2) To investigate the contribution of digital media in the development of an inquiry-oriented learning environment; (3) To enhance students' skills in the use of digital media; and (4) To develop, implement and evaluate the use of inquiry-based learning with digital media through a social constructivist environment.

2.1 Research Questions

In order to provide a focus for these objectives, the following research questions were formulated: (1) Can digital media contribute to and enhance inquiry-based learning within the secondary classroom? (2) What is the impact of using digital media on students' abilities in the classroom learning environment? (3) How does digital media enable the student to develop higher-order thinking skills? (4) How can constructivist strategies be promoted through the development and use of digital media?

3 Significance

It was anticipated that this research would contribute to future investigations related to the teaching and learning of secondary students within technology-orientated classrooms. In particular, the research study is significant for a number of reasons. Firstly, it is likely to provide new information about the extent to which students can develop higher-level thinking skills using web authoring tools that utilise digital media. Secondly, it is likely to provide information related to the contribution that these tools have on changing the learning environment to be inquiry-oriented. This would support the research conducted by Coulter [5] who investigated the role that technology has played in the provision for and enhancement of an inquiry environment. The third area to which the study is likely to contribute is in facilitating comparisons with the work of Cooper and Maor [4] who utilised multimedia to create a student-centred learning environment. Cooper and Maor [4] based some of their research investigations on the work of Grabinger [6] who posed questions including: How can we design machines to help people learn and think? Can we use machines to help make the learning processes visible and more accessible? Further comparative information can be gathered and considered from the studies conducted by Maor and Taylor [11] who examined student achievements related to higher-level thinking skills, and the investigation of the mediation role of teachers' epistemologies in high school computerised classes. In addition, studies by Maor and Fraser [10] concentrating on how the use of a classroom environment instrument can monitor perceptions in evaluating inquiry-based CAL are relevant. These investigations may provide comparative results related to the analysis of a technology content-based classroom, its environment and the actual and preferred perceptions of the students and teachers. The study is likely to contribute to investigations related to constructivism and the work of Jonassen [8] supports this. In particular, he has examined constructivist perspectives for learning with technology, computers as mindtools for engaging learners as critical thinkers, and using computers as cognitive tools. The findings from this study will refer to the literature and highlight particular findings of significance that support and add to the identified areas of investigation.

4   Research Methodology

4.1   Sample

Fifteen students, aged 14 to 16 years, and one secondary Computing Studies classroom teacher participated in this case study. Participating students were enrolled in a Year 9/10 IST elective course: *Internet and Web Design*. The area of Computing Studies was selected for the study because of the requirements from the New South Wales Board of Studies that students be familiar with the use of database design, digital media, Internet and website development and multimedia programs. The teacher involved in the study had 8 years teaching experience and limited involvement with the promotion of higher-level cognitive and inquiry-based learning.

4.2   Instrumentation

The instrumentation for this case study consisted of curriculum materials that involved the use of digital media with particular emphasis on the utilisation of Macromedia multimedia and web-based solutions for school project work – into a Year 9/10 IST elective course: *Internet and Web Design*. In the *Information and Software Technology Years 7-10* syllabus documentation [13] states that, "People can expect to work and live in environments requiring highly developed levels of computing and technological literacy. Current technologies are becoming obsolete at a rapid rate and new generations will need to be flexible to accommodate changes as they emerge. It is important that students learn about, choose and use appropriate information and software technology and develop an informed awareness of its capacities, scope, limitations and implications. Technological competence in the rapidly evolving area of information and software technology will require lifelong learning". The general purpose of the school-based IST elective course at the NSW secondary school used for this case study was to focus students on designing and building their own websites to solve a given problem. For the duration of the school semester when visits and observations were made, students were required to analyse problems, plan solutions, research possibilities, develop webpages for their solution, design suitable graphics, test and finally evaluate the finished project. Students worked towards gaining a valuable real world experience using industry standard software such as Dreamweaver, Fireworks and Flash. Specifically, the IST course assisted students to develop the knowledge, understanding and skills to solve problems in real life contexts. Through experiential and collaborative tasks, students engaged in processes of analysing, designing, producing, testing, documenting, implementing and evaluating information and software technology-based solutions. Creative, critical and meta-cognitive thinking skills were developed through students' practical involvement in projects.

4.3 Data Collection

A 20-week classroom-based study was conducted to investigate whether the use of digital media programs can facilitate thinking and learning. The projected time for the study was equivalent to two NSW school terms. Both a qualitative and quantitative study was initiated through the implementation of this research. Specifically, the data collection methods implemented for this study included: a pre-questionnaire; field notes (descriptive; observations); informal student and teacher discussions; formal student and teacher interviews; student work samples; computer-based student answer files; and a post-questionnaire. Staff and students responded to a classroom environment inventory prior to using the digital media and again 3 months after use was completed.

4.4 Method

The primary data gathering tool for this study was the 'What is Happening in this Class (WIHIC)' classroom environment instrument [1]. The WIHIC was used to examine how the teacher and students perceived the classroom environment to be with relation to the use of technology. It was used to gather data on both the preferred and actual perceptions of the staff and students involved. The WIHIC instrument was administered to both the teacher and students with a 3 month interval between the examination of each group's preferred and actual perceptions. A computer background survey was implemented with the class to obtain information from the fifteen students about their access to computer technology, use of computers both at home and at school, interest and personal assessment of the ease with which they use technology and regularity of use of the Internet and multimedia programs. The researcher assumed the role of a participant-observer [11] in the classroom of one teacher. This role enabled the researcher to monitor selected students application to task and thinking. Field notes were recorded by the researcher to document observations of both the teacher and students during each lesson. These notes recorded the learning processes taking place, whole-class discussions, individual interactions, student-student interactions and teacher-student interactions. Classroom observations and field notes were further supported by access to online entries made at the end of each lesson by students, during the second half of the school semester, in a diary of classwork to record responses to the following questions: (1) What have you completed in this lesson?, (2) What did you learn?, (3) What did you have trouble with? How did you solve it? An ethnographic or socio-cultural interpretation [12] of student experiences was made through informal interviews and observations of selected students. The understanding of concepts and individual perceptions was reviewed and queried, together with an analysis of thinking skills, processes and reasons for completing a task in a given way. Emphasis was placed on the teacher providing students with frequent opportunities to work individually using computers, to work collaboratively with fellow students, and to participate in whole-class discussions. Informal discussions between the researcher and teacher occurred at the end of each class session during the investigation to focus on issues that may have arisen from the lesson and about teaching plans for the next class or subsequent follow-up sessions. A formal interview was conducted both at the commencement of the 20 week observation period and at the end.

5 Results

In response to the research questions posed for this study, early results suggested that technology allowed learning and motivation of students to be enhanced and that there was a willingness exhibited by individual students to engage in tasks and discussions. As they engaged in practical work during the IST elective course classes, students exhibited a number of characteristics central to this study including inquiry-based learning, improvements in skills (planning, technical, thinking, interacting with others) and a constructivist approach to project development. From the field study observations, it is felt that the implementation of digital media can contribute to and enhance inquiry-based learning. This was evident within the secondary technology classroom observed during the study, as a shift from the traditional teacher-centred instructional paradigm to a more student-centred one occurred. In working independently students in this study demonstrated during the semester that they had gained valuable skills (practical, technical, organisational, interrelationship, thinking) that were transferable to other academic endeavours. In creating a more student-centred approach through the use of technology integration it was observed that the use of digital media involving the Macromedia suite in the classroom, could encourage students to take charge of their own learning. When utilising Macromedia multimedia and web-based solutions for learning, students made a firm transition from simply receiving knowledge to becoming producers (constructivism) of their own school project work within a contextual element. This was further evidenced by student entries in a diary of classwork completed during the later part of the semester when students were working on their major project work for the IST elective course. The design of the digital media and web-based solution enabled students during their program of learning to demonstrate acquisition of knowledge, skills, ideas and understanding. In categorising the thinking skills employed by students during the development of the project work in the IST course being studied, reference to an established thinking skills framework is worthwhile for consideration [2]. Technology can be used as a tool for communication (visual, physical) and inquiry through the implementation of a constructivist approach that aims to foster student learning through real-life applications. Students in the study provided evidence that they had gained knowledge through self-exploration and active learning whilst remaining on task during lessons. Students remained entirely on task because their technology classwork centred on themes and concepts and the connections between them, rather than on isolated facts and information that they had difficulty understanding or making links to. The most obvious benefit of the Year 9/10 IST elective course was that students learnt about the web. They learnt about technologies related to the web, software used to create or control the web, and how to organise and present websites. In addition, students learnt to consider and plan their projects and to interact with others to strengthen or to reinforce a skill learnt.

6   Conclusion

Implications from this study for teaching and learning via a digital media approach include encouraging students to verbalise or to write down their thinking process and to identify patterns in their thoughts and possible gaps in their understanding whilst using technology constructively to allow for greater flexibility by students in terms of their cognitive processes. We need to be able to initiate and encourage learners within our classrooms to demonstrate and use effective thinking practices and for both students and teachers we need to consider ways of modelling, coaching and scaffolding thinking processes – this will allow learners to refine their understanding through articulation and comparison of strategies through the concept of reflection. The use of technology to allow students to reflect and evaluate on their project work and to therefore refine, organise and re-organise processes during the process of knowledge construction is also a key area for consideration.

We live in an information rich society that has been greatly enhanced by the advancement of digital media. As educators we need to consider and draw on the revolution of change and the manner in which information is presented in order to allow our students (learners) to be educated through means which are more relevant to society today. Digital media offers a motivating and imaginative approach to subject matter whereby students can be actively engaged and develop a variety of skills including problem solving, thinking, technical and interactivity. A central part to the learning process and the development of an individuals thinking is the concept of constructivism. The learning process is only effective when meaning is constructed by the student. In creating the product (project), students then own the information that they process more than if they were to simply find or be given it. Brearley [3] aptly captures the essence of what a constructivist approach is by stating that it is by no means a replacement for traditional content areas and strategies but rather "The main work of the school is surely the fostering and developing of mental life, enabling children to experience more fully and consciously all that life has to offer. This large, overall aim is to be achieved by an infinity of small steps. The material we provide children can seldom be thought of as an end in itself but rather as a means through which effective thinking and feeling are fostered".

References

1. J. Aldridge, B. Fraser and T. Huang, Investigating classroom environments in Taiwan and Australia with multiple research methods. *Journal of Educational Research*, **93**, 48-57 (1999).

2. L. Anderson and D. Krathwohl, A taxonomy for learning, teaching and assessing: a revision of Bloom's taxonomy of educational objectives, (Longman, New York, 2001).

3. M. Brearley, *The Teaching of Young Children*. (Schocken books, New York, 1969)

4. M. Cooper and D. Maor, (1998). Mathematics, multimedia and higher level thinking skills. *Proceedings Western Australian Institute of Educational Research Forum 1998*. http://education.curtin.edu.au/waier/forums/1998/cooper.html

5. B. Coulter, Technology for learning: how does technology support inquiry? *Connect* (a publication of Synergy Learning), **13**(4), (March/April 2000).

6. R.S. Grabinger, in: Handbook of research for educational communications and technology, edited by D. H. Jonassen (Simon and Schuster Macmillan, new York, 1996), pp. 665-692.

7. S. Hackbarth, *The Educational Technology Handbook - A Comprehensive Guide: Process and Products for Learning*. (Englewood Cliffs, New Jersey, 1996)

8. D.H. Jonassen, *Computers in the classroom: mind tools for critical thinking*. (Prentice-Hall, Englewoods, NJ, 1996).

9. C. Latchem, J. Williamson and L. Henderson-Lancett (eds.), *Interactive Multimedia: Practice and Promise*. (Kogan Page, London, 1993).

10. D. Maor and B.J. Fraser, Use of classroom environment perceptions in evaluating inquiry-based computer-assisted learning. *International Journal of Science Education*. **18**, 401-421, (1996).

11. D. Maor and P.C. Taylor, Teacher epistemology and scientific inquiry in computerised classroom environments. *Journal of Research in Science Teaching*. **32**, 839-854 (1995).

12. S.B. Merriam, *Qualitative research and case study: Application in education (2nd ed.)*, (Jossey Bass, San Francisco, 1998).

13. New South Wales Board of Studies, *Information and Software Technology Years 7-10 syllabus documentation June 2003*. (NSW Board of Studies, Sydney, 2003).

14. A.J. Romiszowski, *Developing interactive multimedia courseware and networks*. Paper presented at the meeting of the International Interactive Multimedia Symposium, (Western Australia, Perth, 1992)

15. K. Wiburg, Becoming critical users of multimedia. *The Computing Teacher*, **22**, 59-61 (1995).

Practice makes perfect
Role-play – because our students deserve it!

Anders Tveit
Norwegian School of Management, Institute of Economics, Nydalsvn 37,
0442 Oslo, Norway, anders.tveit@bi.no

Abstract. In this paper I present the result from a study of how attitudes towards a course and the feeling of learning can change as the teaching style changes. In a traditional course with regard to style of teaching, the students use words such as difficult, comprehensive, confusing and boring when characterizing the course. In other courses with a different pedagogical approach students use words such as instructive, fun and engaging about the same topics. The alternative course is based on a simulation model and role play. In many ways this is a lot like the way a good video game is developed. The participants learn about complex systems by living the role of the player. Like a game, we build our course to be comfortably frustrating. This is learning by doing instead of theory before practice - a way to deeper learning because the participants are brought into a state of mind which makes them so susceptible to learning.

Practice makes perfect

During my time as a lecturer I have seen many students sink into apathy and dejection because they hadn't mastered the subject. My starting point is not the easiest. I teach economics, a course called the sad science, probably because we discuss topics such as recessions, unemployment, starvation and death. If anyone brings up something positive about a case we might possibly comment by saying: "There is no such thing as a free lunch". Charisma doesn't buy you much either as a lecturer in economics. We have few humorists. You will also find the serious factor when it comes to learning our area of study. Economics is not an easy subject. Before you can start you have to learn our system of concepts, which includes things like domestic product, inflation and voluntary and involuntary unemployment. You also need methods. That means good skills in mathematics and statistics. Maybe this is the reason why we get this kind of evaluation feedback: "I didn't understand a

Please use the following format when citing this chapter:

Tveit, A., 2008, in IFIP International Federation for Information Processing, Volume 281; *Learning to Live in the Knowledge Society*; Michael Kendall and Brian Samways; (Boston: Springer), pp. 127–134.

thing" or "heavy and difficult subjects" and " I felt like a fool, total lack of knowledge despite my long work experience," etc.

In order to get a little more insight into why students seemed to feel this way about our subject I asked them the following question [1]: What words would you use to characterise the course? The most common word they chose to use was difficult (46 %). Almost every second student had the opinion that the course was complicated, complex and troublesome. Such a point of view many economists would agree with. Macroeconomics isn't easy. But the word "difficult" also says something about the lack of "mastering." When students were asked, they had had 15 lectures and still almost half of them were left with the feeling that they couldn't cope with the material. In other words they lacked a feeling of control and felt inadequate when it came to what was expected of them. Such experiences do something to you as a human being and they impact your attitude towards the subject. There may be those who become motivated in such a situation, but are there many?

The next word most chose to use was interesting (28 %). Every fourth student thought the course made them think. It was captivating, but at the same time this says something about distance. They seem to think that the course had potential but they did not describe it more precisely. The following words compounded this feeling: comprehensive (18 %) and confusing/difficult to grasp (17 %). The course was apparently perceived of as being thorough and detailed, but at the same time so detailed that it became indistinct. Not until 12 % came the word instructive. This means that a little more then one out of ten said the course was informative. That is not much after 45 hours of lectures.

My point of departure has always been that there is nothing wrong with the subject, but with the way the material is passed on. In the course described above, the lectures are traditional with regard to their style of teaching, and conducted in an auditorium seating 300 – 400 students. What I wanted to investigate was how attitudes towards a course and the feeling of learning might change as the teaching style changes. Is it possible that a course in macroeconomics can be perceived of as not only instructive -- but also as exciting and even funny -- if the teaching methods are changed?

As a fundamental element of an alternative course, the program TOPSIM MacroEconomics II, was chosen [2]. This is a data based simulation program produced by a German Swiss company to help students learn about macroeconomic terms and contexts. The program is played by taking over the leading roles in the private and public sectors of a country. When the groups have taken their final decisions they get back a detailed report of the economic situation for the country. The report makes the basis for new decisions in coming periods. Altogether we normally play three periods in our course.

During the last ten years we have done many role play courses developed around this program. Most of them have been two to three day courses without ECTS credits. At the end of the course I asked them the same question: What words would you use to characterise the course? The most common word they chose to use was instructive (27 %). One out of four now says they were informative. Other words were fun (25 %) and amusing (7 %). This is in contrast to the other course where the words boring (6 %) and heavy (5 %), were used. The quality of the course was also described by the word good (18 %). In addition, many mentioned the form of instruction by using the words engaging (15 %) and different (6 %). One interesting observation was that among the words the students decided to use, difficult was not included. On the other hand no one used the word easy. There was "a lot to learn" and "the topics was heavy", but also "heavy topics were communicated intelligibly". The course was "pedagogically well done" so "time went fast".

Of course there are big differences between a course running for two to three days without credits and a 6 credit course running for 16 weeks. During three days the participants can be "kept away" from complicated material in such a way that they do not understand how difficult and comprehensive the subject actually is. These participants do have a sort of test, but it is not as extensive as in a course with credits and the seriousness does not become such a burden. This is why I wanted to compare the first course with a credit course using untraditional teaching methods.

The course we are now looking at is a compulsory intermediate macroeconomic 12 ECTS credit course at bachelor level. In this course we also used the data based simulation model as part of the teaching method. At the end of the course the students were asked the same question as in the other courses: What words would you use to characterise the course? The most common word they chose to use was instructive (48 %). Almost every second student mentioned the feeling of learning. Other words were interesting (24 %), work demanding (24 %), engaging (15 %), exciting (15 %) and fun (15 %). These students answered almost like the participants at the two to three day course apart from the comment regarding demands. In this course we used digital portfolios as part of the working and evaluation method. This implied that every week the students had to publish (hand in) individual work. In contrast to many other courses that only consist of final exams; this course was probably a major change for many students because of the weekly hand in exercises. It is nonetheless interesting to see that many students still think the course was fun and exciting. It is my opinion that the reason is the way we teach. Let me therefore explain how we develop our role play courses.

The course starts by choosing a role. By living the role of the player you learn not only about the character but also about the system the character is part of. Consequently, the participants learn to think about their role as part of a system, not only as one in a series of casually occurring events. The problems are analysed from different angles. But at the same time you must take into consideration the overall point of view. As such, the participants learn about connections at the same time as they can experience new. This is an excellent way to learn about complex systems.

At the beginning of the course it is also important to have low entry thresholds. After choosing a role we consequently start with the following exercise: Make a logo, a motto and a physical movement that symbolises the motto. This exercise everybody manages. They all get started and it also creates a good atmosphere. At the same time the participants start the process of living themselves into the role and leaving their mark on the role.

A strong feeling of identity is important to learning [4]. In our courses we often experience participants who identify strongly with their role play figure. One time a group of chief constables were going to negotiate a new wage agreement in our macro play. The representative from the union came to meet the employers and was offered a bucket turned upside down as a chair. Later they regretted their gesture.

The negotiation never got started. It ended up in a strike followed by a lot of extra costs to the company. After ending the day the chief constable was still so mad we found it necessary to gather all the participants for a debriefing. This gave us an excellent example of how involved you actually can get in a role play.

When it comes to macroeconomics it is usually those with good knowledge and comprehension of numbers who comes out on top. In role plays you have a longer list of instruments at hand. One time during a strategy presentation the representative at the speaker's platform had a weak grasp of numbers. But the woman was not without a clue of what to do. Instead of winding herself into the current problem, she took off one shoe and slammed it on the platform while delivering her final comment: "This is how it is," she said, which at least gave her self-confidence that lasted for the rest of the course.

These are examples of why involved students are good for learning. As one student wrote in an assessment report: "We do not like the government now". The student was referring to a play in which the government had raised income taxes by 33 %. They did this by raising the tax from 15 % to 20 %. 5 % up is not that much, they thought. They consequently all obtained a deeper understanding of the difference between percentages and percentage points.

Low entry thresholds are an important quality in a good role play. Another characteristic is that you never feel you are in total control. That is why you need to lay on new aspects in the shape of new challenges in such a way that students meet new predicaments. In other words something difficult follows the easy parts.

My thoughts go to the developmental psychologist, Piaget [5], who was preoccupied with the balance between interpreting surroundings by using the knowledge we have (assimilation) and adjusting and changing our common sense and experience based understanding (accommodation). In other words, you are in the accommodation process when you understand that you have to revise your opinions. In our play we put in such processes by letting the participants take over the country when we are in a business cycle with increasing economic growth. Then it is easy to achieve good results. In the next period we are fronting a depression and the country is facing new challenges. Then you get the feeling that this is not so easy after all. A play should be pleasantly frustrating. The challenge consists of fitting in the right combinations of assimilation and accommodation. The thing that makes the change and therefore leads to learning is the accommodation. When a situation occurs when something is just not right, it creates an imbalance which is the main driver for intellectual development and therefore also in the learning process. The urge towards an inner balance drives you to reorganize and thereby to develop new interpretations and knowledge.

We got good feedback about whether our courses were pleasantly frustrating when a student wrote: "At times very frustrating, but it inspired me to continue the work". Such a series in which students start with limited problem solving and continue by solving more comprehensive challenges gives the course a good balance. At the same time this is an important driver for the course.

In our courses we experience participants who, over a long period of time, are willing to deal with macroeconomic problems without significant breaks. In other words it looks like there is something about our courses that makes the students willing to solve complex problems hour after hour [6]. I think a lot of the power comes from the way we teach. It functions as fire in a haystack. Once it's lit, it burns by itself, but it can often take off in unexpected directions. That is why it is important to put down flame barriers, in this case by marking out a course that is in proportion to the curriculum. As with a quarter horse, blinkers are necessary, but they must not be too uncomfortable. Room must be left for improvisation and the unexpected because the participants must feel their freedom and that they have options that are real. My role as an instructor is to guide them back to current problems by asking questions. The idea is to lead the students to find the answer themselves without telling them everything [7]. Whether they experience success or not depends on several factors. First they need knowledge about their own role. This means they need to know the instruments they have control of and how they can be used to reach their goals. At the same time they are a part of a greater whole. That is why their success depends on what the others choose to do. Many scientists argue that this way of working, both being a specialist in a field and cooperating and sharing with others, is decisive in achieving success in the future labour market [8].

These are the same methods we use in our course. Your own success depends on what others do. If you don't cooperate you will discover that by the results of your own decisions coming back in the shape of an extensive report. Because the roles in the private sector are of major dimension, a strong financial result for the country also means a strong financial result for the companies. You don't get rid of the results but you reap new possibilities through subsequent periods. Such a learning process, through learning by doing, was once described by the pedagogue Dewey [9]. He focused on the learning process as a determined and experimental activity, aroused out of a felt need. In our courses we ask questions like: What do you think about the economic growth, .. the unemployment, ... the inflation? What do you want to achieve? The problems are examined and marked off and make the basis of hypotheses about how the problems can be solved. "We could probably get the unemployment or the inflation down if we do ....". Beneficial processes occur when the participants try, fail, get feedback and try again. In our data model there is a simulation part where the participants can try out the effect of their own tools in the light of assumptions about what the others are doing. We also put in strategy presentations where the groups present their rough draft for solutions with discussions in plenary, before they make their final decisions. The results involve new problems and that's the start of a new period.

That a play allows the players to practice is brought up by several researchers: "Humans think and understand best when they can imagine (simulate) an experience in such a way that the simulation prepares them for actions they need and want to take in order to accomplish their goals" [10]. A role play consequently gives you the possibility to practice before you are competent. The alternative used in traditional education is the opposite. The theory comes first, which means you are not allowed to practice before you know how to do it.

In a traditional teaching situation, students learn to replace words by definitions, but it shows that they can not use the words to solve problems because they have not experienced the words in real situations. We have known about this lack of accordance between knowledge of definitions and the ability to use words to solve problems, for a long time [11]. Both Dewey and the developmental psychologist, Vygotsky [12], differentiate between traditional teaching and good teaching.

Vygotsky characterised traditional teaching as summaries without spirit and words learned from memories; words you have not learned intellectually to use; words you not have learned to think in. "This teaching method is the basic mistake of the school's language-based method of teaching, which has generally been abandoned. It replaces the mastering of living knowledge by the learning of dead, empty language forms."

What is there to learn from a role play in this context? One thing is this: One significant skill obtained is that participants achieve relations to the words because they are related to events that occur. That is why they not only get the words connected to numbers but they also get to see how the meaning of words depends on the situation in which they are spoken. Let me give a typical example from one of our courses: The central bank group choose stability and predictability as a motto. The words are written in blue, the logo (blue and green) shows a banknote with the mark M for Macropoly (the country). The group also comes forward and turn thumps up to symbolise unity. A bit later during the annual speech by the central bank chair, she is explaining that their goals are no longer exchange rate stability but an inflation target of 2.5 %. The number is first something she refers to as a reason why she changed the interest rate. Subsequently, the banks and the companies discuss what consequences this might have for their own sector and for the country as a whole. The results, inflation above 3 %, create a great commotion and result in new discussions and new suggestions on how to solve the problems.

Such discussions imply open solution possibilities. In a traditional macroeconomic course we would inform the students that in Norway the central bank has an inflation target of 2.5 %. In a play situation the participants have the liberty to choose their own solutions. If the central bank decides on a 2 % inflation target, it gives us the opportunity to compare with Norway and to argue the issue's pros and cons. This gives the participants a feeling of freedom, another important motivating factor.

As described, the course is based on a data model which consists of six roles. At the end of each session each group delivers their final decisions to the game management by use of a computer. The decisions are then simulated in a data model and the results in the form of reports for the entire economy as well as for each sector, are produced immediately. The groups then discuss the results and are supported and guided by the teacher. There will be focus on achievements and errors made during the first period and the teachers will point to several factors that were the reason for the results.

By using the results of the previous period and a scenario of the economic situation for next period, the participants will make decisions for the following period. This gives the participants the possibility to repeat previously gained knowledge.

It is a combination of data model, role-play and the teacher as a supervisor that contribute to the successful result. Alone none of the components would make it. Without the data model the role play would have no substance. It would be "only talk". The participants would never actually know the outcome of their talking. On the other hand, the data model alone would only be a lot of numbers. Consequently, they wouldn't see how the meaning of words depends on the situation in which they are spoken. And last but not least, the teacher's role would be different. It would be harder to take the student's experience as a starting point. In such a situation we could lose the foundation of all further learning and it would be a lot harder to provide a plan for development with regard to the expansion and arrangement of the teaching material. And it would be a lot harder to deal with the teaching problem - to get the student's experience to move in the direction of what the teacher already knows.

A role play course like this has provided us with many memorable moments and the opportunity to witness many excellent performances. Moreover, the competences embrace a lot more than merely answering test questions. It is about the ability to perform, judge, feel, decide and solve problems, like a professional. In addition to knowledge about macroeconomic terms and context, the course also enhances the participant's ability to think strategically and to solve complex problems. That is why a course like the one described in this paper is not only popular, but also a way to deeper learning. It becomes deeper because the participants are brought into a state of mind which makes them so susceptible to learning. After ending the course the participants therefore gave the following summary: The course can be characterised by the words instructive, fun, good, engaging, interesting, amusing and different.

References

1. At the last but one lecture in a compulsory macroeconomic 6 ECTS credit course at bachelor level, spring 2007. Altogether 260 students answered of whom many replied using more than one word.
2. For more information: http://www.topsim.com/de/planspiele/macro_economics_ii/
3. Not used
4. The claim is supported by Gee 2004, diSessa 2000 and Shaffer 2004:
Gee, James Paul (2004): Situated language and learning: A critique of traditional schooling. London: Routledge. diSessa, A. A. (2000): Changing minds: Computers, learning, and literacy. Cambridge, Mass: MIT Press. Shaffer, D. W. (2004): Pedagogical praxis: The professions as models for postindustrial education. Teachers College Record 10: 1401-1421
5. Piaget, Jean (1973): Psykologi og pædagogik, København and Piaget, Jean (1973): Barnets psykiske utvikling. Gyldendal Forlag. Oslo.
6. Same experience Gee 2006. Gee, James Paul (2006): Are video games good for learning? Nordic Journal of Digital Literacy, Digital kompetanse 3/2006
7. Heuristic method. Used already by Socrates about 470-399 before Christ.
8. Bech, U. (1999): World risk society. Oxford: Blackwell.Gee, James Paul (2004): Situated language and learning: A critique of traditional schooling. London: Routledge. Gee, J. P., Hull, G. & Lankshear, C. (1996): The new work order: Behind the language of the new capitalism. Boulder, CO.: Westview.
9. Dewey, John (1966): Democracy and Education. New York: Free Press.
10. Barsalou, L. W. (1999): Perceptual symbols system. Behavioural and Brain Sciences 22: 577-660. Clark, A. (1997): Being there: Putting brain, body, and world

together again. Cambridge, Mass.: MIT Press. Glenborg, A. M. & Robertson D. A. (1999): Indexical understanding of instructions. Discourse Processes 28:1-26
11. Gardner H. (1991). The unschooled mind: How children think and how schools should teach. New York: Basic Books.
12. Vygotsky, Lev S (1987): The collected works of L. S. Vygotsky vol 1 in: Robert W. Rieber and Aaron S. Carton (ed.) Problems of general psychology. New York: Plenum Press.

Gearing up for Robotics

An investigation into the acquisition of the concepts associated with gears by teachers in a constructionist robotics environment

Debora E. Lipson[1], John Murnane[2] and Anne McDougall[2]
[1]School of Education, Faculty of Arts, Education and Human Development,
Victoria University, PO Box 14428, Melbourne 8001, Australia,
debora.lipson@vu.edu.au
[2]Information & Communication Technology in Education and Research
Group, Melbourne Graduate School of Education, The University of
Melbourne, 3010, Australia, jmurnane@unimelb.edu.au,
a.mcdougall@unimelb.edu.au

Abstract. This naturalistic, qualitative research investigated the extent and depth to which the perceived embedded educational skills and concepts associated with gears in a robotics environment were realized. The research literature revealed a paucity and confusion of description and definition of gears, and a lack of articulation of the embedded skills associated with gears. Based on some seminal research papers, a novel skills grid was developed as a measuring instrument, against which deep mining of the knowledge progress of the understanding of gears of four teachers was observed. The analysis of results pertaining to considered gear integration in the construction of a robot revealed that learning does not occur serendipitously and, unless taught overtly, the opportunities for the learning of gear concepts are often missed or deliberately bypassed. This lack of desire to learn about, and consider gear integration in constructions, could be attributed to confusion of interpretation of a non-contextualised ratio, or more deeply, the confusion of ratio representation in rational number and colon formats.

1. Background

Robots are rapidly becoming an integral component of everyday life. In order to facilitate an understanding of this future environment, the study of robots, known as robotics, has become a growing field of interest and learning. Historically situated in information technology courses, robotics has developed from an element of investigation in control technology, to a compulsory, selected, or elective subject in schools at all levels. Over the last two decades the inherent complexity in the

---

Please use the following format when citing this chapter:

Lipson, D.E., Murnane, J. and McDougall, A., 2008, in IFIP International Federation for Information Processing, Volume 281; *Learning to Live in the Knowledge Society*; Michael Kendall and Brian Samways; (Boston: Springer), pp. 135–142.

construction and programming components has been reduced, making the robotics educational environment more available and accessible for students of all ages. This multi-component approach to teaching and learning, situates robotics as both a process and a content curriculum, involving deliberation about the environment (group work, construction, problem solving), the material to be transmitted (physics, mathematics, spatial skills), and the method for transference of material (higher-order thinking skills, programming, and group work). Investigation into the learning opportunities revealed a plethora of skills, issues, and embedded knowledge including personal and inter-personal learning, and the studies of Mathematics, Science, English, History, and Sociology.

1.1 Claims

This emergent field of study has been supported by a developing literature of claims that robotics is rich in potentially embedded depth and breadth for the teaching and learning of a range skills and concepts including improvement in engagement [1, 2] and self-esteem [1]; improved problem solving skills [2]; improved understanding of scientific [2] and mathematics concepts [3-5]; and, close links with real life scenarios [1, 2]. These claims support the seminal ideas of Papert's theory of constructionism [6], whereby construction of a publicly inspectable artefact is evidence of understanding the principles inherent in the artefact, and that learning occurs serendipitously in this environment.

This learning is evident in the cyclical processes of model generation, revision, and evaluation for model construction [7]. This perfect medium appears to enable deep understanding of the embedded concepts including the transmission of a deep understanding of simple machines. In spite of the increased interest in robotics in schools, little research appears to have been done in the short recent time to study the effect of this medium on the multitude of opportunities as touted in the literature [8].

1.2 Science Teaching

As part of a general science curriculum, it is seen as important that students develop knowledge, understanding, and appreciation, of machines in every day life, to raise their appreciation and understanding of the world they live in. The essence of these machines is the integration of simple machines i.e. gears, levers and pulleys, in various configurations. However, it appears that much of the science teaching about simple machines only emphasizes the mere recognition of gears, levers, and inclined planes, in everyday environments, and rarely addresses the scientific rationale and background of working machines [4, p23]. Further, even when there is a deeper investigation into the machinations of simple machines, instruction does not appear to be informed by the kinds of conceptions that children bring to the table [4, p23].

As a simple machine, although gears are small and apparently insignificant, they are the essential and most common components in the creation of a moveable model. An appreciation of the many various types of gears, gearing configurations, and their impact in everyday objects, is generally only studied to a superficial level and, unless there is a need to understand the intricacies of gearing to control the speed of motion of an object, students rarely gain the educational opportunity to investigate and encounter the many cognitive concepts embedded in a gears environment. With consideration for the provision of an engaging, manipulative environment that allows student exploration and contextualised learning, the construction of robots provides an ideal medium for the transmission of knowledge of contextualised simple machines.

1.3   Informal Author Observations

Over years of involvement in a robotics environment, the dichotomy between the potential and the observable skills acquisition has been raised. When students appeared to lack sufficient knowledge to appropriately integrate simple machines, they would select one of three alternative ways to compensate for this lack of understanding. These were modifying the robot construction; altering the programming; or modifying the original brief and objectives for the construction. Anecdotally, most students appeared to prefer the last option, with few students willing to reconstruct their models. These three tactics demonstrated two main problems: (i) the avoidance of good integrated use of gears through alternative modifications, and (ii) the non-realization of the skills and concepts embedded in this environment.

2. The Study

This study did not set out to establish a "truth or......build a warranted representation of the world" [9, p270]. Rather it set out to deliver a "story, ... produce a narrative and give voice to different viewpoints or understandings" [9, p270], and investigate and analyze observations in the light of contextualised activities and constructions, seeking to reveal what gear concepts are manifested and learnt in this environment. It is essential at this point to clarify two aspects:- (i) the consideration of all aspects associated with gears, including descriptions, definitions, skills and concepts housed in these artefacts will be restricted to the educational setting, focusing on the gears contained in the LEGO® construction kit of ROBOLAB®; (ii) the gearing concepts, although sufficiently complex at a school level will remain at a relatively low level in comparison to gears used in heavy industrial machinery or cars by engineers, and are not extended to the full range of available, and more complex, engineering gears.

2.1   The Methodology

There are a large range of skills and abilities developed in a natural and collaborative construction and programming robotic environment. As such, the most appropriate way to examine acquisition of any skills and concepts is to observe and document any progress. Thus, to investigate any knowledge growth, a naturalistic qualitative study was conducted in situ, using a human as a researcher/evaluator/data collector [10, p124] to reveal the developing "story" of knowledge acquisition. Information was gathered by the participant observer through multiple sources of video capture, journals and pencil and paper tests.

2.2   Research Setting

Each week for a period of six weeks, four teachers attended a three-hour, after hours, *Robotics in Education* course as part of one of their selected academic subjects towards a higher qualification of a Masters of Information Technology in Education. They were presented with a series of construction and programming tasks of increasing difficulty and complexity, entwined with discussions of educational theory and issues, as raised through the literature. The construction component used the standard set of LEGO® construction kit called ROBOLAB®. The iconic programming language used was MindStorms® where, using the click and drag feature, icons representing motors, lights, and sensors were 'placed' on ports (input and output) in the programming sequence.

2.3   The Subjects

The focus on these self-motivated, articulate, and high achieving teachers, with divergent academic backgrounds and teaching foci, was seen as essential, as teachers are facilitators of student learning, guiding and directing knowledge acquisition. To support the inclusion and integration of robotics in an educational program, teachers need to be aware of the embedded skills and concepts, and ensure sufficient self-confidence to enable facilitation on this course. As teachers are more articulate than students, observation of teacher discussions and constructions, as indicative of their acquisition of gears skills and concepts, would provide greater insight into how students learn in this environment. Hence, a focus on teaching learning in this environment was seen as an opportunity to begin to create a rich and developing story of learning in a robotics environment.

2.4   Measuring Tools

The journal - as a component of assessment in this subject, the teachers were to develop a journal of reflection and planning. These journals were photocopied and used alongside the video to expand the analysis and development of each case study.

The pencil and paper test - based on a range of studies [3, 4, 11-13], pencil and paper tests are an accepted component for measuring and assessing knowledge of gears. Drawing on these tests, a pre and post-test was designed focusing on planar gear trains.

The video - in spite of some limitations associated with the use of a video to capture data, this method of data collection allowed the analysis and reporting of thick, rich descriptions of observations in a natural setting. It also provided opportunity to capture postures, gestures and interpersonal body language. Repeated viewings and analysis of episodic units enabled the development of deep probing and refined analysis after transcription of relevant units of discussions or constructions associated with gears and gearing. It also provided an opportunity to experience classroom events vicariously.

The grid - as preparation for the study, examination of the research literature and reference text books revealed a paucity and confusion of descriptions, definitions and identification of associated embedded concepts of gears. To enable clear articulation and measurement of the development of knowledge of gears, it became evident that there was a need to produce a grid that delineated the often overlooked and assumed understanding of gearing concepts. After analysis of a range of research papers that utilized gears as a testing medium, Lipson then developed the following novel evaluation grid (Table 1) [14].

3. The Results

As an evolving story of learning in a robotics environment, there were many observable outcomes in a number of areas. However, documenting and interpreting the learning process focused on gears revealed some significant results.

An analysis of the pencil and paper test revealed that little learning appeared to occur throughout the program. Review of the video during this testing phase provided some contrary and valuable insights into the diverse methods of solutions of gear ratios. 'Talk-aloud' protocols exposed obvious confusion between the reciprocal relationships of the ratio of cogs to the ratio of turns of planar gear configurations. Further confusion occurred when gears were not exact multiples of each other and resultant fractions were difficult to simplify.

Analysis of the weekly video data, as reported through the case studies, revealed some interesting issues related to the teachers' learning outcomes as identified through the skills grid.

Identification

In spite of the expectation that teachers would have the ability to discern the exact difference between gears, it was found that there was consistent confusion and inability to identify and name the spur gears according to the number of cogs, or discern the function of the idler, bevelled edged, crown, worm, rack and differential gears. There was, however, a demonstration for an appreciation for the consistent relationship between the diameter and the circumference of a spur gear.

Motion

In general, the teachers understood the difference between rotational and linear motion when associated with the gross motion of a buggy travelling either in a straight line or turning a corner. However, there was some difficulty in appreciating that the rotational motion of gears created linear motion, and the use of a differential gearing configuration created pivotal motion where the object rotates on a fine point.

Causality

Adults have an intuitive appreciation for the requirement of gears to be connected (meshed) to produce motion throughout the construction (Connectivity). There is also an intuitive understanding that meshed gears results in simultaneous turning or motion (temporal causality), and that in a gear train the idler gears can be used as "spacers" between the initial point of motor contact (driver gear) and the desired point of action (follower gear).

Direction of rotation

Prompted by the pencil and paper tests, the teachers began thinking about the direction of rotation of meshed gears, and although construction further raised awareness of direction of rotation, they were unable to move beyond the 'by inspection' analysis to develop a generalised formulation.

Ratio

There are many opportunities for ratio learning in this environment. However, during construction there was no direct application to appreciate, or find, π (the mathematical ratio of circumference to diameter).

Teacher discussions revealed an obvious awareness of the identical ratio of turns for same sized gears, with explicit appreciation for different ratio of turns between different sized gears. Quantification of meshed planar gears of different sizes was, however, more difficult to calculate.

During construction, all teachers appeared to appreciate the non-effect on the ratio of idler gears, although this component was not evident in the pre or post-tests.

Regardless of size, same shaft gears initially produced ratio responses as if they were meshed planar gears.

The calculation of the gear ratio of a compound gear configuration was often difficult as it appeared to be based on the teachers poor understanding, and resultant lack of desire, to manipulate fractional rotations and their confusion between the two ratio formats (colon and rational number formats).

Problem solving

The teachers were unable to extract general solutions from a range of specific situations with regard to the rotational effect of idler gears. However, to enable calculation of the various planar and compound gear configurations all teachers decomposed the complex into parts.

4. Conclusion

Even though the teachers in the study were knowledgeable, self-motivated, articulate, and high-achievers, there was confusion in understanding and manipulation between a ratio presented in rational number format and a fraction. Further, there was a lack of durability and transferability of various gear concepts that demonstrated a fragility of concept retention.

This suggests that, for this study, construction in a robotics environment does not necessarily support the many claims of the embedded learning potential. It is obvious that there is a need for clear descriptions and definitions of gears and gear ratios, a need to ensure clear articulation of the two representations of ratios, and the need to identify the difference in operation and meaning between ratios and fractions. This indicates that there is a need for explicit teaching of ratios.

At the completion of the course there was an intensive analysis of the gear ratio of a compound gear configuration. The teachers then noted that this manipulative could be used as a visual representation for teaching fraction multiplication to students.

Identification	• One-to-one correspondence identifying and naming gears • Appreciation and identification of varying sized gears and the relationship between number of cogs on each gear and its size. • Appreciation for the relationship between the diameter and the circumference of a gear including the consistent relationship between the diameter and circumference for various sized gears.
Motion	• Understanding the difference between rotational (pivotal) and linear motion
Causality - *This involves understanding the need for connectivity for causality and the effect of this connectivity on direction of rotation*	
-Connectivity	• Recognition of effect of meshed gears vs. non-meshed
-Temporal Causality	• For planar gears: - simultaneous turning • For three or more gears in a gear train - effect of idlers as "spacers" • For compound gear configuration - emphasis on "use" to create movement in configuration
-Direction	• Opposing direction for sequentially meshed gears • Same direction for alternating gears • Same direction for gears (regardless of size) on same shafts • Use of worm gears to create unidirectional motion
Ratio	• Ratio of diameter to circumference to find π. • Ratio of turns for same sized and different sized meshed, planar gears • Ratio of same sized or different sized gears on a single shaft or axle • Calculating ratios for compounded gear configurations • Using ratio to enable an understanding of speed
Mechanical advantage	• Transfer force through the use of rack gears • Mechanical advantage
Higher order thinking (Problem Solving)	• Breaking whole into parts (decomposition) • Progress from specific to development of general rules (abstraction) • Development of symbolic representation (deduction) • Conditional statements • Prediction

Table 1. Novel grid of skills and concepts embedded in the use of gears

References

1. Waddell, S., *Why teach robotics?* Tech Directions, 1999. **58**(7): p. 34.
2. Mauch, E., *Using Technological innovation to improve the Problem Solving Skills of Middle School Students: Educators' Experience with the LEGO Mindstorms Robotic Invention System.* The Clearing House, 2001. **74**(4): p. 211.
3. Bartolini Bussi, M.G., et al., *Early approach to theoretical thinking: gears in primary school.* Educational Studies in Mathematics: An International Journal, 1999. **39**(1-3): p. 67-87.
4. Lehrer, R. and L. Schauble, *Reasoning about Structure and Function: Children's Conceptions of Gears.* Journal of Research in Science Teaching, 1998. **35**(1): p. 3-25.
5. Norton, S.J. *Using Lego Construction to Develop Ratio Understanding.* in *MERGA 27: Mathematics Education for the Third Millennium: Towards 2010, 27-30 June 2004.* 2004 (a). Townsville, Australia: Mathematics Education Research Group of Australasia Inc.
6. Papert, S., *Mind-storms: Children, Computers, and Powerful Ideas.* First ed. 1980, Sussex: The Harvester Press. 230.
7. Li, S.C., N. Law, and K.F. Liu, *Cognitive Perturbation through Dynamic Modelling: A Pedagogical Approach to Conceptual Change in Science.* Journal of Computer Assisted Learning, 2006. **22**(6): p. 405-422.
8. McRobbie, C.J., S.J. Norton, and I.S. Ginns, *Student designing in a robotics classroom,* in *Annual meeting of the American Educational Research Association.* 2003 (b): Chicago, IL. p. 7.
9. Evers, C.W., *From Foundations to Coherence in Educational Research,* in *Issues in Educational Research,* J.P. Keeves and G. Lakomski, Editors. 1999, Pergamon: Oxford. p. 264-270.
10. Royce Sadler, D., *Intuitive Data Processing as a Potential Source of Bias in Naturalistic Evaluations,* in *The Qualitative Researcher's Companion,* A.M. Huberman and M.B. Miles, Editors. 2002, Sage Publications: Thousand Oaks. p. 123-135.
11. Perry, M. and A. Elder, *Knowledge in transition: Adults' developing understanding of a principle of physical causality.* Cognitive Development, 1997. **12**(1): p. 131-157.
12. Metz, K.E., *The Development of Children's Problem Solving in a gears Task: A Problem Space Perspective.* Cognitive Science, 1985. **9**: p. 431-471.
13. Metz, K.E., *Development of Explanation: Incremental and Fundamental Change in Children's Physics Knowledge.* Journal of Research in Science Teaching, 1991. **28**(9): p. 785-797.
14. Lipson, D.E., An investigation into the acquisition of the concepts associated with gears by teachers in a constructionist robotics environment., in ICT in Education and Research (Including the International Centre for Classroom Research). 2008, The University of Melbourne. p. 316.

Chapter 6

Online Distance Learning

Approaching TEL in university teaching: the faculty training need

Guglielmo Trentin [1], Jane Klobas [2,3] and Stefano Renzi [2]

1 Institute for Educational Technology, National Research Council,
Genoa, Italy (trentin@itd.cnr.it – http://www.itd.cnr.it)
2 University of Western Australia, Perth, Australia
(jane.klobas@uwa.edu.au - http://www.uwa.edu.au)
3 Bocconi University, Milan, Italy
(stefano.renzi@unibocconi.it - http://www.unibocconi.it)

Abstract. The introduction of ICT in university teaching is a long process and is strongly conditioned by many variables, first of all the level of knowledge the faculty members possess about the educational uses of ICT and the related instructional design approaches. This is the key issue on the basis of which the two specific training projects referred in this paper have been launched. After describing the related training approaches, some considerations will be made on the different role and status of those teachers who no longer restrict themselves to classroom teaching but who intend to complement or replace it with online education activities.

1 Introduction

Faculty members play a significant role in introducing the educational use of ICT in university teaching and should be capable of assessing the value that Technology Enhanced learning (TEL) [1] adds to their teaching [2, 3, 4]. They therefore need to acquire a fresh culture that envisages these approaches not so much as an antagonism or alternative to face to face teaching but as a further possibility. For example, there are cases where time and space impose severe constraints on attending classroom lessons or situations where TEL methodologies prove to be more effective didactically by being able to play separately on the element of "space" (doing as much as possible at home, locally, perhaps assisted at a distance or involved in group learning) and "time" (when conditions enable it).

Teachers generally face an awkward moment during their initial experiences of using TEL when it would be useful to provide them with support in their choice of methods in accordance with the teaching objectives. Bearing this in mind several

Please use the following format when citing this chapter:

Trentin, G., Klobas, J. and Renzi, S., 2008, in IFIP International Federation for Information Processing, Volume 281; *Learning to Live in the Knowledge Society*; Michael Kendall and Brian Samways; (Boston: Springer), pp. 145–148.

Italian universities have promoted training projects aimed at culturally developing faculty members in use of ICT in teaching and learning. The two cases presented here highlight two different approaches.

2   The ODL experience at the University of Turin

The ODL Project [5] at the University of Turin (started in 1999) consisted of a series of initiatives to channel methodological/technological abilities towards teachers already active in the educational use of ICT and towards training those who, despite being aware of the new opportunities offered by TEL, had not yet been given the chance to come to grips with using them. For teachers accustomed to TEL, this meant taking action to consolidate and systemize existing approaches; for the others, ad hoc project-oriented training courses focused on creating a personal TEL project.

The training model is broken down into two levels: basic training and advanced training.

Basic training is aimed at all teachers involved in the training programme and is provided during the first year. The main purpose is for teachers to acquire the minimum skills for designing and developing their first ICT application to support their own teaching. During basic training, topics related to networked learning are tackled fairly lightly, and the teachers' first approach to TEL almost always starts out by creating websites with learning materials.

Advanced training is therefore meant for teachers who, after their first experience of educational ICT uses (as a result of basic training or previous personal experience) intend to acquire TEL methods more deeply, both in the design of educational e-content (and more specifically learning-objects) and the management of networked collaborative learning.

In other words, while basic training envisages a sort of annual "call for participation" for the recruitment of those who want an introduction to TEL, advanced training, on the other hand, is based on explicit request from faculty members interested in acquiring greater skills to teach with ICT.

3   The BEL experience at the University "Bocconi" of Milan

The Turin experience could be described as bottom-up, in the sense that the diffusion of knowledge about TEL, beginning with the teacher, leaves the teacher to choose "if", "how" and "when" to use TEL in their own teaching. This approach works well if the objective is cultural. On the other hand, systemic approaches can be adopted by universities that provide strong organizational commitment to adoption of TEL. The BEL (Bocconi E-Learning) project illustrates one such approach.

Bocconi University, a prestigious business university in Milan, had significant success in introducing TEL, but eight years later wanted to move further forward.

In 1998, Bocconi began its TEL journey with the "B-learning" project. As part of this project, the university bought a learning management system (LMS) and established the technical infrastructure to support university-wide use of TEL. Five pilot teachers participated with three courses re-designed with the assistance of LMS experts. Subsequently, other teachers spontaneously adopted the platform and within three years 25% of the courses used TEL [6]. By the 2004-2005 academic year, almost all of Bocconi's courses incorporated some form of TEL, but most TEL usage was limited to upload of teaching material. Few courses involved students in online activities or computer-supported collaborative learning.

In the meantime, the increased number of Bocconi students spending a semester off-campus as interns or on exchange led the University to reconsider it use of TEL. A new project was initiated with the goal of enabling Bocconi students who were temporarily off-campus to participate in courses they would otherwise have taken on-campus. Six optional courses, involving nine teachers, were selected for participation in the first year. They were granted funds to buy technology, expertise and teaching relief.

Although the University's brief to the teachers was quite open, a number of requirements were set. They included: (1) the participation of the teachers in formal course design activities; (2) the online version of the course had to be offered in the same semester and by the same teacher as the classroom version of the course; (3) student participation in online activities should be compulsory.

The teachers selected for the new initiative included one of the original BEL project pilot teachers. He provided initial leadership, recommended they work together as a project team, and encouraged them to incorporate activities based on online collaborative learning where it was appropriate. The group agreed and decided to invite an experienced instructional designer to work with them.

The instructional designer held two introductory half day seminars, then worked individually with the teachers on design of the online versions of their courses. All teachers agreed to work to the same schedule for course design during the semester that preceded initiation of the online course:

- macro-design: definition of course objectives and goals, evaluation criteria, the types of activities to be incorporated, and preparation of an initial course outline;
- micro-design: detailed design of course modules, activities and timeline, reflected in a more detailed course outline;
- development of learning materials;
- "audit" of the revised courses by the instructional designer and participants.

Throughout these stages, teachers experimented with a range of technologies and activities. The first two re-designed courses were introduced to postgraduate students in September 2007. At the time of writing, they are being formally evaluated.

4   Some concluding remarks

Research carried out on the Turin and Bocconi University projects highlights two key conditions for fostering the process of introducing TEL in university teaching: cultural development of faculty members in the use of TEL approaches; and renegotiation of the teachers' new role as 'e-teacher'. In the first case, it is necessary:

- to adopt ad hoc training courses for faculty aimed at establishing initial contact with TEL and at steadily introducing the learning/teaching processes;

- to support faculty members in their first experience as an instructional designer of an online course.

In the second case, careful reflection is needed to understand how the teachers' role will change due to adopting innovative teaching methods with and through the use of ICT. In fact, although teachers continue to play a central role in TEL, their function inevitably tends to change with respect to classroom teaching: from a classroom teacher to a facilitator of the learning process where they are content experts. They contribute towards preparing e-materials and supervise online interactive activities. How much one changes clearly depends on the type of learning process to be fostered and whether it is partly or entirely based on the use of ICT. However, this often entails a work-overload, above all when teachers, besides TEL solutions, are anyway required to hold classroom lessons.

The importance of the role of e-teacher can be observed particularly when approaches based on networked collaborative learning are adopted.

To sum up, we may conclude that the study of and experimentation with TEL models is quite well developed, even if there is still significant room for improvement in their application. On the other hand, the training of faculty members, the norms (including those related to intellectual property of e-content), the organization, logistics and infrastructure still constitute serious obstacles for a solid university-wide implementation of the relative practices. Nevertheless it is comforting to observe that an increasing number of teachers are currently involved in experimenting with the use of TEL as a support for their teaching.

References

1. TEL Committee, University of Texas (2004). Report of Technology Enhanced Learning Committee. Available: http://www.utexas.edu/provost/planning/reports/TEL_Report_2004.pdf.

2. Clulow, V., & Brace-Govan, J. (2003). Web-based learning: Experience-based research. In A. K. Aggarwal (Ed.), *Web-Based Education: Learning from Experience* (pp.49-70). Hershey, PA: Information Science Publishing.

3. Hazemi R., & Hailes S. (2002). Introduction. In R. Hazemi and S. Hailes (Eds.), *The Digital University: Building a Learning Community*. London: Springer.

4. Zemsky, R., & Massy, W.F. (2004). Thwarted innovation: what happened to e-learning and why. Final Report for The Weatherstation Project of the Learning Alliance at University of Pennsylvania. Available: http://www.csudh.edu/dearhabermas/WeatherStation_Report.pdf.

5. Trentin, G. (2008). TEL and university teaching: different approaches for different purposes, *International Journal on E-Learning*, 7(1), 117-132.

6. Klobas, J.E., & Renzi, S. (2003). Integrating online educational activities in traditional courses: University-wide lessons after three years. In A. K. Aggarwal (Ed.), *Web-Based Education: Learning from Experience* (pp. 415-439). Hershey, PA: Information Science Publishing.

Merger of Knowledge Network and Users Support for Lifelong Learning Services

Christian-Andreas Schumann, Claudia Tittmann and Sabine Tittmann
University of Applied Sc.Zwickau, PF 201037, 08012 Zwickau, Germany
schu@fh-zwickau.de; clt@fh-zwickau.de; sati@fh-zwickau.de
WWW home page: http://www.fh-zwickau.de

Abstract. Nowadays knowledge acquisition takes place in a lifelong process within diversified phases and styles. The complexity of knowledge transfer processes permanently increases. This specialization leads to the development of competence clusters and their intercross-linking to knowledge networks. It will be tried on the part of the knowledge acquisition to realize the knowledge transfer in a transparent and effective way by using high information density and high-grade knowledge representation. While the learning process itself and while using electronically learning- and knowledge transfer systems the learners will be supported by special services. Focus is on the process of interconnection and integration of levels, knowledge network and user support, in a useful and efficient way for mutual advantage. This process will be described in this paper.

1 Diversity and Complexity of Knowledge Transfer

In the past, the learning and knowledge transfer processes were much simpler and uncomplicated than today. With the development of the industrial and later information and knowledge society the information flood was augmented by new means of media permitting to transfer information in higher volumes and with higher density. At least, the half-life period of validity of the existing knowledge decreases continuously. Therewith the learning process became a life-long procedure with a lot of different kinds of learning objects, knowledge transfer methods, means and technologies as well as multimedia and computer aided information systems. Briefly worded a diverse and very complex network of methods, systems, and tools to control the efficient transfer of knowledge and information was generated.

The approach of knowledge management and learning procedures related to the required competencies is characterised by several views e.g. social view as network of the participating partners with diverse competencies, technical view as technology driven, and infrastructural development of competencies. The complexity will be augmented not only by the different views, subjects, and relations of the solving

Please use the following format when citing this chapter:

Schumann, C-A., Tittmann, C. and Tittmann, S., 2008, in IFIP International Federation for Information Processing, Volume 281; *Learning to Live in the Knowledge Society*; Michael Kendall and Brian Samways; (Boston: Springer), pp. 149–152.

problem, but also by the required networks for the different kinds of services especially for knowledge sharing and transfer as well as knowledge workers and learners support [1].

2   Genesis of Competence Clusters for Knowledge Sharing

The growth of knowledge and competence is limited by the resources of the single organisation. Therefore, the development of networks of knowledge as well as networks of competence is forced by the scientific communities, the public organisations, and the private enterprises in order to generate the conditions for knowledge integration and sharing within the networks [2]. Knowledge management and engineering deal with the interconnectedness of particular information, and knowledge to complex, interconnected solutions in networks of competence. The competence networks and knowledge networks between organisations are precondition and enabler for knowledge transfer and knowledge sharing. In this context knowledge networks support inter-organisational cooperation and linking with external experts, associations, educational institutions for common knowledge application and diversification of the knowledge base [3]. Because of the ontological constitution of knowledge networks they are a suitable methodology for structuring, organising, and extending intra- and inter-organisational knowledge.

Knowledge sharing expatiates with the problem how to transfer collected knowledge into relevant organisational divisions and to initiate the lifelong learning process.

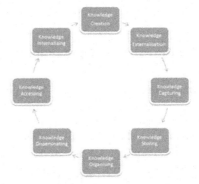

Fig. 1. Knowledge Sharing Lifecycle [4]

While the knowledge sharing lifecycle [3] the created knowledge will be externalised, structured, saved and organised. The knowledge base can be enhanced by external knowledge sources. Finally, this knowledge is – depending on authorisation - diffused inside the knowledge network and internalised by the users. This is premise for creating new knowledge and to continue or rather to iterate the lifecycle. For the creation of clusters of competence concepts the development of a knowledge base are necessary. Out of knowledge networks highly specialised competence and knowledge clusters can be developed and used for advancement of existing knowledge. Otherwise, existing competence clusters are able to be integrated into knowledge networks [1].

3   Class of Learners and its Access to the Knowledge

The ambition of a didactic strategy for e-learning is to arrange the learners to reach certain learning targets. However learners dispose of different attributes which aid or block the learning process [5]. Thus, the learners have to be classified [Fig1.].

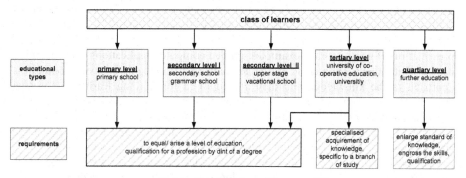

Fig. 2. Classification of Learners [6]

The requirements of learners of level schooling are basically consistent: own an equal level of education and get a qualification for a profession by dint of a degree. Learners of high level education aspire a specialised acquirement of knowledge by choosing a specific branch of study and by getting an academic degree. The level of further education includes lifelong learners, mostly learners in work life, who want to enlarge the standard of their knowledge. Concerning the previous knowledge, the learning contents have to be conceived according to this. [7] Another basic fact is the experiences with self-directed learning and the familiarity with diverse didactic methods or previous knowledge in diverse media. Different learners need different forms of learning instructions adjusted to their competencies. In all probability the scholars and first-year students are unversed in self-directed learning whereas students in higher semesters or active workers are able to deal with teaching material themselves. Homogeneity of learners eases the conception of the learning contents respectively the learning location [5]. All these described requirements of the learners provide a basis for requirements of an effective knowledge sharing. Ideally the learning content has to be developed in the level where it shall be used. Although the generated knowledge is available level comprehensive.

4   Merger of Knowledge Worker's Supply and Learner's Demands

A rough structuring in the framework of a systemic approach allows to pick up the main subsystems working together in order to provide the end user interface for e-education. Special main levels are essential for a successful, practical working of all the different kinds of systems and processes. They form a three level architecture for application of e-education.

The first level is composed of the e-platforms, computer-based training and web-based training systems, etc. as a first level backbone network from the users view.

The second level cooperation network is formed by the e-education specialists pushing the development and application of e-learning in the framework of competence clusters. The third level support network is characterised as user's support network including the personal services for the end users. Therefore, it is necessary to develop a special tutoring and coaching system. For this purpose experiences and knowledge of e-learning specialists are fundamental. All the experiences have to be assembled to one tutoring system which helps the learners in getting basic principles and particularly avoids typical beginner's mistakes of e-learning. The practical realisation is multi-level organised and contains primarily a presentation of good practice examples, guided computer applications and e-learning basics. With those competencies the learners of all categories have a boundless approach to the knowledge and they are qualified for lifelong learning. It is also important to ensure a permanent information flow between specialists and learners - organisational as well as technological in use of the e-learning platform. Thus, it is possible to integrate all levels to one consistently standard and assure knowledge sharing among the universities and beyond it. [8]

To realise a transparent and effective knowledge transfer, specialised competence and knowledge clusters have to be developed and linked to knowledge networks. Learners of all classes will be supported by special tutoring and coaching systems to have a boundless approach to these networks and therewith practice knowledge transfer while using electronically learning- and knowledge transfer systems. This offers the opportunity of lifelong learning to young and adult learners.

References

1. C.A. Schumann, C. Tittmann, Multilevel Cross-Linking and Offering of Organisational Knowledge. In: Martins, B., Remenyi, D.: Proceedings of the 8th European Conference on Knowledge Management (Volume Two). Barcelona. Reading: Academic Conferences. 2007. 878-883. (ISBN: 978-905305-52-0)

2. C.A. Schumann, C. Tittmann, J. Weber, E-Education Competence Cluster as Knowledge Transfer Hub in a Multilayer Architecture; Proceedings IT Towards Empowerment (ITE) International Conference 2007, Bangkok/Thailand, 2007.

3. M. Haun, Handbuch Wissensmanagement, Springer Verlag, Berlin/Heidelberg, 2002.

4. F. Kappe, Knowledge Management with the Hyperwave eKnowledge Infrastructure, White Paper, Hyperwave, 2001.

5. S. Walter, Blended Learning in der Hochschullehre, Rudolf Haufe Verlag, Freiburg i. Br., 2007.

6. Hochschule Zittau/ Görlitz (FH), Fachbereich Sprachen (March, 27, 2008); http://www.hs-zigr.de/~bgriebel/bildungswesen.gif, Quelle: Zahlenbarometer vom Bundesministerium für Bildung und Wissenschaft

7. M. Kerres, Multimediale und telemediale Lernangebote – Konzeption und Entwicklung, Oldenbourg Verlag, München, Wien, 1998.

8. C.A. Schumann, S. Tittmann, current results of research work in project "multilevel approach for last-mile-solutions supported by e-education competence clusters" at Zwickau university, 2007, 2008.

Development of Instruments for Evaluation of Quality of Distance Studies

Lina Tankeleviciene[1]
1 Siauliai University, Distance Education Study Centre,
Visinskio St. 15 a, LT-77156 Siauliai, Lithuania
linat@splius.lt

Abstract. The popularity of declaring quality assurance seems to be growing significantly in the last decade, including the field of distance studies and e-learning. Unfortunately, the implementation of quality assurance mechanisms on the operational level faces considerable problems. In this article we describe different conceptions of quality of distance studies, the stage of research and implementation of quality assurance in Lithuania, and especially at Siauliai University. We present analysis of two case studies where different methods of the evaluation of distance studies were used: 1) Expert evaluation can prove that distance studies meet posed requirements, and therefore is acceptable in the organization; 2) Students' questionnaires allow to investigate distance studies as a process. Also we present problems that arise while seeking to enhance developed instruments.

1   Introduction

New possibilities of distance learning also bring new risks and contradictions. For example: 1) Tailoring study programs to the individuals' needs highlights the differences in requirements of different groups of stakeholders; 2) The possibilities to develop study materials of high quality that are better structured and presented in different forms also require more investment in financial and human resources [1]. One of the aims of instructional design specialists in distance studies is to help to decrease the negative impact and to increase the positive impact of factors, mentioned above, among others. In order to achieve this aim, both scientific research and practical case studies in the real context are carried out.

The infrastructure of distance studies and the amount of distance study courses (DSC) have increased rapidly in Lithuania during the last decade [2]. Therefore, the problem of quality of distance studies becomes more topical. Higher education institutions have the biggest experience in the delivery of distance studies in Lithuania. The quality aspect in these studies, which are formal and supported by government, is of high importance.

Please use the following format when citing this chapter:

Tankeleviciene, L., 2008, in IFIP International Federation for Information Processing, Volume 281; *Learning to Live in the Knowledge Society*; Michael Kendall and Brian Samways; (Boston: Springer), pp. 153–156.

The aim of this paper is to analyse mechanisms for assurance of quality of distance studies implemented at Siauliai University and to propose recommendations for its enhancing.

2 Different Conceptions of the Quality of Distance Studies and its Evaluation Methods

The 'quality' concept is defined diversely [1, 3], for example: 1) The totality of features and characteristics of a product or service that bear on its ability to satisfy stated or implied needs; 2) Conformance to requirements; 3) Fitness to use. In the terms of quality management, distance studies must be considered as products, services and processes. Different strategies for measurement of different mentioned categories are supposed.

The quality of distance studies is not defined unambiguously in scientific literature. In order to assess, whether the particular case of distance studies is successful, we must know the its main purpose. It can be, for e.g., to decrease training period. The list of indicators for measurement depends on this purpose.

One of the major problems is to define criteria or indicators showing quality of distance studies. Different criteria lists are used, for e.g. 10 axes as in [4]: 1) Content; 2) ODL adaptation and integration; 3) User interface; 4) Use of technologies; 5) Interactivity with the instructional material; 6) Students' support; 7) Communication channel; 8) Acquisition of knowledge; 9) Projects and 'learning by doing'; 10) Assessment and self-assessment. Some of the criteria are not suitable for formal studies, for example: 1) Formal courses must not be 'Open to everybody', because it will bring some confusion over the activities dates, students' support, communication etc. If similar situation occurs, we duplicate courses and adapt one of them for self-learning with no responsibility. 2) 'Understandability of the instructional material' must be acceptable at the University level. Some of the criteria are difficult to achieve with the limits of budget and existing infrastructure. Different users' groups also formulate different needs for quality of distance studies.

Siauliai University was one of the first institutions in Lithuania to begin formalising DS quality assurance using internal documents. The Regulations on the preparation, accreditation and delivery of DSC were approved in the meeting of Commission for Accreditation of DSC at Siauliai University on March 9, 2004. The similar regulations in other institutions are: a) The temporal regulations for accreditation of materials of distance learning modules, prepared at Vilnius Gediminas Technical University; b) The model of quality for DSC material which is used by the Department of Science and Higher Education of the Ministry of Education and Science while organizing competitions for preparation of distance courses; c) The regulation for DSC accreditation, prepared in 2004 by Lithuanian Distance Network project and the Ministry of Education and Science. Janilionis [2] presents contribution towards quality assurance in other Lithuanian organizations.

On the background of the analysis of the mentioned documents, we can draw the conclusion that distance learning course is explored by expert as a static product, not as a process.

3 Procedures of Evaluation of DSC at Siauliai University

Two methods are used for quality evaluation in the domain of distance studies: expert evaluation and evaluation of final users. Here we briefly describe both methods, as they are applied at our University.

The Regulations on the preparation, accreditation and delivery of DSC consist of three parts: a) Requirements; b) Regulations on submitting of DSC for accreditation; c) Regulations on process of evaluation. The following groups of DSC evaluation criteria are used in the accreditation process: a) Information about the course; b) Structure of DSC; c) Content of DSC; d) Students' activities while working alone; e) Organization of evaluation; f) Representation form and design of learning materials. They are listed in the regulations, which are intended for DSC authors, and in the review form, which is intended for evaluators. The criteria are subdivided into separate concrete items, so called sub-criteria. An expert defines, whether the concrete item exists in the DSC. Further he/she draws a conclusion on appropriateness of the concrete criterion. Sub-criteria are used in order to avoid the narrow view on the structure of DSC and to support different teaching strategies.

The members of Commission for Accreditation of DSC are not experts in the subject domain. Therefore, the review from subject domain expert and propositions to delivery DSC from department and faculty must be presented to Commission. The accreditation procedure lets to avoid lecture notes, delivered electronically, treating as DSC. A DSC that was approved by the Commission for Accreditation of DSCs is acknowledged as a methodical aid published by an academic staff.

Despite of all advantages, limitations of the mentioned system can be seen: 1) Used technologies sometimes don't correspond to our present viewpoint on the methodology of distance learning, and confrontation between known best practices and real context arises. 2) The dominant educational aims are often changing. Therefore, documented regulation can come into conflict with new ideas. For example, requirement to assurance of enough quantity of prepared study material leads to demand of transferring information, rather than empowering student to learn. 3) The conclusions of experts are in some aspect subjective: in the ideal model, an evaluator must be an expert in the human-computer interaction domain and in the branch of course knowledge (for example, social sciences).

The conclusions of the experts don't empower us to decide unambiguously about the fitness of DSC, because DSC is not investigated as a process. For that purpose the empirical evaluation is conducted. The results of the study process are influenced not only by well prepared study material and support system, but also by readiness of students, learning competencies, advanced attitudes toward distance learning. Readiness of students and advanced attitudes were investigated by the author in 2001 and 2003 [6]; research has confirmed positive attitudes towards distance learning.

The attitudes of students towards delivered DSC are investigated by the initiative of lecturers at Siauliai University. The results of research are used locally. Usually the assessment of DSC is recorded using Likert scale and the main idea is to identify more important advantages and shortcomings. The following schema for the improvement of DSC was foreseen:
1. Formulation of shortcoming of DSC.

2. Matching of students' demands and requirements of organization:
   - Identifying the importance of characteristics of DSC for final user; identifying intensiveness and frequency of shortcomings.
   - Identifying technological tendencies, necessary technologies, educative tendencies, priorities of organization, aims and restrictions of study program or subject module, regulating documents.
3. Improvement of DSC.

This schema was used in surveys, conducted in 2005-2007. The different questionnaires were chosen, gaps in different aspects (course structure, support, etc.) were obtained and improvement directions for each DSC were highlighted.

4   Evaluation and Conclusion

Absence of common agreement on some strategies and main criteria for evaluation of quality of DSCs doesn't allow to achieve reliable and widely used results.

The competencies of an academic enable him/her to improve DSC from these aspects: study material for DSCs, methodology, planning of learning activities, solving technological problems. A DSC must be investigated as a heterogeneous object (product, service, and process) in the aspect of total quality management.

Expert evaluation can prove that DSC meets posed requirements, and therefore is acceptable in the organization. In order to gain high quality, formative and improvement-oriented evaluation mechanisms must be used rather than summative and expert based evaluation.

It is recommended for an academic, who seeks to improve DSCs: to obtain thorough students' opinion; strive to constructive critique; to use open questions in questionnaires – then the responses provide with more qualitative information.

References

1. J. P. Wilson (Editor), *Human Resource Development: Learning & Training for Individuals & Organizations* (Kogan Page, London, 2005).
2. J. Janilionis et al., Analysis of evaluation of quality of distance studies in Lithuanian and foreign institutions of higher education (in Lithuanian). Final report, made during executing project 'Creation of regulations for evaluation of quality of distance studies and its application', 2006.
3. P. Vanagas, *Total quality management* (Kaunas, Technologija, 2004).
4. A. Karoulis, A. Pombortsis, Heuristic Evaluation of Web-Based ODL Programs, in: Usability Evaluation of Online Learning Programs, edited by C. Shaoui (Information Science Publishing, London, UK, 2003).
5. Regulations on the preparation, accreditation and delivery of distance studies courses. Approved in the meeting of commission for accreditation of distance studies courses at Siauliai University (March 9, 2004); http://distance.su.lt.
6. L. Tankeleviciene, S. Turskiene, Research on attitudes towards distance learning, Pedagogika, No 69, 2003, pp. 223-229.

Knowledge Network Internetworking

Kirstin Schwidrowski
Universität Siegen, Institut für Didaktik der Informatik und E-Learning
Hölderlinstr. 3, 57076 Siegen, Germany
schwidrowski@die.informatik.uni-siegen.de,
WWW home page: http://www.die.informatik.uni-siegen.de

Abstract. The convergence of informatics systems and media systems has caused a lack of educational concepts for long-term knowledge. We assume that gaining informatics competencies enables adults to meet the demands of today's society. Therefore, didactics of informatics has to contribute educational concepts. In this paper, we introduce a strategy to structure the domain Internetworking. Aim of our research is to develop a Didactic System for Internetworking. By applying the presented strategy a knowledge network is constructed. It represents knowledge with an educational value for handling informatics systems as well as various possibilities of sequencing this knowledge for learning processes. Thereby, findings in informatics and didactics of informatics are considered. The knowledge network is improved by results of a case study. Dimensions of knowledge networks are informatics principles, knowledge level, application, and matter.

1 Media Upheaval and implications to Didactics of Informatics

Informatics systems and media systems have converged. Therefore, media usage has changed. As a result a lack in educational frameworks has emerged. Therefore, didactics of informatics contribute concepts. Research objective is development of an e-learning framework [1]. Thereby, we concentrate on the domain Internetworking. We regard its structure, communication, and information security.

In this paper, we present a strategy to structure learning processes for acquiring informatics knowledge regarding Internetworking. Thereby, we consider adult learners with no prior knowledge informatics and heterogeneous experience in handling informatics systems. A knowledge network is the result of applying the strategy. The network represents a structure of a domain from a didactic point of view. Arrangement of knowledge objects provides various learning sequences. Findings in informatics, didactic of informatics, and adult learning are considered to deduce sequence of learning matter.

Please use the following format when citing this chapter:

Schwidrowski, K., 2008, in IFIP International Federation for Information Processing, Volume 281; _Learning to Live in the Knowledge Society_; Michael Kendall and Brian Samways; (Boston: Springer), pp. 157–160.

2   Approaches for Structuring Learning Processes and Domain

Brinda and Schubert have introduced a Didactic System [2]. This educational framework combines a knowledge network, exercise classes, and exploration modules. We follow up this approach to deduce a Didactic System for Internetworking. Stechert has applied a learner-centred cognitive approach for improving informatics system understanding [3]. Observable behavior, internal structure, and implementation are characteristics of informatics systems. These characteristics structure the learning matter. Voß has proposed an educational concept for using standard software [4]. She has addressed adult learners. Her approach offers a cognitive access based on informatics modelling. Learners get to know the internal structure of a text or table document. This knowledge is combined with applying standard software. In our assumption, informatics knowledge enables to analyze, evaluate, and reflect functioning of informatics systems. In particular, learners know structure of Internet-based media systems, states of media processes, and the combination of both.

3   Learning Barriers

The design of an educational framework includes structuring of learning matter. At first, informatics principles with an educational value have been identified. Therefore, we have evaluated their relevance for Internet structure and processes. Two additional criteria have been generality and appropriate complexity. Identified informatics principles have been protocols, client-server model, and IP-addressing. Integrity, availability, and confidentiality are introduced as quality factors of an informatics system. During a case study several problems of using the Internet have been identified [1]. The result is summarized in Tab. 1. We have used it for deducing a strategy to structure the domain Internetworking.

	Problem
P_1	Domain specific terminology (e.g. client, server, html) is not understandable.
P_2	Basic IT-knowledge like working with common data formats is not known.
P_3	Explanations that are based on experience lack in integrity.
P_4	Informatics knowledge is restricted to specific software.
P_5	Personal benefit of learning informatics is not obvious.
P_6	No alternative learning matters are offered.
P_7	Learning objectives are not useful for ordinary computer users.

Table 1: Problems of using the Internet

4   Strategy for a Multi-Dimensional Knowledge Network

A knowledge network offers information about the intended learning outcome and the relation of knowledge within a domain. Criteria for generating a knowledge network are deduced and listed in Tab. 2.

	Requirement	Related Problems
R_1	Modeling alternative sequences of knowledge objects	P_6, P_7
R_2	Modeling optional knowledge objects	P_7
R_3	Modeling knowledge objects according to their intensity	P_1, P_2, P_3
R_4	Defining prior knowledge	P_1, P_2, P_3
R_5	Using prior experience more obvious	P_3, P_4, P_5, P_6
R_6	Reflecting individual experiences and learning goals	P_6, P_7

Table 2: Requirements for refining knowledge network structure

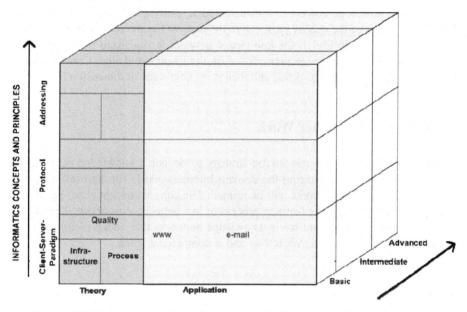

Fig 1. Multi-dimensional knowledge network 'internetworking'

We address elements of a knowledge network as knowledge objects. A knowledge object is a combination of an intended learning outcome and a domain specific location. The location is determined by dimensions *informatics principle* (IP), *knowledge level* (KL), *application* (A), and *matter* (M). Dimension IP explains basic structures and processes of the Internet. Dimension KL deals with complexity (see R_3). Three levels are suggested: basic, intermediate, and advanced. The basic level emphasizes on terminology since this is a precondition for understanding (see R_4). The intermediate level addresses handling with informatics systems under regular circumstances. The advanced level offers additional, not mandatory knowledge (see R_2, R_6). The dimension A assigns either a certain application (e.g. World Wide Web, email, groupware) or theory to every knowledge object. Thereby, theoretical aspect offers an abstraction of concrete applications of an informatics principle. It helps to transfer knowledge. The practical aspect exemplifies the theoretical knowledge by real life applications. This supports goal-oriented learning (see R_6). The dimension matter reflects the problem that informatics systems are very complex such that is very difficult to analyze and evaluate them. Every informatics system has a structure. That is a static perspective. An informatics system is included in processes. This is a dynamic perspective. At least informatics systems are used in a specific context. According to it, they can be evaluated. Therefore, quality factors or preconditions have to be known.

A sequence of knowledge objectives is defined by the following rules. Regarding dimension IP, the default sequence is (1) client-server model, (2) protocols, and (3) addressing. Dimension KL has a fixed order. If a learner has already reaches a knowledge objective of basic or intermediate level, it can be omitted. All advanced knowledge objects are optional. A learner can decide whether to start with a theoretical or a practical knowledge object (see R_5) at dimension A. But they are mandatory. The sequence of knowledge objects in dimension M is partly given. Before handling a knowledge object of the quality perspective the ones of the structure and the process have to be handled. In Fig. 1, the knowledge network is visualized by a cube. The initial points of the knowledge network are on the lower, front side. Learners cross this cube from there to the backside and then up to next stage of dimension IP.

5   Remarks on Further Work

In this paper, we have presented a strategy to deduce a knowledge network. It puts the emphasis on structuring the domain Internetworking. In the next step, the concept of knowledge networks will be refined. The current concept either results in a representation of a specific learning process or in a large, confusing one. Therefore, we will introduce macro and micro knowledge networks that address learning outcomes at the level of learning objectives and at competence level.

References

[1]   K. Schwidrowski, Introducing Internetworking in Vocational Training, in: Proceeding of the IFIP Joint Working Conference iTET2007 "Information Technologies for Education and Training 2007", edited by C. Abbott and Z. Lustigova (ETIC, Prague, 2007), pp.154 - 161.
[2]   T. Brinda and S. Schubert, Didactic System for object-oriented modeling, in: Proceedings of networking the learner/Computers in education, edited by D. Watson and J. Andersen (Kluwer, Boston, 2002), pp. 473 - 482.
[3]   P. Stechert, Informatics system comprehension: A learner-centered cognitive approach to networked thinking, in: Education and Information Technologies 11(3) "Imagining the future for ICT and education", edited by B. Munro and D. Watson (Springer Netherlands, Dordrecht, 2006), pp. 305 - 318.
[4]   S. Voß, Informatic Models in Vocational Training for Teaching Standard Software, in: Proceedings of ISSEP 2005 „Informatics for Secondary Schools - Evolution and Perspectives: From Computer Literacy to Informatics Fundamentals", edited by R. Mittermeir, (Klagenfurt, 2005), pp. 145 - 155.

Chapter 7

ICT Issues in Education

Virtual Learning Communities: a learning object integrated into e-learning platform

Patricia Alejandra Behar, Ana Paula Frozi de Castro e Souza
and Maira Bernardi

Education College – Federal University of Rio Grande do Sul (UFRGS)
Av. Paulo Gama, 110 – 90.046-900 – Porto Alegre – RS – Brazil
{pbehar, mairaber}@terra.com.br, nanafrozi@yahoo.com.br
home page: http://www.nuted.edu.ufrgs.br

Abstract. COMVIA (COMunidades VIrtuais de Aprendizagem – in portuguese language, is a learning object that cares about virtual learning communities based on standard interaction. In this paper we describe the final results of this study highlighting the ways in which the students interact through the COMVIA object in e-learning situations. Also present in the article are the main characteristics of a learning objects and how it can be integrated into a virtual platform.

1 Introduction

The present article is a reflection upon the theoretical references of the learning object COMVIA[1], its building steps and its application for tests and validation in a post graduate[2] discipline that has resulted in the formation of virtual learning communities. It is an object about Virtual Learning Communities, the use of COMVIA in the afore mentioned discipline was precisely to check the level of the object resources in relation to these requirements. It was used in the Federal University of Rio Grande do Sul, Brazil, in the graduate and post graduate courses of the Education College. It was integrated in the virtual learning environment called ROODA[3] used by this institution.

---

[1] Available in: http://www.nuted.edu.ufrgs.br/instrumentalizacao_em _ead/comvia
[2] Discipline SA: Oficinas Virtuais de Aprendizagem - in post graduate level in Education and Computer Education throughout 2007/1.
[3] Rede cOOperativa de Aprendizagem – distant learning education platform from UFRGS. Available in: www.ead.ufrgs.br/rooda

---

Please use the following format when citing this chapter:

Behar, P.A., Frozi de Castro e Souza, A.P. and Bernardi, M., 2008, in IFIP International Federation for Information Processing, Volume 281;
Learning to Live in the Knowledge Society; Michael Kendall and Brian Samways; (Boston: Springer), pp. 163–166.

2   The Learning Object COMVIA

In this study, Learning Object is understood as any digital resource such as: texts, animations, videos, images, applications, Web pages combined. Its utilization is aimed at learning situations, either distant or presential. According to LTSC[4], these can be defined by any entity, digital or non digital, that can be utilized, re-utilized or referenciated during technology-mediated learning.

COMVIA is a Learning Object about virtual learning communities based on interactionist premises. This tool fosters students'active participation in the construction of knowledge and cognitive development. Its utilization is aimed at learning situations, either presential or distant.

COMVIA was developed in four main phases: project concept, planning, implementation and evaluation, observing necessary criteria for the development of learning projects as defined by Amante & Morgado [1]. These phases are: (1) Project Idea, when the project, key lines and intended applications were defined following the groups´ initial idea. (2) In the Planning phase research was made for its development, the study of storyboard and navigation paths due to its non-linear structure. (3) The implementation phase refers to the development per se, where the programming tool to be used is defined and the first prototypes of the object are elaborated until they reach their final version. (4) In the Evualution phase, were perform tests to verify the functionality of the object. COMVIA was finalized with eight resources. Among COMVIA resources are: Base Theories, Contents, Challenge Bank, COMVIA TV, Library, COMVIA guide, Glossary and Help.

3   Validation of COMVIA in post graduate level through a long distance education platform

Throughout 2007/1, COMVIA was piloted in SA discipline: Virtual Learning Workshops, in the Computer Education Science and the Education post graduate courses at UFRGS. This discipline covers a multi disciplinar area of knowledge that integrates Digital Technology with Education, innovative in the use it makes of distant learning environments. The objective of this discipline is the study through workshops to be carried out in the virtual learning environment ROODA. In such post graduate discipline, students had contact with COMVIA through the workshop about Virtual Learning Communities. Therefore, the students were, at the beginning, invited to explore the resources of Learning Object, among them Base Theories, Contents, Library and Glossary. All the activities were carried out with the support of the virtual learning environment ROODA, using the Forum, Webfolio, Diary, Class, Chat, Groups and A2 tools. There were four meetings, three of them presential and one virtual, a total of 20 hours.

---

[4] Learning Technology Standards Committee - http://ltsc.ieee.org/wg12

3.1 Integrating COMVIA object and ROODA platform

Workshops were structured so that the learning object COMVIA could present its contents and challenges to participants in a dynamic and interactive way, through challenges, videos, texts and links. ROODA virtual environment was used so students could have a place to carry out their interactions. Experience exchange and interaction among students were encouraged during the discussions about the themes being worked on, through the ROODA environment.

During the presential classes, aspects regarding the conception, creation and pedagogical implications of virtual learning communities in different educational contexts were discussed. In the virtual meeting, students met online, using the ROODA environment in order to solve the challenges assigned.

The challenges were carried out in groups. The students needed to meet virtually or face-to-face out of class time. This necessity made it possible for these students to constitute a virtual space with their groups, through the environment ROODA that resulted in the constitution of collective spaces among participants. It was possible to observe, thus, the formation of virtual learning communities within the group to carry out the challenges that were proposed.

3.2 Why integrate DL platforms and learning objects?

The use of a distant learning platform integrated with the learning object was paramount for synchronous and assynchronous interaction among students, through the functionalities it offers. This way, during the class period, several themes/challenges made available by the learning object were discussed and collective spaces were created, allowing for cooperative work. Such endeavor made it possible to observe the actual experience of a learning community among participants during the workshops. Interaction is a dialectical and complex process of exchange and of meanings from which subject and object change [2]. In this perspective, action becomes the exchange instrument, and knowledge is built through schemes and coordinated actions. The subject is understood as a totality constituted by internal factors (maturation) and external factors (environment). Such interactive process allowed the students themselves to be mediators of their learning, learning through a cooperative process [3].

Hence, as a result of the application of this learning object through ROODA environment, students (and support team) created a moment of reflection and of knowledge production about the concepts of virtual learning communities, registered throughout the production and elaboration processes, published by the groups.

The concept of communities was developed through the COMVIA object and it presents communities as a group of subjects that establish interdependent relationships, within a complex social framework, with specific and individualizing characteristics [5]. The Virtual Learning Communities set themselves as electronic networks of interactive communication, organized round a mutual project. They constitute themselves from common knowledge interests, shared goals and exchange values, established through a cooperative process. The formation of such networks could be observed in the course, as well as its maintenance for study of new contents. According to Paloff e Pratt [2], the community is the vehicle through which learning occurs. As a result, it was also necessary to promote autonomy, initiative and creativity of each group, so that a sense of belonging to the community could be observed by participants of the discipline.

Because of its non-linear character, the object contributed for actions that did not take certain pathways determined a priori, observing linearity but built upon connections, additions, what Lemos [4] defines as a "stroll through cybernetic space". It is understood that this adequation encompasses the formation of a concept about the actions that were taken. The intended goal was not to have the students do the activities using the tools of the environment but that they expressed their awareness about their actions.

In this perspective, we could observe that the students dealt with the information available in the object as their own, through the experiences exchanged throughout the period the class was going on. This was possible because they themselves formed virtual learning communities with the support of ROODA's functionalities.

4   Final Considerations

To conclude we can say that integration between the learning object COMVIA and the platform ROODA made interaction possible among students of the workshop, constituting a collectivity among them. Such collectivity culminated with the formation of virtual communities that could be observed throughout the presential and long distance meetings, resulting in good quality final productions by the groups.

Thus COMVIA is a tool to be used by teachers in their formative process, students and other web users. It is believed that the object can help the theoretical and practical instrumentalization of its subject matter, through different technological resources that can be employed in different areas of knowledge. For this matter, the object was published in the CESTA[5] repository of learning objects. Such repository allows for publication and reutilization of learning objects by any user in any course.

References

1. Amante, Lúcia. Morgado, Lina. (2001) "Metodologia de concepção e desenvolvimento de aplicações educativas: o caso dos materiais hipermídia". In: Discursos. Lisboa, Portugal. [III Série, número especial]: 27-44, junho.
2. Behar, P. A. ; Leite, Silvia Meirelles ; Bordini, Sandra ; Souza, Lúcia Barros De ; Siqueira, Luciano Goularte (2007b). Avaliação de Ambientes Virtuais de Aprendizagem: O Caso do ROODA na UFRGS. Revista Avances en Sistemas e Informática, v. 4, p. 81-100,
3. Duran, David; Vidal, Vinyet. (2007) Tutoria: aprendizagem entre iguais: da teoria à prática. Tradução Ernani Rosa. – Porto Alegre: Artmed.
4. Lemos, André. (2002) "Cibercultura: tecnologia e vida social na cultura contemporânea". Porto Alegre: Sulina.
5. Paloff, Rena M. e Pratt, Keith. (2002) "Construindo comunidades de aprendizagem, no ciberespaço: estratégias eficientes para salas de aula on-line". Porto Alegre: Artmed.

---

[5] Available in: http://www.cinted.ufrgs.br/CESTA

The development of ICT networks for South African schools
Two pilot studies in disadvantaged areas

Ingrid Siebörger [1], Alfredo Terzoli [1], and Cheryl Hodgkinson-Williams
[1] Computer Science Department, Rhodes University
Grahamstown. South Africa, 6139 [i.sieborger,a.terzoli]@ru.ac.za
WWW home page: http://www.cs.ru.ac.za
[2] Education Department, Rhodes University
Grahamstown. South Africa, 6139 chodgkinsonwilliams@gmail.com

Abstract. Information and Communication Technologies (ICTs) are increasingly considered valuable tools in education, promoting the development of higher cognitive processes and allowing teachers and learners access to a plethora of information. This paper reports on two pilot studies conducted in South Africa in proto-typical previously disadvantaged schools and their surrounding communities. Each pilot study deployed a local loop network within impoverished communities, connecting schools to one another and central services such as email and voice communications. The benefits of these networks were that teachers, learners and the local community had access to information, and communication and collaboration channels, providing potential test beds for investigating the use of computers as mind tools.

1. Introduction

Computers can be used in education as cognitive tools, or what Jonassen [1] calls Mindtools. For computers to be used as effective knowledge construction tools, networking of computers is essential, organizing them in local area networks (LAN) as well as connecting them to the Internet [2, 3, 4]. Cornu maintains that networking within the school will result in a change from the old form where knowledge circulated from the teacher to the learners, to a networked form where both learners and teachers are involved in the knowledge process and work together to generate knowledge and ideas via access to different resources such as libraries and the Internet [3]. This transformation is problematic in all institutions of formal learning, but is much more so in an environment such as the "previously disadvantaged" schools in South Africa where relations are steeply hierarchical and the separation between "teaching" and "learning" appears very strong. Besides, before we can realise the effects of the introduction of networked computers as tools of transformation, we need to build the physical infrastructure that is absent in large parts of South Africa.

Please use the following format when citing this chapter:

Siebörger, I., Terzoli, A. and Hodgkinson-Williams, C., 2008, in IFIP International Federation for Information Processing, Volume 281; *Learning to Live in the Knowledge Society*; Michael Kendall and Brian Samways; (Boston: Springer), pp. 167–170.

2. Computer networks in South African schools

The e-Education White paper [5], published in 2004, revealed that of the 6300 schools in the Eastern Cape 8.8% had computers, while only 4.5% deployed computers for teaching and learning purposes. The White paper expressed the objective that "Every teacher and learner in General and Further Education and Training must have access to an educational network and the Internet" [5, p 24]. In order for such a goal to be realised in the Eastern Cape there would need to be a substantial roll-out of ICT facilities to all the schools in the province.. An ICT roll-out of this nature would require substantial financial assistance from the South African government and executed according to a carefully devised plan.

As there is not much information available about building computer networks within poorly resourced schools and communities, a pilot study was undertaken in two disadvantaged areas in the Eastern Cape. The first pilot takes place in the township of Grahamstown where the schools and the community are located in an peri-urban area, with basic general infrastructure, such as electricity, sanitation, telephone lines and road networks. The second pilot takes place in Dwesa, a deep rural, semi-marginalised community located on the Wild Coast in the former Transkei homeland of the Eastern Cape, which generally lacks basic facilities [11].

3. The Grahamstown schools' ICT network

Since its inception in 1998, the Rhodes University Telkom Centre of Excellence in the Computer Science Department has been conducting research into cost effective last mile Internet access solutions. One of the aims has been the identification of solutions that would be affordable and sustainable for previously disadvantaged schools. This research has included Digital Subscriber Lines (DSL) type connections [4, 6], WiFi (IEEE 802.11b/g) connections [4, 7, 8], and WiMAX (IEEE 802.16a) connections [9, 10], all with promising results. In the Grahamstown district in the Eastern Cape of South Africa, the Telkom CoE has built a local loop network which connects schools in the area to one another and shared resources and consists of these multiple technologies. This education local loop connects the schools to the Rhodes University network in such a way that each school is part of the greater Rhodes network. Each school then has access to central services housed on Rhodes campus such as email, Voice over IP (VoIP) and the Internet.

4. The Dwesa ICT Network

The Dwesa network employs WiMAX technologies only in local loop education network, which connects all the schools in the project to the shared Internet connection (via VSAT from Telkom) and to central services such as VoIP. This project is a joint venture between the Telkom CoEs at Rhodes University and the University of Fort Hare respectively. The original objective of the project was to develop and field-test the prototype of a simple, cost-effective and robust, integrated e-business/telecommunication platform, to deploy in marginalized and semi-marginalized communities in South Africa, where a large number (42.5%) of the South African population live. The project has evolved into an experiment on the adaptation of the Internet to rural areas in South Africa, based on the deployment of ICTs in schools, which together realise a distributed access network [12].

5. Recommendations and lessons learned

Both the networks in Grahamstown and Dwesa serve the school communities by firstly allowing them the opportunity to share commonly required resources, such as Internet connections and computer servers which run commonly required central services such as email and VoIP. Secondly the networks allow the teachers and learners to collaborate with one another through communication channels such as email, VoIP and chat programs. Thirdly, the schools, can share the cost of one or perhaps two technicians to support and maintain the network [4].

Thus far in both projects we have seen a keen uptake of ICTs among teachers and learners at the various schools. Besides the perception of a more critical engagement with knowledge among the various school actors, which is currently difficult to quantify, there have been noticeable practical effects of the introduction of ICT in Grahamstown and Dwesa First, learners involved in the Grahamstown project have entered into tertiary education institutions, still a very rare event here, with one notable student achieving a 90% aggregate in his first year at Rhodes University. In addition, we have also begun to see the teachers use the ICT facilities to break down traditional hierarchies and to start to engage with computers as thinking tools. One teacher from Grahamstown used the ICT facilities to this end through the Global teenager project allowing learners to interact and learn with others from around the world. This eventually resulted in some of the learners winning the competition and being provided the opportunity to travel to Italy, an experience they would never otherwise have had. While, in Dwesa, one of the primary schools involved in the project has been extended into senior school and has been selected within the province to take part in a new e-learning programme.

Lessons learned throughout both pilot studies include the importance of champion teachers; ICT literate teaching staff and ICT training; good leadership by the principal; and community engagement at all levels, which seems to encourage ownership and lead to sustainability [13]. From the benefits we have seen in both the Grahamstown and the Dwesa schools we propose that a local loop networks be built in each district that will connect all schools in the district to one another and central services. Central services would include email, web services, domain name systems (DNS), proxy services, voice over IP (VoIP) services and videoconferencing.

6. Conclusion

In this paper we reported on the deployment of two local loop networks in South Africa in proto-typical, previously disadvantaged schools and their surrounding communities, one peri-urban and the other rural. Each network connected schools to one another and central services. The benefit of these networks is that teachers, learners and the local community have access to information, communication and collaboration channels. These network deployments will progressively expand; have constructed test beds for the potential exploration of using computers as Mind tools. Without the deployment of these networks and facilities to schools within South Africa we can not even begin to ask how ICTs can be used to engage learners in critical thinking.

7. References

[1]   D. H. Jonassen, C. Carr, and H.-P. Yueh, "Computers as Mindtools for Engaging Learners in Critical Thinking," *TechTrends*, vol. 43, no. 2, pp. 24-32, 1998.

[2]   C.-C. Tsai, "A review and discussion of Epistomological Commitments, Metacognition, and Critical Thinking with suggestions on their enhancement in Internet-assisted Chemistry classrooms," *Journal of Chemical Education*, vol. 78, no. 7, p. 970.

[3]   B. Cornu, *World Year Book of Education 2004: Digital Technology, Communities and Education - Chapter2: Networking and collective intelligence for teachers and learners*, A. Brown and N. Davis, Eds. Routledge Falmer, London and New York, 2004.

[4]   I. Brandt, "Models of Internet connectivity for secondary schools in the Grahamstown Circuit," Master's thesis, Rhodes University, Jan. 2006.

[5]   Department of Education, "White Paper on e-Education: Transforming learning and teaching through Information and Communication Technologies," Sept. 2004.

[6]   G. A. Halse and A. Terzoli, "Open Source in South African Schools: Two Case Studies," in *Highway Africa Conference*, 2002. [Online]. Available: http://mombe.org/%7Eguy/papers/highway-africa-2002/HALSE-Highway-Africa-2002.pdf

[7]   I. Brandt, A. Terzoli, and C. Hodgkinson-Williams, "Wireless Communication for Previously Disadvantaged Secondary Schools in Grahamstown, South Africa," in *SATNAC 2005, Convergence - Can technology deliver?*, Sept. 2005. [Online]. Available: http://ings.rucus.net/Brandt.pdf

[8]   I. Brandt, A. Terzoli, and C. Hodgkinson-Williams, "Wi-Fi as a last mile access technology and The Tragedy of the Commons," ISBN 978-1-4020-6265-0 Innovative Algorithms and Techniques in Automation, Industrial Electronics and Telecommunications. Springer, 2007, pp. 175-180.

[9]   I. Siebörger and A. Terzoli, "Field testing the Alvarion BreezeMAX as a last mile access technology," Sept. 2007.

[10]   P. Beyleveld, "Deployment and Testing of WiMAX Wireless Network Technology," Computer Science Honours thesis, Rhodes University, Grahamstown, South Africa, 2006.

[11]   R. Palmer, H. Timmermans, and D. Fay, *From Conflict to Negotiation: Nature-based development on the South African Wild Coast*. Pretoria: HSRCPress, 2002.

[12]   M. Thinyane, L. Dalvit, A. Terzoli, and P. Clayton, "The Internet in rural communities: unrestricted and contextualized," Submitted to *the International Conference on Distributed Computing and Internet Technology, Bangalore, INDIA*, 2007

[13]   C. Hodgkinson-Williams, I. Siebörger, and A. Terzoli, Enabling and constraining ICT practice in secondary schools: case studies in South Africa, *International Journal of Knowledge and Learning*, 3(2/3), p171 – 190.

Supporting Teachers to Plan Culturally Contextualized Learning Activities

Ap. Fabiano Pinatti de Carvalho, Junia C. Anacleto, Vania P. de Almeida
Neris
Advanced Interaction Laboratory (LIA)
Department of Computing - Federal University of São Carlos (DC/UFSCar)
Rod Washington Luis, Km 235 – São Carlos – SP – 13565-905
{fabiano, junia, vania}@dc.ufscar.br
+55 16 3351-8618

Abstract. This paper presents PACO-T, a common sense-aided computational tool that helps teachers on planning culturally contextualized learning activities supported by common sense knowledge. The tool is based on the framework PACO, a seven-step framework for planning learning activities that concerns pedagogical issues, for an effective learning. It implements the framework seven steps and makes available common sense knowledge from the Brazilian Open Mind Common Sense (OMCS-Br) knowledge base, so that teachers can analyze how people with the same profile of their target group talk about themes related to the learning activity which is being planned, and therefore possibly identify the target group's previous knowledge and contextualize the learning activity to its needs. In this way teachers can approach themes which they consider relevant to reach the intended pedagogical goals with that specific target group.

1 Introduction

In order to reach effective learning, it is important to take into account pedagogical issues during the planning of learning activities with the purpose of offering learners conditions to build and acquire new knowledge. Concerning Learning Theories of renowned authors, it can be noticed the importance of contextualizing learning activities to the target group's previous knowledge in order to make possible knowledge retention [4]. Here it is considered as target group the learners who participate of the learning activity or the members of the social group with whom the learners are going to interact in order to apply the knowledge acquired during the learning activity.

Although several authors, such as [3] and [6], mentioned the importance of considering the learning activity target group previous knowledge in the learning

Please use the following format when citing this chapter:

de Carvalho, A.F.P., Anacleto, J.C. and de Almeida Neris, V.P., 2008, in IFIP International Federation for Information Processing, Volume 281; *Learning to Live in the Knowledge Society*; Michael Kendall and Brian Samways; (Boston: Springer), pp. 171–174.

process, until early 2006, it was not possible to find in the literature how teachers could assess it easily. However, recent researches have shown that common sense knowledge, i.e. the knowledge people acquire since their childhood, considered as truth in the cultural environment where they are inserted into, can be used to state the target group's previous knowledge and to identify its needs [4] [5] [2]. Therefore, we have been investigating how computational technology can make possible the use of common sense to plan learning activity, taking into account the importance of contextualizing the learning activity to the target group's needs in order to reach pedagogical issues. As common sense knowledge expresses cultural knowledge [1], it is considered that learning activities planned based on it is culturally contextualized.

The paper is organized as follows: section 2 presents PACO, the framework for planning learning activities which PACO-T is based on; section 3 presents PACO-T; finally, section 4 presents some conclusion remarks and points to future works.

2   The Framework PACO and Common Sense

PACO is a framework designed to support teachers on the **P**lanning of Learning **A**ctivities supported by **CO**mputers, which is composed by seven steps [8]: (1) define the learning activity theme, target public and general goal; (2) organize the learning activity topics; (3) choose a pedagogical/methodological reference; (4) plan the learning tasks; (5) choose computer tools to support the tasks execution; (6) edit the learning objects which are going to be used in the learning activity; (7) test pedagogical and technological issues.

PACO has already been used by teachers from different areas such as computer science, nursing and occupational therapy. One of the learning activities planned by nursing professionals using PACO was specially proposed to analyze the possibility of using common sense knowledge during the planning of learning activities, in order to contextualize them to the target group's needs. For details on the case study that show how common sense knowledge can help teachers answer questions which they face with along the framework seven steps so that they can contextualize the learning activity planning to their target group needs see [4] and [5].

3   PACO-T

Based on the requirements elicitation performed during the planning of the case study learning activity, it was possible to design PACO-T. This tool maps the questions which teachers should answer during the planning of a learning activity, according to PACO proposal, and offers teachers access to the common sense knowledge stored in the OMCS-Br knowledge base, so that teachers can use common sense as it was previously discussed. For this purpose, the tool uses the semantic networks and the API (Application Program Interface) provided by OMCS-Br.

PACO-T has seven steps, as the framework on which it is based, which should be performed in order to get a learning activity planned. The first thing that should be done in PACO-T when a new learning activity planning starts is to define the learning activity target group's profile and, consequently, tell the system to which ConceptNet it should connect. ConceptNet is the name given to the semantic networks of OMCS projects. This name was first used in the American OMCS project [7] and later it was adopted by OMCS-Br [1]. Both projects adopt semantic networks to represent the knowledge collected in natural language in the project web site.

In OMCS-Br, there are several ConceptNets. This is because the Brazilian project offers the possibility of generating a ConceptNet to each combination of the profile parameters (age group, gender, geographical location and education level), allowing the system to use only the common sense knowledge collected from people who fit to the target group's profile. Figure 1 presents an interface of PACO that brings common sense knowledge support. In this interface, teachers should define the learning activity theme and justification. On the right in the interface, it can be seen the common sense support available in this step. As it was discussed in section 3, teachers can use this knowledge in this sub-step to answer the questions that they face with.

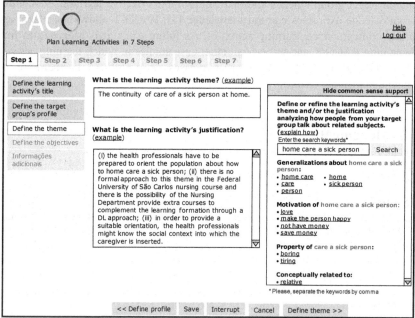

Figure 1. PACO-T Step 1 – Define the theme

In order to analyze how people talk about subjects of interest, teachers have to provide some keywords in the search text field and click on the button "Search". Doing that, the system retrieves the context related to the keywords provided and presents the related common sense knowledge expressed in the ConceptNet in the common sense support box.

The common sense support box is always presented when there is the possibility of teachers to decide something based on this kind of knowledge. By following the steps of the computational representation of PACO, answering the questions presented in each step and exploring the available common sense knowledge, teachers can plan their learning activities taking into account pedagogical issues and fit it to their target group needs. It is worth pointing out that teachers can go back to steps that they have already passed, modify their answers, interrupt a planning and resume it in another moment or even cancel a planning already started. At the end, teachers can export the learning activity plan to text format so that they can print it.

4 Conclusions and Future works

This paper has presented PACO-T, a computational tool to support PACO, a framework to plan learning activities following pedagogical principles. The tool aims to support teachers on planning learning activities, taking into account the seven steps defined in PACO. For that, it was performed a study about what information teachers should provide in each step in order to build up the learning activity plan. Moreover, it was performed a case study which allowed to identify how common sense knowledge can be useful to teachers in order to help them to answer some questions that are inherent in learning activity planning.

With PACO-T, it is intended to make the task of planning learning activities easier for teachers and to give teachers conditions for planning learning activities that fit to their target group's needs and that can promote effective learning. As common sense knowledge expresses cultural knowledge [1], PACO-T allows the planning of culturally contextualized learning activities. As future work, it is proposed to finish implementing PACO-T and to perform other case studies in which learning activities should be planned using the tool in order to assess its usefulness. Furthermore, it is also intended to apply usability tests in the tool.

Acknowledgments
We thank FAPESP and CAPES for partially support this project.

References
1. Anacleto, J. C.; Lieberman, H.; Tsutsumi, M.; Neris, V. P. A.; Carvalho, A. F. P.; Espinosa, J.; Zem-Mascarenhas, S.; Godoi, M. S. Can common sense uncover cultural differences in computer applications?. In *Artificial Intelligence in Theory and Practice – WCC 2006*, vol. 217, Bramer, M. (Ed). Berlin: Springer-Verlag, 2006. p. 1-10.

2. Anacleto, J. C.; Godoi, M. S.; Carvalho, A. F. P. de; Lieberman, H. L. A Common Sense-Based On-line Assistant for Training Employees. In: *Proc. INTERACT 2007,* Rio de Janeiro – Brazil. Heidelberg: Spring-Verlag , LNCS 4662, 2007, p. 243-255.

3. Ausubel, D.P. *Psicología educativa:* un punto de vista cognoscitivo. Mexico: Editorial Trillas, 1976. /in Spanish/

4. Carvalho, A. F. P. de; Anacleto, J. C.; Zem-Mascarenhas, S. Planning Learning Activities Pedagogically Suitable by Using Common Sense Knowledge. In: Proc of the 16th International Conference on Computing, 2007, Mexico City - Mexico. p. 1-6.

5. Carvalho, A. F. P. de; Anacleto, J. C.; Zem-Mascarenhas, S. . Learning Activities on Health Care Supported by Common Sense Knowledge. In: *Proc. of 23rd SAC*, 2008, Fortaleza – Brazil. New York: ACM Press, 2008 p. 1385-1389.

6. Freire, P. Pedagogia da autonomia: saberes necessários à prática educativa. 31 ed. São Paulo: Paz e Terra, 1996. /in Portuguese/

7. Liu, H.; Singh P. ConceptNet: a practical commonsense reasoning toolkit. *BT Technology Journal*, v. 22, n. 4, p. 211-226, 2004.

8. Neris, V. P. A.; Anacleto, J. C; Zem-Mascarenhas, S. Z.; Carvalho, A. F. P. de PACO - A Framework for Planning Learning Activities Supported by Computers. In *Proc. of the 18th Brazilian Symposium on Informatics and Education (SBIE 2007)*, 2007, São Paulo – Brazil. Porto Alegre: SBC, 2007. p. 597-606.

The Web as a learning environment
Focus on contents vs. focus on the search process

Francesco Caviglia[1,2] and Maria Ferraris[1]
[1] CNR- Institute for Educational Technology, Via De Marini 6, 16149 Genova, Italy
[2] Ph.D. student at Doctoral School in Education and Learning Sciences, Ca' Foscari University, Venezia, Italy
{caviglia,ferraris}@itd.cnr.it,
WWW home page: http://www.itd.cnr.it

Abstract. The Web is typically used, in educational settings, as a repository of contents to be learned. Within this approach, the Web-searching process tends to be perceived merely as an obstacle on the way to the contents. This paper suggests instead that searching the Web requires information problem solving competences which are in themselves key requisites for literacy in a knowledge society and deserve to be fostered as explicit goals in educational settings. Given the complexity of the competences involved, it is suggested that educational intervention focus on practice with information problems which should be thin in content, but rich in opportunities for bringing to the foreground some critical areas of the information problem solving process.

1 Introduction

If one takes into account the most widespread metaphors of the Web [1], at least of the Web 1.0 which is the focus of this paper, two main patterns emerge. The first corresponds to a focus on the information contained in the Web, and considers the Web as a *container*, a *virtual library*, an *encyclopedia*. It is a static and tangible view, which gives value to the *places* one can arrive at, and to the quality of the information they deliver. A second cluster of metaphors corresponds instead to a more dynamic and abstract view of the Web as a *space for traveling*. In this case, not just the destination places are valued, but rather the *paths* one walks to reach them, and the quality of the journey.

In considering how the Web can be used in educational settings, the container or library metaphor corresponds to a focus on the *contents* the learner is required to access. From this point of view, learning how to move through information to reach a goal is indeed important, but only as a prerequisite for accessing valuable contents. Therefore, teachers often choose to provide the learner with a list of pre-selected

Please use the following format when citing this chapter:

Caviglia, F. and Ferraris, M., 2008, in IFIP International Federation for Information Processing, Volume 281; *Learning to Live in the Knowledge Society*; Michael Kendall and Brian Samways; (Boston: Springer), pp. 175–178.

websites, to spare time or to prevent bad encounters on the Web. Such a protective attitude, however, fails to promote the learner's ability to find her/his way around and to develop her/his own maps and connections. To foster autonomy, it is necessary instead to shift focus from the *contents* to the *processes* activated by the learner in conjunction with the task of solving an information problem on the Web; that is, to shift from the *web-as-container* to the *web-as-space-for-traveling* metaphor.

Research on Web searching suggests that information problem solving on the Web is a complex, highly dynamic process, under the influence of factors such as the user's familiarity with the Web, her/his cognitive style, motivation, perseverance, as well as her/his prior knowledge on the topic and the type of problem [2, 3 and others that can not be mentioned due to space constraints]. Knowing the way search engines operate and the way information is organized on the Web seem no warrant that a user will be successful in solving information problems: several experiences of educational intervention ([4], Kuiper, Volman and Terwel in [5], Walraven, Brand-Gruwel and Boshuizen in [5]) suggest indeed that learning the technicalities of the Web should go hand in hand with the development of the broader competences, strategies and attitudes that lay at the basis of a knowledgeable use of information resources, such as being able to identify one's information needs and translate them in questions, to understand a text, to assess the trustworthiness and relevance of a piece of information, to adapt one's strategy to the results of the search process.

This paper, based on research and teacher education activities carried out since 2002 and in part accounted for in [6, 7], suggests that those competences can be fostered by means of frequent, unassuming practices on the web, based on information problems designed to highlight crucial issues of the search process.

2   Highlights on the process

Let us imagine to engage a group of students with questions out of pure curiosity: "Was Einstein indeed a bad student?"; "What is the name of the Botswana currency and why is it called so?"; "You are traveling to Easter Island in February. Will you take your swimsuit with you?"; "Why does Genoa Football team wear red and blue?". These questions are not especially relevant in themselves and do not require any specialized content knowledge, nor advanced Web proficiency. However, they are nontrivial as long as no ready-made solutions are available (which was true at the time of our experiences) or the existing answers contradict each other.

The students and teachers with whom we tried these and other questions differed widely in their search strategies. Some of them tried to locate a pre-defined "correct answer", while others showed a more flexible attitude and tried to figure out by themselves some possible answers, maybe based on wrong assumptions such as "It is cold in February, I should not need my swimsuit". Some of them got rid of the problem ("I looked in the Genoa website and it does not say anything. There is nothing on this on the Web"), others drew hasty conclusions from the information they encountered ("This site shows Einstein's school report, it's full of 4 and 5, he was indeed a bad student"). But when the teacher managed to promote doubts and further questioning – for example, by suggesting, in the case of Einstein's reports, that mark systems differ across countries – the enacted process made it possible to highlight some unfortunate attitudes and to exercise some competences that are critical for the use of information resources. In the following, we will focus on three of such competences.

Asking questions The most distinctive feature of the Web, compared with paper-based material, is that the user has to ask questions to gain access to information. In a way, the Web restores the natural order of things: asking comes before answering. We use the verb "to restore" because learning at school is typically a matter of acquiring *answers*. On the Web, asking questions is easy, almost unavoidable, and does not put one's face at risk, while incremental refinement of the search string is always possible. In the whole, the Web is an excellent environment for cultivating doubt and curiosity, that is for *initiating* the learning process by recognizing one's lack of information and one's interest in broadening one's understanding.

Building hypotheses While navigating on the Web, at any moment the user is faced with choices: "Shall I start reading this or that?"; "Shall I rephrase my search?"; "Is this piece of information reliable"? Many of these decisions will be taken on the basis of *abductive* inferences. For example, choosing a link to follow from a list of results of a query implies making a prediction about the content of a web pages, on the basis of cues from the page description. Abduction is also behind the construction of possible answers to the information problem. For example, when some of our students discovered that Genoa Football Club had been founded by Englishmen, they wondered whether there was a link between this British background and the team colors, and looked on the Web to confirm this (correct) hypothesis. The Web, as a place where abduction is ubiquitous in the process of information problem solving, can thus become a place for raising awareness of a crucial cognitive tool which has long been neglected in scholarly tradition [8] and hence in educational practice.

Recognizing trustworthiness Information problem solving on the Web does not only require asking questions and building hypotheses, but also understanding answers, assessing them for relevance and trustworthiness, recognizing contradictions. For example, Web searches about Einstein as a student return a majority of pages stating that he was indeed a bad student, but also pages stating the contrary. To settle the controversy, the user needs to further look for more pieces of evidence and to decide which sources are the most reliable. The high rate of information pollution on the Web thus highlights the need for 'critical literacy' skills. However, these skills are also crucial outside the Web. Therefore, the variable quality of information on the web can be regarded as an opportunity for real-life practice in critical literacy and for conveying the message that not everything is on the Web, and that Web-based information is not always the best information. In other words, that the Web is a good place for asking questions, but not necessarily the best place for finding answers.

3 Conclusions

As any new technology, the Web is being used after the model of pre-existing ones. It is therefore not surprising that the Web has become, in educational settings, an alternative to books as a source of information for schoolwork, with some negative effects, such as plagiarism, shallowness, disregard for other sources. However, these effects should not be ascribed as much to the Web itself, but rather to the kind of tasks the students are required to perform, as far as those tasks focus on reproduction or, in best case, integration of contents; such tasks reveal a view of learning as expanding the *quantity* of the contents the student is asked to acquire. But, paradoxically, it is the Web itself, with its ever-growing number of pages, to reveal how such a view is unrealistic face to the huge and fast-changing body of knowledge in today's society. What has become important, inside and outside the Web, is being able to move through information in a knowledgeable way, to ask questions, to assess answers, to deepen one's understanding. These competences seem indeed to be lacking even among young people who are highly familiar with technology [9]. A focus on the *process* of Web searching and navigating – as suggested throughout this paper – emerges therefore as a fruitful area for educational intervention.

References

1. L. Ratzan, Making sense of the Web: a metaphorical approach, *Information Research*, **6**(1) (2000); http://informationr.net/ir/6-1/paper85.html.

2. C. Hölscher and G. Strube, Web search behavior of Internet experts and newbies, *Computer Networks*, **33**, 337-346 (2000).

3. D. Bilal and J. Kirby, Differences and similarities in information seeking: children and adults as Web users, *Information Processing and Management*, **38**, 649-670 (2002).

4. E. Kuiper, M. Volman, and J. Terwel, The Web as an Information Resource in K-12 Education: Strategies for Supporting Students in Searching and Processing Information, *Review of Educational Research*, **75**(3), 285-328 (2005).

5. S. Brand-Gruwel and P. Gerjets (Eds), Instructional Support for Enhancing Students' Information Problem Solving Ability. *Computers in Human Behavior*, **24**(3), 615-1914 (May 2008).

6. M. Ferraris, Navigare sul WWW a scuola. Ma per andare dove? [Navigating on the WWW at school. To go where?], *TD-Tecnologie Didattiche*, **28**, 29-41 (2003).

7. F. Caviglia and M. Ferraris, Web-searching for learning: observing proficient web users working out an information problem, *Proc. IADIS Conference on Cognition and Exploratory Learning in Digital Age*, 440-442, (2006).

8. L. Magnani, N.J. Nersessian, and P. Thagard, Preface to "Model-based reasoning in science: learning and discovery," *Foundations of Science*, **5**(2), 121-127 (2000).

9. J. Nielsen, Usability of Websites for Teenagers (January 2005); http://www.useit.com/alertbox/teenagers.html.

How to favour know-how transfer from experienced teachers to novices?

Thierry Condamines

Knowledge Team of the Modelling , Information and Systems (MIS)
laboratory , Université of Picardie Jules Verne, 33 rue Saint Leu, 80039
Amiens Cedex 1, France.
thierry.condamines@amiens.iufm.fr

Abstract. The first years in a teacher's career are known to be very hard. In fact, know-how, resulting from experience, is rather poor. And at the same time, there are seeds of know-how distributed in each experienced teacher and constituting a real gold mine. Finding the means of transferring this know-how constitutes a challenge for the knowledge society. We propose here a solution based on a know-how capitalization using both a knowledge base and a case base. Know-how is collected from a large number of experts, using collection scenarii. In addition, as it's impossible to collect all know-how, problems encountered by novices are discussed with selected experts and, when solutions are found, the cases are stored in a case base.

1 Introduction

In many countries, young teachers' professional identity construction is an increasingly important concern. The control of all knowledge necessary for this work is difficult bringing teachers, during the first years of their career, to balance between pleasure and suffering, and sometimes to resign. According to Saujat [1], young teachers must face a double training: that of their pupils and theirs.

While it's easy enough for a teacher to increase his knowledge on subjects like mathematics, history or physics, it's more difficult to learn class management for example. It's a field where young teachers have the poorest knowledge or, when knowledge exists, it often rests on false representations coming from their own experience as pupils. Unfortunately it's difficult to teach this kind of knowledge at university because it comes primarily from experience which, by definition, is absent at the beginning. And beside that, there is a gold mine of know-how distributed in each experienced teacher. Thus how can we effectively prepare young teachers with class reality, making them able to face every day difficulties and unforeseen situations?

Please use the following format when citing this chapter:

Condamines, T., 2008, in IFIP International Federation for Information Processing, Volume 281; *Learning to Live in the Knowledge Society*; Michael Kendall and Brian Samways; (Boston: Springer), pp. 179–182.

2 Knowledge transfer from experienced teachers

According to Nonaka [2], teachers' know-how belongs to tacit knowledge and is difficult to formalize and communicate. It can be shared by oral communication or observation of experienced teachers in action: how to control noisy children, conflicts. According to Tardif [3], a teacher employs routines built by a trial and error approach to react to new situations, which enable him to pay more attention to children learning.

The first idea is to say that if know-how is difficult to formalize, it can be learned by observation. But a teacher has to manage his own class and has no time for observation. Another way is to discuss with experienced colleagues in the same school. But this implies to show its weaknesses and, in fact, when we question young teachers on this subject, we note that discussions are very limited because of a fear to be perceived like an inefficient teacher by colleagues. A third way is tested in Canada. It's a "mentor" program where an experienced teacher follows a novice over a long period. Studies enumerated in [4] show the interest of such a program. But a problem is that it's difficult and complex to find a mentor adapted to a particular beginner. Moreover, the beginner can copy the mentor, without a sufficient reflexive analysis. Another approach is based on electronic forums. It can be forums between only beginners or with participation of some experts. The main problem of this process, quoted by Depover [5], is that the artefact gives a very poor structure to discussions. Thus knowledge is drowned in the flood of messages.

3 A know-how capitalization approach

To try to find a solution, we turned to the industry world where techniques of knowledge management were developed to identify and store crucial knowledge of experts and make it available for new workers, new projects. But can we compare knowledge necessary to manufacture an object with knowledge for class management? In our case we are confronted with knowledge very difficult to model because we are not in a technical field but in human sciences. This difficulty is proven by the little of work on this subject. These works are generally based on capitalization of explicit knowledge by indexing [6] or annotation [7] of texts. Others as [8] are based on a computer supported collaborative work to exchange knowledge. About tacit knowledge for teachers we can quote the IPAS project [9], where knowledge is exchanged in the field of pedagogical scenarii construction, and the Te-Cap project [10], based on a community of practice for online tutors in a distance learning system.

3.1 Expertise seeds

Each teacher, thanks to a pedagogical freedom, has built a very effective individual know-how. Thus our postulate is that there is not a small list of well-known experts (which is often the case in an industrial field) but on the contrary, "expertise seeds" disseminated in the population of experienced teachers. If we consider only a "representative" list of experts we will have to face an important loss of knowledge.

This scattering of expertise seeds makes them difficult to identify and collect. The first stage of our work is then to find a process to collect them at a large scale. Traditional methods based on discussions with some experts cannot be employed here. Our approach is based on three stages:

- to identify crucial know-how by discussions with young teachers, experienced teachers and the observation of discussion forums. For example: how to manage workshops in a nursery school?
- to characterize each know-how. For example for a workshop: composition of groups, duration, subjects, place of the teacher, instructions, evaluation
- to build a collection scenario for each know-how. From the characteristics of a know-how, we build a tree structure questionnaire.

The collection at a large scale brings a certain richness but raises the question of the value of these know-how seeds. If it's quite easy to evaluate knowledge implied in the manufacture of objects, it's more difficult in human sciences. An a priori evaluation is impossible. We thus chose an evaluation of this knowledge on the level of its use by the beginner. For example, when a beginner wonders how to manage workshops, the system returns several ways of doing it (coming from several experts). He chooses the most appropriate one (with his situation, his character). Then, following its implementation in his class, he will be able to give an evaluation.

3.2   Case base reasoning

Know-how, in particular in class management, is often related to a quite precise situation and often corresponds to the solution of an encountered problem. We cannot a priori capitalize all know-how allowing to solve all the problems. To help a beginner, an expert must know the context with precision to give a possible answer to the problem. This is why we use a case base to enrich our base.

The beginner describes his problem with precision. If elements appear in the knowledge base or similar cases in the case base, they are returned. If he is not satisfied, the case is put on standby and sent towards several adapted experts. The beginner exchanges then with the experts until a solution which is appropriate to him is found. The solved problem is then put in the case base.

3.3   Importance of a teacher profile

It's crucial to define a teacher profile to allow to measure the degree of expertise of a teacher (general experience, experience in the current class, domain of expertise, utilization ratio and evaluation of his know-how,…), to connect an expert adapted to a beginner (type of school, type of class,…), to return a knowledge adapted to a request. It's a dynamic profile which is constantly updated. For example, a teacher works in a urban nursery school (in a difficult social area, with 5 classes) for 10 years, has 4 years old pupils for 5 years with sometimes a handicapped one, 28 children in the class. He prefers teaching mathematics and science. His know-how evaluations are: discipline (30%), workshop management (80%).

4   Conclusion

Know-how transfer from experienced teachers to novices is an important challenge for the knowledge society. A huge progress has been made in industrial applications of Knowledge Management but a lot of work has to be made in Education. A system based on knowledge capitalization and case base reasoning seems to be interesting for several reasons:
-   to preserve know-how of experienced teachers even if they stop working (retirement,…);
-   to tutor young teachers ;
-   to allow pedagogical innovation starting from existing know-how;
-   to allow education managers to better know what problems are really encountered by teachers and to optimize their decisions (lifelong training programs,…);
-   to identify good practices.

Our experiments are at their beginning and the results, although encouraging, require being refined. We also work on a domain ontology allowing a better knowledge management (indexing, research) and the use of inferences.

References

1. F. Saujat, Spécificité de l'activité d'enseignants débutants et genre de l'activité professorale, *Polifonia*, N°8, pp. 67-93 (2004).
2. I. Nonaka, and H. Takeuchi , *The knowledge-creating company : How Japanese Companies Create the Dynamics of Innovation* (Oxford University Press, 1995).
3. M. Tardif, and C. Lessard, *Le travail enseignant au quotidien. Expérience, interactions humaines et dilemmes professionnels* (De Boeck, 1999).
4. C. Bergevin, and S. Martineau, Le mentorat (2007); http://www.insertion.qc.ca/article.php3?id_article=126
5. Ch. Depover, B. De Lievre, and G. Temperman, Points de vue sur les échanges électroniques et leurs usages en formation à distance, *Sciences et Technologies de l'Information et de la Communication pour l'Education et la Formation (STICEF)*, Vol. 13 (2006).
6. M.H. Abel, A. Benayache, D. Lenne, and C. Moulin, E-MEMORAe : A content-oriented environment for e-earning , *E-Learning Networked Environments and Architectures : A Knowledge Processing Perspective* (Springer, 2005).
7. F. Azouazou , and C. Desmoulins, Teachers Document Annotating : Models for a Digital Memory Tool , *Int. J. Cont. Engineering Education and Lifelong Learning (IJCEELL)*, 16 (1/2), pp. 18-34 (2006).
8. J. Carroll, et al., Knowledge Management Support for Teachers , *Educational Technology Research and Development*, 51 (4), pp. 42-64 (2003).
9. Tzu-Chien Liu, and Yih-Ruey Juang, IPAS – Teacher's knowledge management platform for teachers professional development , *the International Onference on Engineering Education, Manchester*, England, August 18-22 (2002)
10. E. Garrot, S. George, and P. Prevot, "The development of TE-Cap: an Assistance Environment for Online Tutors", *2nd European Conference on Technology Enhanced Learning (EC-TEL 2007), Crete, Greece, Sept. 17-20 (2007)*.

Chapter 8

Educating ICT Professionals

Where Will Professional Software Engineering Education Go Next?

Bill Davey and Arthur Tatnall
1 School of Business Information Technology
RMIT University, Melbourne, Australia
Bill.Davey@rmit.edu.au
2 Centre for International Corporate Governance Research
Victoria University, Melbourne, Australia
Arthur.Tatnall@vu.edu.au

Abstract. In 1998 Lethbridge surveyed software engineering professionals and found that there were aspects of their degree that they saw as being useless to their jobs. This study was repeated in 2005 with very similar results despite a significant tightening of the research method. Inspired by this input to the curriculum development process we studied 20 years of curriculum at a University chosen for its very close ties to industry. The study showed that there has been a continual and growing move towards integrating specific technical issues into organisational context. The indication is that curriculum valued by industry will involve students being immersed in business problems rather than learning technical skills and then finding a place to apply them.

1 Introduction

To produce a competent software engineer takes at least 4 years of undergraduate education and a minimum time of professional experience. This means the educators must be able to look at least 4 years into the future. In many countries there is overlaid on this need for precognitive powers a strange anomaly. The general public sees the job of software engineers to be producing computer programs. The same general public in many countries have heard disturbing rumours of the off-sourcing of coding jobs to other places such as Russia or India. This is in the same climate that sees not only considerable deficit in Information and Communication Technology (ICT) professionals, but undergraduate numbers that can never be expected to meet known demands for ICT staff. A seminal point in this discussion happened in 1998 when Lethbridge [1] conducted two studies into computing and software engineering curricula. Lethbridge found, using two methods, that the same set of curriculum materials was uniformly seen as having been a waste of time by professionals. This work showed that it is possible, not only to lack foresight, but to

Please use the following format when citing this chapter:

Davey, B. and Tatnall, A., 2008, in IFIP International Federation for Information Processing, Volume 281; *Learning to Live in the Knowledge Society*; Michael Kendall and Brian Samways; (Boston: Springer), pp. 185–192.

continue to include curriculum elements that are no longer valid. In an attempt to allow us to see what picture should be painted of the future of the industry we have looked at the past of ICT education in an attempt to draw some trend line that will help make the future picture clear. This paper will report on a study of a sample curriculum over 20 years. The study seeks to find trends that can inform our decisions on where to take curriculum in the next 20 years.

2   A View of the Future from the ICT Industry

In 2006 a report to the Australian Commonwealth Government [2] underlined the value for Australia of a highly skilled ICT workforce able to make innovative use of ICT as the key to business productivity improvement. It went on to state that: "The combined impacts of the ageing workforce, changing generational patterns of work and the apparent failure of many employers to upgrade workplace skills could mean that Australia risks being unable to sustain key ICT-based economic capabilities, operations and services in the future" [2]. In particular it identified as "a major concern" what it considered as an outmoded and negative perception of ICT occupations and careers. It pointed to a poor understanding of the diversity of ICT occupations and opportunities and suggested the urgent need: "for action to address negative perceptions of ICT careers in the community which lead many young people and those who influence their career choices (such as parents, teachers, career advisers) to underestimate the opportunities available in ICT and thus to turn away from considering a career in ICT" [2].

In Australia ICT represents about 3.6% of the total workforce which is higher than for Europe (about 2.5%) and the United States (about 2.8%) [2].

Also as a part of this Australian Government report the Committee noted the views expressed by Gartner [3] on the future of the ICT profession. This Gartner Report predicts that by 2010 the ICT profession will be split into four main areas of expertise:

- *"Technology Infrastructure and Services,* with growth in service, hardware and software companies. Network design and security will remain strong everywhere, with routine coding and programming off-shored to developing economies.
- *Information Design and Management,* with growth in business intelligence, online consumer services, workplace enhancement. Search-and-retrieval practices and collaboration, particularly in ICT-user, systems integration and consulting companies. In this area Gartner predicts there will be a demand for professionals with linguistics, language, information design and knowledge management skills.
- *Process Design and Management,* involving standard operational processes (for outsourcing vendors), competitive business processes (for ICT-user companies) and design of automation software (for software vendors).
- *Relationships and Sourcing Management,* requiring ICT professionals to acquire skills in this area which demands strengths in managing intangibles, negotiating among different parties and coordinating outcomes among

geographically distributed parties with different work agendas and cultures. In some instances ICT professionals in this area will serve as relationship managers between overseas service providers and domestic customers."

Gartner also notes that by 2010, six out of ten people working in ICT will be undertaking business roles based around information, process and relationships [3]. They point to four chief areas of knowledge that will inform and enrich the domains of expertise listed above [3]:

- "Technical knowledge. How does this technology work? What are its effects? How does it interact with other technologies? What are its dependencies?
- Business-specific knowledge. What makes this company tick? Business-specific knowledge breaks down further into knowledge of enterprise objectives, operational activities, social and knowledge networks, and cultural behaviors.
- Core process knowledge. What processes fuel this company's competitive edge? In other words, which processes make this company unique?
- Industry knowledge. What forces, markets and models characterize this industry? Which parties or industries are traditional or emerging buyers and sellers? How does regulation affect this industry? Which industries does this industry resemble?" [3]

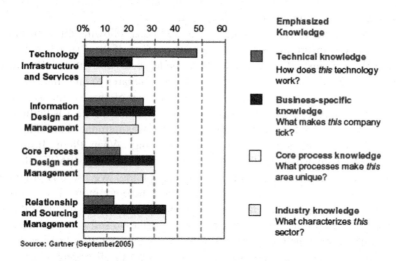

Source: Gartner (September 2005)

Figure 1: Relationship between areas of knowledge and domains of expertise

It is instructive to look at views from the industry itself. In Australia, over the last few years the Australian Computer Society has noted with irony the decline in University enrolments across the IT field in comparison with the growing shortage of ICT professionals in the industry [4]. In the United Kingdom (UK) in 2006 at a meeting of the Information Technology Professors, a senior technical executive from IBM responded to a question about the future of software engineering in the UK by agreeing that most of the basic programming jobs would continue to be outsourced to countries like India. He went on to stress, however, that business-related ICT jobs would and must remain in the country [5]. These jobs would involve areas such business analysis, and customising solutions for local businesses.

3   Verifying a Trend

When Lethbridge [1] found gaps in software engineering curricula it was by surveying professionals. Later work by [6] found almost identical results but made sure that the people surveyed were relevant to the University curriculum being studied by careful selection of the population. There are still two problems with this method:

- Graduates in the profession know what goes on in their workplace now. Not necessarily all workplaces, and not into the future
- The survey asks a negative question: "what do you not use?" rather than "what will you need to know?"

Our study was centred in one Australian University. Australian because that is one part of the world that is known for having introduced broader curriculum alternatives than many. For example Dieste recognises "SE-specific programs have proliferated in several countries, such as the US, the UK, Australia, and Canada. Although these programs focus on SE knowledge, they might also offer electives related to advanced CS knowledge, depending on the university. This proliferation hasn't occurred throughout the European Union."[7]

In Australia there have been a number of traditions following different streams in the formation of institutions of tertiary education. One of these steams is that of the vocational or industrial University. This model sees a tight link between the University and industry, where undergraduates are prepared to take immediate places in industry through tailored programs. An indicator of this stream is where the University favours 'applied' research. One institution of this type was Philip Institute of Technology. In 1985 an undergraduate program was introduced at Philip Institute to provide a Bachelors degree in Data Processing. When Philip Institute later amalgamated with Royal Melbourne Institute of Technology (RMIT) this course continued as a bachelor degree in Business Computing. We use this program as a case since there is the suspicion that the programs here are more closely influenced by what the direct needs are in the local industry, rather than by more theoretical consideration within the various disciplines that make up software engineering. The program has always included compulsory paid employment after two years of study and before the final year. This period of employment of all undergraduates means, among other factors, that the program is tested by current students every year against the ability to perform in up to 150 workplaces (one for each enrolled student in each year level.)

4   The Sample Points

To draw our trend lines we need a number of points spread out over the short history of our discipline. It is not very sensible to start much before a complete degree program was introduced and so we start with the program description of a whole program introduced in 1986 and the writings of 1984 and 1985 that were the principal influences for that course. We then describe the programs that were offered in 1990 and 1995 and compare them with the 2000 programs and the newly accredited program that will be delivered starting in 2008. This sample of approximately 5 years, keeping the environment of the University constant, provides some lessons for what might happen over the next 5 years.

5 Results

To attempt to find some patterns across the history of this one program, each of the course description documents was read, with attention to both stated intentions of the program and actual contents of the courses that made up the programs. The aims of the program have remained remarkably stable over the 20 years of the study. When first proposed in 1985, the program was intended "to provide a sound understanding of information structuring and processing concepts, system building techniques and computing technology as a framework to facilitate the continual development of professional competence" [8]. As we will see, this was interpreted in the subject construction in a very technical way. However, from the very first, these programs were intended to ally as closely as possible to industrial needs. As the program developed from an initial offering the aim continued to be fairly stable. By 1990 the program was "to provide the opportunity for the student to apply concepts and procedures and to develop technical computing skills on assignments representative of those in industry, commerce or government" [9]. The amalgamation of the two institutions to become a university came with a move to focus more on the application of skills to program aims with an almost complete lack of the word skill. In 1995 the program was to "produce competent graduates with a level of professionalism appropriate to work in business computing and information systems" [10]. The current program talks about skills with a totally different meaning, but maintains the close ties to industry. In 2007 "The program allows you to develop both generic business and specific business information systems capabilities through experiential learning to meet current and future expectations of employers. By applying real and relevant knowledge, the program is aimed at developing you as a highly skilled, 'well-rounded' ICT professional" [11]. The changes that have happened over the 20 years have also come about through consideration of the same set of forces. The current proposal for 2008 reflects practices recorded for previous changes to the program: "proposed changes are the outcome of a series of workshops involving academics involved in the delivery of the program. Documentation prepared for the 2005 Australian Computer Society Accreditation Program Review Process was also reviewed together with its subsequent recommendations for improvements. Also sourced was literature pertaining to the required skills and knowledge required of future ICT professionals. Subsequent discussions drew on the participants' experiences and research, collected through conversations and feedback from students, discussions with employers on co-op visits, and readings from industry reports and research papers." [11]

6   Classifying Subjects

The analysis of program components consisted of examining each subject in each incarnation of the program. The examination sought to identify some useful distinction between subjects so that a track could be made from 1985 to the present day. A distinction that became immediately obvious was that between subjects built around a particular technology: COBOL programming (such as the first versions of the subjects Commercial Programming A and B), Networking and Machine Language subjects, and those that generally taught 'how to run a computer'. Alternatively there were always subjects built around means of identifying and applying technology to business problems. These subjects still often contained some technology based skill, but the descriptions and syllabi were oriented around the needs of the problem area rather than the technology solution. We decided to call these 'technology' or 'integrative' subjects, integrative in that the technology was to be integrated into a study involving the finding of solutions. Over the years the program has generally included 24 subjects, plus a year of work integrated learning giving students a work load of 8 subjects each year. As a degree in the Faculty of Business, there have always been a number of compulsory non-IT subjects and a varying number of elective subjects that must be taken from the IT stream. We took as an indicator of trend the number of elective subjects offered as an indication of the perceived educational need of students. Table 1 (below) shows the breakdown of subjects over the period studied:

Table 1: Classification of subjects taught from 1985 – 2008

Year	Core technology subjects	Elective technology subjects	Core integrative subjects	Elective integrative subjects	Total technology subjects	Total integrative subjects
1985	6	5	0	3	11	3
1990	9	5	3	3	14	6
1995	3	8	5	5	11	10
2000	3	8	5	6	11	11
2005	3	3	7	13	6	20
2008	0	2	13	11	2	24

The first thing to note about this table is that the total number of IT subjects rapidly rose in the first five years. From the original 14 subjects thought to cover all of undergraduate IT to a total of 20 subjects was a large jump in the scheme of curriculum change. Subjects added to the list included another language (FORTRAN), Assembly Language and Graphics Programming and a second computer hardware subject. The only change in integrative subjects was to take the 3 electives in Business Information Systems and make them compulsory. By 1995 the move to cover every technical skill had reached its peak with VB, PICK, COBOL, Pascal and C being taught as programming languages. Graphics programming had been dropped, as not being commercially relevant, and commercial programming had changed in fundamental nature. It became and was now called Applications Development. The subject content no longer was written around syntax of a programming language, but described the process of determining requirements and planning a system to meet those professionals using a language. The next significant change happened in 2005 after a major review of the program. At this change almost all the programming subjects delivering skills narrowly defined by a programming language were removed. Two networking subjects were sufficiently oriented to the technology that these were defined as technology subjects, despite a significant move to problem solving within the technological environment.

7 Conclusion

In 1986 the program was intended to "provide a professionally recognized business oriented data processing course" [8]. By 1995 students found "your job can involve the planning, design, implementation and management of information systems that your organization depends upon" [8]. The current student is told that they will be popular because "companies choose RMIT graduates because of their IT skills and business acumen" [12]. There is now a specific set of envisioned outcomes for graduates. They can look forward to positions like the following: "Typical positions include business analyst; Internet service provider; database designer and administrator; systems operations manager; systems analyst; IT consultant; programmer/analyst; information centre manager; client server administrator; network administrator; object oriented systems developer; training officer in IT area; applications developer; software engineer; user liaison officer; computer marketing executive; and information systems manager" [12]. So the first trend line we see is one from a focus on the data to a focus on the business. This tells educators to focus even more in the future on understanding the impact of technology rather than the intricacies of a particular technique. It also advises us to market what we do for students in terms of solutions rather than skills. Tell parents and high school students what our graduates have done for their companies, rather than how much fun it is to write computer programs, show them pictures with clients rather than with terminals and develop programs of study that integrate learning rather than isolate discipline lines. This also fits well with what the industry suggests is the future of the IT professional in countries like Australia. Gartner [3] identifies four areas of knowledge that they predict will be needed in the future:

- Technical knowledge.
- Business-specific knowledge
- Core process knowledge.
- Industry knowledge.

If we look at the change in our sample over 20 years it is clear that this set of four areas of knowledge is what we have been moving towards.

References

1.   Lethbridge, T. *A Survey of the Relevance of Computer Science and Software Engineering Curricula*. in *Proceedings of the 11th International Conference on Software Engineering*. 1998. Silver Spring MD: IEEE Compuetr Society Press.

2.   Department of Communication; Information Technology and the Arts, *Building Australian ICT Skills: Report of the ICT Skills Foresighting Working Group*. 2006, Department of Communication, Information Technology and the Arts: Barton, ACT.

3.   Gartner, *The IT Professional Outlook: Where Will We Go From Here?* 2005, Gartner: Orlando, Florida.

4.   Australian Computer Society. *ICT Professionals Shaping Our Future*. 2007 [cited November 2007]; Available from: http://www.acs.org.au/.

5.   Thompson, J.B., *The Future of ICT Education in the UK*. 2006: Newcastle, UK.

6.   Kitchenham, B., et al., *An investigation of software engineering curricula*. The Journal of Systems and Software, 2005. **74**(3): p. 325.

7.   Dieste, O., N. Juristo, and Ana M. Moreno, *How Higher-Education Systems Influence Software Engineering Degree Programs*. IEEE Software, 2004. **21**(4): p. 78.

8.   Philip Institute of Technology, *A Submission for Accreditation to the Accreditation Board for a UG1 Bachelor of Business (Data Processing)*. 1985.

9.   Philip Institute of Technology, *1990 Handbook*. 1990, Bundoora: PIT Publishing.

10.   RMIT, *Faculty of business undergraduate and post graduate proghrams 1995*. 1995, Melbourne: RMIT.

11.   Dick, M., *Draft Program Guide BP138 Bachelor of Business (Business Information Systems)*. 2007, RMIT University: Melbourne Australia. p. 58.

12.   RMIT, *Program Guide BP138 Bachelor of Business (Business Information Systems*. 2000.

Maintaining Industrial Competence
The Challenges for Continuous Professional Development and the Role for Universities

J. Barrie Thompson and Helen M. Edwards

School of Computing and Technology, Informatics Centre,
University of Sunderland, St Peter's Campus, St Peter's Way, Sunderland,
Tyne and Wear, SR6 0DD, United Kingdom.
barrie.thompson@sunderland.ac.uk, helen.edwards@sunderland.ac.uk

Abstract. Poor quality software and projects that fail to deliver are a too-frequent occurrence. There is thus a clear need for greater professionalism throughout the sector and this must be supported by appropriate Continuous Professional Development (CPD). Details are presented of foundation work, undertaken since 2000, relevant to the on-going professional development of IT practitioners. Information is then given on a current project that is concerned with identifying successful industrial practices and the teaching of such in academic programmes including programmes that support CPD. The major challenges that this work has exposed are detailed, current conclusions are outlined and suggestions are given with regard to possible solutions for the problems that clearly exist.

1   Introduction

Although there have been many significant developments in computing during the last 50 years too many software projects still fail to meet all their objectives, and the termination of partially completed projects is also a frequent occurrence. The on-going problem of poor quality software has been repeatedly highlighted in published studies (e.g. Glass [1]), and in major conference presentations (e.g. keynote address by the 2005/2006 President of the British Computer Society at IFIP's 2006 World Computer Congress [2]). The cost of these failures is enormous: a recent article [3] reported that in the UK, between 2000 and 2007, the total cost of abandoned central government computer projects had reached almost two billion pounds. Yet many of the types of problems that act against successful IT project delivery have been clearly identified in an in-depth study which was undertaken by a working group of the Royal Society of Engineering (RSE) and the British Computer Society (BCS). The resultant report [4] on the situation with regard to Complex IT projects included conclusions and recommendations with particular regard to: Professionalism,

Please use the following format when citing this chapter:

Thompson, J.B. and Edwards, H.M., 2008, in IFIP International Federation for Information Processing, Volume 281; *Learning to Live in the Knowledge Society*; Michael Kendall and Brian Samways; (Boston: Springer), pp. 193–200.

Education of practitioners, Project management issues, Role of risk management, Role of systems architecture, Adoption of best practices, and Research in the field of complexity. In the section on Professionalism the report highlighted the following [4] with regard to Continuous Professional Development (CPD):

"Customers should therefore ensure that all senior IT practitioners involved in the design and delivery of 'high consequence' systems have attained Chartered status (the highest level of professional status) and maintain their technical currency through Continuing Professional Development" and "The Office of Government Commerce, together with the Professional Institutions, should assess means of enforcing the registration, and maintenance of professional competence through CPD, of senior practitioners working on high consequence systems"

We see no reasons to assume that the situation in other parts of the world is significantly different to that in the UK and that there is an ongoing international requirement for high quality CPD. It is also clear that there is a major role for Universities to provide education and training programmes that would support CPD requirements.

In the reminder of this paper, we detail work that we have been undertaking in recent years that is relevant to the ongoing professional development of IT practitioners. This is an area that is key to the work of IFIP Working Group 3.4 - the group that is concerned with IT professional and vocational education (it is also the group that the first author of this paper currently chairs and within which the second author is a member). In section 2 we provide information on initial work that we have undertaken relating to professionalism. We then follow this in section 3 with details of an ongoing funded project that commenced in 2005 which is concerned with identifying successful industrial practices and then incorporating the teaching of such into academic programmes including programmes that support CPD. In section 4 we summarise what has been undertaken so far. Then in section 5 we provide details of the major challenges that we perceive to exist, our current conclusions, and some suggestions as to possible solutions to the problems that clearly exist.

2   Contextual Information and Early Work

During the 1990s the International Federation for Information Processing (IFIP) undertook work directed towards defining an international approach with regard to professional standards throughout the whole of the Information Technology sector. In 1999, committees within IFIP approved a document entitled "Harmonization of Professional Standards" [5]. The document addresses six specific areas:

*   Ethics of professional practice,
*   Established body of knowledge,
*   Education and training,
*   Professional experience,
*   Best practice and proven methodologies, and
*   Maintenance of competence.

Starting in autumn 2000, we undertook a series of activities aimed at both promoting and evaluating the IFIP document primarily within the Software

Engineering community. Some 15 international activities were undertaken over the next two years. The most informative of these were: a workshop held at the 2001 Conference on Software Engineering Education and Training (reported in [6]), a workshop held during the 2001 International Conference on Software Engineering (reported in [7]), and an International Summit which was co-located with the 2002 International Conference on Software Engineering (reported in [8]). The overall reaction to the IFIP Professional Standards document by the Software Engineering community was very encouraging [9]. It was recognised that the document defines a framework which should assist the advancement of professional standards. However, the evaluative work also highlighted community concerns that were associated with the areas of: best practice and proven methodologies, maintenance of competence, and the educational support for these areas [9].

Subsequently some further work was undertaken in 2004 on investigating best practices in the Software Engineering sector and their role in the curricula [10]. This did much to reinforce the earlier findings and concluded that: "... there are already what appears to be best practices (or what could become best practices) in operation. But what is too often lacking is the empirical evidence that these practices are really effective, that they can be transferred from one project to another, or from one organisation to another, or that they are scalable."

3 The Current Project

In 2005 the first author of this paper was awarded a prestigious UK National Teaching Fellowship from the UK Higher Education Academy [11] and with it funding to carry out an individually determined research project related to teaching and learning. It was felt that a project related to best practices which built on the work that had already been undertaken in evaluating the IFIP Professional Standards document and which would support the activities of IFIP Working Group 3.4 would be most appropriate. Such a project would also:
- Make use of the knowledge gained from involvement in the ACM and IEEE-CS supported international curricula effort for undergraduate degrees in Software Engineering [12] (both authors of this paper were involved in this effort).
- Reach-out to the wider professional/practitioner IT community.
- Feed into the development of the curricula and appropriate teaching and learning approaches.

The overall aim set for the project was to develop guidelines and recommendations regarding:
- The identification and incorporation of proven industry-related best practices into both undergraduate and post-graduate computing curricula (including curricula that relate to maintenance of competence for existing professionals), and
- Best practice mechanisms for the delivery of such enhanced curricula in a variety of contexts (e.g. remote distance learning).

It was felt that the particular benefits which could follow from the project were:
- Improved working relations between academia and industry.

- Closer agreement between academic outputs and industry requirements.
- Improved teaching and learning approaches.
- More attractive academic programmes (and hence more students).
- Opportunities to support Life Long Learning (e.g. short courses to support "Maintenance of Competence" requirements).

4 Progress

The work which had been undertaken in 2004 [10] had shown that identifying proven best practices would be far from easy. It was therefore decided to progress the new project on two fronts:
- To investigate the various links that already exist between industry and academia to see if information gained via such links could be used as a means of determining truly effective practices.
- To progress work via existing industrial and academic contacts and those formed from activities associated with professional bodies. This was also to be supported by attendance at conferences and meetings where one would expect there to be a reasonable representation from industry.

4.1 Direct Links between Industry and Academia

Four international workshops have now been undertaken to support the project. The first workshop [13] was held at the 19th Conference on Software Engineering Education & Training in April 2006. In addition to highly interactive discussions the there were presentations on papers [14] which addressed: the role of adjunct professors, an Indian company's Academic Interface Program, the importance of industry experience for students, and the role of guest speakers from industry. In addition trials were carried out on a preliminary template which could be used to record interactions. This concentrated on: context, the actors involved, the interaction, analysis, and evaluation.

The second workshop [15] was held at the 28th International Conference on Software Engineering, in May 2006. In addition to discursive sessions there were short presentations to support seven position papers [16] which were organised into four themes. Theme 1: Types of Interaction - this addressed the importance of dialogue with industry. Theme 2: Projects and Solutions for Industry - this addressed collaborations that are driven by projects, strategies for collaboration, and the use of a SE laboratory. Theme 3: Courses for Professionals - this addressed how such could form a two-way communication channel. Theme 4: Industry Assisting Academia – this addressed courses run by industry and how industry could provide data to support research. In addition to support Theme 2 a paper [16] was circulated that addressed technology transfer to small and medium sized enterprises. Further trials were also carried out on an enhanced template which could be used to record interactions. The workshop participants were divided into groups representing each of the four themes detailed above and each group was requested to complete a template for an interaction relevant to their theme and then feed back their feelings about its use. Finally there was a general appraisal session that addressed particular issues relating to the study of interactions and the use of the templates.

The third workshop [17] was held in August 2006 and formed the first event within the IFIP's Conference on Education for the 21st Century. This in turn was one of the constituent conferences which formed IFIP's World Computer Congress. The main purpose of this workshop was to provide a forum for a group that would not only be Software Engineering orientated. The event took the form of a series of "round table" discussions that addressed various experiences relating to interactions between universities and industry relating to specific academic programs. This event attracted a very different set of attendees compared with the previous two events. There were attendees from several countries that had not been previously represented including: Chile, Ecuador, Puerto Rico, Oman, South Africa, Portugal, and Japan.

The fourth workshop [18] was held at the 14th Asia-Pacific Software Engineering Conference, in December 2007. This was purposefully very interactive in nature with working in groups throughout the day. It consisted of three distinct discussion sessions plus an introductory and plenary session. The discussion sessions addressed: the Industry /University Gap, University and Industry Collaboration, Achieving Real World Experiences. Each session commenced with a short presentation on a relevant position paper [19]. Of particular interest was a particular approach used at a University in Indonesia where to gain group and personal skills the students do not only construct software artifacts but also build boats from old car tyres and bamboo and then have to sail them [20].

4.2 Industry, Academia, and Professional Bodies

The funding provided by the project has enabled the first author to become involved in the British Computer Society's Professionalism in IT programme [21] as a member of its executive committee. This is an ambitious three year managed programme that began in 2005 and which is aimed at proactively addressing various issues relating to professionalism throughout the IT sector. The programme has two key objectives [21]:
1. By increasing professionalism, to improve the ability of business and other organisations to exploit the potential of information technology effectively and consistently.
2. To build an IT profession that is respected and valued by its stakeholders- Government, business leaders, IT employers, IT users and customers – for the contribution that it makes to a more professional approach to the exploitation and application of IT.

The importance of the BCS programme has been recognised by the International Federation for Information Processing (IFIP) and has led to the creation of a Task Force to address key issues that are facing the global ICT industry today with regard to professionalism [22]. An obvious consideration is whether and to what extent the BCS's Professionalism in IT programme can be developed so that it can be used by IFIP's other member organisations. A detailed account of the programme and its development to date, including the work with IFIP, can be found in a paper [23] in the proceedings of an IFIP Working Conference on Education Training and Life Long Learning that was held in Prague in September 2007.

In addition, to involvement with the BCS's professionalism activities, the project funding has provided support to attend relevant workshops at international conferences [e.g. 24] and various one day events in the UK such as:

- UK Government IT Conference 2007 [25] which addressed IT issues relevant to local government.
- The launch of the UK National Computing Centre's Enterprise Architecture and Systems Engineering (EA-SE) Programme [26] which is related to the BCS's Professionalism in IT Programme.
- A Westminster eForum Keynote Seminar "A UK IT Skills Gap" [27] which involved Members of Parliament.

5   Challenges and Conclusions

The various activities and related research detailed in the proceeding sections have provided many insights into the IT sector and its problems. It has also revealed the many and various interactions that exist between industry and academia. Unfortunately the one area that still remains generally elusive is hard information on proven best practices. Industrial contacts made at conferences and meetings often result in promises to send details of their organisations proven practices. However, in every case what has resulted is a subsequent communication informing us that their practices are confidential to their own company. Clearly there can be no independent evaluation of such practices and the claims of their worth. Also, as was made clear during the 2007 workshop on Realising Evidence-Based Software Engineering [24] there is very little concrete evidence in the literature that stands up to detailed scrutiny. In addition, small surveys undertaken at various conferences have failed to produce any significant evidence that provable best practices do exist. In fact the nil returns could be interpreted to indicate that the reverse is actually the case.

We have recognised that trying to collect information on University/Industry interactions via a paper-based system was likely to have very limited success. Thus during the 2006/2007 academic year we sponsored a number of Master's level projects that had as their goals:

- The development and evaluation of a range of different web-based interfaces for collecting data about interactions
- The development of a database that can be used to hold the data and which will support subsequent interrogation

As yet we have not yet received an easy-to-use system and there is the further challenge that once such a system is delivered we will still have to persuade academics and industrialists to make real use of it.

We have still to complete a detailed analysis of the content of each of the workshops and there are still many hours of audio recordings to be transcribed, analysed, and reported on. However, what has clearly emerged, from the preliminary analysis is that with the exception of student projects, few of these interfaces are ever formally documented and evaluated.

What has become clear is that to a great extent there are two distinct communities – Industry and Academia - and the two interact much less than is desirable. Go to a major international Software Engineering conference and you find relatively few industrialists. Go to a UK government-supported conference that supports the Information, Communications and Technology (ICT) sector (the government's preferred term) and you will find very, very few academics. Also, perhaps too many academics, at least in the UK, are driven by the demands of successive Research Assessment Exercises [28] where to publish high quality academic research papers is a clear aim and applied work with the industrial ICT sector is largely avoided. In addition, we must recognise that currently the normal career progression for an academic in computing is: undergraduate degree, postgraduate degree, enter academia, do worthwhile "academic" research and teach. There is obviously much to be done to bring the two groups closer together.

References

1. R.L. Glass, *Facts and Fallacies of Software Engineering*, Pearson Education, Boston, 2003.
2. C. Hughes C. (2006), Professionalism in IT, Keynote Address, 19th IFIP World Computer Congress (WCC 2006), Santiago, Chile, August 20-25, 2006, Presentation available from: http://www.ifip.org/projects/IT-Pract-main.htm [accessed October 3 2006].
3. B. Johnson And D Hencke, Not Fit For Purpose: £2bn Cost Of Government's IT Blunders, Guardian, Saturday January 5, 2008, p11.
4. Royal Academy of Engineering, The Challenges of Complex IT Projects, Report of a working group from The Royal Academy of Engineering and The British Computer Society, 2004, available from: http://www.bcs.org/upload/pdf/complexity.pdf [accessed October 12 2006].
5. I. Mitchell, P. Juliff, and J. Turner, Harmonization of Professional Standards, International Federation of Information Processing, 1998, at: http://www.ifip.or.at
6. J.B. Thompson and H.M. Edwards, Achieving a World-wide Software Engineering Profession: Report on the CSEET 2001 Workshop, *Journal of Education and Information Technologies*, 6/4, December, 2001 pp 267-293.
7. J.B. Thompson, Report on the ICSE Workshop to Consider Global Aspects of Software Engineering Professionalism, *ACM Software Engineering Notes*, November 2001, vol. 26, no 6, pp 40-48.
8. J.B. Thompson and H.M Edwards, A tale of two summits, Part 2, SEA Software, *The Journal of Software Engineering Australia*, October 2002, pp36-37.
9. J. B. Thompson, Evaluations of IFIP's Proposed Standards for Professionals, in Proceedings of the 8th IFIP World Conference on Computers in Education, (WCCE 2005), Session P10.3. University of Stellenbosch, Cape Town, South Africa, July 4-7, 2005
10. J.B. Thompson and A.J. Fox, Best Practice: Is this the Cinderella Area of Software Engineering? Proceedings of 18th Conference on Software Engineering Education and Training (CSEE&T 2005), Ottawa, April 18-20, 2005, pp. 137- 144.
11. UK Higher Education Academy details of this and the and National teaching fellowship Scheme can be found via: http://www.heacademy.ac.uk .
12. IEE-CS and ACM, *Software Engineering 2004* (Curriculum Volume) available from: http://sites.computer.org/ccse/SE2004Volume.pdf

13. Workshop on Best Practice in Software Engineering: The Role of Industry in Software Engineering Education and Training. Held during the 19th Conference on Software Engineering Education & Training (CSEE&T2003), Turtle Bay, Hawaii, April 2006.
14. The position papers by: D.J. Frailey; R. Narayanan, R.B. Vaughn Jr. and J. Carver; S.M. Young, H.M. Edwards and J.B. Thompson for Workshop [13], are available from IEEE-CS Digital Library.
15. Third International Summit on Software Engineering Education (SSEE III) Bridging the University/Industry Gap. A workshop held within the 28th International Conference on Software Engineering, Shanghai, May 2006.
16. The position papers by L. Jaccheri and S. Morasca; S. Jarzabek and U. Pettersson; T.J. Reichlmayr; M. De Gids and T. Vos; B. Pimentel et al; S. Morasca; K. Kesavasamy; Q. Liu and R.C. Mintram for the Summit [15] are available from the ACM digital library.
17. International Workshop on Informatics Education: Bridging the University/Industry Gap. A Workshop held within IFIP Conference on Education for the 21st Century - Impact of ICT and Digital Resources which was part of the 19th IFIP World Computer Congress, Santiago, Chile, August 2006.
18. J.B. Thompson, M. Noro, and H.M. Edwards, Software Engineering Education Workshop: Bridging the University/Industry Gap, 14th Asia-Pacific Software Engineering Conference, December, 2007, pp 560-561
19. The position papers by J.L. Díaz-Herrera, M. Makabenta-Ikeda, M. Ardis, and D. Coleman; I. Liem and A.M., Karsono; T. Mahmood, K. Lister, S. Karunesekera. and E. Kazmierczak; Y. Wang and H. Shi, that supported the workshop [18] appear in Proceedings Workshop on Software Engineering Education, publisher: Information Processing Society of Japan, 2007.
20. I. Liem, A.M. Mulyanto, E. Karsono, Industry based Learning in Software Engineering: Successes and Challenges, in Proceedings Workshop on Software Engineering Education, publisher: Information Processing Society of Japan, 2007, pp10-15.
21. British Computer Society (BCS), Professionalism in IT Programme, Information on this is given in a series of articles in the May 2006 edition of the BCS publication IT Now. The programme was formally launched at PROF IT 2006 conference, London, May 8, 2006.
22. IFIP, Global IT Profession Comes Nearer, IFIP press release January 23, 2007
23. J. B. Thompson, The Professionalism in IT Programme: The Answer to a Global Problem? Published in: Education, Training and Lifelong Learning, International Federation for Information Processing, Austria, 2007, pp 113-123.
24. D. Budgen et al, 2nd International Workshop on Realising Evidence-based Software Engineering, A workshop held within the 29th International Conference on Software Engineering, Minneapolis, May 2007, Companion Volume pp 137-138.
25. Government IT 07: Transformational Government - Reshaping Service Delivery through IT, February ,1 2007, QEII Conference Centre, London
26. The launch of the UK National Computing Centre's Enterprise Architecture and Systems Engineering (EA-SE) Programme, May 31, 2007, Institute of Engineering and Technology, London.
27. Westminster Forum Keynote Seminar: A UK IT Skills Gap, London, October 25, 2007, A seminar supported by Institute of Engineering and Technology, London.
28. Research Assessment Exercise 2008, information via: http://www.rae.ac.uk/

EUCIP in Italian Universities

C.R. Alfonsi[1], E. Breno[1], M. Calzarossa[2], P. Ciancarini[3], P. Maresca[4],
L. Mich[5], F. Sala[6] and N. Scarabottolo[7]

[1] Fondazione CRUI, Roma, Italy {alfonsi,breno}@fondazionecrui.it
[2] Università di Pavia, Italy mcc@unipv.it
[3] Università di Bologna, Italy cianca@cs.unibo.it
[4] Università di Napoli Federico II, Italy paomares@unina.it
[5] Università di Trento, Italy luisa.mich@unitn.it
[6] AICA, Milano, Italy fulvia.sala@aicanet.it
[7] Università di Milano, Italy nello.scarabottolo@unimi.it

Abstract. EUCIP (EUropean Certification of Informatics Professionals) is a pan-European qualification scheme for people entering the IT profession and for IT professionals wishing to assess their professional development. This paper presents the experiences of the Italian Universities in the framework of the EUCIP programme. We illustrate both the institutional perspective of the Universities and the personal perspective of a set of students who received the EUCIP *Core* level certification during their University studies. The results of our investigations have shown a good interest of the Universities towards the EUCIP programme. Students in general recognize the importance of this certification for their future professional career and show a good interest in improving their certified knowledge and competences.

1   Introduction

The fast technological innovation has increased the ICT skills gap at the European level [1]. Industries call for professionals capable of driving and managing innovation, by creating production processes based on new technologies and anticipating ICT trends. Such a situation requires more articulate educational and evaluation systems, based on technological competences, and on capabilities of using and developing technologies in multicultural, dynamic, unstable innovation contexts. The EUropean Certification of Informatics Professionals (EUCIP) [2] is a programme defined by the Council of European Professional Informatics Societies (CEPIS) [3] for the verification and assessment of the ICT skills. Unlike the other certifications – such as the well known European Computer Driving License – EUCIP is conceived as a certification for ICT professionals. This target clearly

Please use the following format when citing this chapter:

Alfonsi, C.R., Breno, E., Calzarossa, M., Ciancarini, P., Maresca, P., Mich, L., Sala, F. and Scarabottolo, N., 2008, in IFIP International Federation for Information Processing, Volume 281; *Learning to Live in the Knowledge Society*; Michael Kendall and Brian Samways; (Boston: Springer), pp. 201–208.

emerges from the structure of its *syllabus*, that is, the set of competences required to acquire the certification. In particular, as we will discuss in more details in Section 2, EUCIP defines two levels of competences, associated with two different certifications:

- EUCIP *Core*: a "cultural" level, aimed at providing all ICT professionals with a common terminology and a set of basic competences related to the implementation of ICT systems, including their planning, construction, and actual operation; and
- EUCIP *Elective*: an "operative" level, that identifies competence profiles related to some typical jobs offered by ICT industries.

The integrated and flexible view of EUCIP – that allows the evaluation of competences coming from a variety of different learning activities – has convinced the major Italian bodies involved in the EUCIP, namely, the Italian Society of ICT professionals (AICA), the Italian University consortium for ICT (CINI) and the operative section of the Conference of the Rectors of Italian Universities (Fondazione CRUI), to launch the EUCIP4U (EUCIP for University) project, with the objective of promoting the introduction of EUCIP *Core* level in academia. Some 40 Universities were involved in the project with a total of about 70 degrees of Computer Engineering and Science.

This paper is organized as follows. Section 2 describes the main features of EUCIP; Section 3 discusses the experiences of the Italian Universities in the framework of EUCIP. In particular, we will focus on the perspective of the Universities and on the perspective of a set of students who obtained the EUCIP *Core* certification during their University studies. Finally, the lessons learned from these experiences and some concluding remarks will be presented in Section 4.

2 Main characteristics of EUCIP

In advanced countries where technological innovation is a major social and industrial force, there is a clear evidence of the importance for people and industry to measure ICT competences and skills by means of certifications. *"Within the ICT industry, certifications are credentials that result from a voluntary evaluation process whereby an individual's knowledge and/or skill in a particular subject area is verified against a set of predetermined skill standards by means of an objective assessment"* (CompTIA, 2004, pp. 18-19) [4].

EUCIP is an international certification scheme aimed at developing and keeping up-to-date the competences of ICT professionals. Its specific goals are to:

- define the minimal core of competences necessary to all ICT professionals;
- establish a network of educational services to promote the advancement of ICT competences;
- help to fill the skills gap in the field of ICT; and
- offer guidelines for lifelong learning and training of ICT competences.

The EUCIP programme [5] dates back to the year 2000. Today (December 2007) the countries participating to the programme are: Croatia, Estonia, Greece, Ireland, Italy, Latvia, Norway, Poland, and Spain.

As already pointed out, the EUCIP programme includes two certification levels, namely, a EUCIP *Core* level and a EUCIP *Elective* level. The learning effort required to acquire these certifications is evaluated in 400 study hours for the EUCIP *Core* level and in 800 study hours for the EUCIP *Elective* level, including both the time spent for classes and the time spent for personal study. If we compare this effort with a University degree, the EUCIP effort is equivalent to 16 credits for the *Core* level and 32 credits for the *Elective* level. We remind that one credit corresponds to 25 study hours, and that one student-year is conventionally equivalent to 60 credits. Hence, by taking into account the effort measured in terms of credits, we can conclude that the two levels of EUCIP are equivalent to slightly less than one year of a University degree.

2.1   EUCIP *Core*

The EUCIP *Core* certification defines the minimum set of competences of an ICT professional. These competences are structured in 18 modules organized in three different knowledge areas: *Plan, Build, Operate*. The *Plan* knowledge area includes seven modules dealing with the economic and managerial planning and use of an IT system in a business environment. The *Build* knowledge area includes four modules concerning how the software architecture of an IT system is designed, implemented, and deployed. The *Operate* knowledge area includes seven modules on how an IT system is operated, namely installed, supervised and maintained.

The exam for obtaining the EUCIP *Core* level certification is based on online tests consisting of multiple choice questions drawn from a *Question and Test Base*, namely, 40 questions for the *Build* and *Operate* areas each and 45 questions for the *Plan* area. The time allotted for each test is 90 minutes. At least 60% of correct answers for each area are required to pass the corresponding test.

2.2   EUCIP *Elective*

While the EUCIP *Core* level requires a broad knowledge of basic topics in the ICT field, the EUCIP *Elective* level defines specialized competences of an ICT professional in terms of educational modules and practical experiences. The current EUCIP *Elective* certification (version 2.4, February 2007) includes 21 profiles, corresponding to the 21 main professional roles required by the ICT industry. Thus, each profile is defined by a list of learning modules and practical skills with their associated proficiency levels.

The examination process for a EUCIP *Elective* level certification is based on two steps consisting of the presentation of a *portfolio* of competences and related certificates and of an oral exam that assesses the candidate's knowledge and skills.

The EUCIP *Core* level certification is a pre-requisite for the EUCIP *Elective* certification.

3   EUCIP in the Universities

The Italian Society of ICT professionals, AICA, has been active for a long time in promoting the ICT culture in Italy, with particular emphasis to schools and Universities. Since 1997, it has been addressing the issues of ICT certifications. To analyze the introduction and the impact of certification programmes in academia, in the year 2001 AICA founded, in cooperation with CINI and Fondazione CRUI, the "Observatory of the ICT certifications in Italian Universities" [6] whose main goal is to collect and spread experiences and good practices of the Universities in the framework of informatics certifications [7, 8].

In this section, we summarize the results and the trends of the EUCIP projects in the period 2004-2006. We will present both the institutional perspective of the Universities and the personal perspective of the end users, that is, the students who obtained the EUCIP *Core* level certification during their University studies.

3.1   University perspective

The Observatory monitored the diffusion of the EUCIP *Core* level certification since 2004. In 2004, only five out the 51 Universities that participated to our investigation offered this kind of projects. The results in the following years were definitely more promising: EUCIP projects were available at 23 out of 63 Universities in the year 2005 and at 26 out of 65 Universities in the year 2006. This trend denotes a tight correlation with the launch of the EUCIP*4U* project.

Among the Universities that offered the EUCIP in the year 2006, the vast majority, namely 17, is either large or very large. Concerning their geographic distribution, there is a slight prevalence of Universities located in Northern Italy (11), whereas there are nine Universities located in Southern Italy and six in the Central regions of Italy. Figure 1 shows the details of the choices made by the Universities with respect to EUCIP *Core* projects in the year 2006.

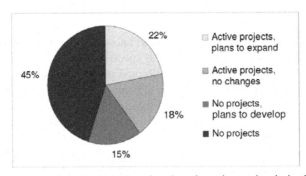

Figure 1. Diffusion of the EUCIP *Core* level projects in academia in the year 2006

We can notice that more than 50% of the Universities have demonstrated an interest to the EUCIP *Core* level certification. In particular, 22% of the Universities plan to expand their existing projects and 15% plan to develop new projects. Universities without EUCIP projects include the ones where no IT degrees (i.e., Computer Engineering and Computer Science) are offered to students, thus where EUCIP does not fit student interests (actually, scientific and technical faculties were present in only 75% of the Universities that participated to our investigation).

The distribution of the years of activation of the EUCIP projects, shown in Figure 2, outlines once more the strong impact of the EUCIP*4U* project. The majority of the Universities activated their projects in the years 2005 and 2006, and only nine Universities activated EUCIP projects earlier, that is, between 2002 and 2004. Note that, in 2004, CINI launched a pilot project that involved some Universities spread all over Italy, and some students of Computer Engineering and Science enrolled in the third and fourth year of their degree.

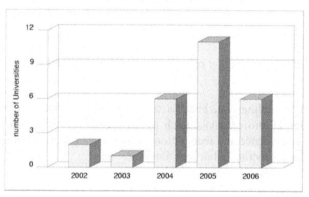

Figure 2. Distribution of the years of activation of EUCIP projects

The relevance of the EUCIP *Core* level certification in terms of number of credits earned by the students is shown in Figure 3. The most frequent values, that is, three and five, are in line with the recommendations of the two Italian groups of the University professors of Computer Engineering and Computer Science. The figure shows three Universities that associated nine credits with the EUCIP *Core* level certification: this choice was probably due to some local peculiarities.

The quantitative analysis of the EUCIP projects focused on the number of students involved in these projects and on the number of certifications awarded to the students. Despite the increasing interest shown by the Universities towards EUCIP, these numbers are not very encouraging. For example, in 2005, the Universities involved in their EUCIP projects 3,123 students in total and awarded 504 certifications. In the year 2006, we noticed a decrease of these numbers, namely, 1,808 students involved and 189 certifications awarded. A possible explanation of this trend relies on some peculiarities of the EUCIP*4U* project, which granted students a free access to e-learning material and a discount on the Skills Card required for the online tests. These two aspects might have led students to enroll earlier in the EUCIP projects. However, Universities might have not given them sufficient incentives (for example, credits) for pursuing the corresponding certification.

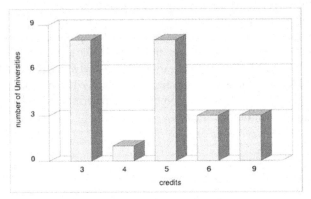

Figure 3. Maximum number of credits associated with the EUCIP *Core* level

It is important to outline that, because of the novelty for the academic world of certifications for IT professionals, such as the EUCIP *Core* level, their diffusion requires a strong evidence and recognition by industries which, in turn, require long and complex dissemination and penetration processes.

3.2   Student perspective

The investigation on the institutional aspects of the EUCIP projects has been integrated by telephone interviews of a set of students who obtained the EUCIP *Core* level certification in the years 2004, 2005 and 2006 during their University studies. These interviews were aimed at collecting the student perspective on EUCIP with respect to their degree of satisfaction, their choices and motivations.

The interviews involved in total 85 students enrolled at 20 different Universities. While the Universities were uniformly distributed all over Italy, the majority of the students (i.e., 70%) was enrolled at Universities in Northern Italy. Moreover, about two thirds of these students belonged to Computer Engineering, and about one third to Computer Science. The analysis of the motivations that led students to obtain the EUCIP *Core* level (see Figure 4) has shown a strong prevalence of professional motivations. Only 35 students had to perform a specific preparation before taking the exams required to obtain the EUCIP. For 50 students, the competences acquired during their University studies were enough. Even though the large majority of these students have Informatics as their major, it is interesting to point out a different behaviour between the students of Engineering and Science.

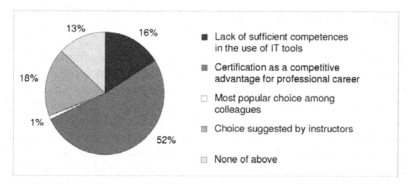

Figure 4. Motivations of the students to obtain the EUCIP *Core* level

Our investigation has shown that the majority of the students perceived the certification as either very useful or useful for their future professional career.

Concerning the competences certified by EUCIP *Core* level, about two thirds of the students involved in the interviews expressed the need to improve them. This need was stronger among the students of Science (77%) than among the students of Engineering (61%). Figure 5 shows the choices of the students with respect to three EUCIP areas – *Plan*, *Build* and *Operate* – and to other topics not covered by these areas.

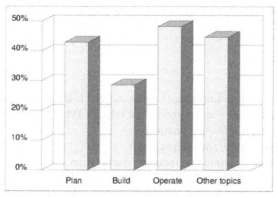

Figure 5. Topics to be improved after the acquisition of the EUCIP *Core* level

Each student was allowed multiple choices. It was surprisingly to discover that the most popular choice of the students, namely 48.2%, referred to the *Operate* area that covers topics related to operating systems and computer networks.

In summary, we can then conclude that students recognize the importance of the EUCIP *Core* level for their future professional career and show an interest in improving the knowledge and the competences certified by EUCIP. These results represent an important starting point for the design of new University programmes.

4   Concluding remarks

The results of the investigation of the EUCIP activities performed by Italian Universities have shown a good interest towards this type of certification. Many Universities offer EUCIP in their degrees. Moreover, the students who obtained a EUCIP *Core* level certification during their University studies are in general satisfied of their experience, and express a need to improve the certified competences.

Our investigation has also outlined the possibility of extending such a certification to a larger audience, that is, to students with major other than Informatics.

Moreover, the main feature of the EUCIP programme, that is, the integration between University studies and on-the-job experiences, makes it particularly suitable to become part of the University degrees. Hence, the experiences described in this paper could represent a good basis for the ongoing revision of University programmes in Italy. The integration of the EUCIP in Bachelor degrees in scientific and technical areas would definitely increase their attractiveness for the market.

Acknowledgements

Authors would like to thank the representatives of the Universities who participated to these investigations. Fabrizio Agnesi and Paolo Schgör of AICA deserve a particular mention for their valuable suggestions during the preparation of this manuscript. A special thank goes to Marcello Beccaria, Pietro Marzani and Ilaria Scarabottolo for their support. Finally, authors acknowledge the continuous encouragement of AICA, CINI, and Fondazione CRUI.

References

[1]   Commission of the European Communities, E-skills for the 21st Century: Fostering Competitiveness, Growth and Jobs, COM(2007) 496 final.
[2]   EUCIP website: http://www.eucip.com.
[3]   CEPIS website: http://www.cepis.org.
[4]   The Computing Technology Industry Association – CompTIA, The Situation and the Role of E-Skills Industry Certification in Europe (August 2004).
[5]   The EUCIP Model - A standard approach to the definition and measurement of ICT Competences, AICA report (2007). Available at: http://www.eucip.it.
[6]   Website of the Observatory of ICT Certifications in Italian Universities: http://osservatorio.consorzio-cini.it (in Italian).
[7]   M. Calzarossa, P. Ciancarini, P. Maresca, L. Mich, and N. Scarabottolo, The ECDL Programme in Italian Universities, *Computers & Education* 49(2), pp. 238-243 (2007).
[8]   M. Calzarossa, P. Ciancarini, P. Maresca, L. Mich, and N. Scarabottolo, The ECDL Certification of ICT Usage Skills in the Italian Universities, *Proc. of the Twelfth Int. Conf. on Distributed Multimedia Systems*, pp. 238-243 (2006).

Competence Based Tutoring Online

A Proposal for Linking Global and Specific E-Learning Models

Monica Banzato[1] and Gustavo Daniel Constantino[2]

[1] Università Ca' Foscari di Venezia, SSIS del Veneto (School of specialization secondary teacher), Fondamenta Moro 2978 Cannaregio – 30121 VENEZIA Italy, banzato@unive.it
WWW home page: http://www.univirtual.it/ssis

[2] CIAFIC/CONICET, Information Communication Technology Department (TICIAFIC), Av. Federico Lacroze 2100, 1426 Buenos Aires, Argentina, gustav@wamani.apc.org,
WWW home page: http://www.didaxis.com.ar/constantino

Abstract. The paper suggests crossing global e-learning models with specific ones so as to determine their possible correlation in order to infer online tutor competence profiles. These are found at the intersection of the pyramid, matrix and e-learning instructional design models. Hypothetical setups of the pyramid e-learning systems are discussed. The competence matrix is described in more detail as a complex and potentially useful instrument to guide OLT training and evaluation. It is concluded that the synergy resulting from the interplay among the competence matrix, e-learning instructional design models and e-learning environments will make it possible to assess instrument potential and conceptual schema appropriateness. It will also show their limitations, with a view to improving them.

1 E-learning models and tutoring competences

Cooperative or collaborative online learning [6, 7, 10] appears as the most complex and qualitatively rich of the three models –independent, assisted and collaborative- proposed by Banzato & Midoro [9]. Collaborative activities entail task-sharing and the explicit intention 'to add value', i.e. to produce something new or different through a deliberate and structured collaborative process, as opposed to just exchanging information or executing instructions. Collaborative learning may be thus defined as the acquisition of knowledge, skills and attitudes by individuals through collaborative group interaction aimed at creating a product or service or providing a solution to a certain group task [9].

Please use the following format when citing this chapter:

Banzato, M. and Constantino, G.D., 2008, in IFIP International Federation for Information Processing, Volume 281; *Learning to Live in the Knowledge Society*; Michael Kendall and Brian Samways; (Boston: Springer), pp. 209–216.

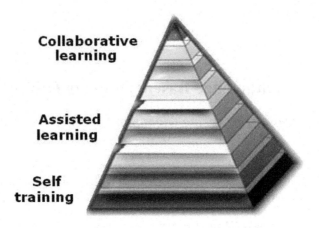

Fig. 1. Pyramid: collaborative, assisted, autonomous learning [9].

The collaborative model places interaction between tutors and learners at the very core of e-learning as instruction in virtual spaces or on virtual platforms. The added value of this active and joint construction of knowledge (collaborative learning) cannot be reduced to the mere sharing of instructional materials or to individual tutoring. Specific online tutor (OLT) training has become therefore crucial to the success and quality of the process and its outcomes. The importance of OLT competences does not decrease even in the case of blended courses, in which a different and integrated strategic plan is required to mobilise them around set activities. The OLT competence matrix, proposed by Banzato [1], was developed to reflect the abilities needed to design and implement courses to acceptable standards. It was developed, and has been tested, in international online university environments of Veneto's SSIS ONLINE, ITALS online master's programme, courses and OLT master's courses in Italy, Spain, Portugal, Brazil, Paraguay and Argentina, to name but a few. We are currently involved in ALFA-Miforcal, a project in which universities from six European and Latin American countries take part, whose main features will be discussed.

Beyond the necessary and sufficient conditions for OLT training, the competence profile or matrix points to professional qualification in order to ensure quality education. The evaluation of online tutoring should be conceived not only in terms of the dynamic selection of the agents that will devise and implement instructional activities, but also as an opportunity to make use of the strategic instruments of continuous quality improvement. The issue of OLT certification, which appears as central to e-learning quality management systems, needs therefore to be addressed. Quality OLT training is key to intervention strategies, constituting a chief priority of all the systems proposed at the international level (i.e. the EQF in Europe).

Only an accurate definition of the matrix of OLT competences and roles will enable the construction of different competence profiles, especially in relation to quality education standards such as personalised instruction and the encouragement of critical and creative thinking. Taking into account both the current literature and our own work, the paper put forward a conceptual framework that employs the OLT competence matrix [1] to evaluate OLT training programmes with regard to the effective and differentiated instruction provided. This will impact on online tutor selection, ensuring that the candidates' competence profiles meet the requirements of educational institutions. The framework consists in a knowledge, skills and competence matrix that accounts for about 500 OLT micro-competences seen – beyond any behaviourist connotations- as valid and reliable indicators of middle- and higher-order competences. Thus, we offer an analytic approach and an instrumental matrix that may be integrated or completed with other instruments in different instructional contexts or situations.

2   The online tutor macro-competences matrix

The online tutor macro-competences matrix [1] has been conceived as the three dimensional product of 4 knowledge dimensions, 7 competence areas and 4 macro-phases of the training process. Fig. 1 represents the product of the first two. The first group includes: (1) theories of e-learning environments; (2) theories of online instruction design; (3) social theories of Internet-mediated communication; (4) theories of e-learning media. The second group consists of: (A) management and control of the learning processes; (B) implementation of differentiated instructional methodologies; (C) effective communication with e-learners; (D) efficient use of the e-learning environment; (E) organization and timing of tutoring work, activities and resources; (F) information technology support (help desk), and (G) applied research and testing of new standards. The resulting 28 macro-competences are developed through the macro-phases of the training process in which tutors are daily involved. For the sake of simplicity they have been summed up as: (1) diagnosis/prognosis, (2) planning, (3) delivery, (4) monitoring and evaluation. Thus, 500 micro-competences and micro-skills have been obtained.

Our three-dimensional matrix provides a structure to describe all OLT profiles, and not just that of the ideal tutor. Even experienced tutors do not necessarily master all the professional skills in terms of knowledge, competence and ability. The whole training staff is often responsible for instructional decisions and actions, which are based on context requirements, project/programme demands, etc. Furthermore, no instructional system, no matter how complex, calls for the simultaneous exercise of all the skills. But while low-skilled tutors could distribute curriculum content materials and provide learning checks, a higher level of expertise would be needed to build a learning community and facilitate interpersonal relations. Sometimes novice tutors can keep forum interaction going, but in other cases specific micro-competencies are required to encourage the development of higher-order thinking skills, such as metacognition.

Online Tutor Macro-Competences Matrix (Banzato M., 2007)

Knowledge Areas of competence	01 Theories of education in elearning environment	02 Theories of instructional design (ID)	03 Theories of social communication network	04 Theories of virtual media environments
A. Managing the processes of learning on-line.	A-01 Able to understand process of learning online, assessing/evaluating human/professional/cultural students' needs.	A-02 Know how to teach in relation to instructional design (ID) choose by course	A-03 Able to build a social network and to support the growth of social group.	A-04 Able to create and introduce links between topics and online resource.
B. Using differentiated teaching methodologies.	B-01 Able to design and plan different types of learning activities (ID) in relation to the models of the project.	B-02 Able to teach and mange individual and collective educational activities (ID).	B-03 Able to interact and diversify communication in relation to the groups and ID.	B-04 Able to choose specific software tools to develop learning activities (ID).
C. Communicating online in effective ways.	C-01 Able to establish meaningful relationships with students: create a sympathetic and positive atmosphere in virtual classrooms.	C-02 Able to organize and support individual or group communication in learning activities (ID).	C-03 Able to organize social events to raise the indices of social presence.	C-04 Know how to detect appropriate media (e.g. audio, video etc.), social software, spaces/times of communication.
D. Using of the virtual learning environment in efficient ways.	D-01 Know how to design online learning activity in efficient ways in different learning platforms.	D-02 Know how to teach online learning activities (ID) in relation to elearning platforms.	D-03 Able to detect social ideas (knowledge sharing), develop arguments, promote valuable threads.	D-04 Able to draw on different technological systems: e.g. adaptive systems; tutorial; simulations, games etc.
E. Planning own workplace activities, time, resources.	E-01 Able to design curriculum and sequence content.	E-02 Able to evaluate and assess learning activities (ID).	E-03 Know how to devise instructional and social activities.	E-04 Able to programme media tolls and platform configuration.
F. Providing technological assistance.	F-01 Know how to organize help desk course for student in relation to the professional/cultural students' needs.	F-02 Know how and when to use normal and special features of software to help learner's use.	F-03 Know how to select and suggest social interaction tools and their uses.	F-04 Able to use software to create and manipulate locations in space for elearning platforms.
G. Developing research.	G-01 Being determined and motivated to explore new learning ways in virtual environments.	G-02 Being able to try out new learning models (ID), methods and roles.	G-03 Being able to explore and to try out the social network and communication features.	G-04 Being able to try out and to implement new media tools and media instructional use

3. Linking tutor competence profiles and e-learning instructional design models

The pyramid model shows three clearly defined e-learning types or systems consistent with different instructional design models and tutor competence profiles. The matrix model shows the micro-competences obtained by crossing online education knowledge areas with the whole range of instructional and curriculum action (macro-competences). It is put forward as a heuristic tool to enquire into the micro-competences found in each tutor competence profile.

Instructional design models are theoretical hypotheses, i.e. conceptualisations arising from the application of instructional models to concrete e-learning systems, each with its own peculiarities and constraints. Their outcomes may therefore be empirically assessed, and thus they are both heuristic and experimental in nature. The instructional design models proposed specify those represented in the pyramid.

OLT competence profiles no doubt underpin our connection of the three groups of models. Within a holistic framework, the matrix provides a 'universe' of competences that may be used to identify the capabilities included in each ideal profile or to assess OLT's concrete skills. Heuristically, it might be seen as a neural network, in which most frequently activated nodes (micro-competences) would make up a basic profile, whereas those that are only sporadically operational would give rise to differentiated profiles, whose structural and situational contexts could be analysed. This might have a huge impact on OLT training and selection.

4 E-learning Instructional Design Models and OTL Matrix: The Miforcal Case

The competences matrix has been applied to the European Project Alfa Miforcal [4]. The project aims to design a online training quality program degree for European and Latin American secondary teachers candidates. The project spreads over many research areas, in particular the design of a shared curriculum. The project has not chosen a single model ID, but different training models that extend over the entire e-learning system pyramid [9].

The training program is still in progress, but we can recognize the different tutor profile's choice according the ID.

1) The common curricular area (pedagogical disciplines) would only need tutors that administrate access to instructional documentation and learning activities, answering the student content questions, and testing the student achievement. The tutors/instructors' role does not differ much from that of traditional teachers: they 'produce' lessons that will be delivered through content distribution networks. According to the competence matrix, in this case the OLT should have at least the following competences: A-01, B-01, C-04, D-02, E-04.

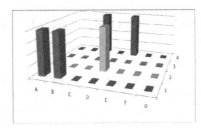

Fig. 2. OLT profile for the self-learning model: 3-D representation of the competences involved

2) For specific curriculum content areas (science, humanities and language) has been chosen a model ID assisted. Online tutors must, in this model, offer educational guidance and assistance to a group of students. They facilitate document content learning and the sharing of views and experiences among the participants. It is not their job to provide information technology support, in which they differ from technical assistants/operators, or to coordinate collaborative work. The basic OLT skills required by the model, as can be seen in fig. 3, are: A-01; A-02; A-04; B-01; B-03; C-01; C-02; E-02; E-03. Our graphical representation does not include instructional design (E-01, E-02, E-03, E-04) or advanced (G-01, G-02, G-03, G-04) competences, such as subject matter research.

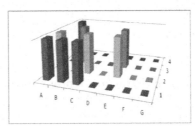

Fig. 3. OLT profile for the assisted learning model: 3-D representation of the competences involved

3) Otherwise, for laboratories areas have been chosen a collaborative learning model. The OLT, as moderator, focuses of the organization and management of collaboration and cooperation of the working groups. This model has been borrowed, as some writers point out, from communications and group dynamics studies. The minimum OLT competences required by these learning communities can be seen in fig. 4: A-01, A-02; A-03; A-04; B-01; B-02; B-03; C-01; C-02; C-03; C-04; E-01; E-02; E-03; F-03; G-02.

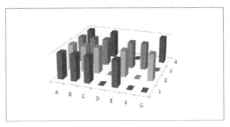

Fig. 4. OLT profile for the collaborative learning model: 3-D representation of the competences involved

5   The matrix and the construction of differential profiles

The competence matrix might prove helpful in constructing OLT differential profiles, insofar as:
a) It provides guidance on theoretical and practical issues. Instructional designers and planners can use it, for example, to assess the impact of tutor performance in online courses on the other components of the instructional system.
b) It can serve as a monitoring instrument for project managers seeking to maintain instructional system quality while focusing on possible solutions to specific problems or necessary adjustments.
c) It could even help design e-learning environment simulations for OLT training purposes.
d) Finally, it constitutes a powerful heuristic instrument for tutor (self-) evaluation and, therefore, may contribute to the development of a more balanced professional profile and competence portfolio.

6   Conclusion

We have outlined three approaches to e-learning systems grounded in three different theoretical perspectives. Their main features have been discussed in order to show that they do not exclude but rather complement each other.

Therefore we suggest crossing the global theoretical models (e-learning pyramid) with specific ones (profile matrix and instructional design models), which will enable an in-depth theoretical and practical consideration of conceptual structures. This in turn will provide functional quality criteria for e-learning systems designers and those in charge of course coordination and tutoring management.

Our proposal aims at developing efficiency hypotheses, concepts and criteria in order to work out operational management and instruction profiles in the competence, procedure and strategy areas. This will enable the construction of e-learning environments centred on quality teaching and learning processes.

The instructional design models applied within the framework of the Alfa Miforcal project show how the competence matrix captures the concrete OLT profiles 'in action'. Our goal has been to test the performance of OLT profiles as well as of e-learning environment design instruments.

The synergy resulting from the interplay among the competence matrix, e-learning instructional design models and e-learning environments will make it possible to assess instrument potential and conceptual schema appropriateness as well as their limitations, with a view to improving them.

References

1. M. Banzato, La mappa delle competenze del tutor ondine, in M. Banzato, D. Corcione, G. Guardagli, Il tutor online. Un quadro di riferimento per la certificazione delle competenze e della qualità, Bologna, CLUEB, 2007, pp. 97-102.
2. C.R Clark, R.E. Mayer, E-learning and the science of instruction, San Francisco: Jossey-Bass, 2003.
3. G. Collison et al., Facilitating online learning, Madison (WI): Atwood, 2000.
4. G.D. Constantino, M. Banzato, Modelos de Organizaciòn Docente para la Formaciòn Online. El caso del Proyecto Alfa Miforcal. – Proceedings TE&ET'06 (vol. 1), Redunici, La Plata, 2006, pp. 285-294.
5. G.D. Constantino, M. Banzato, J. Raffaghelli, Research in virtual worlds: linking quantitative and qualitative data in e-learning environments, Proceedings IHSRC 2007- International Human Science Research Conference, 13-16 June 2007, Rovereto (ITALY), 2007.
6. D.H. Jonassen, M.Tessmer, W.H Hannum, Task Analysis Methods for Instructional Design. Mahwah, NJ: Lawrence Erlbaum Associates, 1999.
7. D.H. Jonassen, (Ed.).(). Handbook of research on educational communications and technology, 2nd. Ed. Mahwah, NJ: Lawrence Erlbaum Associates. 2004.
8. U. Margiotta, Qualification Framework. Un terreno di ricerca per la formazione degli insegnanti secondari italiani, in Rivista Formazione&Insegnamento, vol 1°, n. 3, Multimedia Pensa, Lecce, 2003, pp 9-30.
9. V. Midoro, M. Banzato, Modelli di e-learning, TD - Rivista Tecnologie Didattiche, vol. 36, 2005, pp. 60-71.
10. C. Reigeluth, (ed.), Instructional-design theories and models: Volume II A new Paradigm of Instructional Theory. London: Lawrence Erlbaum Associates, Publishers, 1999.
11. G. Salmon, E-Moderating. The key to Teaching and Learning Online, London (UK): Kogan Page, 2000.

In this paper, Monica Banzato wrote the paragraphs: 2, 5 and 6; Gustavo D. Constantino wrote the paragraphs 1, 3 and 4.

Chapter 9

Innovative Learning Environments 2

An Ontology-Based Modeling Approach for Developing a Competencies-Oriented Collective Intelligence

Mihaela Brut[1], Florence Sedes[2], Toader Jucan[1], Romulus Grigoras[3],
Vincent Charvillat[3]
[1] Alexandru Ioan Cuza University of Iasi, Romania,
{mihaela, jucan}@infoiasi.ro;
[2] Institut de Recherche en Informatique de Toulouse, France, sedes@irit.fr;
[3] ENSEEIHT, France {romulus.grigoras, charvi}@enseeiht.fr

Abstract. Expressing the user competences through domain ontology concepts is a prerogative for developing well managed and semantically enriched user profiles, transferable from a system to another. If, supplementary, the available documents are also ontology-based annotated, the add-on value will concern not only the document semantics, but also the relations and dependencies between users and documents. In such approach, the ontology constitutes the binder between peoples, as well as between peoples and documents, and also between documents. Its reasoning support sustains the development of a collective intelligence, as well as the most suitable knowledge sharing, according to the users common competencies. In this article we present such modeling approach, and also some methods for user and document model development, as well as the advantages for personalized and collaborative facilities.

1 Introduction

An E-learning platform is a real source of knowledge due to the available materials, but also to its users' competences. Our paper goal is to provide a solution for interconnecting these two resource types in order to provide platform users with access to the most suitable documents and collaborators, according to their profile.

The solution considers the same domain ontology set for modeling both the documents annotations and the user profile. After presenting the two models and their development techniques, our paper will expose the modeling approach advantages and applications, followed by conclusions and further work.

Please use the following format when citing this chapter:

Brut, M., Sedes, F., Jucan, T., Grigoras, R. and Charvillat, V., 2008, in IFIP International Federation for Information Processing, Volume 281;
Learning to Live in the Knowledge Society; Michael Kendall and Brian Samways; (Boston: Springer), pp. 219–222.

2 Ontology-Based User Competences Model

The idea of managing user competencies through one or more ontologies was explored in multiple systems. The CommOn framework uses self-defined competence schemes, organized as ontology, in order to develop Competency-Based Web Services dedicated to Human Resource Management [10]. In [4] is presented an system for storing and reasoning about competencies of students at universities, based on a fine-grained representation of skills and competence ontology.

General user models consider five most popular features for user as an individual: the user's knowledge, interests, goals, background, and individual traits [2]. The overlay model enables to represent these features as a subset of the domain model, which could consist in one or more domain ontologies.

Our goal is to integrate such overlay model focused on competences inside the user model provided by the e-learning standards and to find a solution for automatically developing it. For an e-learning platform aiming the user competences management and development, two features are essential for the user model:

1. *Knowledge* – the user actual, acquired, competences, expressed through ontology concepts selected according his acquired certificates and qualifications.
2. *Interests* – the user desired, foresighted, competencies, expressed through ontology concepts selected according the courses in which the students is currently enrolled (each course aims at developing a set of competences);

Among the two main user profile models standardized in the e-learning domain - IMS Learner Information Specification and IEEE PAPI Public And Private, we choose PAPI for our user profile model, because we intend to use IEEE LOM standard for structuring the educational content. PAPI model structure includes 6 categories [11], the Learner Performance category being in charge with competence management, including support for tracking the competences level and validity.

Because the two layers user profile development is related to certain events such as exams upholding or course enrolment, a *rule-based solution* for it's automatically updating is suitable [7]:

- When a user pass an exam and gains a certificate, its associated competences (ontology concepts) are transferred into the user knowledge level, being deleted from the interest layer profile.
- When a user is enrolled to a certain course, the course assigned topics (ontology concepts) are included automatically in his long term interests profile.

3 The Domain Model

The IEEE/LOM (*Learning Objects Metadata*) standard for the educational materials structuring is considered as the most enabling for semantic extensions. Its *Classification* category enables to specify that the LO belongs to a certain classification system such a domain ontology, by identifying the ontology and the particular concept which want to refer.

For enhancing the *expressive power* of annotations that create links between documents and ontology concepts, there were conceived some techniques of associating *roles* and/or *weights* with these relations. The most common role is "prerequisite" [1]. In the KBS-HyperBook system, the documents could be marked as "problem statement", "example", "theory" for a certain concept [6].

Because our goal is to identify the most relevant documents for a certain user competence profile, we propose the usage of 3 roles (as relation types) for expressing the relevance of a document for a certain concept. These could be integrated into Classification IEEE/LOM category as a new attribute, relationType, with 3 possible values expressing this relevance into a decreasing order:
- isOnTopic – for a document which is especially destined to a certain topic;
- usesTheConcept – expressing the concepts encountered into document;
- makesReferenceTo – for marking the other referenced concepts from ontology.

For automatically generating this relations, our solution first distributes the document in 3 classes, which are relevant for our considered relations: the document title and subtitles will be considered for the isOnTopic relation, the hyperlinks and the bibliographical references – for the makesReferenceTo relation, and the document body (the rest of the document) will be processed in order to obtain the usesTheConcept relation. The existing Web Information Retrieval techniques consider a larger number of classes, corresponding for example to 12 categories [7].

For each class concept-based annotation, the existing approaches consider the *Latent Semantic Indexing* techniques [5], which represent a document through concepts rather than through index terms, as in term-based classical information retrieval. First the matrix of terms frequency is built, and then the matrix of concepts frequency is obtained, by applying the *Singular Value Decomposition* technique [8]. Thus, for each of the above mentioned 3 document classes, there is obtained the corresponding set of concepts, together with their occurrence number.

4   The Modeling Approach Advantages

The documents and users modeling in the exposed manner provides a permanent connection between users and materials which could be exploited for many purposes:
- *recommending* a user the potential collaborators (in general or in specific projects)
- *filtering* and *ranking* the existing materials according to a user profile,
- *adapting* the navigation system to a user profile (by re-ordering the links, emphasizing the most important ones, or eliminating those which are not useful).

Because each such facility is focused on a sub-set of the ontology competencies set, the selection of the suitable materials, as well as the user selection could be reduced in fact to a *query process*. Thus, all the mentioned situations could be reduced to the case of querying the users and materials XML databases by a ontology concepts based query. A ranking algorithm processes such queries, considering as most relevant the documents which contain:
- the query concepts linked through strong semantic relations (e.g. *isOnTopic*);
- the concepts related to the query concepts;
  These criteria are adapted from ILEX *(The Intelligent Labeling Explorer)* system [9]: (i) information becomes less relevant the more distant it is from the focal

object, in terms of semantic links; (ii) different semantic link types maintain relevance to different degrees.

- which has a good temporal relevance (recently created or updated);
- which author is competent concerning the query concepts.

These facilities could be exported from an e-learning system to another if they are implemented in the form of Web services [3]. Thus, the user mobility is facilitated by his user competencies profile recognition by other systems.

5   Conclusions and Further Work

In this article, we presented a modeling approach for the content annotations and user competences profile within e-learning platforms, based on the same domain ontology set. This approach considers all the system resources from the perspective of enhancing user competencies and collaboration, contributing to the collective intelligence development.

A further research direction consists in exploring the implementation and optimization techniques details for the particular case of personalized recommendations, considering also the collaborative filtering criterion.

References

1. Brusilovsky, P., Eklund, J., Schwarz, E.: Web-based education for all: A tool for developing adaptive courseware. In: Ashman, H., Thistewaite, P. (eds.) Proc. of Seventh International World Wide Web Conference. Vol. 30. Elsevier Science B. V. (1998) 291-300
2. Brusilovsky, P., Millán, E., User Models for Adaptive Hypermedia and Adaptive Educational Systems, in P. Brusilovsky, A. Kobsa, W. Nejdl (Eds.): The Adaptive Web, LNCS 4321, Springer 2007
3. Brut, M., Buraga, S., Ontology-Based Annotation Grid Services for E-Learning, in Xhafa F., Barolli, L., Proceedings of Conference on Complex, Intelligent and Software Intensive Systems, IEEE Computer Society Press, ISBN 0-7695-3109-1, 2008
4. Dorn, J., Pichlmair, M., A Competence Management System for Universities, Proceeding of the European Conference on Artificial Intelligence, St. Gallen, 2007
5. Dumais, S.T.: Latent semantic indexing (LSI) and TREC-2. In: Text REtrieval Conference (TREC) TREC-2 Proceedings (1993) 105–116 NIST Special Publication 500-215.
6. Henze, N., Nejdl, W.: Adaptation in open corpus hypermedia. International Journal of Artificial Intelligence in Education 12, 4 (2001) 325-350
7. Lin, W., Alvarez, S.A., Ruiz, C.: Efficient adaptive-support association rule mining for recommender systems. Data Mining and Knowledge Discovery 6 (2002) 83–105
8. Micarelli, A., Sciarrone, F., Marinilli, M.: Web document modeling. In Brusilovsky, P., Kobsa, A., Nejdl, W., eds.: The Adaptive Web, LNCS 4321, Springer 2007
9. O'Donnell, M., Mellish, C., Oberlander, J., Knott, A.: ILEX: An Architecture for a Dynamic Hypertext Generation System. Journal of Natural Language Engineering 7(3) (2003)
10. Trichet, Leclere, A Framework for building competency-based systems, in N. Zhong et al. (Eds.): ISMIS 2003, LNAI 2871, pp. 633–639, Springer, 2003.
11. * * *, IEEE P1484.2.25 - Draft Standard for Learning Technology. Public and Private Information (PAPI) for Learners (PAPI Learner) Learner Performance Information, 2001

Maintenance of Learner's Characteristics by Spreading a Change

Michal Šimún, Anton Andrejko and Mária Bieliková
Slovak University of Technology, Faculty of Informatics and Information
Technologies, Institute of Informatics and Software Engineering
Ilkovičova 3, 842 16 Bratislava 4, Slovakia
simun.michal@yahoo.com, {andrejko,bielik}@fiit.stuba.sk
WWW home page: http://www.fiit.stuba.sk

Abstract. Learners have different knowledge, interests and also goals in any educational process. If all the learners are provided the same content the process will probably not meet expected goals. A personalized approach to a learner increases the efficiency of the learning process. It is based on information about the learner that is subject of change. Several adaptive educational systems exist. However, they usually do not consider changes in user behavior and relationships that may exist among contents in order to maintain learner characteristics. In this paper we present a novel method for maintenance of user's characteristics based on spreading activation.

1 Introduction

Good educational process strongly depends on a combination of the best learning sources aimed at achieving high quality while using the most effective methods of education as possible. Web-based educational applications provide huge amounts of information from various areas that are presented to learners, but usually do not consider the learner's individual knowledge or interest. Such a learner might be provided with content that he/she is not ready to study at that time, is not interested in, or can not find suitable information in large knowledge spaces. Increased efficiency of learning process requires a personalized approach to a learner where characteristics for each learner are modeled in a user oriented model which is used to select the most suitable study material for an individual learner. In this approach the key requirement is to accurately estimate the individual learner's characteristics.

There are several ways to model characteristics in a user model. The most common approaches are *stereotype* [1] and *layered* [2, 3] user model. In the stereotype approach learners are divided into groups according to the selected difficulty of course. Each learner is assigned to one stereotype only and is provided

Please use the following format when citing this chapter:

Šimún, M., Andrejko, A. and Bieliková, M., 2008, in IFIP International Federation for Information Processing, Volume 281; *Learning to Live in the Knowledge Society*; Michael Kendall and Brian Samways; (Boston: Springer), pp. 223–226.

with studying materials assigned to the particular stereotype. The stereotype can be changed after successfully completing the competency for that material (e.g. test, skills demonstration, etc.). In the layered user model the user's characteristics are modeled according to educational documents within a particular course. In this case, evaluation of user characteristics' for a visited document and for related parts of the course (*characteristic propagation*) is employed. Actualization of a characteristic for the course can be based on defined rules [3] or on analysis of learner's activity [2].

In this paper we focus on modeling user's characteristics while learning. We propose a novel method for maintenance of user's characteristics based on spreading adaptive change in a layered user model.

2   Adaptive Web-Based Educational System Models

In the personalization process it is desirable to know the document's attributes (educational content) in an educational course (domain model) and also the user's characteristics (user model). In this paper we provide examples on adaptive learning programming. Individual learner's characteristics are mapped against characteristics of educational materials that express the semantics of educational materials. Therefore, for the domain (and user) model ontology representation [4, 5] is used. Having reusability of the models in mind we divide the domain model into *Knowledge item space* and *Learning objects space* as shown in the Fig 1.

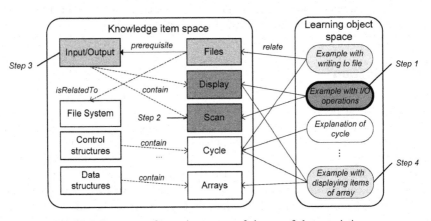

Fig 1. Sequence of steps in process of change of characteristic.

The *Learning objects space* consists of learning objects and relations between them. This part of the domain model merges with a standard view of the domain model for adaptive web-based systems. A *Knowledge Item* (KI) represents a *topic* or a *key word* that represents key terms of the domain. Its aim is a categorization of available learning objects into knowledge items (using the linkage *relate*) according to learning goals of particular learning objects. We have added knowledge item level to the domain model to be able to model personalization at the knowledge items level. It allows for a determination of the learner's characteristics for all learning objects related to the knowledge item. Our approach also supports the changing of learner's characteristics for the learning objects, even he/she has have not visited them yet. A knowledge item can be connected using relations *prerequisite* (knowledge items necessary to be understood or known in order to study other subjects), *contain* (hierarchical content of knowledge item) or *isRelatedTo* (logically related knowledge items). Personalization in an educational course is based on presentation (recommendation) of appropriate learning objects to an individual learner who is represented in a user model. Furthering the developed user model is influenced by [2]. It consists of records about user's visits, interest and knowledge.

3   User's Characteristics Maintenance by Spreading a Change

While a user works with a learning object we obtain his/her characteristics for that learning object (e.g. interest). Since there is a connection between learning objects and other parts of the domain model we incorporate any changes to other related parts of the domain model, even if the user has not worked with these parts yet. The process consists of four steps.

In the first step characteristics for actual learning object (e.g. *Example with I/O operations* in Fig 1) are set. Its characteristics *knowledge* and *interest* are changed according to the variety of views and each view defines a strategy for characteristics to be updated. Furthermore, *interest* and *knowledge* have assigned *characteristic's value* (numeric value) and a *probability* of modeled value (how likely a real value of user's characteristic matches a modeled value of the characteristic). Analyzing learner's activity we directly change following views for actual learning object:

- *Feedback:* user adjusts interest (knowledge) in a graphical user interface directly;
- *Classification:* every defined level of the characteristic (e.g. expert) creates a class of classification. According to the selected strategy a model of classification is created that assigns a user into one of the defined classes in regard to user's activity.

In the second step, changes of characteristic's values from actual learning object are applied to knowledge items (knowledge item *Display* and *Scan*). For instance, if user studied a learning object focused on cycles it is desirable to increase *knowledge* for the knowledge item *Cycles*. Characteristic's value for related KI is computed using all related learning objects that initialized a characteristic with changed view.

Spreading or applying changes of characteristic's values from knowledge items (*Scan* and *Display* in our example) to other related parts of knowledge item space (*Input/Output* and *Files*) is processed in the third step. A change of a characteristic for knowledge and interest is applied through the modeled relations between knowledge items. Spreading user's characteristic to other knowledge items is based on spreading activation [7, 8] where initial energy of a selected node is spread to other nodes, and fades with increasing distance. Energy is a couple (*value, probability(value)*), where *value* is a quantified representation of the spread characteristic. Fading is accomplished by sequentially decreased probability of value.

The last step is spreading characteristic's change from the knowledge items to the related learning objects (*Example with writing to file*). After the change of value and probability of a characteristic for the knowledge item occurs it is necessary to process the change of the characteristic for all learning objects. These changes in characteristics occur in the learning objects space that have assigned selected knowledge item. Characteristic's value for related learning object is computed from characteristics of all related knowledge items that have initialized the characteristic.

4   Conclusion

A personalized approach to learners provides a way to improve the educational process. We present a method for modeling and maintenance of user's characteristics based on spreading activation. In the first step, characteristics in a source of activation (i.e. learning object a user is working with) are set. Afterwards, spreading is processed to knowledge items related to the selected learning object. Changes in knowledge item characteristic affects also related learning objects.

For evaluation purposes a simple programming course was created. It consists of 16 learning objects and knowledge items are imported from ACM classification. We developed an adaptive web-based educational application that recommends learning objects. It is built on three architectural layers – user, application and data. The data layer contains learning materials and semantics of the course – domain ontology and user's characteristics (in OWL-DL). The application layer is responsible for maintaining of user's characteristics using our method and is implemented in Java SE 6. The user layer is implemented in JRuby and it is responsible for generating views in the educational course and acquiring information about user's activities.

Acknowledgement: This work was supported by the Cultural and Educational Grant Agency KEGA 3/5187/07 and by the Scientific Grant Agency VEGA 1/3102/06.

References

1. C. Seeberg et al., From User's Needs to Adaptive Documents. In: *Proceedings of the Integrated Design & Process Technology Conference*, 2000.
2. E. Schwarz, P. Brusilovsky, J. Eklund., Web-based Education for All: A Tool for Developing Adaptive Courseware. In: Computer Networks and ISDN Systems 30 (1-7), 1998, pp. 291–300.
3. P. De Bra et al., AHA! The Adaptive Hypermedia Architecture. In: *ACM Hypertext Conference*, Nottingham, UK, 2003, pp. 81–84.
4. P. Brusilovsky, Methods and techniques of adaptive hypermedia. User Modeling and User-Adapted Interaction 6 (2-3), 1996, pp. 87–129.
5. P. Šaloun, Z. Velart: Adaptive Hypermedia as a mean for learning programming. In: ICWE, Palo Alto, ACM, 2006, pp. 1–5.
6. A. Andrejko, M. Barla, M. Bieliková. Ontology-based User Modeling for Web-based Information Systems. In G. Knapp et al. (Eds.): Advances in Inf. Sys. Development New Methods and Practice for the Networked Society, Vol. 2, Springer, 2007, pp. 457–468.
7. F. Crestani, P.L. Lee: Searching the Web by Constrained Spreading Activation. In Proc. IEEE Forum on Research and Technology Advances in Digital Library, 1999, pp. 163-170.
8. J. Suchal: Caching Spreading Activation Search. In M. Bieliková (Ed.): IIT.SRC 2007 – Student Research Conference 2007. Bratislava, Slovakia, 2007, pp. 151–155.

Future Learning Strategy and ePortfolios in Education

Christian Dorninger and Christian Schrack

Austrian Federal Ministry for Education, the Arts and Culture

www.bmukk.gv.at; www.e-portfolio.at

Abstract. Based on the experience of a long running eLearning initiative the "Futur(e)Learning"-strategy was started October 2007: New forms of learning and "Web 2.0" didactics were launched at Austrian schools. The current results of this educational project will be outlined. The introduction of ePortfolios in education is part of this strategy: Portfolios are powerful tools to realize individualised learning in formal education (process portfolio) and they also support the documentation of skill oriented knowledge and informal acquired competences for the later professional career (application portfolio).

1   The Futur(e)Learning Strategy

The internet loses its pure "publication" function and is getting more and more interactive and user oriented in the sense of Web 2.0. This change concerns technical issues as well as all areas of application and using. In this context a new strategy for Austrian schools has been launched, based on the following focus points:

1) New forms of learning: by using non-directive learning arrangements it would be possible to gain results from group, partner and individual work.

2) Promotion of creativity: according to their natural talent the youth should get the chance to prepare their own creative thinking environment. Appropriate instruments like communication machines and learning management systems should help to find new ideas, realise own visions and learn important knowledge and behaviour patterns.

3) Using communication machines for mobile learning: all electronic devices like notebook PC, sub notebook, communicator, Classmate PC, PDA and web phone could become a communication machine for mobile learning!

Futur(e)Learning is part of the quality management initiative which is responsible for the implementation of evaluation culture at Austrian schools (Ministry of Education in Vienna, 2007). At the moment 220 schools are involved in Futur(e)Learning. The schools are supported by two eLearning knowledge networks, which were founded 2002: eLearning im Schulalltag (eLSA- lower secondary level)

Please use the following format when citing this chapter:

Dorninger, C. and Schrack, C., 2008, in IFIP International Federation for Information Processing, Volume 281; *Learning to Live in the Knowledge Society*; Michael Kendall and Brian Samways; (Boston: Springer), pp. 227–230.

and eLearning Cluster Project (eLC – upper secondary level). Following projects have been launched in this framework:

1. eContent for all subjects and mid term IT-services for complete education
2. Social Software Support (Wikis, Weblogs, ePortfolios, Learning Communities)
3. Mobile phones for learning (connection with MOODLE platforms)
4. Teachers training with online academies and real time platforms
5. Equipment guidelines and equipment initiatives (for standardisation)
6. Educational offers for adult learners and employed persons (in an EU-ESF-project, especially for migration students)
7. Reduction of barriers for special target groups (isolated children and children in hospitals – project IICC)
8. Quality projects in schools and safer internet use (school development and educational standards, content production by teachers and students; IT-security)
9. Artistic-creative projects together with cultural institutions like the ARS Electronica Center Linz.
10. Introduction of ePortfolio in education

2   Why ePortfolio Projects?

ePortfolio captures the idea of lifelong learning and supports individuals moving along episodes of school, study, training and employment. The educational system should also prepare pupils and students for an active role on the modern labour market, which requires a dynamic evaluation of competencies. Due to the inherent portability of portfolios the smooth transfer of verifiable information about learning, evaluation and competences between the levels of education is ensured.

Based on experiences of several years of practice ePortfolios seem to demonstrate successfully the potential of serving individuals as well as organisations in a comprehensive way. According to the Chief Executive of the European Institute for eLearning (EIfEL), Serge Ravet "*ePortfolios are now a central element in some national learning policies.*" [1] (RAVET, 2005). So it is safe to conclude that schools, higher education as well as enterprises are well advised to engage in the potentials of ePortfolios.

Portfolios are products of self organisation to support individual and collaborative learning processes at schools and they can deliver first experiences of students achievement maps on the way of lifelong learning. Portfolios can be seen to balance rather strict school quality management issues like education standards with prototypic tasks and test items. Both elements, strict and open approaches, must be implemented in a proper mixture to shape schools of tomorrow. Portfolios are personal reflection instruments to enrich traditional school work and university lectures. For students it is now possible to collect know-how and skills-oriented knowledge for their later professional careers. This approach also offers the chance for integrating informal und non-formal acquired knowledge and know-how in this personal competence tool.

Portfolios can be used as personal learning instrument for students, as new assessment instrument at vocational schools and to prove competences and qualifications in the transition to the labour market as well. The process portfolio for reflected learning and the application portfolio are the two matching parts of this essential learning instrument (see fig. 1). On special occasions corresponding parts of the process portfolio would be extracted and prepared for assessment purposes and job application.

Learning ePortfolio

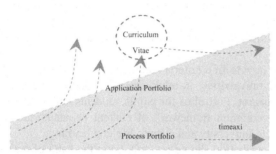

Fig. 1: Process and application portfolio

3 ePortfolios in Austrian Schools and Adult Education

Since examinations are not suitable for further teacher training, institutions like the "Pädagogischen Institute/Pädagogische Hochschulen" started using portfolios ten years ago. The experiences with Portfolios could be assumed as very well: Most of them include a learning diary, a documentation of lesson modules, personal reflections and evaluations of teaching and learning processes.

The idea of the Portfolio based on electronic documents (ePortfolio) was especially promoted by a conferences hold by "Salzburg Research" in 2005. Several secondary schools of the eLearning Cluster Austria decided to adapt the five-to-five model of Helen Barrett [2] (BARRETT, 2001) and launched first ePortfolio Projects with their students. The progress at secondary level also depends on the change of the final school leaving examination regulations ("Reife- und Diplomprüfungs-vorschriften" in the Austrian VET-sector), which includes the management of larger engineering or business projects with focus on team work.

A good software environment can help to develop portfolio structures easily. One of the basic ideas behind ePortfolio concerns the transformation between the working/process portfolio and the presentation/application portfolio especially for graduation at school, during university studies and for job application.

There have been made lot software test on ePortfolios within the eLearning Cluster Project. Simple schemes like Wiki-lists or learning platform courses are under discussion as well as more complex structures like LMS – portfolio environments with comprehensive export functions. Benefits of the web 2.0

transformation like social software or learning community tools are tested to establish a useful culture also for university demand. The portfolio module has been realized within the Moodle Platform with a special extension named Exabis portfolio (www.moodlekurse.org).

4   Further Proceedings

Portfolios are instruments for reflective and self - organized learning. Learning should be organized in groups using the classroom setting. Learning Management Systems (LMS) are the good tools for co-operative and collaborative learning. The LMS offers structural support to work with learning projects and case studies and , enables instances for individual or partner reflection and feedback of the peer group" (Peer Evaluation).

The main challenge is now to find criteria and indicators for the implementation of ePortfolios at schools, universities, in adult education and even for personnel managers for the labour market. Portfolios for pupils, students and any learners are only useful, if there is a common framework of content demands and technical environments from school to university and even to lifelong learning.

The expertise and the evaluation should not only be in the hand of teachers, the students themselves can give support to each other. In LMS groups it is common that students read contributions of others, especially if they are encouraged to do so. The students get an active role to knowledge-"acquisition" and the teachers are coaching this process as experts. The coaching role in a constructivism manner means that the teacher enables the learners to reach the self directed targets in different ways.

To optimise this learning process social effects and the teamwork should be explicitly enforced. Community learning spends higher motivation as learning single [3] (Lave und Wenger, 1991). To copy others´ work is welcome. This kind of learning offers chances for complex peer coaching processes in classroom. In this way Learning Management System and ePortfolio are ideal complementary instruments for sustainable learning processes against the state of art educational background of differentiation and individualisation.

References

[1]   RAVET, S., (2005) *ePortfolio for a learning society,* eLearning Conference, Brussels, May 19-20 2005,
http://www.elearningconference.org/key_speaker/ravet.htm
[2]   BARRETT, H.C.; (2001) *ePortfolios in K-12 and Teacher Education, ISTE-Presentation, Anchorage.* Methodically their role in
[3]   LAVE, E,; WENGER, E.; (1991) *Situated Learning. Legitimate peripheral participation, Cambridge.*

"What is it?": A Culture Sensitive Educational Game

Eliane Pereira, Junia Anacleto, Alexandre Ferreira, Aparecido Carvalho,
Izaura Carelli
Advanced Interaction Laboratory (LIA)
Department of Computing - Federal University of São Carlos (DC/UFSCar)
Rod Washington Luis, Km 235 – São Carlos – SP – 13565-905
{eliane_pereira,junia, alexandre_ferreira,fabiano}@dc.ufscar.br,
imcarelli@gmail.com
+55 16 3351-8618

Abstract. When teachers want to introduce a discussion about the use of cigarette to a group of teenagers, it can be interesting to know what this group thinks about it in order to contextualize the approach to their profile. It is proposed here a framework to instance web game supported by common sense knowledge to approach the called "transversal themes" of the school curriculum, like healthcare, sexual education and ethic. The quiz game framework called "What is it?" is presented as a support for teachers in contextualizing the content to the students' local culture, promoting a more effective and significant learning, where a new knowledge is related to a previous one in the student's cognitive structure. Teachers can set up a web quiz game based on common sense knowledge in the prototype presented.

1   Introduction

"What is it?" (http://lia.dc.ufscar.br/jogo_lia/game) is an online common sense-based game framework being developed in the context of the Brazilian Open Mind Common Sense (OMCS-Br) Project [1] to collects and uses common sense knowledge. It is intended here to make possible the use of common sense knowledge in web-based educational games, aiming at stimulating the learning contextualization the knowledge's construction in the learning process. Furthermore, it intends to collect common sense knowledge from teachers and learners who use the generated games.

The use of common sense in the learning process is suggested by several educators who defend that by contextualizing the learning it is possible to promote

Please use the following format when citing this chapter:

Pereira, E., Anacleto, J., Ferreira, A., Carvalho, A. and Carelli, I., 2008, in IFIP International Federation for Information Processing, Volume 281; *Learning to Live in the Knowledge Society*; Michael Kendall and Brian Samways; (Boston: Springer), pp. 231–234.

the meaningful learning [2, 3]. The "What is it?" ("O que é, O que é?" in Portuguese) is a project supported by FAPESP, CAPES and PDTA/FPTI-BR.

The game bear these issues by supporting teachers to work on themes related to the transversal themes [4], allowing teachers to have a picture of the language, believes and habits from a certain group considering these themes. The "What is it?" framework is divided in two modules explains in section 2 and 3, and in section 3 describes a future works and conclusion.

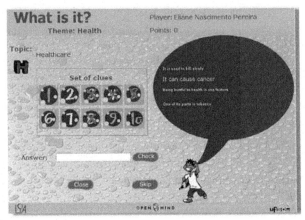

Fig. 1. Player's Module

2   The Player's Module

Figure 1 presents the "What is it?" player's module main interface. To illustrate the game's use, it was developed a game's instance considering the theme "Health". To start the game the player should, first of all, click on the dice, represented in Figure 1 by the letter "H" (by "Healthcare"), whose faces represent topics related to the transversal theme on which the teacher intent to work. Other topics which can potentially compose the "Health" theme's dice, according to the teachers' necessities, are "human development" and "risk factors". Also, the letters which represent the topics are presented to the player fast and randomly. When the player clicks on the dice it stops and says which topic the secret word is about and should be guessed. Each topic has a set of cards associated related to different secret words. These cards are defined by teachers in the game's editor module, using the support of a common sense knowledge base.

The clues play the role of supporting the player to guess which the secret word is. Each card can have a maximum of ten clues that can be selected by the learners clicking on a number into the "Set of Clues" area, which can be seen in Figure 1. After having the topic defined by the dice, a card with clues is presented to the player and, as s/he selects a clue, it is displayed on the blue balloon. The players can select as many clues as they consider necessary before trying to guess the word.

As the players try to find out the secret word, the system collects common sense knowledge, storing the relation between the word they suggested and clues that were already displayed. This collecting process is interesting (1) to teachers, who can identify possible misunderstanding by analyzing the answers that learners with the profile of their target group give to a specific set of clues, and therefore, approach those misunderstandings in classroom to clarify them; and (2) to the Brazilian OMCS knowledge base, which will increase the number of stored common sense statement.

3   The Game's Editor Module

The game's editor is a seven-step wizard to guide the teacher to create game's instances, which fit to their pedagogical goals. This module is supported by the common sense knowledge stored in the Brazilian OMCS knowledge base.

In order to create a new game's instance, the teacher must define three items: (1) the game's main theme, which should be chosen from the six transversal themes [4] available; (2) the topics, which are specifics subjects related to the transversal theme chosen (as it was previously mentioned, the topics compose the game's dice faces); (3) the cards, which have a group of clues related to a secret word from one of defined topics, an optional secret word's synonym list.

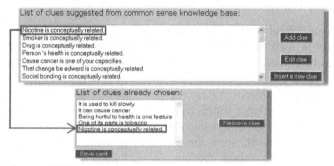

Fig. 2. Games Editor Module

During the cards' definition the teachers receive the support of the common sense knowledge. For that purpose, in the framework's editor Step 1 teachers have to define the population profile which should be considered in the search for common sense statements in the knowledge base. In this way, the system guarantee that the statements recovered to be offered to the teacher were gathered from people who have the desired profile to fit the game's instance to his/her pedagogical goals, i.e., the statements are contextualized to the target group. This process is called common sense filter definition. Once the filter is set up, the teacher can choose the secret words for each card. In the following, the teacher can define a list of synonyms for each one secret word, and these synonyms are also accepted as expected answers in player module.

The next step consists of defining the set of clues for each secret word. For each secret word defined, it is performed a search on the Brazilian OMCS semantic network, called ConceptNet-Br [1]. The ConceptNet's search mechanisms allow increasing the number of words associated with the secret work. The concepts associated with the secret word and their synonyms are presented to teachers as natural language statements and, based on these statements, teachers can compose the cards. For example, the relation "ConceptuallyRelatedTo nicotine, cigarette", found in the ConceptNet, is presented to teachers as "Nicotine is conceptually related". Then the teacher can select a common sense statement as a clue, adding it to the card's set of clue, edit a statement to make it suitable to the game's purpose, or just ignore the suggestions and compose others clues. It is worth to point out that the sentences edited or composed by the teachers are also stored in the Brazilian OMCS knowledge base as new common sense statement of that teacher. Figure 2 presents in the box "List of clues suggested from common sense knowledge base" some statements retrieved from the OMCS knowledge base which can be used as clues, as it was explained before. Those statements are related to the secret word "cigarette". The box "List of clues already chosen" lists the clues already chosen to compose the cares.

4 Conclusions and Future Work

This paper shows "What is it?", an educational game framework whose purpose is to help teachers to work on the transversal themes proposed by the Brazilian Secretary/Minister of Education: sexual education, ethics, healthcare, environment, cultural plurality, market and consumers. The intention is to give teachers some support for teaching these themes concerning their students' context and culture through common sense knowledge usage, and at the same time promoting a way of learning with fun. As future works it is intended to being planned to perform a case study with teacher and students from the Brazilian public education system, in different cities, in order to assess the game's usefulness and to gather new requirement to fit it to the teachers and learners necessities.

References

1. Anacleto, J. C.; Carvalho, A. F. P. de; Neris, V. P. A. ; Godoi, M. S.; Zem-Mascarenhas, S.; Talarico Neto, A. How Can Common Sense Support Instructors with Distance Education? In: SBIE 2006, Brasília. Anais, 2006a. v.1. p.217-226.

2. Freire, Paulo Reglus Neves. Pedagogia da autonomia: saberes necessários à prática educativa. 31 ed. Rio de Janeiro: Paz e Terra, 1996.

3. Freinet, C. (1993). Education through work: A model for child centered learning. Edwin Mellen Press, New York 1993. 438 p.

4. SEF (Secretaria de Educação Fundamental). Parâmetros curriculares nacionais: terceiro e quarto ciclos: apresentação dos temas transversais. Brasília: SEF/MEC, 1998. 436 p

Chapter 10

Knowledge and Technology

The Contribution of Computer Science Education in a Creative Society

Ralf Romeike
University of Potsdam
Department of Computer Science
A.-Bebel-Str. 89
14482 Potsdam, Germany
romeike@cs.uni-potsdam.de

Abstract. This article builds on the assumption that learning to live in the knowledge society requires creativity; it points out how the school subject of computer science (CS) can contribute to that issue and presents results of a study concerning how students think about CS and creativity after experiencing creative programming. A strong connection between creativity and CS was described by the students. Diverse possibilities of how CS contributes to creativity, applies creativity and ways of how the students can include gained CS knowledge in order to be creative were explained. The results are discussed in the context of current research.

1 Introduction

It is not a new idea that we are educating our students for a "new" society which is greatly influenced by the increasing role of technology and the expanding growth of available information and knowledge. Since about the 1990s it is called the Knowledge Society. With its consideration comes a new perspective of learning: life long learning. Several educators are facing the issue and publishing ideas of how to cope with this challenge. Creativity seems to appear as a key factor in the discussion. In the position paper on life long learning of the International Federation on Information Processing (IFIP) the role of ICT is seen as "one of empowerment, enhancement of creativity and support" [1]. In the IFIP/Unesco ICT Curriculum for secondary schools creativity is considered in the "transforming approach" at the highest stage of school development [2]. Resnick [3] extends the picture of the knowledge society. He claims that knowledge alone is not enough. Rather, he suggests speaking about a Creative Society because "[i]n today's rapidly changing world, people must continually come up with creative solutions to unexpected problems. Success is based not

Please use the following format when citing this chapter:

Romeike, R., 2008, in IFIP International Federation for Information Processing, Volume 281; *Learning to Live in the Knowledge Society*; Michael Kendall and Brian Samways; (Boston: Springer), pp. 237–244.

only on what you know or how much you know, but on your ability to think and act creatively" ([3] p.1).

With CS exists a subject in schools that does not only make use of ICT but which has the creative use and design of technology in the centre of its focus[1]. Given that an understanding of the underlying principles and concepts of ICT is essential for its efficient use, CS can contribute a lot to the qualification and preparation of the students for everyday challenges and life long learning. Unfortunately CS curricula and the preconceived notions of CS in public do not necessarily reflect this creative view; CS often is perceived as technical, uncommunicative and uncreative. We investigated how this view can be changed when confronting an 11th year high school class with a creative introduction to programming (cp. [4]). In the survey after the course a strong connection between creativity and CS was described by the students. Diverse possibilities of how CS contributes to creativity, applies creativity and ways of how they can include gained CS knowledge in order to be creative were explained.

2 Creativity

The term creativity is used with different meanings and is discussed controversially in psychology. Common speech usually defines something as creative when coming from the arts or something extraordinary. But not just artists can be creative. Everyday life requires creativity – and so does CS. There is agreement in psychology that something is creative if it is new, original and useful. Boden [5] describes two aspects of creative achievements. Historical creativity (h-creativity) describes ideas which are novel and original in the sense that nobody has had them before. Something that is fundamentally novel to the individual Boden describes as psychologically creative (p-creativity). In an educational context the latter is more interesting and can be aimed for in the classroom. In this paper we want to call something creative if it leads to personal new, unique and useful ideas, solutions or insights (cp. [6, 7]). As summarized by [8], in the classroom creativity can enhance learning through improved motivation, alertness, curiosity, concentration and achievement.

3 The Contribution of CS to Creative Life Long Learning

Creativity is a phenomenon of human behavior which is generally valued, admired and desired from politics and industry. As such the encouragement of creativity found its way into schools and curricula. Creativity is also aimed for as a superior learning objective in CS education. Keeping in mind the role of ICT in life long learning as enhancement and support of creativity, the subject of CS is in a fortunate position: Technology, software and skilled teachers are part of the learning environment in CS classrooms. Many of the specific tasks for creativity supporting software

[1] We refer in this paper to the school subject of computer science / informatics in German high schools. Topics include various aspects of CS, such as programming, practical, theoretical, technical and social aspects of CS.

tools [9] are fulfilled by the software used in CS education. Furthermore CS concepts which are essential for the efficient, creative use and understanding of ICT are central to the subject. In addition the possibilities CS offers for working creatively can have a major impact on students' motivation and interest. These three drivers for creativity in CS education are explained in more detail in [10].

Nevertheless the possibilities that CS education offers for creativity are not well reflected in practice (e.g. [11-13]). As Resnick points out for schools in general, in CS "many students learn to solve specific types of problems, but they are unable to adapt and improvise in response to the unexpected situations that inevitably arise in today's fast-changing world" [3]. We see a reason for this in the character of assigned problem-solving tasks in CS education. The curriculum and the corresponding tasks which teachers assign within the CS classroom concentrate very much on solving specific tasks and problems. However, students have a hard time seeing problems themselves and find getting comfortable with new, unexpected situations difficult.

For us it seems to be important to disclose the creative potential of CS to the students. This can be done by actively engaging the students with tasks that require the application of creativity. This approach has been successfully applied, even if only by a few researchers. Some examples include after school clubs [14] and introductory college courses (e.g. [15, 16]). In CS high school lessons, creativity still is hardly utilized [17].

For establishing a framework that helps designing creative CS lessons we proposed criteria for creative lessons. Applying these resulted in an improved perception which students have about CS and also improved achievements (cp. [4]). However, we also experienced that it is sometimes not easy to change a firm stereotype of CS, as illustrated by the following example. After the lessons one student seemed quite unhappy and uncertain. When she was asked about what was bothering her she answered that she found the lessons a bit strange and asked when we will start with "real" CS. The experienced lessons in her opinion have been so "c-r-e-a-t-i-v-e". In the students opinion other subjects are supposed to be creative – but not CS. Asked about if she understood the content and if she enjoyed the lessons she agreed. The lessons just had not met her pre-conceived notion of CS. Taking this students' dilemma into account we were wondering what the rest of the class thought about the creativity vs. CS dichotomy. What is their understanding of creativity? Do students think CS is creative? Will creativity help them in CS? Did the creative programming course help them to discover the creative possibilities of CS? Answers to these questions may help to situate creativity better into the learning process and lead students' actions towards a proper understanding of what the essence of CS is. Generalizing the results may encourage teachers of other subjects to consider creativity as well in their classes and thus better prepare the students for life long learning.

4 Students' Perception and Understanding of Creativity in CS

4.1 Methodology

The aforementioned questions were addressed by using a qualitative research approach. A quantitative approach using detailed questionnaires in the evaluation of the course revealed to us an abstract overview about the success of the creative teaching unit and changes of the students' perceptions of CS. However, the qualitative approach allows us to look behind standardized answers and to investigate the issues concerning creativity in CS in more detail. Data-collection consisted of brainstorming sessions and short essays written by the students. The objective of the study is to enhance understanding of how creativity is perceived by the students after being confronted with creative programming tasks but without bringing up the topic explicitly. The survey also built a starting point for an in-class discussion regarding what CS can do for creativity and vice versa.

4.2   Data Collection and Analysis

The survey was performed following a creative introduction to programming (cp. [4]). This was done in a German high school class with 21 students of whom 18 students (11 male, 7 female, ages 16 to 17) participated in the survey. The survey consisted of two open tasks:

1. A visual brainstorming task with the keywords "creativity" and "computer science" in the middle of a sheet of paper and the headline question: "What comes into your mind about the topic creativity and CS?" The students worked about 10 minutes on this task.
2. Secondly, a writing task was given: "Now summarize in your own words, what comes into your mind about creativity as related to CS. You may explain the results of your brainstorming or describe other aspects. You can use examples to illustrate your explanations. Start with describing what you understand of creativity." The students worked about 20 min on this task.

First, the brainstorming sketches were analyzed and categorized. Then specific ideas within the brainstorming sketches corresponding to the previously found categories were collated. In the next step the short essays were analyzed with content analysis techniques to better understand how students perceive the connection between CS and creativity. This enabled us to identify the dimensions of the phenomenon described in the answers. The Analysis led to the following results.

4.3   Results

Analyzing the brainstorming sketches

Almost all students initially see connecting ideas between creativity and CS. While most of the students drew connections between the two subjects, two students were looking at both separately. However, in the explanations in the second task these two students also described connecting characteristics.

The students' brainstorming task led to results which can be assigned to 3 categories: results associated to creativity, results associated to CS and results somewhere between the two. The most popular results of each category are summarized in table 1. The resulting categories from the brainstorming session overlap in relation to how the question was understood. The analysis gives us a general idea about the students' experiences and interpretation of the question. The most frequently named ideas for creativity as well as CS are stereotypical: Half of the students mentioned "art" as representative for creativity and also half mentioned "computer" as typical for CS. Half of the students saw the connection between CS and creativity in "programming". The next named item in this category was the programming language Scratch. Also several other ways of practically working with the computer were named as connecting creativity and CS.

Table 1: Brainstorming about CS and creativity. Most popular answers/category.

Creativity		Connecting Items		Computer Science	
art	9	programming	9	computer	10
realizing ideas	5	Scratch	6	data	3
coming up with ideas	5	Webpage development	4	logic	3
create	4	Photoshop/photo processing	3	programming	3
handicrafts	3	music editing/creating	3	school lesson	2
paint	3	creative writing (e.g. with Word)	3	internet and applications	2
free possibilites	3	computer games	3	information	1
imaginative	2	ideas	3	new ideas	1
human ability	2	internet	2	new technology	1
music	2	e-mail writing	2	abstract	1

Analyzing the short essays

All students describe items and activities that are connected to both; creativity and CS. While the analysis of the brainstorming items shows a quite homogeneous picture with answers corresponding to three categories, the analysis of the individual opinions in the short essays reveals a multidimensional perspective of how creativity and CS can be perceived. By their description of how the two are related the diverse student answers can be arranged in five main categories:

CS is creative by its nature

Many students mention that in their eyes creativity is a necessity for CS, e.g. because programming requires creativity: *"Connecting the two topics I immediately thought of programming. There you need to involve your own ideas."*
Related to this viewpoint is the perspective of seeing CS as a form of applied creativity. This is based on the product orientation in CS. This perspective also involves a personal standpoint where creativity is seen as self-realization and self-fulfilment in realizing ideas by creating things. Hereby CS is seen as a way of doing so: *"In regard to CS I see that with every program new things are made."*
For us it seems interesting, that the students here comply with the p-creative view of creativity, where it is important for them to come up with personally new ideas, regardless if someone else has had them before. In addition when engaging in programming the feeling of doing something creative is motivating to the students.

CS provides creativity support

"CS for me is fostering creativity because it is not only opening one door, it is opening several doors [with possibilities]. Everyone can do something with it."

ICT can support creativity and the students are also aware of this. Furthermore they extend the view on the strategies and concepts they learn in CS lessons for using ICT efficiently and creatively. This perspective also includes the application of utilities which enable the students to express themselves creatively: *"For example when writing an e-mail creativity can be very important: If you want to write a love letter to a person by e-mail and it shall be a special one, you really need to be creative."* This can by the appropriate use of tools and methods.

Art perspective of CS

In this perspective the students identify procedures in the CS field that are comparable with art, e.g. when visualizing information: *"For making problems and relations more demonstrative (clips, charts, diagrams) in CS creativity is applied."*
This view finds its application in the many crossover domains like media-design or computer-graphics where both, CS knowledge and artistic expression are combined creatively.

Holistic perspective

In this perspective the impact of CS products in the society and its creative development are reflected. Here the personal aspect is out of focus, but the overall development is observed. *"CS nowadays is everywhere. It is so powerful, this I consider as creative." "Creativity in CS is responsible for the technological progress."*
With respect to the creative misuse of technology (i.e. hacking) and the critical awareness of the technological progress, these are crucial perspectives CS educators also should consider in their lessons when encouraging the students to become critical thinkers.

Focusing on the difference

For a few students, it was important to underline the difference between creativity and CS. They see creativity as a superior human characteristic which they do not want to bind too close to CS: *"Programming fosters creativity of the programmer, and creativity is essential to programming. CS needs creativity, but creativity does not need CS."*

5 Discussion

Summarizing, the students' answers revealed several perspectives of creativity and CS. It is interesting to see that the students perceived their own activity in CS as creative. Taking into account that this is motivating to them, emphasizing this characteristic of CS can be taken as an opportunity for fostering motivation and interest in the field as well. The results of the study described here support findings where creativity was named as a major driver for very successful students getting deeply involved with CS in school and in their free time as well [18]. Also, in studies with open source programmers creativity related factors were named as the most pervasive drivers and responsible for project involvement [19]. Following up on the results of the course evaluation described in [4] which showed a drastic increase of motivation, interest fun and other positive factors we now know more about the circumstances surrounding increased motivation.

Especially interesting are those student answers, where a development of the stereotype becomes visible: *"Generally CS and creativity obey different laws. CS needs logic and mathematical structures while creativity generally breaks out of these. Creativity bursts laws and algorithms while CS is dominated by those. Nevertheless CS doesn't work without creativity. For writing new programs and code a creative spirit is needed."*

However, not all students formulated their understanding of creativity this way. A few focused on the creative use of ICT only. The positive side is that these students also had discovered the creative use of ICT for themselves. Nevertheless, from a CS perspective there is more to this that they can discover. Every student has his own concept of creativity and thus the answers are very diverse. Indeed the diversity of the answers is what makes it so interesting for a CS educator as several approaches for a creative look at CS are revealed. As it is a main task of the school to broaden students' horizons, the different ideas and perspectives students have on this issue can be utilized. In the course described in this paper we encouraged group discussions on where creativity helps in CS and vice versa. The students shared and discussed their views and even came up with good examples for the points made.

Can there be too much creativity? Undeniably, fostering creativity in the classroom can be unexpected and confusing to students if they are not used to it. The student cited above who was uncomfortable experiencing CS so creatively explained her standpoint in the survey in more detail. She did not like that *"In CS lessons creativity means that the task is so open that (1) you need to come up with your own ideas (e.g. Which game shall I realize?), (2) you need to think about how you can realize these ideas and (3) everybody has different results!"* With these statements the student exactly described some of the key criteria which the course was built on. The discomfort obviously came from the unfamiliar situation where she was not exactly told which steps she has to take and from a lack of ideas. While most of the other students did not have problems with coming up with ideas, this was really bothering her. Before starting the following course on creative computer graphics, some creativity techniques were introduced and practiced. This time all students enjoyed open and creative tasks. With this enjoyment of creative computing and the gained insights into underlying principles CS lessons can make an important contribution to the students' preparation for life long learning.

6   Conclusion

The resulting attitude of the students towards creativity in connection with CS after implicitly engaging creatively with the subject is a very attractive one. It is a perception that encourages young people to involve themselves with ICT for fun and as seeing it as enriching their personal life. By engaging creatively with CS they also develop digital literacy and skills that are essential in the Creative Society. Furthermore if this picture is transferred to the parents, other students and finally to the society we believe the perception of CS as boring and technical etc. soon may become obsolete. Warnings about to less people caring for getting involved in IT related jobs would be a thing of the past. Of course computer scientists need to evaluate for themselves if this picture actually reflects their understanding of the nature of CS. For us it certainly does.

References

1. M. Kendall, B. Samways, and J. Wibe: Position Paper Lifelong Learning (Lll) Version 1. International Federation for Information Processing (IFIP), Laxenburg (2002).
2. T. van Weert, and D. Tinsley: Information and Communication Technology in Secondary Education – A Curriculum for Schools. UNESCO, Paris (2000).
3. M. Resnick: Sowing the Seeds for a More Creative Society. In: Learning & Leading with Technology, International Society for Technology in Education (ISTE) (2007).
4. R. Romeike: Applying Creativity in CS High School Education - Criteria, Teaching Example and Evaluation. In: 7th Baltic Sea Conference on Computing Education Research, Koli Calling, Koli (2008).
5. M.A. Boden: The Creative Mind: Myths & Mechanisms. Basic Books, London (1990).
6. M.A. Runco, and I. Chand: Cognition and Creativity. Educational Psychology Review. 7(3), 243-267 (1995).
7. J. C. Kaufman, and R. J. Sternberg: Creativity. Change: The Magazine of Higher Learning. 39(4), 55-60 (2007).
8. D. Fasko: Education and Creativity. Creativity Research Journal. 13(3-4), 317-327 (2000).
9. B. Shneiderman: Creativity Support Tools. Commun. ACM. 45(10), 116-120 (2002).
10. R. Romeike: Three Drivers for Creativity in Computer Science Education. In: IFIP-Conference on "Informatics, Mathematics and ICT: a golden triangle", Boston, USA (2007).
11. R. Mittermeir: Informatik-Unterricht: Bastel-Unterricht, Eine Intellektuelle Herausforderung oder "Preparation for the Information-Age". Medienimpulse. 9/33, 4 – 11 (2000).
12. R.B. Sweeney: Creativity in the Information Technology Curriculum Proposal. In: 4th Conf. on Information Technology Curriculum, pp. 139-141, Lafayette, Indiana, USA (2003).
13. M. Guzdial, and E. Soloway: Teaching the Nintendo Generation to Program. Commun. ACM. 45(4), 17-21 (2002).
14. M. Resnick: Rethinking Learning in the Digital Age. In: Kirkman, G., (ed.) The Global Information Technology Report: Readiness for the Networked World, pp. 32-37. Oxford University Press, Oxford (2002).
15. E. Sutinen, and J. Tarhio: Teaching to Identify Problems in a Creative Way. In: 31st Frontiers in Education Conference. IEEE Computer Society (2001).
16. G. Lewandowski, E. Johnson, and M. Goldweber: Fostering a Creative Interest in Computer Science. In: SIGCSE '05, St. Louis, MO (2005).
17. R. Romeike: Kriterien Kreativen Informatikunterrichts. In: 12. GI-Fachtagung "Informatik und Schule - INFOS 2007". Köllen, Siegen, Germany (2007).
18. R. Romeike: Creative Students - What Can We Learn from Them for Teaching Computer Science? In: the 6th Baltic Sea Conference on Computing Education Research, Koli Calling. Uppsala University, Uppsala, Sweden (2006).
19. K. Lakhani, and R. Wolf: Why Hackers Do What They Do: Understanding Motivation Effort in Free/Open Source Software Projects. In: J. Feller, B. Fitzgerald, S. Hissam, and K. R. Lakhani (eds.) Perspectives on Free and Open Source Software, pp. 3-22. MIT Press (2005).

The Medium And The Message

Building an Online Learning Community to Implement
Curriculum Planning and Assessment in Primary Schools,
New South Wales, Australia

Vicki Lowery
New South Wales Department of Education and Training, Sydney,
Australia

Abstract. Teachers of primary students aged 5 – 12 years in government schools in New South Wales, Australia, are implementing curriculum planning and assessment frameworks which provide a model for the integration of the six subjects taught to primary students into one manageable teaching program. This paper discusses how 120 schools, supported by Australian Federal Government funding, are trialling the program, providing valuable feedback for their peers, developing deeper understanding of the curriculum, sharing their knowledge and gaining greater confidence in the consistency of their teacher judgement. They are achieving much of this through their participation in an online community of learners. This online community is supported through a variety of ICT tools such as the Internet, videoconferencing and online meeting software. The teachers are gaining skills and expertise not only in curriculum and content but also in the use of interactive technologies which will provide a positive collaborative learning experience for them and their peers no matter where they are located.

1   Background

For many years primary teachers of students aged 5 – 12 years in New South Wales, Australia, have worked with a curriculum they perceived as overcrowded. In 2002 the NSW Government commissioned a study to identify the demands created for teachers as a result of the introduction of a new way of assessment and reporting based on syllabus outcomes. Eltis [1]

The terms of reference included:

- assess the impact different approaches to recording and reporting have had on the workload of primary teachers;
- identify the features and characteristics of best practice models;

Please use the following format when citing this chapter:

Lowery, V., 2008, in IFIP International Federation for Information Processing, Volume 281; *Learning to Live in the Knowledge Society*; Michael Kendall and Brian Samways; (Boston: Springer), pp. 245–252.

- provide advice about the nature of support required to promote best practice within the context of a manageable workload.

The recommendations included developing program frameworks into a 'total teaching program that is manageable and directed at promoting productive learning opportunities for all students' [1].

As part of the response to the Eltis report, the New South Wales Department of Education and Training (NSW DET) developed *Curriculum planning and assessment frameworks*. The frameworks provide a total teaching program for primary students aged 5-12 years in the major learning areas of English and Mathematics and an integrated program for the four key learning areas; Creative arts, Human society and its environment, Personal development health and physical education and Science and Technology. Included are 30 complete units of work incorporating ideas and suggestions for planning, programming and assessing. Thus a common focus made connections between syllabus outcomes from different subject areas. This grouping of outcomes is called Connected Outcome Groups or COGs. [1]. As the Eltis report suggested: "It need not be mandatory for schools to implement the *Program Frameworks* but it can be confidently expected many will choose to do so, especially if the Frameworks are presented in such a way as not to be a strait-jacket for schools" [2] This paper focuses on the strategy adopted for the implementation of COGs in NSW DET primary schools.

2   Challenges

The role of the curriculum support area of the Department to promote the frameworks to teachers, to encourage them to implement them and provide support to assist them is made especially challenging because the frameworks are not mandatory. Financial support has been made available to NSW DET through the Australian Government's Quality Teacher Programme (AGQTP). AGQTP provides funding to all school sectors across Australia to support teacher professional development. In NSW the COGs project is one of the projects to receive funding over four years, 2006-2009. The project budget includes funding for a senior curriculum adviser and a senior project officer (the author)

3   The Project Begins

COGs became available for implementation in schools late in 2005. The AGQTP project began at about the same time. There are 1644 primary schools in NSW [3] ranging from large metropolitan schools (up to 1,000 students) to one-teacher schools (up to 25 students) in isolated rural areas across a total area of 800,628 sq kms. Obviously the AGQTP project could not target them all within available budget and human resources. Two of the many challenges for the project were: 1: how to best use the resources available to work with a critical mass of teachers across the state and 2: how to make the benefits and achievements of the project available to all primary teachers who wanted support to implement COGs. The project brief was to provide professional learning opportunities to teachers and to target a number of primary schools covering the range of large, small, metropolitan, rural and to cater for students of all needs. From early discussions with teachers, focus areas were identified for the first phase of the project. A total of 115 schools participated in this first phase for two years.

4   Development of Project Networks

Early adopters made up the initial focus group. The early adopters were teachers from 5 schools who had participated in the writing of the COGs units. These teachers therefore had a good understanding of the framework and its content. Their role was to teach the units and collect work samples from their students which the teachers then assessed. These work samples and assessments were published on a web site which could be accessed by all teachers to assist them in their own assessments. The other teachers provided feedback on manageability, resources and suggestions for possible modifications and to modify COGs units for multi-stage classes. The units had been written for 'standard' classes and did not take into account the large number of small mainly rural schools which have multi-stage classes ranging from all students Kindergarten to Year 6 (K-6, ages 5-12) in one class to composite classes of two grades in the one class. Teachers requested that the COGs units be modified to provide for these needs. While the focus groups would work separately it was important that the results could be shared initially within the groups and later across the groups so that all teachers could benefit, firstly those in the project and ultimately all interested K-6 teachers. How could this be achieved effectively and efficiently within the available resources?

5   A Learning Community

Much has been written about learning communities – their roles, benefits and constraints but in general it is agreed that the primary aim is for the participants to learn with and from each other by developing intelligence and abilities beyond what is possible by any one individual [4] and, as Mitchell and Sackney suggested, to work with others in a spirit of experimentation and risk taking to improve the educational experience of all [5]. The research was outlining the needs of this project. Another desirable feature of learning communities is that participants can scaffold one another through sharing of information and experiences thus providing good learning opportunities [6]. Establishing a learning community to provide information, support, resources and models of implementation appeared to be the logical next step.

Mitchell and Sackney [5] also point out that the shared understandings that are built up in a learning community need to develop slowly through team building. However this project did not have the leisure to develop slowly but rather needed to work quickly to provide the support teachers were asking for while still adhering to the aims of AGQTP; to provide professional development opportunities for teachers. Few researchers clarify just how a learning community is built and maintained [5] but the project officers appreciated the importance of establishing the networks so as to build a sense of community among and between the members.

6   Developing a Delivery Model

Budget and resource constraints meant that much of the development, support and sharing between the members of the learning community would need to be online. Face-to-face course costs of teacher relief, travel and accommodation are the largest items in any school education project. For example, one day's teacher relief costs approx A$300 and if teachers have to travel several hours to a venue, overnight accommodation must be offered. Thus it can happen that for one teacher to attend one day's professional development, that teacher spends one day traveling to the venue, one day's attendance and one day traveling from the venue resulting in A$900 for 3 day's relief, travel costs (intrastate airfare costs are very high) and accommodation. This does not include the costs incurred in development, presentation, venue costs, etc.

Appreciating teachers' preference for face-to-face professional development and based on the evidence from evaluations of similar projects, it was decided to provide a blended learning approach combining face-to-face and online. Ewing et al in their evaluation of *CTJ (Consistent teacher judgement) Online for Science and Technology K-6* (a previous AGQTP project managed by the author) found that 'the next most important factor was the opportunity for face-to-face meetings. This finding supports evidence from other research in on line programs that face-to-face support is essential [7]. Research also shows that the extent of the mix of face-to-face and the ICT tools and how the tools are applied can greatly impact the learning outcomes [8]. The face-to-face workshops making up the blended approach provide excellent opportunities for ICT skill development to counteract the hesitancy on the part of many teachers about their ability to be involved in online learning. The blended approach seems to offer the best of both worlds: face-to-face meetings for everyone to get to know each other thereby encouraging the feeling of communicating online with colleagues rather than strangers and to have hands-on practice in a supportive environment with the ICT tools to be used [9]

7   ICT Tools Used to Develop the Online Community

In order to maximise the opportunities which ICT could provide, it is important, where possible, to tailor the learning experiences to preferred learning styles to make the learning more effective for those teachers who are unconvinced of the potential of online learning [10]. The technologies selected were those which were already available in schools: the Internet for presentation, staying up-to-date, sharing of information and resources; online discussion board which is collaborative and supports a learning style which includes solitary, verbal and reflexive modes; video conferencing which simulates face-to-face interaction and supports learning styles which are visual, social, verbal and active; interactive white boards which support whole group and small group work and suit learners who are active, kinesthetic, visual and social and online meetings using audio, video and shared computer screens to support learning and to share developments suiting learners who are visual, social, aural and active.

The project web site monitors the progress of the project as well as providing links to resources developed specifically to support the curriculum planning frameworks. Using video snapshots, the site showcases the achievements of schools, teachers and their students as they make their COGs journeys. School presentations and curriculum support presentations were filmed at conferences around the state during 2007. These were edited and published on the project web site. The videos are proving to be a successful way of 'spreading the word' and are being used to stimulate discussion in teacher meetings, both face-to-face and online. Teachers present a credible voice to their peers and provide a powerful support for the online learning community.

An online discussion board provided the communication tool for the teachers providing student work samples which were in a variety of formats including word documents, graphics, sound and video files. As part of the process, the teachers were to engage professional dialogue around the assessment of their work samples. Using the blended technologies approach, a face-to-face meeting was held at the beginning of the project to introduce the teachers to each other, to provide an overview of the project and to explain the ICT tools to be used for the majority of the interaction. A further face-to-face meeting was held in the following school term to discuss progress, solve problems and provide further support in the use ICT. The discussion board would also be used to facilitate professional dialogue between teachers about the assessment and moderation of their student work. The author has been an online facilitator for a number of similar projects and is fully cognisant of the benefits and limitations of online discussions. In many discussions with teachers, they have reported that they find that, while the process of writing can assist in reflecting on their learning, this can be limited by an inhibition to express their thoughts for reading by their peers, which in turn leads to a hesitation at sharing the result of their teaching for critiquing by others. Therefore the need for protocols during the moderation process was emphasized so as to limit any possible feeling of intimidation. The example used was based on: Looking Collaboratively at Student Work: An Essential Toolkit [11].

8   Online Meetings

Over the last few years the NSW DET infrastructure has increased its broadband speeds and improved school computer networking which has greatly enhanced distance education using video conferencing. More recently the NSW Government announcement of the rollout of a videoconferencing unit, an interactive white board

(IWB) and a data projector to all schools has dramatically increased the potential for collaborative communication for all schools. Meeting online will save time, money and make it possible for teachers who would not otherwise have the opportunity to meet, to work together as peers. As schools provide access to these ICT tools, teachers will begin to appreciate their potential for teaching and learning for their students and for themselves.

The online meeting tools include videoconferencing and software such as *Bridgit* which enables computer screen sharing and communication by video (web cam) and audio (headphone/speaker/microphone). Meetings using *Bridgit* have provided opportunities for clarification of project issues, demonstration of products of the project such as work samples, modified units, and small group meetings. These opportunities have been embraced by many.

Even before the rollout, schools have purchased over 5,000 IWBs and are finding that the IWB acts as a central focus for group work and can provide a stimulating collaborative tool for learning. The IWB can be used as a standalone tool in the classroom but can also be used in conjunction with video conferencing and software such as *Bridgit*. This combination of tools enables project participants to join online meetings to access professional development while at school, collaborate with peers and be involved in professional dialogue around the implementation of COGs. The potential for ICT used in this way to support the sustainability of online communities is only just beginning to be explored.

9   Progress to Date

Evidence has been collected so far, based on exit evaluations from workshops, comments made in interviews and from conference presentations. This clearly shows that teachers in the project are very positive about the COGs units which are part of the curriculum planning and assessment frameworks and their implementation in schools. Through the project, they have developed a deeper knowledge and understanding of teaching practice, an enhanced appreciation of assessment and reporting and feel the framework facilitates whole school planning, evaluation and decision making. In addition the majority of teachers say their teaching has been re-energised. Many teachers are overcoming their apprehensions of online professional development and realising the power of working together as an online learning community to achieve better learning outcomes for their students. These outcomes could not have been realised without the use of ICT. The technology provided a new way to bring together a community of teachers in K-6 schools across NSW. The project will continue to increase the use of these tools over the next two years.

10 Sustainability of the Learning Community

The project has at the time of writing, completed two years of the scheduled four years. A growing body of work is now available to inform and support the adopters and the hesitant. New resources are being constantly added to the project web site. New student work samples and assessments will continue to be collected, edited and published. The project is currently in the early days of evaluation by an external evaluator.

In 2008 60 new schools will join the project to continue the work achieved 2006-2007. Several of the current project schools will act as mentors to new schools; each mentor school will support about 4 other schools. The mentor schools are already developing online networks with the schools they are supporting through videoconferencing and later through online meetings. Anecdotally those teachers who have never used videoconferencing before (a large majority) are agreeing that the experience is very positive and 'almost like being there'. Additional project schools from 2007 will collaborate online to assess and moderate their student work. Their results will provide additional student work samples for publication on the web.

The new schools will provide sustainability by their active participation in the project. The networks forming the online community will continue to develop and provide multiple pathways for teachers to engage in learning and networking activities, sharing their practice, learning with and from each other to extend their professional understanding of curriculum planning, assessment and reporting.

References

1.   Getting the balance right. The Department's response to Time to teach, time to learn. (New South Wales Department of Education and Training, Sydney, 2005).

2.   Eltis, Ken J. Time to teach, time to learn. Report on the Evaluation of Outcomes Assessment and Reporting in NSW Government Schools, (New South Wales Department of Education and Training, Sydney, 2003).

3.   New South Wales Department of Education and Training (https://www.det.nsw.edu.au/reports_stats/fastfacts/index.htm)

4.   Matthew Campbell and Philip Uys, Building learning communities of practice for professional development in open and distance learning: the CELT experience, ODLAA (Open and Distance Learning Association of Australia) Conference, Adelaide (9-11 November, 2005).

5.   Coral Mitchell and Larry Sackney, Building capacity for a learning community, *Canadian Journal of Educational Administration and Policy,* **19** February 24 (2001)

6.   Ken Ryba, Linda Selby and Mandia Mentis, Analysing the effectiveness of on-line learning communities, HERDSA (Higher Education Research and Development Society of Australasia) Conference, Perth (7-10 July, 2002)

7.   Robyn Ewing, Evaluation of the Australian Government Quality teaching consistency of teacher judgement online phase 2 project, Sydney, University of Sydney (2005).
8.   Ron Oliver, Using blended learning approaches to enhance teaching and learning outcomes in higher education, (November 30, 2007) http://elrond.scca.ecu.edu.au/oliver/2005/iaup2.pdf (2005)
9.   Vicki Lowery. Connected not isolated; emerging communications technologies: tools to maximise access to teacher training and development programs; an Australian perspective. International Federation of Information Processing. World Computer Congress. Vienna and Budapest. (1998)
10. Lisa Cluett and Judy Skene, A new(er) dimension to online learning communities; using web tools to engage students, Teaching and Learning Forum, Perth (30-31 January 2007).
11. Looking Collaboratively at Student Work: An Essential Toolkit (November 30, 2007) http://www.essentialschools.org/cs/cespr/view/ces_res/57#3
12. Janette R. Hill and Arjan Raven, Online learning communities: if you build them, will they stay? University of Georgia, College of Education, IT forum paper 46. Posted on ITFORUM October 10, 2000. (30/11/2007) http://it.coe.uga.edu/itforum/paper46/paper46.htm

Project Websites

1.   What do I really know about COGs; dispelling some of the myths around COGs http://www.curriculumsupport.education.nsw.gov.au/cogs_myths/index.htm
2.   AGQTP Implementing the curriculum planning and assessment frameworks http://www.curriculumsupport.education.nsw.gov.au/agqtp_cogs/
3.   Work samples supporting COGs units http://www.qtp.nsw.edu.au/assessment_framework/index.asp

Accessing knowledge through narrative context

Giuliana Dettori[1] and Francesca Morselli[2]
[1] ITD CNR, Via De Marini 6, 16149 Genova, Italy
dettori@itd.cnr.it
http://www.itd.cnr.it/personalescheda.php?Id=12
[2] Dipartimento di matematica, Università di Genova, Via Dodecaneso 35,
16146 Genova, Italy
morselli@dima.unige.it,
http://www.dima.unige.it/~morselli

Abstract. In this paper we discuss how narrative may contribute to create meaningful learning contexts. Starting from a socio-constructivist and situated learning perspective, we acknowledge the crucial role of context in accessing knowledge. Then we point out the potential of narrative in education and discuss the positive role it can play in the creation of meaningful learning contexts. To this end, we focus on different examples of narrative contexts within technology-enhanced learning environments, drawn from the literature. We analyze what kind of contexts raise from different ways to set up narrative activities. Our study points out that narrative can be a powerful tool for the creation of a variety of contexts suitable for different learning situations, by stimulating learners' direct involvement and offering a concrete starting point for reflection.

1 Introduction

What is context? This term is widely used, in different ways and for different purposes, in many research fields somehow related with accessing knowledge, such as philosophy, linguistics, psychology, education, cognitive science, problem solving, theory of communication and artificial intelligence. Its definition can range from *"a set of features in the world"* to *"a set of assumptions on the world"*, hence viewing it as an objective state of affairs, on one side, or as a subjective representation of the world, on the other side [14], or any combination of these two extreme positions, based on the underlying reference theory and on the application at hand.

In order to restrict and better focus our analysis, we will concentrate on the educational field, where context is increasingly attributed a major role. Here, under

Please use the following format when citing this chapter:

Dettori, G. and Morselli, F., 2008, in IFIP International Federation for Information Processing, Volume 281; *Learning to Live in the Knowledge Society*; Michael Kendall and Brian Samways; (Boston: Springer), pp. 253–260.

the influence of social constructivism and situated cognition theories, learning is widely considered as a context-dependent activity [3] that takes place by interacting with content and context. Content is the information to be learnt, while context is the set of all circumstances that are relevant for the learner to build his/her knowledge. According to socio-constructivism, content and context are dual elements interwoven with each other: *"context holds in itself the seed of content and content holds in itself the seed of context"* [11].

The connection among content and context is even more emphasized in situated learning, where knowledge is seen as characterized by the situation (or context) within which it is constructed, which includes physical, emotional, intellectual, social and cultural aspects of the learning environment [12]. In this view, which includes both external, objective elements and subjective, cognitive ones, context is also influenced by the behavior and past experiences of the learner him/herself [13]. Therefore, it appears important to plan activities for the learners that could allow them to take part in shaping learning contexts that suit their needs and attitudes.

In this paper, we argue that narrative can be a good tool to create learning contexts that deeply involve the learners. We focus in particular on narrative contexts within technology-enhanced learning environments, i.e., contexts which are heavily determined by stories and narrations related to the learning task, and take advantage of some technological means to facilitate the creation of narrative or amplify its effect. To this end, we analyze several examples of narrative contexts, discussing their potential role and value.

2 Learning potential of narrative

Narrative is increasingly used in education, since it has been recognized as a natural expressive form for people of any age and culture [4], as well as a privileged way to help develop cognitive abilities and organize knowledge [17]. It is a form of meaning making where human beings engage in symbolic activities to construct and make sense of themselves and work out a coherent meaning for their experiences [6].

The roots of this rich cognitive potential clearly appear in the definition that Bruner [4, p. 43] gives of narrative: *"...a unique sequence of events, mental states, happenings ... But these constituents do not have a life or meaning of their own. Their meaning is given by their place in the overall configuration of the sequence as a whole..."* . This definition, which is in agreement with the definitions of narrative given by scientists with different focus and orientation [8], highlights the presence of logical constraints among the elements of a story: all elements contribute to form a whole which, in turn, gives meaning to each single part [6]. This allows people to understand more than it is explicitly reported, and hence leads both producers and receivers of a narrative to access knowledge by carrying out a meaning construction process.

This applies to both invented narratives (stories) and true ones (history and experience narrations), as pointed out by Ricoeur [15, p. 288], who recognizes *"a family resemblance at the level of sense or structure between these two narrative types"*.

The literature highlights that narrative's positive influence on learning concerns not only cognition, but also motivation and emotions. As Bruner [6] points out, *"narrative in all its forms is a dialectic between what was expected and what came to pass"* (p.15), as well as *"an invitation to problem finding, not a lesson in problem solving"* (pg. 20). For this reason, the use of narrative in learning can result challenging and stimulate curiosity and fantasy, which are major components of intrinsic motivation, according to the taxonomy proposed by Malone and Leppers [16]. The support to emotions raises from the fact that stories are based on an interplay between characters and causation [2], which leads the user to highlight aspects of personality, emotional state and social standing, as well as the motives and intentions which underlie the characters' actions.

The context-making potential of narrative is also underlined in the literature. Arnold, Smith & Trainer [1], for instance, argue that narrative can help make more visible the context of individuals and is an important way of revealing and negotiating contexts in virtual settings.

We add that narrative can help creating meaningful learning contexts by offering a simple way to connect context knowledge and external setting with the learner's experience and by supporting his/her engagement in a deep meaning-making process. This is due to several reasons:

- Narrative always has a narrator, hence it is always told from an explicitly declared perspective, which can help people get aware of the plurality of possible points of view and information sources.
- Narrative, including (implicit and explicit) logical constraints among the narration elements, stimulates the users (be they narrating or receiving a story) to make inferences and deductions, and hence to become aware to *"know more than they thought"* [6].
- Narrative concerns actions and events, which are something concrete and hence can constitute solid, objective ground for discussion and reflection.
- Sharing stories is traditionally a social activity, hence narrative is particularly suitable to create social contexts; this is important from the point of view of learning, in that *"the cultural contexts that favor mental development are principally and inevitably interpersonal"* [5, p. 68].

In the next sections, we support our claim by describing some narrative contexts that appear particularly interesting, and by discussing their characteristics and potential.

3 Examples of narrative learning contexts

Stories can be used in different ways, within technology-enhanced learning environments, to shape a context apt to facilitate learning, as illustrated by the following examples, drawn from the literature.

3.1 Creating context by role-playing

Revolution (by The Education Arcade, http://www.educationarcade.org/revolution) is a multi-user, role-play, educational game on the American Revolution, to be played in 45-minute sessions in a networked environment. The users take the roles of seven different kinds of characters (such as upper class lawyer, patriotic craftman, or African American house slave) who formed the society of the American colonies at the time of the Revolution. Starting from a background story, chosen among a number of available ones that refer to historical facts, and from general guidelines on characters' behaviours (which include compliance with the social rules of the period), participants create always new stories by means of their actions (i.e., conversations with other characters and execution of professional activities). The environment includes also some synthetic characters, whose function is to guide the role-players, by means of suitable conversations, to respect historical and semantic constraints. Experiencing different roles, the learners are led to focus on the life in the considered historical period from different social, economic and cultural perspectives, hence deepening understanding of the historical facts which are object of study.

In this educational game, the story construction by participants' actions provides a context for the intended historical learning. Taking a role, each player becomes part of the unfolding narrative actions, which can positively influence understanding and memorization, as well as support motivation to get interested in an event that would otherwise be far from the learners' life. The historical background constraining players' actions induces learning. Knowledge is built by interacting and discussing with peers. Like with all role-playing games, however, the activity must be carefully prepared in order to give rise to meaningful stories and actually favor the expected learning.

3.2   Creating context by taking part in a given story

Crystal Island [16] is an environment for middle-school students, supporting inquiry-based learning in microbiology and genetics, to be played individually. The user is led to engage in a problem solving activity by taking part in a given story: he/she is travelling in a far country with a scientific expedition which is decimated by an epidemic disease; in order to stop it and save the expedition, a genetic problem needs to be solved. The learner navigates the environment and, interacting with a number of synthetic, semi-autonomous characters, gets information on the topic of study and suggestions to work out a solution. The fact that the characters are implemented by means of semi-autonomous agents implies that they behave in a (partially) new way every time they interact with the user, so that the user can repeatedly interact with the same character without passing through the same conversation again and again, as it would be the case with simple multimedia environments.

The background story provided creates a context for the assigned task and helps the user to make sense of the data. It works as a container to highlight the different kinds of elements to take into consideration when solving microbiology and genetics problems, helping the learner to build an overall picture from a plurality of data and hence supporting a meaning-making process which is functional to the construction of a solution. Instead of simply being handed information, the student draws out meaning by interacting with the context. This data-highlighting role is not trivial nor irrelevant in relation to learning: some research studies underline that problem solving is more often hindered by an incomplete or inaccurate analysis of the data involved than by the lack of suitable solution strategies [18].

3.3 Creating context by sharing reflective narrations

In a regular face-to-face foreign language course at university level, one of the teachers sets up a blog and asks a group of volunteers from her course to narrate the language learning experience they are undergoing during the course. This activity usually lasts about 10 weeks and involves a limited number of students (6 to 10). The assignment is not to report reflections but actually to narrate one's own learning story as it is taking place during the course.

As a consequence, over the weeks, personal stories develop and intertwine in the blog, creating a social context in which learning is highlighted and becomes itself an object of study. Learning-related actions become visible (to each narrator and to her/his peers) and provoke reflection and reaction. Students have under their eyes, and can compare, difficulties, strategies and achievements, hence learning from each other and improving awareness of different ways of learning as well as of their own strengths and weaknesses as language learners.

3.4 Creating context by sharing experience online

LODE [7] is a virtual environment supporting teachers' collaborative work on Learning Objects (LOs). It allows users to share not only educational material in the form of LOs, but also personal views, experiences of use and reflections, by providing discussion spaces associated to each LO. It aims to help teachers learn from each other and to favour by this means teachers' professional growth, as well as the diffusion of innovation in the school. Among the discussion spaces associated to each LO, there is a "narrative corner" where teachers are invited to narrate their use experience with the associated LO.

The possibility to post and read such narrations creates a context for improving the use of LOs, giving concreteness to the shared materials and helping to make the pedagogical intention behind them clear. The presence of narrations by different teachers in relation to every single LO helps the users gain an articulated, multi-dimensional view of it, hence turning the re-use experience into a learning opportunity for all teachers involved, including the original producer of the material. Therefore, this narration sharing also creates a social context for teachers' learning from each other and professional growth. This base of personal stories of use constitutes a shared ground on which pedagogical reflection can develop. This task could not be done as effectively by sharing only reflections instead of personal stories, since reflections are filtered by personal judgement while stories, though including the narrator's point of view, are closer to raw data and can better allow prospective re-users to look at the material and related experiences from their own point of view.

3.5 Creating context by collective narration

Dolk & Den Hertog [10] describe a face-to-face training activity for Mathematics teachers they carry out in the Netherlands. In such activities, a small group of teachers firstly watches a video showing a classroom episode where some pupils are experiencing difficulty with solving a mathematical problem. The teachers are then asked to jointly produce a story of what they saw in the video before starting analyzing it. This task, which aims to improve observation and entails negotiation among the group participants, is much less trivial than one could think; as a matter of fact, experience highlights that teachers may need to see the movie several times before being able to make a precise, shared account of what happens in the movie. Precise observation, on the other hand, is a key skill for teachers, crucial to be able to correctly diagnose learning difficulties so as to be in condition to effectively help the students to overcome them.

The joint construction of stories from observed videos, as carried out in this example, creates a social context where the teachers involved can support each other in enhancing observation skills, and finally leads to a deeper understanding of the educational situations taken into consideration. Narrating before reflecting results more effective than only reflecting, in that it creates a shared view of the situation and gives rise to something concrete -the jointly reconstructed story- on which a meaningful reflection and discussion can develop, hence finally supporting professional development.

4 Discussion and conclusion

These five examples presented widely differ from each other as concerns the population involved, the expected learning and the ways narrative is used, as well as what context is created and in which way it influences learning.

As regards the target population, the examples address learners of different ages: middle school and university students as well as adult, in-service teachers. Moreover, it is easy to figure out to adapt each of the mentioned narrative activities to learners of different ages; De Vries [9], for example, describes a case of reflective narration carried out with primary school children in the framework of science classes. This fact suggests that narrative contexts can be suitable for a wide range of learners, independently of their age.

Also the knowledge to be learned varies from example to example, ranging from curricular topics (history in Revolution and biology in Crystal Island), to meta-cognition and self-regulated learning (in the Narrative blog), up to collaborative and teaching skills in the last two examples. Also in this case, it is reasonably possible to create analogous narrative contexts for other topics or to make use of similar narrative activities in different fields. This underlines that narrative activities have wide possibilities of applications.

An even wider difference can be noticed in the way narrative is used: in the first two examples, a background story is given, even though the learners contribute to shape more detailed stories starting from it, while in the last three examples the narrative is completely determined by the users. In the first group, the story is completed through the learners' actions, while in the second group, the narratives created are expressed in words. Inside these two groups, however, we notice again deep differences.

In Revolution, the background story is just sketched, giving the main lines of the situations that can be developed and assigning constraints for the possible behavior of the characters. A precise plot is not given, and the users create the actual story by means of their activity. In Crystal Island, on the other hand, the background story is much more developed; taking part in it, the user does not influence its expected conclusion (solving the proposed problem), but develops his/her own way to reach it. The plot in this case is given; only the way to develop it (sequence of interactions with the synthetic characters and the program's features) is determined by the user's behaviour. These different ways to use narrative are very much in line with the two cognitive tasks assigned. In Revolution, the need to generate the story puts into play creativity, which can likely be useful to explore the socio-political situation of the historical period of interest. Not having to create a story, on the contrary, gives freedom to Crystal Island's user to concentrate on data collection, organization and elaboration, which likely facilitates problem solving.

As concerns the contexts where a narrative is completely created by the learners, we notice a strong similarity between those in the Narrative blog and in the LODE environment, since in both cases a narration of experiences is produced. The aim, however, is different: in the first case it is to stimulate meta-reflection, while in the second it is to support learning from each other and a thoughtful re-use of LOs. The last example in this group, the Teacher Training, shows a strong similarity with storytelling, in that a story to be told is given in a video, and the assigned narrative activity stimulates careful observation and recognition of crucial points.

From the above discussion, however, it is clear that, beyond the differences pointed out, all the considered narrative contexts share a few important aspects:

- Stories constitute a starting point to boost reflection.
- The narrative activity that shapes the context is always strongly connected with the learning content.
- Learners actively take part in shaping the context through the narrative activity they carry out. This gives rise to learning contexts that are suited to the learners' characteristics and needs, and also treasure their experience.

Finally, we remark that in all examples technology does not appear essential, but is certainly very useful. For instance, as concerns Revolution, a similar role play could be carried out by traditional means, i.e., by writing a plot and performing it in class. The use of technology offers several advantages: backgrounds, characters and props are provided, lowering the production effort; synthetic characters control the historical consistence of stories without teacher's interventions, that could result intrusive and hinder creativity; giving life to virtual characters helps avoiding the embarrassment of playing in person. Analogously, the use of technology to share stories in the Narrative blog and in the "narrative corner" of LODE makes experience sharing easier than with traditional means, and facilitates recording for future reference.

References

[1] Arnold, P., Smith, J. D. and Trayner, B. (2006). Narrative: Designing for Context in Virtual Settings. In: Figueiredo, A. D. & Afonso A.P. eds., *Managing Learning in Virtual Setting: the role of context* (p. 197-218). *Hershey* PA: Information Science Publishing.

[2] Aylett, R. (2006). And they both lived happily ever after? In G. Dettori, T. Giannetti, A. Paiva & A. Vaz (eds.), *Technology-mediated narrative environments for learning* (p. 5-25). Rotterdam: Sense Publishers.

[3] Blandin, B. (2006). The Role of Context When Implementing Learning Environments: Some Key Issues. In: Figueiredo, A. D. & Afonso A.P. (eds.), *Managing Learning in Virtual Setting: the role of context* (p. 62-83). *Hershey* PA: Information Science Publishing.

[4] Bruner, J. (1990). *Acts of meaning*. Cambridge, MA: Harvard University Press.

[5] Bruner, J. (1996). *The culture of Education*. Cambridge, MA: Harvard University Press.

[6] Bruner, J. (2003). *Making stories: law, literature, life.* Cambridge, MA: Harvard University Press.

[7] Dettori G., Forcheri P. and Ierardi M.G. (2006) Endowing LOs with a Social Dimension, In Wenyin Liu, Qing Li and Rynson W.H. Lau (eds.), *Advances in Web Based Learning* (p. 189-202). Lecture Notes in Computer Science, 4181, Springer.

[8] Dettori, G. (2007). *Towards a classification of Narrative Learning Environments*. ITD-CNR Report 05/07 (Genova, Italy), available at http://telearn.noe-kaleidoscope.org/open-archive/browse?resource=1542

[9] De Vries, B. (2006). Reflective narration with e-mail: Issues concerning its implementation. In G. Dettori, T. Giannetti, A. Paiva & A. Vaz (eds.), *Technology-mediated narrative environments for learning* (p. 41-54). Rotterdam: Sense Publishers.

[10] Dolk, M. and Den Hertog, J. (2006). Teachers' storied lives: narratives in teacher education, *Proceedings NILE 2006*, P. Brna ed., p. 13-26.

[11] Figueiredo, A.D. and Afonso, A.P. (2006). Context and Learning: A Philosophical Framework. In: Figueiredo, A. D. & Afonso A.P. (eds.), *Managing Learning in Virtual Setting: the role of context* (p. 1-22). *Hershey* PA: Information Science Publishing.

[12] Forret, M., Khoo, E. and Cowie, B. (2006). New Wine or New Bottles: What's New about Online Teaching? In: Figueiredo, A. D. & Afonso A.P. eds., *Managing Learning in Virtual Setting: the role of context* (p. 253-273). *Hershey* PA: Information Science Publishing.

[13] Milhauser, K.L. (2006). The Voice of the Online Learner. In: Figueiredo, A. D. & Afonso A.P. (eds.), *Managing Learning in Virtual Setting: the role of context* (p. 219-235). *Hershey* PA: Information Science Publishing.

[14] Penco, C. (1999). Objective and Cognitive Context. In P. Bouquet et al. (eds.), *CONTEXT'99* (p. 270-283). Lecture Notes in Artificial Intelligence, 1688, Springer.

[15] Ricoeur, P. (2005). *Hermeneutics and the human sciences. Edited and translated by J.B. Thompson* (17th edition). Cambridge: Cambridge University Press.

[16] Rowe, J. P., Mcquiggan, S. W., Mott, B. W. and Lester, J. C. (2007). Motivation in Narrative-Centered Learning Environments. Proceedings of the Workshop on Narrative Learning Environments at the 13th AIED Conference. Marina del Rey, CA, July 2007, p. 40-49.

[17] Shank, R. C. (2000). *Tell Me a Story: Narrative and Intelligence*, 3rd printing, Northwestern University Press, Evanston, IL.

[18] Sutherland, L. (2002). Developing problem solving expertise: the impact of instruction in a question analysis strategy, *Learning and Instruction*, 12, 155-187

Design of Exercises and Test Items for Internetworking Based on a Framework of Exercise Classes

Stefan Freischlad

Didactics of Informatics and E-learning, Universität Siegen
Hölderlinstraße 3, 57068 Siegen, Germany
freischlad@die.informatik.uni-siegen.de

Abstract. Student teachers and teacher novices need an aid to design high quality exercises and test items for Internetworking. In this paper the design of exercises respectively test items is described based on a framework of exercise classes for Internetworking. This framework is composed of content, process, and representation dimension. The content dimension is based on exercise classes for Internetworking and knowledge categories. The process dimension is based on the cognitive process which is needed to solve an exercise and therefore directly influences formulating the question. The third dimension is based on modes of representation and affects the design of the context. The framework was evaluated during a case study in secondary education.

1   Toward High Quality Exercises and Test Items

Informatics education has to face the difficulties associated with the use of the Internet. International curricula for informatics education describe selected contents [1, 2, 3] in this field. But there is still no concept for classroom practice. This paper is part of a research project which is promoted by the German Research Foundation (DFG). The aim is to develop and prove a didactic concept, i.e. to describe a concept by means of three components of the Didactic System "Internetworking"[1]: Knowledge Networks, Exercise Classes, and Learning Aids. Exercise classes defining and structuring informatics concepts in the field of Internetworking shall support teachers especially novices like teacher students to create or adapt exercises and test items. But we found that there is a gap between applying exercise classes and the design of exercises which is hard to overcome by teacher students. Thus, a concept is needed

---

[1] The term Internetworking is made up of internetwork and networking. Referring to Merriam-Webster (http://www.webster.com) the author understands networking as the establishment and use of internetworks.

Please use the following format when citing this chapter:

Freischlad, S., 2008, in IFIP International Federation for Information Processing, Volume 281; *Learning to Live in the Knowledge Society*; Michael Kendall and Brian Samways; (Boston: Springer), pp. 261–268.

which provides teacher students with a framework for the creation of new and for adaptation of existing exercises. This framework will lead to a strategy for the design of exercises. Brinda proposed an approach for a framework in the field of object-oriented modelling [4]. It is derived from an analysis of exercises in this field and is based on a catalogue of identified exercise types which combine several attributes of exercises. An important requirement of the framework which is presented in this paper is to enable teachers to combine several attributes without the inherent restrictions of predefined exercise types.

The overall research project started in 2005. The author started analysing characteristics of informatics systems based on the Internet to identify necessary competences for using Internet applications [3] and described the theoretical approach towards the components of the Didactic System "Internetworking". Learning material was developed based on the Didactic System and implemented into classroom practice. After these two projects exercise classes for Internetworking were defined based on the analysis of textbooks. This classification was applied to existing items [5]. In the third project phase these exercise classes were used in teacher education. Teacher students had to design test items during the practical training in school. This lead to the refinement of the framework for exercise classes which is described in this paper. It was used for the design of a test which was performed during the third classroom project. The question which is targeted in this paper is: What are defining attributes of exercises which have to be considered when selecting the informatics core of the exercise and the context, i.e. when defining stimuli, question, and solution?

2   A Framework for the Design of Exercises

Exercises and test items must be aligned to the learning objectives and to the prerequisites of course participants. Therefore, decisions about the terms or concepts in the field of Internetworking, the type of knowledge about the terms or concepts, the activity of learners, and the level of abstraction concerning the clearness of context and instruction have to be considered. These aspects can be described by (1) the content dimension, i.e. informatics core and knowledge type, (2) the process dimension, i.e. activity for solving an exercise or test item, and (3) the representation dimension, i.e. representation of stimulus, question, and answer. The attributes of an exercise considering these dimensions control the level of difficulty of an answer: The interconnectedness of concepts and the knowledge type influence the difficulty level of an exercise within the content dimension. The cognitive complexity of an activity influences the level of difficulty within the process dimension. And the level of abstraction affects the level of difficulty within the representation dimension.

Anderson et al. [6] describe Bloom's revised taxonomy for the design of assignments based upon clear definitions of learning objectives. They discern the knowledge and the cognitive process dimension. Bruner [7] describes levels of representation. These conceptions permit the assessment of assignments in terms of cognitive levels. But they abstract from the context of a subject. The author proposes the enhancement with subject specific exercise classes (EC). The development of learner adequate exercises is facilitated by the structuring of exercise classes within a taxonomy which follows subject specific and didactic criteria, as well as the development of a strategy for the design of exercises from exercise classes on different levels [4].

The Content Dimension

Freischlad and Schubert describe a hierarchical classification of EC for the Didactic System Internetworking. They derived this structuring from the analysis of textbooks [5]. Each EC represents the informatics core of an exercise. Apart from previous knowledge about computer networks and information security they discern five classes at the first level which are refined at the second level. For example, the major class "Addressing" (EC_3) comprises identification of hosts within computer networks. Additionally, this class includes directory services that support information about an address. It is made-up of the sub-classes IP addressing (EC_{31}), Domain Name System (DNS) (EC_{32}), directory services (EC_{33}), and Network Address Translation (EC_{34}). As Freischlad and Schubert explain EC are suitable to explain the level of interconnectedness of a concrete exercise.

But to specify the content of an item we need a finer grained differentiator. Anderson et al. [6] provide such a differentiation with the knowledge dimension of the taxonomy of educational objectives. They discern factual, conceptual, procedural, and metacognitive knowledge. "These categories are assumed to lie along a continuum from concrete (Factual) to abstract (Metacognitive)" [6, p. 5]. Factual and conceptual knowledge is declarative knowledge, i.e. to "know that". Procedural knowledge is the "knowledge of how" instead of the "knowledge what". Thus, the content dimension is described by exercise classes and knowledge category.

The Process Dimension

The cognitive level is not defined by the selection of an exercise class since the concrete question or instruction defines the cognitive process. The concrete question refers to the content, i.e. the exercise class, but it is not defined by the content. Therefore, it is possible to use this category to contextualize an item. The author proposes to apply the cognitive dimension of Bloom's revised taxonomy. It comprises 19 cognitive processes assigned to six categories where the first category "Remember" focuses on retention and the following five categories focus on transfer, i.e. "Understand", "Apply", "Analyze", "Evaluate", and "Create". "The continuum underlying the cognitive process dimension is assumed to be cognitive complexity; that is, Understand is believed to be more cognitively complex than Remember, Apply is believed to be more cognitively complex than Understand, and so on" [6, p. 5].

The following example illustrates the relation between the content dimension and the process dimension. The informatics core is defined by EC_{21} (protocols of the application layer) and it is concretised by the selection of conceptual knowledge, i.e. the behaviour of the interacting processes. The first exercise is contextualised with the following question: "Compare the state diagrams of the Simple Mail Transfer Protocol (SMTP) and the Post Office Protocol (POP) of the server process. What is your conclusion regarding the authenticity of the client process?" The cognitive process is "Inferring" because the learner has to draw a logical conclusion from the information presented by the diagrams. Another exercise which is assigned to the same category within the knowledge dimension is: "Illustrate the given state diagram of an SMTP server by means of an interaction diagram which describes the transmission of an e-mail!" This exercise is assigned to the cognitive process "Exemplifying" because the learner has to find a concrete example of the principle which is given by the state diagram. Both cognitive processes are of the category Understand. Therefore this differentiation does not describe different levels of cognitive complexity.

The Representation Dimension

Bruner [7] specifies three representations which were used within the learning process. According to Bruner learners pass the levels of representation, i.e. "enactive", "iconic", and "symbolic". An example within our course is the unit about Hypertext Transfer Protocol (HTTP). The enactive representation is retrieving a web page with HTTP commands via Netcat. Learners get direct feedback whether the next step has been correct and about the reaction of the web server. An iconic representation could be an interaction diagram which illustrates the data exchange between client and server. The symbolic representation could be the formal description of HTTP. While learners have to consider syntactical correctness of the Netcat commands as well as linefeeds and whitespaces using HTTP commands on the enactive representation level they abstract from these details using interaction diagrams. At the iconic level they have to consider the data exchange between client and server for establishing a logical connection. On the symbolic level they abstract from these details focussing on the structure of HTTP commands. This example illustrates, that the modes of representation are linked to levels of abstraction. The hypothesis is that the level of difficulty increases with the level of abstraction.

Assignments of an exercise to the content category and the representation mode have to be done from a holistic point of view, i.e. considering stimulus, question, and answer. Thus, it doesn't matter whether the least abstract representation is part of the question or part of the answer. In contrast the cognitive process is determined by the separation of question and answer.

3   Design of the Case Study

The classroom project was performed by four teacher students during their practical course which is combined with a seminar. Furthermore the supervising teacher and the researcher attended the course with 24 students. The project spanned nine weeks and comprised seven learning units. The test was performed after eight of the nine weeks of the course and was marked as a regular test. Learners had 30 minutes to work on the test, due to the legal framework. 22 learners took part in the examination. The items were designed according to the design principle of the PISA studies [8], i.e. each of the items is composed of stimulus and related questions. Three items were selected. Each item consists of three questions. Every item was constructed with two simple questions, i.e. focusing on informatics concepts, and one question which combines concepts of the proceeding questions and is closely linked to a concrete phenomenon. The design was closely oriented to the learning objectives.

Within the first item learners should show if they are able to assess whether a correctly given domain name provides reliable information about the authenticity of an Internet resource which is accessed.

A1. Julia called a web page and suspects that the displayed page is not the true web page. Answer the following questions to explain if this is possible.
a) Describe the logical Internet structure by arranging the following domain names as a tree diagram representing the namespace hierarchy: www.google.de, de.wikipedia.org, en.wikipedia.org, www.die.informatik.uni-siegen.de
b) Explain the components of the domain name www.ifip.org (*domain changed*)!
c) Explain why in the case of DNS resolution with or without caching spoofing is not possible.

Thus, it is about the exercise class Domain Name System (EC_{32}). The first two questions address factual knowledge about the DNS hierarchy, i.e. the structure of the DNS namespace, and the third question addresses conceptual knowledge about the process of domain name resolving. The cognitive process category is alternating from Understand to Remember to Understand. This implies the lowest cognitive complexity of the second question. Question a) is based on an iconic representation while questions b) and c) use a symbolic representation. The first question is at the lowest level of abstraction. Thus, the third question is proposed to be at the highest level of difficulty.

The second item is about checking the authenticity of an e-mail and to assess the reliability of the result. The application e-mail is just the context in this case. The informatics concepts were represented by sub-classes of EC_3 (Addressing), and EC_4 (Data Transfer).

A2. Mario wants to find out the origin of an e-mail. He proposes to check an IP address. Explain if it is possible to determine the location of a host by an IP address.
a) The Internet is composed of several interconnected computer networks. Explain how they are connected and what is the functionality of the connecting component considering data exchange?
b) Insert the IP addresses 141.99.64.200 and 141.99.200.200 into the empty fields of the figure and complete the addresses in field 3 and 6. (*Assign IP addresses to empty fields of a diagram representing hosts in two networks.*)
c) Substantiate your proceeding for address allocation!

The questions are about conceptual knowledge. The first question addresses interconnected networks (EC_{52}) and packet switching on the Internet (EC_{42}). Learners have to name and to explain the functionality of a router. The second question asks for the connection between the components of an IP address (EC_{31}). And within the third question learners have to explain why and how addresses (EC_{31}) are assigned to one of several interconnected networks (EC_{52}). This assignment is a necessary prerequisite for packet switching (EC_{42}). Thus, the third question combines exercise classes of the other questions. The first question is assigned to the cognitive process dimension Understand. The second is assigned to Apply, because learners have to execute a familiar task. And the third question is assigned to Understand, because learners have to explain the assignment of IP addresses to different networks. Thus, the first question is at the lowest process level and the second at the highest. Furthermore, the second question is at a lower representation level (iconic) while questions a) and c) are at the same level (symbolic).

The third item is about whether learners are able to plan and process an indirect search. It focuses a specific Internet application.

A3. Julia wants to borrow a book from the school library. She decides to look in advance on the web if the book is available. Where does she have to look for the book?
a) Describe the functionality of search engines completing the given activity diagram!
b) Explain the terms web crawler and index each with two items.
c) How should Julia proceed using a search engine and when would she not succeed? Substantiate your answer!

The first question addresses conceptual knowledge about the functionality of a search engine. It is about the dynamic view on this informatics system (EC$_{12}$: World Wide Web). The second question aimed at factual knowledge about web crawler and index which are important components of a search engine. Therefore, the static structure of the search engine is examined regarding its components (EC$_{12}$). The third question addressed procedural knowledge about search strategies based on knowledge about the functionality of a search engine (EC$_{12}$). The first question asks for an explanation of the functionality of a search engine which is assigned to the category Understand and the representation mode is iconic. The second and third questions refer to a symbolic representation. But the second is assigned to the lower process category Remember while the third question is assigned to the higher process category Apply.

4   Findings of the Case Study

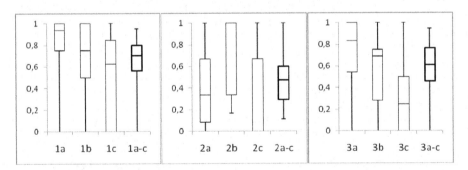

Fig. 1. Box plots of results of test items 1-3

The left diagram in Figure 1 shows the results of test item 1 relative to the total number of points for each assignment. The boxes comprise the quartiles around the median, i.e. the boxes comprise half of the results. The appended whiskers visualise the interval from maximum to minimum results. Most learners could answer these questions. Eight learners could not answer question 1c. But there were four learners who achieved the full amount of points. The middle diagram shows the results of test item 2. While less than half of the learners could answer the first question sufficiently, i.e. they have got more than half of the points, the second question was answered completely correct by 12 learners. The third question was answered correctly by four learners. But the median is 0 points. Therefore the median of item 2 is at 0.47. The right diagram shows the results of test item 3. Three-fourths could complete the activity diagram with more than 50 per cent of the points. Question two could be answered by most learners with more than half of the points. But the third question was answered by three-fourths in a way that they achieved less than half of the points. Just four learners could apply indirect search to the described situation.

The results are discussed considering the assignment of the questions within the framework. The framework does not provide a weighting of the three dimensions regarding the level of difficulty. The results of the test are interpreted regarding the influence of the dimensions to the level of difficulty. Just the questions of a single test item were compared to avoid effects related to the prerequisites of the learners regarding the differing contents. In Table 1 the assignment of the items according to the predefined framework is shown. As far as applicable within parentheses the level of the attribute within the dimension is shown.

Table 1. Test items in the framework

Test Item		Content	Process	Representation
A1	a	EC_{32} / Factual (0)	Understand (1)	iconic (1)
	b	EC_{32} / Factual (0)	Remember (0)	symbolic (2)
	c	EC_{32} / Conceptual (1)	Understand (1)	symbolic (2)
A2	a	EC_{42}, EC_{52} / Conceptual (1)	Understand (1)	symbolic (2)
	b	EC_{31} / Conceptual (1)	Apply (2)	iconic (1)
	c	$EC_{31}, EC_{42}, EC_{52}$ / Conceptual (1)	Understand (1)	symbolic (2)
A3	a	EC_{12} / Conceptual (1)	Understand (1)	iconic (1)
	b	EC_{12} / Factual (0)	Remember (0)	symbolic (2)
	c	EC_{12} / Procedural (2)	Apply (2)	symbolic (2)

The results of A1 indicate that the representation mode strongly influences the level of difficulty. Although question b) would be assigned to a lower level of difficulty according to the cognitive process question a) is answered better. The explanation which is derived of the framework indicates that the iconic representation of question a) and therefore the lower level of abstraction is the reason for better results. Furthermore, the comparison of the questions b) and c) indicate that the knowledge category and the cognitive process category affect the level of difficulty. The comparison of the question A2 a) and b) do not allow conclusions because they are items of different exercise classes. But the interconnectedness of exercise classes in question c) (compared to a)) respectively in combination with the representation mode (compared to b)) results in a higher level of difficulty. The results of A3 indicate that the representation mode mostly affects the level of difficulty because question a) is assigned at a higher level of difficulty according to the content and the process dimension than question b). Nevertheless the results are better. Furthermore the effect of the content in combination with the process dimension to the level of difficulty is confirmed comparing question b) and c).

The results indicate that the level of difficulty is varied by the modes of representation and the combination of content and process dimension. Thus, the framework is applicable to explain levels of difficulty. Whilst the content category and the cognitive process are derived from the learning objectives which are used for the design of the learning process, the representation mode is independently chosen to vary the level of difficulty. This knowledge can be used when creating new or modify exercises respectively test items.

5 Conclusion

The aim of this framework is to enable teachers respectively teacher students and teacher novices to design high quality items in the field of Internetworking. Attributes which affect the level of difficulty are defined. The content, process, and representation dimension are appropriate to describe the design strategy of exercises and test items. The results of the case study indicate that the design of exercises can be aligned to this framework. The framework has to be validated in further empirical studies with more items so that the distinction of the attributes for the evaluation becomes clearer. And the framework has to be applied in teacher education to affirm its feasibility. In 2008 we will conduct practical training in school with teacher students. Thus, we will get feedback to this approach.

References

1. Tucker, A. (ed.): A model curriculum for K–12 computer science: final report of the ACM K–12 task force curriculum committee. ACM, New York 2006. URL: http://www.csta.acm.org/Curriculum/sub/CurrFiles/K-12ModelCurr2ndEd.pdf (January 2008)
2. Anderson, J.; van Weert, T. (eds.): Information and communication technology in secondary education – A Curriculum for Schools. UNESCO, Paris 2002. URL: http://wwwedu.ge.ch/cptic/prospective/projets/unesco/en/curriculum2000.pdf (January 2008)
3. Freischlad, S.: Learning Media Competences in Informatics. In: Dagiene, V.; Mittermeir, R. (eds.): Proceedings of Second International Conference on "Informatics in Secondary Schools. Evolution and Perspectives – ISSEP", November 7–11, Vilnius (Lithuania) 2006, pp. 591–599, ISBN 9955-680-47-4.
4. Brinda, T.: Development of the exercise culture in informatics. In: [9]
5. Freischlad, S.; Schubert, S.: Towards High Quality Exercise Classes for Internetworking. In: [9]
6. Anderson, L. W.; Krathwohl, D. R. (eds.): A taxonomy for learning, teaching and assessing: A revision of Bloom's Taxonomy of educational objectives. Addison Wesley Longman, New York 2001.
7. Bruner, J. S.; Olver, R. R.; Greenfield, P. M.: Studies in Cognitive Growth. John Wiley, New York 1966.
8. OECD: Learning for Tomorrow's World – First Results from PISA 2003. Organisation for Economic Co-operation and Development, Paris 2004. URL: http://www.pisa.oecd.org/dataoecd/1/60/34002216.pdf (January 2008)
9. Benzie, D.; Iding, M. (eds.): Proceedings of IFIP-Conference on "Informatics, Mathematics and ICT: A golden triangle", June 27–29, Boston (USA) 2007, ISBN-13: 978-0-615-14623-2.

Chapter 11

Digital Literacy for a Knowledge Society 2

Transitions towards a Knowledge Society
Aspectual Pre-evaluation of a Culture-Sensitive Implementation Framework

Mamello Thinyane, Alfredo Terzoli and Peter Clayton
Department of Computer Science, Rhodes University,
Grahamstown – 6140, South Africa
mthinyane@rucus.net, {a.terzoli,p.clayton}@ru.ac.za,
WWW home page: http://www.cs.ru.ac.za

Abstract. Information and Communication Technology (ICT) is aiding the transition of society into information society and ultimately knowledge society. Embedded within ICT are the cultural and philosophical undercurrents of the society in which the ICT solutions are developed, currently predominantly the Western culture. The proliferation of ICT is therefore inadvertedly leading to more Westernization of the world. It is important, therefore, that ICT solutions are culture sensitive and flexible enough to be situated within different cultures. To that end, we utilize Herman Dooyeweerd's Theory of Modal Aspects to analyze a framework we has developed for implementation of locally situated knowledge based systems, to determine its efficacy in addressing the different modal aspects, which make up the total experience and cultural expressiveness of societies.

1. Introduction

The 21st century is seeing increased multi-culturalism and higher levels of globalization which has been aided by the proliferation of Information and Communication Technologies (ICTs). In this dynamic cultural interaction, there's however a dominance of the Western culture and as a result a general Westernization of the world [1]. This phenomenon has been termed by some observers as neo-colonialism and it occurs at the expense of a possible assimilation of less prominent, marginalized cultures and societies [1]. The process of Westernization of the world, through the proliferation of ICT, happens because these technologies encapsulate a culture and world-view from which they were conceived. For example, the Human Computer Interaction (HCI) components and usage metaphors would extensively reflect the culture and the language within which they were developed. There are two possibilities when such systems are introduced into different cultural setting. One results in a culture synthesis out of the amalgamation of differing aspects from the two cultures and the other allows for a functional integration of technology while maintaining the cultural integrity of the communities adopting the technology.

Please use the following format when citing this chapter:

Thinyane, M., Terzoli, A. and Clayton, P., 2008, in IFIP International Federation for Information Processing, Volume 281; *Learning to Live in the Knowledge Society*; Michael Kendall and Brian Samways; (Boston: Springer), pp. 271–278.

The culture specific influences in the world of ICT and computing have been observed particularly within the discussions on computing and the politics of gender identity. Extensive literature recognizes the masculine and military culture out of which computing and ICT was birthed, which has resulted in the exclusion and marginalization of many females [2, 3]. Tedre et al also recognize the cultural positioning of computing in their discussion on ethnocomputing [3]. Cultures play a pivotal role in the realization of ICT solutions and in their usage. An example is from the Eastern cultures, some of which seek meaning in the harmony and order of relationships between human elements and nature, the spiritual and the natural [4]. Zhang highlights, within the context of education and pedagogy in Eastern cultures, the outworking of the fundamental epistemological beliefs of a culture, in the values the society embraces, the nature of the examination process and the manner in which education systems are organized. He contrasts the Eastern notion of ICT within education as a new information source with the Western view of ICT as an open-content productivity tool [5].

The rest of this paper discusses the worldviews and philosophical theories that underpin the Western culture by highlighting the ground motives that the reformation Dutch philosopher, Herman Dooyeweerd, identifies as primary in Western thought. The Western culture's influences on ICT are then discussed with a particular focus on knowledge-based systems. This is followed by a juxtapositioning with alternative conceptualizations of knowledge and then a basic analysis of PIASK, a culture sensitive framework for implementing knowledge based systems.

2. The ground motives

Dooyeweerd, in his book "In the twilight of Western thought" calls the influences and factors that have shaped the western philosophical landscape, the 'ground motives' of western philosophy. Ground motives are pre-theoretical presuppositions that shape a worldview. These are the beliefs, which are either true of false, which are held by faith and which form the foundation for conceptualizing and understanding reality. It's important to highlight Dooyeweerd's Theory of Ground Motives and Religious Presuppositions which recognizes the inherently religious nature (the faith commitment) and inclination of every philosophy and theoretical thought [6]. The same observation was made by Clouser in "The myth of religious neutrality" [7]. This is necessary to highlight because it challenges and nullifies the assumed autonomy of theoretical thought, and places it on the same plane as other modal aspects [8].

The following are the four basic ground motives that have influenced the western philosophical landscape [6]:

- The form-matter motive – which is traditionally the Greek philosophy. It makes a distinction between the form motive and the matter motive. The former deified the cultural and social life of the classical Greek society, and the latter emphasized the biotic component of our existence.
- The word-revelation motive – encapsulates the biblical theme of creation, fall and redemption. It identifies the concentration-point of creation/reality in connection to an absolute creator, God.
- The nature-grace motive – sought to reconcile the Greek and the biblical motives, and since Renaissance sought to accommodate biblical and humanistic motives. It makes a sharp distinction between the secular and sacred, between priest and laity, between natural and spiritual.

- The modern humanism motive – since Emmanuel Kant has been referred to as the nature-freedom motive. It sought emancipation from the supra-natural influence of religion and emphasized nature and the creativity of the modern man as the master of his destiny and of the world. It absolutized the theoretical-logical aspect and reason.

3. The West and ICT

Tedre et al highlight the fact that the roots of computing are in the cultural context of the West, and that the science itself is Western, middle or upper class and male in origin [3]. The developments and advancements, the philosophies, tools, concepts and methodologies that have been used in computing have been predominantly Western. For example:
- Falsification as a positivist tool and method is still used extensively in computing to validate correctness of programs. [3]
- The reductionist view of knowledge and reality within the western culture which has influenced the ontological underpinnings of knowledge based systems.
- The Western notion of mutual exclusivity, teleology and hierarchy through local division and dominance has influenced classificatory thought in computing [11]. For example, the classification within the SUMO ontology (Figure 1) reveals a specific worldview and way of organizing reality, which would be different from a different philosophical perspective.
- Reason and logic within the computing domain still reflect its western roots
- The learner focused, constructivist pedagogies are still the more prevalently supported on eLearning tools and Virtual Learning Environments (VLEs).

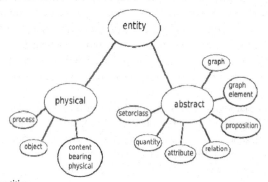

Figure 1- SUMO top level entities

The tools that have been developed have therefore embodied these cultural perspectives and their use is in harmony within cultures with aligned perspectives. These tools become problematic in contexts where there is a conflict with the local cultural perspective and this is exemplified by: perceived lack of user friendliness of applications and systems; extremely high learning curves for new applications and systems, often requiring one to acquire a new way of conceptualizing reality. For example, the Object Oriented Programming (OOP) paradigm is aligned with a reductionist view of the world but not with a view of the world that is unitary and where determination of types and relationships of objects is not a sufficient way to analyzing reality (e.g. the Vedanta of Sankara philosophy) [9]; lack of a cultural fit (intrinsic alignment) in the usage of applications and systems; and user's experience in using the applications being separate, distinct and disconnected from their reality.

The assumption of universality of computing and that it is an a-cultural discipline is not valid. It is necessary, within the discipline, the tools and the systems developed, that an ethnographic critique is undertaken. The tools and the systems need to be culturally localized. An awareness of the different philosophical perspectives can also enrich the discipline and the systems developed.

4. Alternative philosophies and limitations in ICT

This section is centered on highlighting specific areas of conflict between the underlying philosophy in ICT and other philosophies, in particular looking at African and Asian worldviews. The focus on these regions is due to the fact that most Least Developed Countries (LDCs) are situated there (approximately 67% in Africa and 21% in Eurasia [10]), and in the process of exploring possible interventions for development, technology and ICT are usually taunted as good enablers. These regions also have significantly contrasting worldviews to the post-modern Western worldview. The majority of worldviews in these regions share a common undercurrent of Animism. This is expressed in the notion of unity and harmony between matter and spirit, and the immanent role of the gods or ancestors in everyday life. These worldviews also have a cyclic teleology (versus the linear view of history of the West [11]) and this is evident, for example, in the concept of rebirth of reincarnation in the Hindu religion. These distinctions in the basic presuppositions on which the worldviews are based contribute to the differences in conceptualizing reality. A good distinction is also made by Eco in 'the name of the rose' [12] and by Borges in 'the library of babel' [13] where they each present a different way of formalizing knowledge and reality. Eco's narrative presents a more empirical, logical and Western perspective. Another excellent and contrasting view is developed by Guattari et al in 'a thousand plateaus' [14] where he presents a rhizome metaphor for articulating the nature of knowledge, which is in contrast to the common hierarchical tree metaphor (Figure 1).

A few immediate examples where current computing tools would be limited, due to the difference in underlying philosophies, include:

- Upper ontologies (e.g. SUMO, CYC) that do not encapsulate and cannot represent knowledge from a different ontological perspective. Figure 2 indicates the high level classification of entities within Nyaya-Vaisesika philosophy [15]. A domain ontology that is developed based on the classification thought in that philosophy, would be difficult to merge or align (via an upper ontology) with other ontologies, simply because the ontology manipulation mechanisms and the underlying concepts in the upper ontologies are not directly equitable to concepts encapsulated in the Nyaya-Vaisesika ontology.

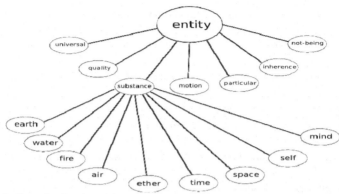

Figure 2 - Example oriental ontology

- Modeling knowledge from a non-Kantian perspective (*'ding an sich'* – presupposed on the existence of entities independent of our experience of the entity [8]), where the essence of knowledge is not the concepts in themselves but rather the process of knowing. Where meaning and structure precedes being. Dooyeweerd refers to the essence of knowledge as the multi-aspectual knowings [16]. The whole of the knowledge modeling discipline is predicated on this Kantian notion of *'ding an sich'* as such knowledge bases are simply entity-relationship specifications. It is difficult therefore to conceptualize, from a Western perspective, a knowledge base as anything but concepts and entities and how they relate to each other.
- Relations of containment - mechanisms are already in place to handle containment relationships of the whole-part type. Therefore representing a relationship that signifies the containment of different vehicle parts in a car is a trivial and well handled problem.

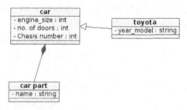

Figure 3 - Whole-Part containment relationship

The whole-part relationships can also be easily modeled using the RDF language constructs: *<rdf:type>*, *<rdf:bag>* and *<rdf:seq>*. In both the oriental and the western philosophies, the car (in Figure 3) contains the different parts that it's made up of. However in the oriental philosophies, the car is also contained in the individual car parts. There is a harmony of interdependence where a whole is said to inhere in the parts while the parts are the inherent cause of the whole.

- Representing enkaptic [17] relations - Enkaptic relationships are a foreign concept in the Western philosophy and are more aligned with philosophies that have sentiments of totality, unity and harmony [17]. The point of departure with the western philosophy is that objects and entities are assumed to 'individuate' from the universal, supra-temporal structures, laws, order and purpose [8]. "Structure and not substance" is the phrase that articulates the philosophy. The different enkaptic relationships, which in Western philosophy are summed up in a single whole-part relationship, include:

foundation enkapsis, subject-object enkapsis, symbiotic enkapsis, correlative enkapsis and territorial enkapsis [8], and the articulation of these relationships using the current tools and techniques is not well supported, if not impossible.

The biggest limitation in having computing and ICT being predominantly western is one that is well articulated by Olson:

"The dominant culture may not acknowledge (and may have to way of acknowledging through linguistic lack of conceptual representation) the discourses of other cultures, such as the cyclical worldview (vs. the teleological worldview) or knowing through Dreamtime, where aborigines "separate time from location". The "all at once" dreamtime (notion of the past, present and future all co-existing) does not counter the aborigines concept of linear time, but rather qualifies and informs it" [11]

5. Multi-aspectual philosophical framework

The lack of an internal ethnographic critique within the computing discipline means that the culture sensitive aspects of computing are left to chance and coincidence. Philosophy, however, provides a critical overview of the thoughts that shape a society and therefore can enrich the ethnographic considerations around computing and ICT.

Because philosophy itself is rooted in a specific culture, it is important to identify and establish a transcendental philosophical framework to guide the implementation of ICT solutions, in particular, knowledge-based local systems. For this task we explore the work of Dooyeweerd, who identified 15 modal aspects (modes that we operate in within our experiential horizon) and articulates the nature, the properties and the relationship between the modal aspects. His work is taunted as "a philosophically sound basis for diversity and coherence, and interdisciplinarity (in this case, interculturality)" [17]. The underlying principle in Dooyeweerd's thinking is *the shalom hypothesis* aka the *simultaneous realization of norms* principle. This principle highlights the need for operating within the laws of a modal aspect in order to maintain sustainability and a deep, rounded, rich well being [8]. An extensive overview of the theory of modal aspects by Dooyeweerd is in his magnum opus "A new Critique of Theoretical Thought" [8] and "In the Twilight of Western Thought" [6]. Dooyeweerd identified the following 15 modal aspects: Quantitative, Spatial, Kinematic, Physical, Biotic, Sensitive, Analytical, Formative, Lingual, Social, Economic, Aesthetic, Juridical, Ethical and Pistic. Dooyeweerd's theory of modal aspects provides a tool for analyzing [17], shaping and assessing various undertakings on the basis of their overall good.

6. Aspectual overview of PIASK

We have developed a framework, PIASK, that we proposed for building multi-modal, multimedia and ontology based knowledge systems [18]. PIASK is a layered architecture that attempts to provide a basis for implementing locally situated and culturally sensitive knowledge based applications. The framework has been utilized in implementing a prototype of a knowledge based ecommerce portal in the context of exploring ICT interventions for development in a rural community in South Africa [19]. A basic aspectual analysis (Table 1) of

PIASK highlights the key areas that are addressed at each of the 5 layers. This analysis is a necessary critique that is needed to determine the adequacy of PIASK as a balanced framework that is coherent across the diverse modal aspects, and across diverse cultures.

Table 1 - Basic Aspectual Analysis of PIASK

PIASK Layer	Modal Aspect	
Presentation	aesthetic	
	lingual	
	sensitive	
	biotic	
	spatial	
Interaction	social	biotic
	sensitive	spatial
Access	formative	
Social Networking	social	quantitative
	juridical	economic
	ethical	
Knowledge Base	pistic	
	analytical	
	lingual	
	formative	

The key layers of the framework, as far integrating the implemented applications and systems within a local culture, are the knowledge base layer (which encapsulates the indigenous knowledge of the community, with its embedded epistemological and ontological presuppositions), the social networking layer (emulating the social systems within the community, and providing an interface to the human, as a participant in a community of Socially Intelligent Agents (SIAs)), presentation layer (handling the primary interfacing to the users in a manner that conveys the user's aesthetics, preferences and sense of beauty and form) and the interaction layer handles the interaction based on the users' preferred usage modality. The PIASK framework encompasses a variety of modal aspects, which allows for an intrinsic consideration of factors within the experiential horizon of the users of the system. Some aspects are less prominently addressed by the PIASK framework because they only come into play indirectly, for example the economic, biotic, and spatial aspects.

7. Conclusion

The current evident transition towards a global knowledge society has its share of (un)desirable outcomes; assimilation of marginalized cultures, loss of diversity (and beauty) through Western-influenced homogenization. We have highlighted examples of the limitations of a mono-cultured solution to be relevant and appropriate in another culture. In order to maintain the harmony in the context of the diversity of cultures and philosophies, it is necessary to situate the ICT solutions on a transcendent philosophical framework, and for this we have proposed

Dooyeweerd's theory of modal aspects. This philosophy can be used to analyze and shape ICT solutions (as exemplified through the analysis of the PIASK framework) in a systematic manner to determine the coherency of the solution, as far as the overall good, well-being and sustainability (i.e. *the shalom principle*) is concerned. The transition towards a global knowledge society needs to be coupled with an understanding and implementation of mechanisms that would direct it towards a desired outcome, and we have proposed one such mechanism.

References

1. S. Latouche, The Westernization of the World: The Significance, Scope and Limits of the Drive Towards Global Uniformity (Polity Press, 1996)
2. P.N. Edwards, The Army and the Microworld: Computers and the Politics of Gender Identity, Signs, 16(1), (JSTOR, 1990), pp. 102-127
3. M. Tedre, E. Sutinen, E. Kähkönen and P. Kommers, Ethnocomputing: ICT in cultural and social context, *Communications of the ACM*, 49(1), (ACM Press New York, NY, USA, 2006), pp. 126-130
4. J. Zhang, A cultural look at information and communication technologies in eastern education, *Education Tech Research Dev,* 55, (Springer, 2007), pp. 301-314
5. H.J. Becker, L.J. Ravitz and Y. Wong, Teaching, Learning, and computing national survey report #3: Teacher and teacher-directed student use of computers and software. *Center for research on Information Technology and Organization* (University of California, Irvine and University of Minnesota, 1999)
6. H. Dooyeweerd, In the Twilight of Western Thought: Studies in the Pretended Autonomy of Philosophical Thought (Craig Press, 1975)
7. R.A. Clouser, The myth of Religious Neutrality (University of Notre Dame Press, 1991)
8. H. Dooyeweerd, A new critique of theoretical thought (Edwin Mellen Press, NY, 1997)
9. S. Dasgupta, A History of Indian Philosophy (Thomas Reed Publications, 1991)
10. List of least developed countries, UN-OHRLLS – United Nations; http://www.un.org/special-rep/ohrlls/ldc/list.htm
11. H.A. Olson, Cultural discourses of classification: indigenous alternatives to the tradition of Aristotle, Durkheim and Foucault. *Proceedings of the 10th ASIS SIG/CR Classification Research Workshop*, p 107-24 (1999)
12. U. Eco, The name of the Rose (Hanser, 1983)
13. J. L. Borges, The library of Babel (Penguin, London, 1989)
14. G. Deleuze and F. Guattari, A thousand plateaus (Athlone Press, London, 1988)
15. S. Saha, Perspectives on Nyaya logic and epistemology (South Asia Books, 1987)
16. H. Hart, Understanding our world: an Integral ontology (Uni. Press of America, 1984)
17. A. Basden, The Dooyeweerd Pages (2007); http://www.dooy.salford.ac.uk/
18. M. Thinyane, L. Dalvit, T. Mapi, H. Slay, A. Terzoli and P. Clayton, An ontology-based, multi-modal platform for the inclusion of marginalized rural communities into the knowledge society, *Proceedings of SAICSIT* (ACM Press, NY, USA, 2007), pp. 143-151
19. M. Thinyane, P. Clayton and A. Terzoli, Exploring a novel service deployment framework, PIASK, through the design and implementation of an e-commerce function for a rural community, *Proceedings of SATNAC* (Mauritius, 2007)

Social networking and the third age
Significance and impact of targeted learning initiatives based on web communities of third agers

Manuela Repetto and Guglielmo Trentin
Institute for Educational Technology, Italian National Research Council
(ITD-CNR)
via de Marini, 6 – 16149 Genoa, Italy
{repetto,trentin}@itd.cnr.it

Abstract. Difficulties with access to ICT and an inadequate use of them risk to increase exclusion of the elderly population and to make the socio-cultural and inter-generational gap greater than it has ever been. Online learning environments based on social networking could not only give an opportunity for individual cultural growth, but also for conceiving a range of practical applications of great social significance such as conscientious access, search and use of information, fruition of a multitude of web services, socialization within online communities, and the sharing of experiences and resources. This article aims at verifying to what extent targeted initiatives of e-learning, like the one referred to here, may facilitate the elderly to gain benefits from what the present knowledge society offers, enabling them to be aware of and at the same time active participants in the current innovative processsest.

1 Introduction

Within the complex and rapidly changing knowledge society individuals are required to adapt themselves continuously and quickly to the changes affecting all the sectors of everyday life. People reaching the third age are increasingly still active, dedicated to furthering their interests, committed in associations or taking part in volunteer activities, and sometimes they are not completely retired from social and professional life. According to the current principles of lifelong learning, elderly people are still able to acquire and develop a broad range of knowledge and skills that make them feel more prepared to meet the emerging challenges, to catch new opportunities, and thus to fully participate in current innovative processes.

Development of skills in the use of information and communication technology (ICT) is an area which most programs of courses targeted at third agers focus on. These skills can be acquired in the context of traditional learning initiatives, onsite activities, but even through more targeted learning courses based on social

Please use the following format when citing this chapter:

Repetto, M. and Trentin, G., 2008, in IFIP International Federation for Information Processing, Volume 281; *Learning to Live in the Knowledge Society*; Michael Kendall and Brian Samways; (Boston: Springer), pp. 279–286.

networking. One of these online learning initiatives was designed and run by the Institute for Educational Technology of the Italian National Research Council (ITD-CNR) in the framework of the experimental project "Informatica per la terza età – ICT for the third age". The course outcomes related to the acquisition of skills in the use of ICT have been investigated, detecting attitudes developed in the participants and analyzing long term follow-up.

2   The targeted learning activity

The people who participated in the online course was selected among participants who had previously attended a theoretical and practical training course on the basic use of ICT successfully. These training courses were organized in the context of an experimental educational plan, run by Liguria Region in the last five-year period, aimed at introducing to the basic use of ICT a consistent number of over-60s [1]. The plan envisaged a mixed learning path organized in onsite and distance activities. The distance activities could take two different forms:

- computer-assisted training, to be carried out autonomously in one's own home and based on the reinforcement of what had been learnt in the classroom;
- online collaborative learning, aimed at an in-depth examination of some topics related to the use of Internet, and targeted at a limited sample of elders who had shown themselves to be totally autonomous in the use of ICT.

This second form of course, identified by the name of "Networked 3rd age", allowed to establish to what extent online learning based on social networking could be considered a complementary way of learning with respect to traditional classroom sessions. The participants, selected among those who attended the previous onsite course, were indicated by their respective classroom teachers on the basis of the satisfaction of a number of conditions, such as basic understanding of the use of e-mail and Web browsing, and availability of internet access in their own home. The participants recruited in this way were then assigned to two separate online learning groups of about twenty persons, each coordinated by an online tutor, fulfilling the criteria of homogeneity in age and gender.

The course, organized in three modules and in twenty-four learning units, was aimed at developing two specific skills which are essential for the typical social networker:

- the optimum use of search engines for information and resource retrieval;
- the establishment and management of web services based on social networking.

The methodological approach adopted in this course was based on a strategy of online learning, characterized by a strong network interaction between all the actors involved (tutor and group of participants) [2]. Each learning unit is initiated by the tutor who, using an asynchronous computer conferencing service, asks participants - with an explanatory message - to perform one or more exercises. Each participant may dedicate time to the learning activity for as long as he wishes, returning the results autonomously or in cooperation with other participants according to dynamics based on self-regulated learning, self-help relations and peer-to-peer collaboration.

The learning environment used is based on social networking tools which ensure, in addition to distribution of learning materials, asynchronous communication one-to-many and many-to-many between tutor and participants and among the participants themselves. Within "Networked 3rd age", a portal offering free spaces and services was chosen with the objective of making participants acquainted with a tool for online communities management that could be used after the course autonomously and at no cost.

3 Activity outcomes

Monitoring and evaluation processes of this initiative, carried out by online tutors and ITD-CNR researchers, was aimed at detecting the achievement of the envisaged learning objectives, estimating participation and involvement level of participants in the proposed online activities, at measuring degree satisfaction and general attitude with respect to the learning methodology adopted to run the online activities. Investigation on the achievement of learning goals and on participation was based on an approach already tested in other online courses [3], focused on analysis of messages and artifacts produced by the participants (in this case exercises) and on the level of individual involvement showed in group interaction. Structured grids were used to establish the correctness of exercises and to perform classification of messages; an incidence table [4] allowed to analyze relations and thus to define the degree of centrality of communication within the online groups. The main tool used to detect participants' attitude was the satisfaction questionnaire delivered at the end of the course; information obtained from this tool were integrated with data from participated observation of participants' interactions and of the more personal messages between the tutor and individual participant.

What follows is a summary of the outcomes of the three aspects on which evaluation of experience - conducted in parallel during the course and at the end of it - was focused.

3.1 Achievement of learning objectives

The assessment of participants' learning achievements took into account the level of correctness of what they produced in relation to the tasks assigned to them. About a quarter of participants completed all the envisaged exercises correctly; one third of them completed three-quarters without mistakes. Thus, more than half of the total number of participants achieved good results.

From the point of view of the complexity of the exercises, about 60% of participants were in the medium-high band, while about 70% correctly completed the exercises considered essential to certificate the achievement of training goals of the online course.

The checks show, therefore, that the acquisition of the contents tackled in e-learning activities was more than satisfactory. However, caution is needed, given the particular conditions in which the experiment was conducted. For example:

- although varied (different entry-level skills, different cultural backgrounds of the participants, etc.) the sample involved was numerically low;
- the content, of a technological nature, lends itself well to training in e-learning courses; it cannot be taken for granted that similar results would be obtained with the same group when tackling other subjects;
- training which had enabled them to acquire the basic notions on the use of network tools and services later used for online interaction beyond the course;
- people were recruited on the basis of pre-screening, made by their classroom teachers, whose key element was a good level of autonomy in computer use.

3.2   Participation and cross-interactions

Analysis of messages shows a fairly high level of participation of both groups though with different dynamics. To analyse in greater detail the dynamics of interaction that developed within each learning group, two separate incidence tables were compiled.

An incidence table is a grid with sender/receiver (S/R) double entry [4]. It is used to record interactions among participants in a discussion group.

Supposing that there are n attendees, the table will measure n by n, and each cell will represent the number of times that each participant has interacted with another group member. The sub-totals of each column represent the number of message emissions, and the sub-totals of each row the number of receptions. The table's total represents the overall number of communications within the group.

Applying two different algorithms to the incidence table yields the centrality index, which measures the extent to which communication centres around each participant, and the participation index, gauging the extent of communication distribution within a group.

In the examined case, only the messages in which there was explicit reference to one or more participants (mentioning the names, or quoting part of a message, etc.) have been recorded in the incidence table. Messages sent to the tutor or socialization messages sent indifferently to the whole group have not been taken into account.

The number of communications were on the whole reasonably distributed throughout one of the groups, even if more centred around four participants; while there was no significant interaction between the participants in the other group, since one-to-one communication between participant and tutor was preferred, aimed mainly at completing the task at hand.

Diversity in the communication dynamics that turned out within the two groups (more "horizontal" in the former and more "vertical" the latter), wasn't influenced by composition of groups, formed using the same homogeneity criteria and started out from almost identical conditions, but rather by the teaching/learning strategy adopted which played a part in such marked diversity. A strategy based on exercises tends, in fact, to give priority to one-to-one communication between the tutor who assigns the tasks and the single participant who completes them, despite a many-to-many horizontal communication triggered where relations are based on self-help.

The presence of the second type of interaction in one of the groups can be influenced by individual factors such as the group members' greater propensity for online socialization, the tutoring style or the tutor's ability to raise participants' interest and to facilitate socialization and collaborative interaction within the learning group.

3.3   Participants' reactions

The general attitude of the participants towards the online course and the learning methodology adopted in online activities, measured by a satisfaction questionnaire delivered at the end of the course, was very positive.

The feeling of disorientation and mistrust towards computer-mediated communication showed in the initial stages, attributed by the participants to difficulties to relating to people that they had never met in person or to uncertainty with technology tools, changed radically about two-thirds of the way through the course, as showed by 78% of the participants who expressed high satisfaction. Instead, average-high and average-low satisfaction were expressed respectively by 10% and 8% of the participants. This positive judgment was accompanied by the desire to follow further similar online courses to deepen other issues linked to the use of ICT.

4   Medium-term effects

The survey on medium-term effects of outputs, conducted six months after the end of the course, allowed to understand to what extent knowledge acquired during online activities was applied to everyday life. The semi-structured questionnaire used to check the application of these competencies was aimed at detecting:

1. frequency of Internet use;
2. type of Web use;
3. type of interpersonal communication used;
4. personal impressions on how the online activity affected their everyday life.

The use of e-mail to send the questionnaire provided a preliminary information on follow-up: questionnaires handed back and duly filled-in by 76% of the participants who had successfully completed "Networked 3rd age" provided a further element of the effective use of internet, or at least of e-mail use.

Quantitative analysis of questionnaire answers (Figure 1) shows that more than half of the total number of participants connect on average several times a day and that almost all people browse the net regularly.

Difficulties with access to ICT and an inadequate use of them risk to increase exclusion of the elderly population and to make the socio-cultural and inter-generational gap greater than it has ever been. Online learning environments based on social networking could not only give an opportunity for individual cultural growth, but also for conceiving a range of practical applications of great social significance such as conscientious access, search and use of information, fruition of a multitude of web services, socialization within online communities, and the sharing of experiences and resources. This article aims at verifying to what extent targeted initiatives of e-learning, like the one referred to here, may facilitate the elderly to gain benefits from what the present knowledge society offers, enabling them to be aware of and at the same time active participants in the current innovative processesDifficulties with access to ICT and an inadequate use of them risk to increase exclusion of the elderly population and to make the socio-cultural and inter-generational gap greater than it has ever been. Online learning environments based on social networking could not only give an opportunity for individual cultural growth, but also for conceiving a range of practical applications of great social significance such as conscientious access, search and use of information, fruition of a multitude of web services, socialization within online communities, and the sharing of experiences and resources. This article aims at verifying to what extent targeted initiatives of e-learning, like the one referred to here, may facilitate the elderly to gain benefits from what the present knowledge society offers, enabling them to be aware of and at the same time active participants in the current innovative processes.

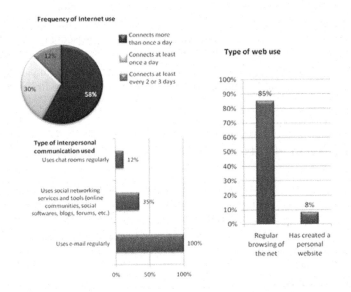

Figure 1. Quantitative data from the follow-up questionnaire

Combination of data given in Figure 1 with the open answers of the participants shows that the Web is used mainly for access to news portals, to local authorities or government bodies websites, to cultural, sports or voluntary associations websites, to those targeted for the third age or concerning health, to online tourism agencies, to websites of museums and libraries, and to use web services of financial nature.

As far as interpersonal communication is concerned, e-mail is the chief means used to correspond with friends and relatives even resident abroad, and to maintain contact with former course companions. It is notable that about one-third of participants uses social networking tools regularly to manage communities similar to that used within the course "Networked 3rd age", and that a little minority created a personal website.

Finally, results of follow-up give evidence for a continuity between the training period and habitual use of what had been learnt; this thus confirm for third age users what had already been found in the application of this methodology with other age groups [2].

5 Considerations

On the basis of results emerging from the analysis of this online learning initiative targeted at elders, some considerations can be drawn which, combined with those already present in research literature on elderly education, can improve the design of similar initiatives and initiate new research activities related to this issue. The great deal of time available for older people and the absence of spatial and temporal constraints characterising asynchronous communication allow high flexibility for participation in online learning activities. On the other hand, the elderly, compared to younger persons, needs for direct personal interaction for practical reasons of uncertainty with technology tools, but even for emotional and social reasons. Thus blended solutions, in which periods of e-learning alternate with onsite activities, would seem more appropriate. Considering the characteristics of these specific age users, older people has response time, cognitive skills, needs and motivations different from those of younger participants in online courses. The complexity of these factors should be taken into account in the design of material, in the selection of the type of online activities and of learning strategies, in the group forming and in the tutoring style to adopt.

Such as it happens in adult learning, elders should acknowledge the intrinsic value of the suggested learning path. Learning must be contextualized, close to their own experiences and to everyday life. The background of older persons is various and consistent; the richness of their experiences should be promoted and their value enhanced through self-regulated learning, which makes feel them responsible and autonomous, and through collaborative learning too, which promotes knowledge exchange, sharing and construction. Taking into account all these elements, the need of specific training both for designers and for the online tutors who are asked to organize and run online initiatives targeted for the third age arises [5], based on a close matching of e-learning design methodologies, network groups management and the most recent theories of andragogy.

Future research on this topic could analyze samples numerically higher; widen or diversify contents, tackling other subjects; and adopt different learning methodologies to that used in this initiative, even if successful. Concerning this last point the alternative methodologies, which should be based on the most recent lifelong learning theories, if applied to social networking tools could generate learning situations virtuous for elder learning. For instance, autobiography as a learning method has many potentialities in transformation and restructuring processes of the self, more evident during adolescence and mainly during the third age, when this practice becomes essential to attribute a sense to one's own life history and to reorient it.

6 Conclusions

The possession of a personal computer, the availability of web access and the mere use of ICT are, as confirmed by recent studies [6], all indispensable elements but far from sufficient to solve the "digital divide". An effective and adequate use of new technologies results to be currently one of the key elements to survive in a knowledge-based society; this implies capabilities which discriminate large social classes, strongly represented by elderly population. The diffusion of an initiative like that described in this article could contribute to close the technological, socio-cultural and inter-generational gap which affects especially elderly population of the present knowledge society. The appropriate use of new technologies, in fact, is not a simply a question of technical skills, but entails the sustenance of one's own self-identity [7] - or its reconstruction - self care, social relationships, dialogue with the new generation. As shown in the present study, basic literacy through onsite training is the first necessary step to spread a culture of the use of ICT among third agers. This first phase should prelude or alternate with an in-depth online course using ICT seen both as the content of training and as learning environment. In such an environment, each learner acquires awareness, creates new horizons of sense, share and negotiate them with others through social networking: in this way he/she progressively achieves those mastery thresholds, not only technical or practical, making him "digitally literate", and thus more able to participate in and contribute to innovation processes taking place in the present society.

References

1. G. Trentin, E-learning and the third age, *Journal of Computer Assisted Learning*, 20 (1) (2004), pp. 21–30.
2. G. Trentin, From distance education to virtual communities of practice: the wide range of possibilities for using the Internet in continuous education and training, *International Journal on E-Learning*, 1, 1 (2002), pp.55-66.
3. V. Benigno and G. Trentin, The evaluation of online courses, *International Journal of Computer Assisted Learning*, 16(3) (2000), pp. 259-270.
4. K. Mackenzie, Structural centrality in communication networks, *Psychometrica*, 31 (1966), pp.17-26.
5. M. S. Knowles, Introduction: the art and science of helping adults learn, in: *Andragogy in action: applying modern principles of adult learning*, edited by M.S. Knowles (Jossey-Bass, San Francisco,1984).
6. N. Selwyn and K. Facer, *Beyond the Digital Divide: Rethinking digital inclusion for the 21st century* (Futurelab, Bristol, 2007); http://www.futurelab.org.uk/resources/documents/opening_education/Digital_Di vide.pdf accessed 30/11/07.
7. Martin, Digital Literacy for the Third Age: Sustaining Identity in an Uncertain World, Conference "web4seniors" (Ulm, Germany, 2007); http://www.uniulm.de/uni/fak/zawiw/content/veranstaltungen/konferenzen/lill_0 7/content/abstracts/martin/Allan_Martin_Digital_Literacy_for_the_Third_Age_ EN_long_version.pdf accessed 30/11/07.

The role of indigenous knowledge in computer education in Africa

Lorenzo Dalvit[1], Sarah Murray[2] and Alfredo Terzoli[3]
[1] SANTED programme, School of Languages, Rhodes University, PO Box 94, 6140 Grahamstown South Africa. l.dalvit@ru.ac.za,
http://www.ru.ac.za/academic/departments/languages/santed/people.html
[2] Education Department, Rhodes University, PO Box 94, 6140 Grahamstown South Africa. s.murray@ru.ac.za,
http://campus.ru.ac.za/index.php?action=category&category=1275
[3] Telkom Centre of Excellence, Computer Science Department, Rhodes Unviersity, PO Box 94, 6140 Grahamstown South Africa.
a.terzoli@ru.ac.za,
http://cs.ru.ac.za/people/staff.php

Abstract. The integration of indigenous knowledge/languages in formal education is a contentious issue in post-colonial Africa. For historical and economic reasons, these are devalued in the formal education system. We argue that appropriate use of indigenous knowledge/languages can empower African students academically even in typically "Western" disciplines, such as Computer Science. We discuss the potential role of indigenous languages/ knowledge in ICT education and then describe an intervention, supporting students from marginalised communities, at a South African University.

1 Introduction

Computer Science promises much too prospective students in Africa: it is potentially empowering both economically and in terms of global access. However, since most computer-related knowledge is produced and consumed in the West, and conceptualised in European languages, it inevitably reflects Western assumptions and ways of thinking. This makes it a difficult subject of study for many African students who, besides having difficulties in accessing the necessary infrastructure, are also unfamiliar with the paradigms informing the discipline. Integrating African indigenous knowledge into the teaching of Computer Science may help to bridge this gap. This, however, needs to be problematised in order to define the role and boundaries within which such integration might benefit African students.

Please use the following format when citing this chapter:

Dalvit, L., Murray, S. and Terzoli, A., 2008, in IFIP International Federation for Information Processing, Volume 281; *Learning to Live in the Knowledge Society*; Michael Kendall and Brian Samways; (Boston: Springer), pp. 287–294.

2 Indigenous knowledge

Indigenous knowledge literally means "knowledge that is specific to one place". In this sense, all knowledge can be considered indigenous in so far as it pertains to a particular geographical location. The term "indigenous", however, is often associated with something exotic and "other", often in a pejorative sense. Western knowledge is usually taken as the reference point for the comparison and the norm against which whatever is indigenous is understood and possibly evaluated [1]. For the purpose of this paper we consider indigenous knowledge as having 3 components: traditional, common and specialised knowledge.

2.1 Traditional knowledge

Traditional knowledge is what, in layman's terms, most people refer to as indigenous knowledge. It is often associated with the religious, spiritual or occult sphere, and is validated by having been part of a specific culture for a long time. Some forms of traditional knowledge, such as those relating to Christianity, have been integrated into formal education, for example, under Apartheid Christian National Education in South Africa. However, African traditional knowledge and, particularly, African religious beliefs were deliberately opposed by missionary education in an attempt to assimilate or integrate the local population [2]. This probably contributed to the stigma attached to indigenous knowledge as a whole. ICT education, with its emphasis on modernity, is often understood in opposition to traditional values and beliefs, be they Western or African.

2.2 Common knowledge

Common knowledge refers to "what everybody knows" and concerns every sphere of daily life. Examples, such as the ones from the health sphere for instance, show how common knowledge is not always scientifically sound and could, in some extreme cases, have dramatic consequences. However, common knowledge is an integral part of the cultural background of a community and as such it should be taken into account by educators. It may be integrated into the curriculum, providing useful examples and metaphors to support teaching. In other cases common knowledge needs to be de-constructed and critically analysed [1]. The inclusion of common knowledge in the curriculum is contentious in Science education, where it may often contradict scientific knowledge.

2.3 Specialised knowledge

Specialised knowledge is specific to a particular field, and is usually possessed by "experts". The boundaries between common and specialised knowledge can be blurred by time and space. While being able to operate a computer through the Graphical User Interface (GUI) can be considered common knowledge among middle class, urban youth in developed countries, it was specialised knowledge until a few years ago and is still so in many parts of most developing countries.

The GUI example also highlights a relationship between specialised and common knowledge. The desktop environment, which contains folders and files and can be browsed through windows, draws on the metaphor of an office desk. For most middle class youth, offices are part of their common knowledge that can be drawn upon when learning to operate a computer through the GUI. For those in developing countries, however, the metaphor may be meaningless [3].

There are other culturally-bound conventions and traits which are taken for granted in the ICT world, such as colour schemes and language. In most Western cultures, for instance, red indicates "danger" or "stop", as opposed to green, which signifies "go ahead". In various African cultures, however, red is the colour associated with tradition, as opposed to blue which symbolises modernity. Likewise, English, the language used in the field of ICT, is not widely spoken or understood by the majority of rural Africans. The lack of terminology in African languages (and the current efforts to develop it [4]) could be seen as marking the still incomplete transition of digital literacy from specialised to common knowledge among their speakers. Within the realm of common knowledge, differences that are important in English (e.g. the one between a menu and a list) are not reflected in many African languages (e.g. in isiXhosa, *uludwe* means both menu and list).

3 Indigenous knowledge and ICT education

The differences mentioned above clearly put African students at a disadvantage when they encounter computers, as they cannot draw on their common knowledge in the way Europeans (and particularly English speakers) do. However, the role of common knowledge in scientific education is the subject of debate. Some scholars have argued that the purpose of education is to replace common knowledge with (Western) specialised knowledge. Two scholars in particular, the Italian philosopher, Gramsci, and the British linguist, Halliday, point to inherent dangers of adopting a relativist position with regard to common knowledge; we take account of their arguments below. In our response to their concerns we also refer to the field of ethnocomputing.

3.1   Gramsci - the role of common knowledge in maintaining hegemony

Gramsci argued that education is the primary tool for the reproduction of inequality in society [5]. In his view, common knowledge (or "folklore") kept people in ignorance and thus in their place. He called for education to take the moral responsibility of combating folklore and substituting it with "higher" (i.e. specialised) knowledge that would make people's social positioning visible to them [6].

Apartheid South Africa offered a striking example of hegemony at work through education. Education for blacks (Bantu Education) made extensive use of indigenous languages and knowledge in the curriculum in order to relegate Africans to an idealised and ideologically constructed African past and deny them active participation in the global community [7]. This was based on a static and "purist" understanding of culture and, as a consequence, of indigenous knowledge. This continues in post-colonial African education, where the dichotomy between traditional (African) knowledge and modern (Western) knowledge is enforced as a clear-cut choice between holding on to tradition and embracing formal education. This does not reflect either the modern understanding of culture and knowledge as dynamic or the bi-cultural and bi-lingual reality of most African students. In this sense, giving African students access *only* to Western specialised knowledge dis-empowers them twice. From the educational point of view, they do not have the scaffolding provided to Western students by their common knowledge. From the ideological point of view, their own traditional, specialised and, to some extent, common knowledge is denied formal recognition within the education system.

3.2 Halliday - Functional linguistics

Functional linguists [8] discuss the specific features of scientific discourse in the domain of education. Science education consists mainly of unpacking technical terms and constructing new classifications to replace existing, commonsensical ones. Halliday and Martin [8] emphasise the creative character of science education and openly criticise the practice of trying to reduce "scientific language" to "common language" in the classroom.

In an African post-colonial context, however, the relationship between scientific and everyday language is often nested within a diglossic situation. For many African students English, which is the language of scientific discourse, is a second or foreign language while everyday communication takes place in one or more indigenous African languages. Given the strong link between language, culture and knowledge, this can be considered as representative of the multi-cultural reality of many African students, who live the tension between tradition and modernity. This is particularly evident in the teaching of scientific and technological subjects which, having been developed within the Western paradigm, are foreign to African culture. For example, while philosophical concepts such as that of *ubuntu* can readily be integrated into Western academic discourse within the Humanities as representing an alternative paradigm [9], indigenous taxonomies for diseases, must be de-constructed and substituted with new ones within the Western scientific discourse.

In Mathematics education, teachers in African schools often code-switch between the dominant European language (often English) and the local African language. New English technical terms are introduced and explained in the students' mother tongue with examples from their everyday lives. The mathematical discourse is then reconstructed in English, which is the only language of testing. Within this model, two aspects seem to be problematic. Firstly, for many African students formal education is the only domain where they are exposed to the powerful Western epistemological paradigm and European languages. Mastery of both is what will determine their opportunities for employment later in life. For this reason, teachers feel the need to expose students as much as possible to these powerful tools in the little time they have available in the classroom.

In South Africa, code-switching is the norm in African schools. This could not be otherwise, given the generally low English proficiency of most African students [10].

However, despite progressive policies nothing has been done to formalise multilingual teaching. Thus, every teacher has to "re-invent the wheel", creating his or her own new terminology and examples. This has two sets of consequences. Pedagogically, it is an inefficient way of organising a process that is so widespread and potentially has such a huge impact on the education system.

Ideologically, it entrenches Western hegemony by reproducing the dichotomy between two paradigms of knowledge. On the one hand, Western specialised knowledge draws on Western common knowledge in a structured and organised way through textbooks and other teaching material. On the other hand, individual teachers draw on African indigenous knowledge, whether it is specialised or common, in a haphazard and *ad hoc* manner. This reinforces the idea, in the mind of the students, that the Western paradigm is indeed superior and Africa has little to offer in terms of knowledge to the global community.

3.3   Ethnocomputing

Ethnocomputing emphasises the importance of integrating cultural elements into software design and the teaching of Computer Science in developing countries [11]. Since computers were invented in the West, they tend to reflect Western values and cultural traits, thus promoting dependency. To counter dependency, the use and teaching of computers must integrate indigenous knowledge and respond to local problems, making technology more relevant and more accessible at the same time.

Duveskog et al [12] provide a practical example, based on their experience in Tanzania, of how the use of fractals in traditional art craft could be used to support the teaching of recursion in the teaching of Computer Science. On a different level, the African philosophical concept of *ubuntu* has named one of the most popular Linux distributions. *Ubuntu*, which literally means "humanity" in isiXhosa and isiZulu, encompasses values of sharing and emphasises the interdependency between all human beings. It therefore captures the spirit of much of the open-source community more precisely than comparable Western terms.

Advocates of ethnocomputing argue that individuals in developing countries need to be given access to meaningful study of how computers work. Like Gramsci's organic intellectuals, they would combine sufficient knowledge of the local context and mastery of the discipline, supporting the development of alternative discourses. However, such individuals are hard to come by, since most Africans with access to ICT (like any other powerful field of study) are usually part of the emerging elite and have internalised Western values and world-views.

4 Intervention

In the last section of our paper we describe an intervention, informed by the considerations above, to integrate African indigenous knowledge in the teaching of Computer Science [13]. Material has been developed and tested at Rhodes University, a *Historically White* South African institution. Like many other South African universities, Rhodes is under pressure from the government to provide access to economically empowering fields of study to members of marginalised communities. In particular, the development of previously marginalised areas and communities requires African graduates and postgraduates in Computer Science who can address local needs [14].

4.1   Focus group

Rhodes provides alternative access to members of marginalised communities through its Extended Studies Programme (ESP). The programme targets mainly African students from underprivileged schools. In most cases, these are first-generation university students who are neither very proficient in English nor fully familiar with Western culture. Most of them are speakers of isiXhosa, the locally dominant African language.

Our intervention focused on the Computer Skills component of the programme. Classes were relatively small (20-30 students) and students used computers both in practicals and in lectures, allowing for the use of a web-based application that supported the integration of indigenous knowledge/languages in teaching practice.

4.2   Material

The material we developed consisted of a glossary of computer terms translated, explained and exemplified in isiXhosa. The development of the material was done collaboratively by a group of experts (mainly isiXhosa speakers) from various disciplines, ranging from computer science to education and linguistics. In an African spirit, the material was developed during long meetings where each term was discussed and people with different levels of computer literacy had a chance to express their views. Team members were representative of the full spectrum of different realities within the Xhosa community, allowing us to capture some of the variety of Xhosa indigenous knowledge.

Each computer term was translated into an isiXhosa equivalent as suggestive as the English one is to a native speaker. The word *wizard*, for instance, was translated as *umvumisi,* a type of traditional healer who asks the patient questions in order to diagnose the cause of a disease. Thus, the term suggests what a wizard does (i.e. guiding the user through a series of steps to achieve something). Each term is then explained and exemplified drawing on the students' knowledge. For example, the relationship between a client and a server is compared to that between a bride and the person designated to assist and equip her for the wedding (*umxobisi*).

The glossary currently comprises more than 150 terms, and is growing. It is available both in print and on-line, and in both versions, related terms are highlighted and linked to show relationships between concepts and build classifications. Students were given access to the glossary at the beginning of 2007 and encouraged to participate in its development with comments and feedback.

4.3   On-line resource

The on-line version of the glossary was integrated into the e-learning course students used in class. Moodle, the Learning Management system used by Rhodes, has a glossary module which was marginally "tweaked" to serve research purposes. This avoided the problem of burdening students who were not familiar with ICT with an additional and unfamiliar on-line resource. Alongside the copy used in the course, the glossary was also made available standalone (see http://www.isixhosa.ru.ac.za).

Moodle allows for numerous interactions between the users and the system. Standard glossary features allowed students to rate entries and give comments. Words which appeared in the explanation and were included in the glossary were hyperlinked, making it easy to follow the relationships between different concepts. System logs allowed us to monitor the use of the resource to see which terms were most popular and which words that students looked for were not in the glossary, so that they could be developed and included.

The on-line glossary is currently being integrated with multimedia. Besides the obvious advantages of using images and video tutorials to integrate text-based material, the use of audio explanations is culturally more appropriate for students from a predominantly oral culture, who may be unfamiliar with the written variety of their mother tongue [10]. The content of the glossary is also being visualised through a concept map using CMapTools, adding a further visual component to explanations, highlighting relationships between concepts and clarifying taxonomies.

5 Conclusions

As we have shown, in the post-colonial African context, local indigenous knowledge is attributed low status and excluded from formal education, disempowering African students educationally and ideologically, by devaluing their knowledge and entrenching Western epistemological hegemony.

Particularly in science and technology education, students' common knowledge must be de-constructed and new concepts and taxonomies created. The function of indigenous knowledge is to support and integrate access to global knowledge, and not to relegate students to marginalised local realities. Furthermore, common knowledge, whether it be Western or African, must be integrated carefully in high-quality teaching and educational material. In the case of Computer Science, this would contribute to the development of programmers who share the background of the majority of the local community and can develop appropriate solutions for local problems.

Our intervention focused precisely on this kind of student. Material in the locally dominant language, using culturally appropriate metaphors and examples, was used to support an existing Computer Skills course. The material was shaped by students through feedback and suggestions. The use of an on-line resource allowed for the integration of multimedia, a medium more appropriate to the cultural background of most students. A preliminary evaluation suggests that the intervention boosted students' confidence in the potential of their own language and indigenous knowledge to help them academically. More conclusive results will be available by the time of the conference.

References

1.Agrawal, A. Indigenous and scientific knowledge: some critical comments, *Indigenous Knowledge and Development Monitor 3(3)*, 3–6, 1995

2.Okere, T., Njoku, C.A., and Devisch, R. All knowledge is first of all local knowledge: an introduction, *Africa Development 30(3)*, 1–19, 2005

3.Thinyane, M., Dalvit, L., and Terzoli, A. The Internet in Rural Communities: Unrestricted and Contextualised. Submitted for ICT Africa, Addis Abeba, 13-15 February 2008

4.Finlayson, R. and Madiba, M. The Intellectualisation of the Indigenous Languages of South Africa: Challenges and Prospects. Current Issues in Language Planning, 3(1), Multilingual Matters, 40-61,2002

5.Borg, C., Buttigieg, J.A., and Mayo, P. Gramsci and Education, Rowman & Littlefield Publishers, 2002

6.Gramsci, A., Hoare, Q., and Nowell-Smith, G. Selections from the Prison Notebooks, Electric Book Company, 2005

7.Kamwangamalu, N.M. The Language Planning Situation in South Africa, *Language Planning and Policy in Europe*, Multilingual Matters, 2006

8.Halliday, MAK, and Martin, JR: Writing science: Literacy and discursive power. Pittsburgh, PA: University of Pittsburgh Press, 1993

9.Kamwangamalu, N.M. Ubuntu in South Africa: a sociolinguistic perspective to a pan-African concept, *Critical Arts 13(2)*, Routledge, 24–41, 1999

10.Heugh, K., and Project for the Study of Alternative Education in South Africa: The Case Against Bilingual and Multilingual Education in South Africa, PRAESA, 2000

11.Tedre, M., Sutinen, E., Kähkönen, E., and Kommers, P. Ethnocomputing: ICT in cultural and social context, *Communications of the ACM 49(1)*, ACM Press New York, NY, USA, 126–130, 2006

12.Duveskog, M., Sutinen, E., Tedre, M., and Vesisenaho, M. In search of contextual teaching of programming in a Tanzanian secondary school, *IEEE conference Frontiers in Education (FIE) 2003*, 5–8, 2003

13.Dalvit, L., Murray, S., Mini, B., Terzoli, A. & Zhao, X.. Production of and Access to ICT-Based Knowledge through English and African Languages at a South African University. *South African Journal of Higher Education (SAJHE)*, 19, 1486 – 1498, 2006

14.Department of Education (DoE) and Department of Communication (Doc): *Strategy for Information and Communication Technology in Education*. Pretoria: Government Printer.

Designing knowledge-rich curricula

Marijke Hezemans and Magda Ritzen
Marijke Hezemans is an educational advisor for Utrecht University of
Professional Education (Hogeschool Utrecht) marijke.hezemans@hu.nl
Magda Ritzen is an educational advisor for Utrecht University
m.ritzen@uu.nl

Abstract. What role does knowledge have in competency based higher education? Many Dutch Universities of Professional Education are struggling with the implementation of competency-based curricula. In view of current practice, this article distinguishes between two sorts of knowledge: vocation-related knowledge and context-free knowledge. In higher education curricula are developed with the aid of various design-models. The resulting curricula are tied to varying degrees with the field of practice, depending on which model is used. Below three models are typified and compared along four aspects: assignment-driven, vocationally related work processes, integral assessment & testing and knowledge development. Recommendations are then made for ways in which knowledge-rich, competency-based curricula can be developed and improved within the given design models. Keywords here are 'good vocational assignments' and 'accountability of results'.

1 Introduction

In the mid-nineties the very first Dutch competency-based project was started. Ten years later we see that the transition to competency-based education is not always going smoothly: the media are full of items where the fear for the incompatibility of knowledge and competency-based curricula comes forward. This paper describes ways in which knowledge-rich competency-based curricula are developed and can be improved. The point of departure is the set of design-models that are in use in the Netherlands today. The paper finishes with a concluding summary of the relationship between knowledge and competency-based education.

Please use the following format when citing this chapter:

Hezemans, M. and Ritzen, M., 2008, in IFIP International Federation for Information Processing, Volume 281; *Learning to Live in the Knowledge Society*; Michael Kendall and Brian Samways; (Boston: Springer), pp. 295–302.

2   Competency-based and knowledge-rich: a paradox?

Competency-based education stands for learning environments that match the future field of practice of the student as much as possible; in the learning environment as well as in the field of practice knowledge, and its application in creating vocational products, is central. Learning is focused on developing competencies in characteristic vocational situations of increasing complexity. Vocational products play an important role here: they make an individual's competency-development visible.

Giving vocational products such a central role is an innovative element in competency-based education. Assessment and testing of developed competencies is based on these (vocational) results and the accounting of their creation. In this way, apart from reproduction, application of knowledge also receives attention: knowledge and its application are prerequisites for arriving at good qualitative results. The results (vocational products and/or services) and accounting for their creation, are a reflection of competent performance.

Creating good qualitative vocational products or results requires knowledge and an ability to apply this knowledge. Both context-free and vocation-related knowledge are needed in creating an accountable vocational product. Both types of knowledge play an important role in competency-based curricula. Where more traditional course-orientated curricula are focused primarily on reproduction of context-free knowledge, competency-based curricula also focus on vocation related knowledge. Making and accounting for a vocational-product (e.g. an auditors'/audit certificate, lessons, research rapport) is cyclical: reflections and feedback on intermediary products (concepts) contribute towards the final product. This 'single loop learning' leads to adjustments during the process which are guided by the requirements that the institute places on the deliverable and the process leading to its creation. The emphasis here is placed on vocationally related knowledge.

When handing in the deliverable a similar process can be organized, by then on a higher level: in 'double loop learning' students compare their products and methods and so come to new insights. At this level of abstraction there is more reference to context-free knowledge.

This 'knowledge development approach' is primarily propagated by 'lectoraten' (Polytechnic research professors) [1].

This leads to the following characteristics of a knowledge-rich competency-based learning-environment:

1.   Assignment-driven: there is an (authentic) assignment, taken from the field of practice the student is being trained for.
2.   Vocationally related work processes: the learning environment provides, in consultation with the field of practice, requirements (quality criteria) that the deliverable and work process that lead to it must satisfy. Within the learning environment the student can also be asked to provide specific requirements.
3.   Integrated assessment and testing: the vocational product (service or deliverable) is the object of the assessment and testing, through which both context-free and vocationally related knowledge are assessed and tested.
4.   Knowledge development: the learning environment provides space and time for double loop learning. Newly developed knowledge is recorded.

3   Three design models

Competency-based curricula can be realized in different ways, depending on the culture and innovation drive within the institute. Here three models are described that are used in the Netherlands to design knowledge-rich competency-based learning environments. These are then assessed along the lines of the previous four characteristics.

3.1   Problem Based Learning (PBL)

PBL has been implemented in Dutch Higher Education since the seventies. The distinguishing aspect of PBL was that it offered knowledge related to the field of practice and that students played an active part in finding relevant knowledge.

Certain aspects of PBL pervade much of Dutch higher education, especially there where the focus is on acquiring new knowledge. Characteristic of PBL is [2,3]:

- problems form a major motivation for learning;
- students are provided with a small case, from which they must distil problems and explanations;
- the problems should (just) not match the foreknowledge of the students and be sufficiently complex and structured.

The learning process is split into seven steps; these steps structure the process of the student group.

3.1.1 PBL as knowledge-rich competency-based learning environment
1.   Assignment-driven

PBL is often used in higher education as a step-up to competency-based learning. Through PBL the ground work is laid for an essential competency, 'learning ability'. PBL works well in that context-free knowledge is presented in an integrated way to vocational problems.

2.   Vocationally related work processes

We now know that a curriculum based solely on PBL assignments does not properly prepare students for the field of practice. The transfer of knowledge to other problems was too scant. For this reason there have been adjustments to pure PBL the previous years: PBL has been made more complex (more authentic) and aids have been developed to help gauge the complexity and the level of structuralization of a case, which have lead to better matching with the foreknowledge of the students. The focus is still on context-free knowledge, but the application thereof is increased.

3.   Integrated assessment

The relationship between the field of practice and context-free knowledge is exposed, although the focus is on context-free knowledge: in some forms of PBL students do make a vocational product / deliverable, but a PBL module is assessed by way of exam and not on the basis of the vocational product or service and the account of its creation.

4. Knowledge development

Until recently PBL was seen primarily as suited to developing context-free knowledge with the help of mainly theoretical vocational assignments.

3.1.2 Conclusions

In our opinion PBL could lead to more knowledge transfer if the student were to work towards a vocational product that was also accounted for and assessed as such. A focus on vocational problems (services) that are not assessed with a knowledge exam but as a product, offers possibilities for competency development and knowledge development and in so doing for innovation in the field of practice.

Many institutes' choice to let go of PBL as the dominant learning style after the first year and focus more on projects fits in well with this view: students are by then more than equipped to formulate their own learning goals, seek out new and relevant information and account for their results.

Writing and working according to a Project Plan and tuning in to the methods in the field of practice initially demand a lot of coaching, but thanks to the PBL ground work these students will probably have less difficulties accounting for their results.

3.2   4 Components of Instructional Design (4C/ID)

The 4C/ID design model originated as a response to PBL. Students work on vocational products as part of the 4C/ID design model and develop competencies in the course of this. Education that is developed through 4C/ID may therefore be viewed as competency-based, more so than in the case of PBL.

The 4C/ID [4] offers a general design strategy for education. This model provides guidelines, suggestions and recommendations for developing an educational programme. The essence of the 4C/ID approach lies in students learning how to work on meaningful, integrational, educational tasks that are derived from professional practice. This professional practice is described in the educational and or vocational profile of the educational programme concerned. By basing the selection of educational tasks on this profile it is possible to secure the level of expertise and competence. The four components of this model are as follows [5]:

- educational tasks represent the rationale for learning. These tasks are authentic and constitute the framework supporting the other components. Educational tasks can vary from complex case studies to a multidisciplinary project which is carried out by a team of students;
- supportive information: this refers to information that may be of assistance when performing educational tasks and is primarily concerned with familiarising oneself with and carrying out non-routine aspects of these tasks;
- "just-in-time" (JIT) information: this is information that is required to familiarise oneself with and carry out educational tasks. It is provided just in time (when needed);
- subsidiary task drills: separately exercising specific subsidiary skills as part of an educational task, so as to automate it in its entirety. This occurs when a teacher is

of the opinion that by working on an educational task alone a student is not acquiring an appropriate routine for work in the field.

3.2.1 4C/ID as knowledge-rich competency-based learning environment
1.   Assignment-driven
The 4C/ID model provides a thorough means of analysing educational tasks to their very core and of producing educational segments based on this analysis. Knowledge that is both related to practice and is contextually neutral can play a clearly defined role in this process. The strength of this model lies in the fact that it highlights four important components that need attention when designing an educational environment: educational tasks, supportive and "just-in-time" information, and subsidiary tasks. These components are covered separately when working on complex practical assignments: work on an assignment is structured in advance with the aid of the 4C/ID model. This provides a basis for the student and his teacher (developer and facilitator).

2.   Vocationally related work processes
Education is structured in such a manner that students exercise subsidiary skills as part of various courses, before they start work on a major assignment. The rationale for this is that it will enable students to be more capable of locating any information that is provided and to acquire skills before commencing the "real work". As a result the work that is to be done on the relevant vocational product is structured in advance.

3.   Integrated assessment
The model focuses on the acquisition of practical expertise. Attention is also devoted to contextually neutral knowledge through courses and lectures. This knowledge is assessed by means of an examination (cf. PBL): a student reveals that he understands a specific model by mentioning its pros and cons. The vocational products are also evaluated, although the achievements of the various student teams are not compared and the students are not (yet) challenged to account for why they have decided on a specific approach or model ("double loop learning").

4.   Knowledge development
This type of education involves the development of knowledge, although it occurs within specified "boundaries" ("single loop learning"): the development of a vocational product is structured in advance with the aid of courses and JIT information. Consequently, there is be little variation in approach and products (results) and this means that there will also be a limited opportunity for the development of knowledge and innovation as part of professional practice in the case of this type of education.

3.2.2 Conclusions
4C/ID involves the use of assignments that are recognisable as ones which have been sourced from professional practice. In the case of these assignments an indication is given of the competencies which they demand. An assignment is analysed by educational developers, and courses and subsidiary tasks are devised on

this basis. The students prepare themselves to work on the assignments with the aid of case studies, amongst other things.

An assessment focuses on contextually neutral knowledge. The latter is evaluated by means of an examination. Any vocational product that is created is also assessed: provisionally in formative terms and later on in summative terms. The students are not invited to account for their achievements and no time is scheduled for them to compare their results with each other. A structured operational approach providing uniform support (subsidiary task drills, courses and just-in-time information) produces well-considered vocational products. There is little variation between these products thanks to the sound support. The exploration of new avenues and innovation as part of professional practice only becomes possible, if one abandons pronounced advance structuring.

3.3   HU educational design model

This educational design model was created after years of working with the above-mentioned and other models, the application of various theories [6] and progressive understanding within Hogeschool Utrecht (HU). It is a model which centres around the qualifications of an educational programme, and which sets out the professional expertise and competencies that are required to ensure appropriate performance (the initial level) as part of the occupation in question. This therefore also guarantees the level of competence and expertise.

In addition to these qualifications, a distinction is drawn between the following two types of educational processes (work processes), which are managed independently of each other:

- the development of competencies – the evolution of personal proficiency, such as the ability to learn, analyse, form judgments and so forth. In the course of assessments students are asked to demonstrate their development of such capabilities: they are the subject of the assessment;
- the development of expertise – the body of knowledge of the occupation concerned. Specific vocational products and what is required to create them are at the heart of it. The development of a student's expertise is assessed on the basis of the quality of products (professional and otherwise) which the student creates in the course of his education: these products (professional and otherwise) are the subject of the evaluation. Both contextually neutral and professional expertise play an important role in this respect. This is reflected in the evaluation criteria that are used.

The development of competencies and expertise are inseparably linked to each other, albeit that each exhibits dynamics which are unique to it. In their assessments students are able to reflect or demonstrate the progress they make in acquiring specific competencies with the aid of those of their products (professional and otherwise) which are positively assessed.

A personal development plan represents the guiding element of competency development. A student regularly determines his own profile in relation to predetermined competencies with the aid of self-assessments, peer evaluations and critical reflection. An assignment (educational or otherwise) constitutes the guiding element for the purposes of developing expertise. The development of this expertise is arranged with the aid of programme modules. The relevant department facilitates the development of expertise by providing guidance in the form of staff-student interaction, a clearly formulated range of modules, unambiguous assessment criteria and the creation of a learning environment (virtual or otherwise).

3.3.1 HU educational design model as knowledge-rich competency-based learning environment
1. Assignment-driven
    Assignments represent the guiding element within the HU educational design model. Such an assignment has two sides to it: students are given an assignment to create and account for a vocational product (development of expertise), and to undergo professional development (development of competencies).

2. Vocationally related work processes
    This model is currently being employed to design part-time Economics studies. This makes it possible to incorporate the educational process as far as possible within the relevant students' work process. The department stipulates requirements for the field of practice of any student (potential and otherwise) concerned and enters into a contract with the student himself and with his superior (employer). Part-time students are enthusiastic about this type of education. They are able to present problems that they experience in the workplace directly in the course of their studies (learning environment) and vice versa.

3. Integrated assessment
    As part of this model a distinction is drawn between two educational processes featuring different dynamics. The assessment that is part of the expertise development process focuses on the quality of the end product which is to be supplied, and how it is accounted for. The assignment is accompanied by criteria (in both concrete terms and at the meta-level) which the end product needs to satisfy. The evaluation of the competency development process is directed towards the student and his development to become a professional. Through assessments a student is able to demonstrate his acquisition of competencies with the aid of positively assessed products or services (achievements), amongst other things.

4. Knowledge development
    There is an explicit place for so-called conceptual modules in the analysis of working methods and models. This occurs with the aid of vocational products which the students contribute where possible. The aim is to produce new and/or improved working models. Students have indicated that this approach enables them to apply the knowledge that they acquire in the course of their studies directly in the field.

3.3.2 Conclusions
The HU model is still undergoing development. To date it would appear to offer a great deal of potential for the design of well-developed, knowledge-rich, competency-based education within a part-time educational environment. Close links

with the students' various fields of practice represent a critical success factor in this respect. It is important that the same close links are established with these fields of practice, if this model is to be successfully utilised for full-time education. The potential for achieving this lies in allowing professional practitioners to play various roles within the educational environment, for example, as a client, assessor or educational developer (the contribution of professional standards for the purposes of assessment and evaluation, amongst other things).

4   Conclusion

This paper explains that competency-based education is impossible without the use of knowledge. Within each model knowledge is assigned an explicit role. The assessment of students' achievements or products clarifies that type of knowledge which is accorded the greatest value within the educational environment. In the case of PBL and the 4C/ID a great deal of emphasis is placed on contextually neutral knowledge as part of assessments, whereas both types of knowledge are evaluated in an integrated fashion as part of the HU model. This model offers great potential for the incorporation of both practically oriented and contextually neutral knowledge within the curriculum. An indication has also been given as to how the other two models may be enriched with relatively simple adjustments.

Using the three design methods that have been outlined, it is possible to produce professionals who are not only capable of being deployed immediately but who can also make a contribution to the development of new expertise, thereby introducing innovation into their fields of practice.

References

1. T. van Weert & D. Andriessen (January 6, 2006); http://www.lectoren.nl/?i=740&t=doc.

2. J. Arts, Innovatieve variant op PGO, *Onderwijsinnovatie maart 2003*, 25-27 (2003).

3. A.E.J.P. Jacobs, e.a., Meten van complexiteit en gestructureerdheid van PGO-problemen, *Onderwijsinnovatie maart 2004*, 17-24 (2004).

4. A.M.B Janssen-Noordman, and J.J.G. van Merriënboer, *Innovatief onderwijs ontwerpen* (Wolters Noordhoff, Groningen, 2002).

5. A. Janssen-Noordman, e.a., Aanleren van complexe vaardigheden, *Onderwijsinnovatie september 2002*, 17-25 (2002).

6. D. de Bie, (red.), *Morgen doen we het beter* (Bohn Stafleu Van Loghum, Houten, 2003).

Chapter 12

Innovative Learning Environments 3

Knowledge Creation Through Engagement in a Personal Learning Environment

Mary P. Welsh

Department of Childhood and Primary Studies
University of Strathclyde
Glasgow G13 1PP, UK.
mary.welsh@strath.ac.uk

Abstract. This paper reports on an action research project involving a complete re-design of a module in Educational Studies undertaken by students in the first year of a B.Ed degree in a university in Scotland. Innovative use of a personal learning environment (PLE), the PebblePad E-Portfolio System, resulted in radical changes in teaching, learning and assessment and produced significant gains in learning and in efficient, effective use of staff time. The lecture programme was restructured in a way that identified five clear, natural breaks, which were named "learning milestones". These occurred at the end of each "mini-series" of lectures. A "core task", designed to consolidate the learning content of each mini-series, was constructed by the faculty member who had delivered the lectures and formative assessment, in the form of self and peer-based assessment, was designed around these core tasks, allowing an incremental increase in the demands placed on students. The project supported the development of skills of self and peer-based formative assessment, reflection and self-regulation in students aiming to be primary (elementary) school teachers. The intervention was funded by the Re-Engineering Assessment Practices in Higher Education (REAP) Project which, in turn, received funding from the Scottish Executive (Government) E-Transformation Initiative.

1 Introduction

In recent years, trends identified in the early sixties and seventies, by commentators such as Umesao [1], Bell [2], and Touraine [3] have come to fruition. We live in an age in which employment is now centred on the service sector rather than the primary and secondary sectors; scientific work, research and development have gained in importance; employers now engage workers for their intellectual capacities rather than their capability to engage in manual labour and, finally, importantly, information and knowledge have become as important, or it could be argued, even

Please use the following format when citing this chapter:

Welsh, M.P., 2008, in IFIP International Federation for Information Processing, Volume 281; *Learning to Live in the Knowledge Society*; Michael Kendall and Brian Samways; (Boston: Springer), pp. 305–312.

more important to production than land and labour. We live in the age of the knowledge society where knowledge is a commodity to be developed, bought and sold as part of a global economy. Governments worldwide have been forced to consider how best they can provide their citizens with the knowledge, skills and training essential to success in this global economy.

One result of this global movement has been an increased desire to widen access to higher education, and for teaching, learning and assessment to adopt more student centred approaches. The language commonly used in government policies seeks the creation of "... successful learners, confident individuals, responsible citizens and effective contributors ..." [4]. Approaches include increased use of formative assessment strategies and evidence based learning supported by the development of new environments for learning and knowledge creation.

In many institutions information and communications technology (ICT) has been harnessed as a tool for supporting student learning; for storing evidence of student attainment; and for facilitating the development of reflective, self–regulated learners with the skills necessary for success in the knowledge society. One important growth area has been the development and implementation of managed learning environments (MLEs), virtual learning environments (VLEs) and personal learning environments (PLEs). Strategies supporting use of such tools have been adopted in the United States, Canada, Australasia, Scandinavia and the countries of the European Community (EC). Increasingly, [5-9], e-portfolios, an important subset of PLEs, are being used as tools for assessment, not just as depositories of evidence-linked materials. Innovative use of e-portfolios to promote formative assessment, in particular self- and peer-based assessment, is the focus of this paper.

1.1   Strategic learning design

The main strategy introduced in this project was one which empowered students to assume responsibility for their own learning. Research in this domain, [10-12], has identified that this notoriously difficult to establish, especially in first year undergraduate study.

The team introduced a learning design based on use of formative assessment to support development of reflection and self-regulation and to allow this to be used as an integral part of the learning process itself. Increasing evidence from literature, [13-19], supported this innovation.

Three main research questions emerged from review and critical analysis of relevant literature and from previous experience of teaching on the module:

- How can we change the assessment system to improve the learning experience of students?

- How can we modify the leaning environment?

- How can we offer timely, high-quality feedback to support student learning and achievement?

1.2   Elements of the intervention

The module discussed here was part of a first year degree course and was designed to provide students (n=175) with an introduction to issues surrounding learners and learning. Students maintained a portfolio recording their engagement with module content which was submitted to tutors for formative evaluation at a mid-point during the academic year. Those who were failing to reach a satisfactory level at this point were offered guidance on how to improve attainment. Tutors were increasingly concerned by a lack of engagement with module content and disappointing quality of resulting student work. There was a perception of mismatch between requirements for final summative assessment and work expected from students during the module. In line with principles of "constructive alignment", Biggs [20], the module underwent a radical re-design. Previously students attended a series of twenty lectures and follow-up tutorials, given by various faculty staff, some of whom were also involved in the delivery of the lectures. During this action research project the lecture programme was restructured in a way that identified five clear, natural breaks, which were named "learning milestones". These occurred at the end of each "mini-series" of lectures. A "core task", designed to consolidate the learning content of each "mini-series", was constructed by the faculty member who had delivered the lectures. Formative assessment was designed around these core tasks and allowed an incremental increase in the demands placed on students. The tasks were spread evenly throughout the year and helped students develop critical skills through consideration of differing theoretical perspectives on learners and learning.

A self and peer assessment methodology was adopted as the basis for formative assessment associated with each core task and a commercially produced e-portfolio system, 'PebblePad', already being introduced in other parts of the course, was adopted as the medium through which the formative assessment strategy could be implemented. It was intended that this would also facilitate links between other course modules.

To maximise the effectiveness of tutor feedback, this was provided to only one sub-group in a tutor's class following each core task submission. Students were then invited to participate in further peer analysis and interpretation of both the submission and its tutor feedback. This promoted development of essential, professional reflective skills and empowered students who were working towards a common future goal.

2   A New Model for Learning

Whilst researching an effective framework to support the intervention, the team considered the work of many researchers in the field. However, it was the work of a researcher from their own institution, Nicol [18-21], which provided a viable framework - detailing ten principles of good assessment and feedback analysed over two dimensions [Nicol 19].

An examination of Nicol's principles 2, 3, and 6, gave rise to the following interpretations and form the focus of the remainder of this paper:

Encourages 'time and effort' on challenging learning tasks.

It was recognised that 'time and effort' on the incrementally challenging learning tasks must be distributed evenly throughout the course. Students in each tutor group of 25 students were allocated to sub-groups comprising a maximum of five students. Core tasks were issued at least four weeks before the submission date for each core task final response, and students were free to offer feedback to sub-group peers during this period. Students were trained in use of the "Two Stars and a Wish" formative assessment strategy which invites individuals to comment on two sections of a response that he/she thinks have been completed well and one section which requires some improvement. An evaluator normally offers some guidance on how this improvement might be achieved or, at the very least, offers comments to prompt consideration of possible solutions. Students were given guidance on appropriate register and vocabulary to use and were advised that this strategy was appropriate for learners at all stages. It was hoped that this process would lead to in-depth discussion of the issues and facilitate deep, rather than surface, learning. It was essential also that a spirit of mutual respect be established.

Submission of core task responses to the e-portfolio environment was therefore developed as a two-stage process. First of all, students were required to post their personal response to the core task to the system, for peer scrutiny and feedback. In the second stage, the sub-group met, face-to-face, or online, to synthesise their group response based on individual responses. The same assessment strategy was recommended to facilitate discussion and allow work to be selected for inclusion in the group portfolio submission.

Deliver high quality feedback information that helps learners self-correct.

Some researchers have questioned the ability of students to offer good quality feedback to peers, however Boud [13], argues that the most effective way of making students "close the loop", Sadler [23], in the 'task-performance-feedback" cycle is to allow students to re-submit work *after* receiving feedback and *before* moving on to the next task. Nicol and MacFarlane-Dick [21], highlight the importance of offering good quality, timely feedback, based on self-regulation. Participants valued both the feedback offered and the opportunity to re-submit, albeit in an altered form. Engagement in a common task enabled students to identify areas of difficulty for peers and to offer supplementary, often contrasting, views of the issue. This contributed to a process of social construction of knowledge and facilitated the development of communal constructivism in which group synthesis responses were stored in the e-portfolio system to be shared by all students in each large tutor group.

Facilitates the development of self-assessment and reflection in learning.

Since the inspirational American philosopher Dewey [22-24] first discussed the importance of reflection for personal and professional growth, educationalists have striven to promote this activity among future, and current, educational professionals [25-30]. Reflection on experience prompts action and results in the development of professional skills, knowledge and understanding and is conceived as one of the hallmarks of a professional practitioner. Through participation in the peer assessment process, this project promoted development of reflection and resulted in an improvement in the quality of written work.

There was no suggestion that the intervention would lead to a predominantly e-learning approach or that traditional approaches to lectures or tutor led seminars would be abandoned. What has now become clear, however, is that the new blend of methodologies has had a feedback effect leading to subtle and sometimes significant, changes in normal operational practice across the whole range of learning experiences. Not only has the adoption of the particular blend improved the quality of student engagement and learning, but it also enabled significant savings in staff time, both in the seminar programme and in the time devoted to assessment activities. This will be discussed further.

2.1 Research Methodology

Action research, with its emphasis on emancipatory involvement in a practitioner setting, through a cyclical process of continual reflection and refinement, was identified as being an appropriate approach for this project [Robson, 31]. A case study evaluation [Robson, 31], with its emphasis on in-depth study of a particular case, supported by engagement with materials gleaned from a range of sources, was deemed a suitable framework for reporting the project. This paper is the result.

2.2 Data Collection and Analysis Research Methodology

A mixed-method approach to data collection allowed both quantitative and qualitative data to be collected and subsequently analysed. Previously evaluation of the module was carried out using a single questionnaire, issued to all students, following the final summative exam. During this project, at the end of the second semester, three weeks before the final summative exam, a modified version of the previous questionnaire was issued. This version was used in order that some comparisons might be made. Data from the questionnaire was subjected to descriptive statistical analysis, using SPSS, by a member of the module research team.
The external REAP evaluation team administered another questionnaire also on the same occasion. This was developed and analysed independently by the evaluators who later conducted focus group meetings, one for students (course student representatives), and one for staff (volunteers, excluding members of the research team), where participants offered opinions on all aspects of the course. This data was also made available to the project research team.

3 Findings and Conclusions

The concepts underpinning the whole process have been the subject of considerable discussion and reflection. Findings from focus groups and questionnaires have shown that, overall, the students were positive about this learning experience with the majority of students (72.3%) agreeing that group tasks supported their learning.

Table 1. The group tasks supported my learning

The group tasks supported my learning

		Frequency	Percent	Valid Percent	Cumulative Percent
Valid	Strongly Agree	20	17.4	17.9	17.9
	Agree	61	53.0	54.5	72.3
	Neutral	19	16.5	17.0	89.3
	Disagree	7	6.1	6.3	95.5
	Strongly Disagree	5	4.3	4.5	100.0
	Total	112	97.4	100.0	
Missing	999	3	2.6		
Total		115	100.0		

Nevertheless, significant anomalies remain. In spite of 67.5 % of respondents finding peer feedback helpful, only 50.9% found group feedback, offered by tutors, relevant to their own work! This would seem to imply that the students themselves have assumed the role of tutors for peers and are perceived as effective in that role.

Table 2. I found the feedback from peers helpful

I found the feedback from peers helpful

		Frequency	Percent	Valid Percent	Cumulative Percent
Valid	Strongly Agree	18	15.7	15.8	15.8
	Agree	59	51.3	51.8	67.5
	Neutral	28	24.3	24.6	92.1
	Disagree	7	6.1	6.1	98.2
	Strongly Disagree	2	1.7	1.8	100.0
	Total	114	99.1	100.0	
Missing	999	1	.9		
Total		115	100.0		

Open responses in the questionnaire indicated that peer based formative assessment had been effective in promoting reflection and self-regulation. Typical comments were:

> "I liked working in groups for the core tasks. It helped me to understand things better when the group discussed it and bounced ideas off each other."

> "The group work really helped me further my development and development of the content."

However there are still some challenges. 52.7% of respondents either "Strongly Agreed" or "Agreed" that use of the e-portfolio environment to support the blended learning approach made an impact on their ability to engage in the course at a distance, but only 23.5% said it helped them organise their course work. Awareness of the wider benefits of blended learning and of ubiquitous PLE, or e-portfolio, systems appears still to be lacking and requires further research.

Furthermore, in spite of better exam results (unknown at the time of the survey), and increased engagement in course materials, some students were still unsure of the benefits of formative assessment - only 51.3% either "Agreed" or "Strongly Agreed" that this method was beneficial.

It is evident that student engagement in different aspects of the course has varied considerably. The research team is considering how these variations in experience might be minimised and welcomes input from interested parties.

Students on this module have generally felt empowered, but there are some for whom the process has been painful,

> "I appreciate the necessity and advantages of working in groups, but this only works if all groups have the same commitment and level of input. Group work does not place the same incentive to study as individual work which is submitted and assessed individually." (Student aged 39+).

To maximise the impact of these developments, education institutions must find ways of promoting formative assessment to improve effectiveness of student learning and also to achieve efficiency gains in the deployment of staff. Skills, which encourage the social construction of knowledge and understanding, leading to collective intelligence, must be developed throughout courses and modules must provide opportunities for students, and staff, to develop knowledge, skills and understanding of the entire learning process and of metacognition. In this project, despite student fears about lack of preparation for the final summative exam, the arithmetic mean score for the written section rose from 59% in the academic year 2005-2006 to 70% in the 2006-2007. Peer based formative assessment has been seen to bring about learning, social and professional gains for all involved.

The use of blended learning, described above, is to support the development of reflective, self-regulated classroom practitioners, skilled in formative assessment strategies and the pedagogy of effective e-portfolio use require further research and development. The role of innovative learning environments is to support these developments.

References

1. T. Umesao, Information Industry Theory Dawn of the Coming Era of the Ectodermal Industry. *Hoso Asahi*, Jan. pp. 4-17, Tokyo: Asahi Hoso (1963).
2. D. Bell, *The Coming of Post-Industrial Society* (Heinemann, London, 1973, 1999).
3. A. Touraine, *The Post Industrial Society Tomorrow's Social History, Classes, Conflicts and Culture in the Programmed Society* (English Edition) Translated by L. Mayhew. (Wildwood House, London, 1994).
4. Scottish Executive, *A Curriculum for Excellence* (Edinburgh, HMSO, 2004).
5. C. Bailey et al., Lifelong learner records to support eLearning. Conference presentation. http://www.alt.ac.uk/altc2004/timetable/abstract.php?abstract_id=153) (2004).
6. B. Collis, The Contributing Student: A blend of pedagogy and technology, in J. Copsey (ed.) *The Next Wave of Collaboration*, Auckland, New Zealand: Educause and The University of Auckland Library, 7-12 (2005).
7. L.A.J. Stefani & S. Diener, The e-Teaching portfolio as a tool to promote professional development, proceedings of Educause, ISBN 0 86869-108-9. (2005).
8. M.B. Ross and M. Welsh, Formative Feedback to Improve Learning on a Teacher Education Degree Using a Personal Learning Environment, proceedings of ICBL, 2007, Brazil. ISBN 978-3-89958-277-2.

9. M.B. Ross and M. Welsh, M. (2007). Formative Feedback to Improve Learning on a Teacher Education Degree Using a Personal Learning Environment, *International Journal of Emerging Technologies in Learning (i-Jet)*, 2 (3), (2007) ISSN: 1863-0383.
10. D. Nicol, Increasing success in first year courses assessment re-designs selfregulation and learning technologies. Proceedings of ASCLITE Conference, Sydney, Dec 3-6, 2006.
11. M. Yorker, *Leaving Early Undergraduate Non-completion in Higher Education* (Flamer, London, 1999).
12. M. Yorker and B. Long den, *Retention and Student Success in Higher Education* (Flamer, London, 2004).
13. D. Bound, Sustainable Assessment: rethinking assessment for the learning society. *Studies in Continuing Education, 22*(2), 151-167 (2000).
14. P. Black and D. Wiliam, (1998). Assessment and Classroom Learning. *Assessment in Education, 5*(1), 7-74.
15. A. Brew, Towards autonomous assessment: using self-assessment and peer assessment, in S.Brown and A. Glaser (eds) *Assessment Matters in Higher Education: Choosing and Using Diverse Approaches* (Open University Press, Buckingham, 1999) pp. 159-171.
16. N. Falchikov, *Improving Assessment Through Student Involvement Practical Solutions for Aiding Learning in Higher and Further Education*. (RoutleldgeFalmer, London, 2005).
17. G. Gibbs and C. Simpson, Conditions Under Which Assessment Supports Students' Learning. *Learning and Teaching in Higher Education* (1), 3-31 (2004).
18. D. Nicol and C. Milligan (2006). Rethinking technology-supported assessment practices in relation to the seven principles of good feedback practice. In C. Bryan & K. Clegg (Eds.), *Innovative Assessment in Higher Education* (Routledge, London, 2006), pp. 64-77.
19. D. Nicol, Principles of good assessment and feedback: Theory and practice. From the REAP International Online Conference on Assessment Design for Learner Responsibility, 29th-31st May, 2007. Available at http://ewds.strath.ac.uk/REAP07 (2007).
20. J. Biggs, *Teaching for Quality Learning at University* (Second ed.). (SRHE/Open University Press, London, 2003).
21. D. J. Nicol and D. Macfarlane Dick, Formative assessment and selfregulated learning: a model and seven principles of good feedback practice. *Studies in Higher Education, 31*(2), 199-218 (2006).
22. J. Dewey, *How We Think* (D.C. Heath, Chicago, 1910).
23. J. Dewey, *How We Think: A Restatement of Reflective Thinking to the Educative Process* (Henry Regnery, Chicago, 1933).
24. J. Dewey, *Experience and Education* (Collier Books, New York, 1938).
25. L. Stenhouse, An *Introduction to Curriculum Research and Development* (Heinemann. London, 1975).
26. W. Carr and S. Kemmis, *Becoming Critical: Education, Knowledge and Action Research* (Falmer/Deakin University Press, Lewes, 1986).
27. J. Elliot, *Action Research for Educational Change* (Open University Press, Buckingham, 1991).
28. D. Schon, *The Reflective Practitioner How Professionals Think in Action* (Basic, London, 1983).
29. K. Zeichner, and D. Liston, *Reflective Teaching An Introduction* (L Erlbaum, Mahwah, N.J., 1996)
30. R.A. Pring, *The Philosophy of Educational Research* (Continuum, London, 2000).
31. C. Robson, *Real World Research* (Second ed.). (Blackwell, Oxford, 2002).

KidSmart: an essential tool for mathematical education in nursery schools

Annarosa Serpe
Department of Mathematics, University of Calabria, Cube 30/A
Via Ponte P. Bucci, 87036 Rende (CS), Italy
annarosa.serpe@unical.it

Abstract. This paper is part of a wide debate and critical reflection on the use of ICT in nursery schools, and focuses on the use of station KidSmart in the classroom to enhance scientific learning within the logical-mathematic field. The study is organized as follows: after presenting the institutional setting within which ICT has been introduced in Italian nursery schools, some considerations are made on the essential characteristics of mathematical education and on the relationship with physical reality through the mediation of ICT, highlighting in particular the pedagogic-educational value of ludic-experiental activities in an early learning context. After that, the characteristics of the KidSmart station are introduced, and some interesting results of the action-research experience aimed at scientifically controlling the conditions and introductory procedures of KidSmart in the field of experience '*exploring, knowing and planning*' are given. Related conclusions round off this work.

1   Introduction

The enhancement of scientific knowledge at all levels is essential to shape a society able to cope harmoniously with today's remarkable scientific progress and rapid technological advancement. A scientific-mathematic education, that is the acquisition of a scientific way of thinking, should form an integral part of any learning programme today, and should make a critical and conscious use of information and communication technology (ICT). On the basis of this, technology has been introduced in Italian schools, with the object of providing innovations and improving the process of teaching and learning. In Italy the introduction of technology in education has mainly concerned secondary schools, while nursery schools, except for a few pioneering experiences, have been totally excluded, despite the regulations introduced in 1991 [1] which recognized the value of multi-media education through the field of experience '*Messages, forms and media*'. In 1995-96 the Programme for the Development of Didactic Technologies (PSTD) was started, which for the first time included infant schools. The real turning-point in the

Please use the following format when citing this chapter:

Serpe, A., 2008, in IFIP International Federation for Information Processing, Volume 281; *Learning to Live in the Knowledge Society*; Michael Kendall and Brian Samways; (Boston: Springer), pp. 313–320.

relationship between technology and infant schools is the 'Act for the re-organization of school cycles' [2], together with a review of the curricula for compulsory education [3], where the use of new technology is strongly recommended.

No specific 'items' or objectives are set out, but reference is made to the field of experience *'Fruition and production of messages'*. In this institutional context the project KidSmart Early Learning was introduced in the scholastic year 2000/01, promoted by the IBM Foundation Italy in collaboration with the Ministry of Education, University and Research, with the object of facilitating the introduction of ICT in the first phase of infant learning. The project, highly innovative in the Italian school context, made use of a model already available internationally, which was then discussed and re-designed around the needs and specificities of the Italian school system [4]. Such a project in Italy involved numerous infant schools located in difficult socio-economic contexts and/or areas geographically isolated, which benefited from the donation of multi-media stations and didactic software programmes [5].

Further details can be found on: http://www.fondazioneibm.it/scuola/kidsmart.htm.

1.1   Mathematical education and utilization of ICTs in nursery schools

In nursery schools, mathematical education represents an important part of the syllabus as the particular field of experience for the development of logical skills, no longer an isolated subject of an abstract nature, but a language useful for the mastering of a scientific way of thinking and reasoning. From this educational perspective, Mathematics becomes not just a system of knowledge organized as a discrete discipline, but a symbolic system which helps the young learners in the processes of decoding real life, in the solution of problems, in the revision and integration of hypotheses, and in the attribution of meaning. Thus, Mathematics provides a powerful conceptual tool which leads children to form general ideas on logical concepts, shaping in them a mental attitude which will later assimilate Mathematics in a way of acting, thinking and doing. From the perspective of didactic methodology, only a suitable approach can provide an effective variable which can promote intrinsic motivation, such as curiosity, lucidity and the pleasure of discovery, all essential factors for the understanding and interpretation of reality. Mathematical education in Italian nursery schools is part of the various fields of experience, in particular of the field of experience *'Exploring, knowing and planning'*, where the following skills are given special relevance: the ability to group, order, quantify and measure, localize, put into relation, plan and invent. This is the field which first helps to organise the child's first knowledge of the world of natural and artificial reality, with special emphasis on exploring and learning through discovery. Such a field of experience, given its special nature, requires dynamic-constructive methodological pathways, able to encourage cooperative activities that can sustain the interest and curiosity of the children, as well as stimulate organization, planning, research and discovery. The evolution of pedagogical practices allow for a diversification of learning situations, so that traditional activities in situ can be supported by technological instruments which make daily education more effective. The introduction of physical instruments (educational technology, media) cannot do without a methodological rationalization (a conceptual scaffolding that supports the organization of the educational process) which should offer stimulating learning environments that contribute to social and cognitive development. As regards the age of the children, the introduction of technological tools should be gradual, privileging the ludic-experiential sphere, and offering elements of continuity with everyday reality. Such a step, to paraphrase Seymour Papert's [6] authoritative thinking, should not be linear and 'sequential' but should gradually be integrated into the different stages of development. Integration of a non-linear nature between experience coming from play and reflexive and metacognitive activities, according to Donald Norman [7-8] should combine experimental learning and reflexive learning. Consequently, the guide lines and theoretical references can only be found in post-Piaget pedagogy, in theoretical reflections inspired by Vigotskij [9] which have been defined as the 'pedagogy of complexity' by Howard Gardner [10-12] or the 'cultural psychology' of Jerome Bruner [13-15]. Thus, the question to be addressed is that of the four sides of a tetrahedron concerning the relationship between age, development and introduction to technology. First of all, the familiar and social context in which children are born and grow up cannot be ignored, an environment which becomes progressively more technologically based. Also, multimedia education should take into consideration the harmonization with different stages of the child's psychological and sensory-motor development, as well as respect for individual maturity and subjectivity [16]. Moreover, the multi code structure of ICTs should be fully exploited through the planning of didactic pathways and Mind Tools [17] so as to enhance, develop and evaluate critically all the possible skills and forms of intelligence that can be taught through multimedia tools, especially relational and communicative intelligence. Last but not least, the introduction of ICTs should be accessible in three relevant aspects: finalization, character based, co-planning [16].

2 'First Mathematics' with KidSmart: an action-research experience

2.1 The KidSmart station [18]

The KidSmart station (Fig.1) contains a state-of-the-art personal computer and a 17 inch screen. It is equipped with big keys sensitive to the touch, a small mouse. Loud speakers are found on the wings of the station, so as to contain sounds which may otherwise disturb other children engaged in different activities nearby. The station also has a microphone and printer, a scanner, video camera and Internet connection facilities, all important aids for didactic activities. It is also equipped with a double seat to encourage cooperation between children. KidSmart uses the much acclaimed software package for children Young Explorer by Riverdeep, which offers a series of different types of educational activities ranging across various fields of experience centred around play and creativity. As an example, in Fig.2 we show the cover of the software package 'IMPARO GIOCANDO' (Learn through Play) where a jolly group of four animals are each linked to a particular field of experience: the mouse relates to the '*Fruition and production of messages*', the cat is linked to '*I, the self and others*'. Lastly, the rabbit and the hippopotamus to the fields '*Exploring, knowing and planning*'. This package is made up of 3 blocks, each one with 30 CD-ROMs.

Fig. 1. The KidSmart station   **Fig. 2.** The software Learn through Play

All the games in the Learn through Play software package use a problem solving methodology as the privileged modality to expand knowledge. Furthermore, the games ensure the synergic and continuous activation of different representational planes (iconic, symbolic, etc.) which ignites the 'sensory machine', making the children a protagonist of their learning.

2.2   The action-research experience

Action-research originated from the need to investigate whether the use of computers and specific didactic software programmes in nursery schools would enhance learning in the ambit of logic and Mathematics. Thus the proposed objectives were:
-   experimenting and scientific control of procedures for new methodological approaches and learning situations relating to the use in the classroom of KidSmart and related software in the field of experience '*exploring, knowing and planning*';
-   promoting opportunities for global and immediate learning which connect the use of computers to direct multi-sensory experience.

The action-research experience, given its specific characteristics, has required a continuous synergy between University and schools, with the direct involvement of a nursery school in the Didactic Circle 'Vittorio Morello' in Bagnara Calabra, in the province of Reggio Calabria, which had already taken part in the KidSmart Early Learning Project. A systematic report of the whole experience has been the subject of a degree Dissertation in the Science of Primary Education at the University of Calabria. Here, in brief, the stages of the experiment and a number of the findings are reported. From a technical point of view, the action-research was carried out in three phases: planning, operation, evaluation and feedback. It lasted two years (2005/07). The planning phase, which followed in-depth studies relating to the use of KidSmart and the research regarding the best practices in the logic-mathematical ambit available in the literature, was organized on the basis of the territorial data and an analysis of the related scholastic context. After that, the scaffolding of the methodological-didactic process was set up, in full respect of the specific biopsychic, social and cultural characteristics of the young learners, as well as of their style and pace of learning. During the operational phase, didactic activities were carried out in order to develop lateral thinking, the perception of shapes and colours, chronological order, the use and interpretation of codes, symbols and signs, knowledge of numbers and figures. All the activities were carried out first in the traditional way (without the use of technology), and subsequently with the use of KidSmart in the classroom using software programmes from the package Learn through Play selected according to the context and to didactic aims. In fact, the software programmes where the adventures of the happy group (a birthday party, at the fairground, etc.) were chosen with regard to the following specific aspects: spatial relations, perceptive discrimination, associations, logical sequences, primary numbers, counting, geometrical figures. The selected software programmes were analysed and evaluated before use for their educational value, and for their potential to stimulate and encourage active learning. As an example one of the activities carried out relating to the concept of quantity, which plays an important role within the field of learning arithmetic will be briefly reported. There are basically two approaches to numbers: non arithmetic (the number is object of reading and writing) or arithmetic (counting as correspondence of numerals to the objects and with cardinal and ordinal meaning). For this purpose, the CD-ROM 'Happy birthday Biff' (Fig.3) was selected. The analogical dimension of the software programme introduces the children to Biff's birthday celebration organized by his friends, who have decorated the room and have put a cake on the table, in full wiew. (Fig.4).

Fig. 3. Home page: 'Happy birthday Biff'   **Fig. 4.** Output: Biff coming home

Tom the mouse invites children to click on his icon to help them prepare the food. The heuristics dimension of the software programme offers the children the chance to take decisions on the following questions: which plate has more sandwiches than the yellow plate? - which plate has fewer sandwiches than the green plate? (Fig.5). Which plate has the same number of cakes as the green plate? (Fig.6) Some children gave the correct answers straightaway, while others had some difficulty, and were helped through further logical stages by the button with the question mark available on the control bar (Fig.5 and 6).

Fig. 5. Output: sandwiches plate   **Fig. 6.** Output: cakes plate

The button with numbers, on the other hand, reminds the child that numbers are used in this game and not the letters of the alphabet, while the series of dots arranged on two parallel rows represent the number of correct answers. For example, in the case of the first question formulated, by pressing the Help button the following situation was recorded:

Help: count how many sandwiches there are on the yellow plate! *Child*: one, two! *Help*: then we must find a plate that has more. How many sandwiches does the green plate have? *Child*: one. *Help*: are there more on the yellow plate? *Child*: yes.
Help: let's count those on the red plate. *Child*: there aren't any.
Help: how many on the blue one? *Child*: one, two, three.
Help: count again the sandwiches on the yellow plate. *Child*: one, two.
Help: so are there more on the blue one than on the yellow one? *Child*: yes!

In order to monitor the activities in the innovation process and their effect on the learning environmen, some protocol observation tables were devised:
- definition of the field and object of observation;
- definition of the categories of the object of observation (description and evaluation function);
- formulation of observation items;
- construction of recording tools (chart, schemes);
- definition of the plan of observation (to establish where, how many, for how long this operation will be carried out).

It should be stressed that all activities with KidSmart were carried out in groups of between 3 and 4 young learners of mixed abilities, as far as starting level, cognitive style, emotional and socio-affective conditions and general skills were concerned. This mode of operation enabled every child to contribute to the group 'whatever their abilities' by playing a role and having a task, while keeping to the agreed rules. For reasons of space, only the synoptic table of the registered results obtained by the young learners during the mathematical activity relating to the concept of quantity is given, leaving any comments to the reader.

The operative and evaluation phases represent, in many ways, the core of the action-research experience. In short, the aim was to 'measure' on a small sample of children any possible improvement and cognitive development in the logical-mathematic field by comparing the results obtained with the use of KidSmart in the classroom with those obtained through traditional learning activities, that is without the use of technology. Below some overall data relating to the KidSmart approach taken from the chart of the activities are shown.

Table 1. Results in the mathematical activity relating to the concept of quantity

Evaluation Educational Objectives	Traditional Activities			Activities with Kidsmart		
	Inadequate	Adequate	Good	Inadequate	Adequate	Good
Comparing Quantities: *many-few*	15	23%	62%	/	21%	79%
Understanding the equipotent sets: *as many as*	34%	7%	59%	13%	34%	53%
Comparing Quantities: *one-many-few*	14%	22%	64%	7%	14%	79%
Quantifying and Counting objects up to number six (6)	23%	14%	63%	23%	21%	56%

Table 2. Some data relating to the KidSmart approach

	never	sometimes	always
Has raised the curiosity of the young learners	/		100%
Has led the young learners to discoveries	/	14%	86%
Has made easy the use of the keyboard and mouse	10%	7%	83%
Has encouraged flexibility of adaptation	7%	5%	88%
Has promoted the acquisition of The skills of:			
- eye-hand coordination;	5%	10%	85%
- Speed of perception;	10%	20%	70%
- Interest in the IT tool;	/	8%	92%
- Peer cooperation and Turn taking	/	38%	62%

3   Conclusions

After analysing the results of our action-research we can state that:
- the introduction of technology into the nursery school curriculum offers young learners the opportunity to cultivate interests and curiosity by taking part in activities within a learning environment organized around the principles of doing and reflecting on doing;
- the teacher, by planning the introduction of KidSmart in the classroom activities and by considering the different opportunities it can offer, is able to extend the experiences available to the children and the educational and cognitive processes activated by the didactic activities on a daily basis;
- the play element in an interactive context has had positive effects on motivation, has effectively increased interest in the technological tool, thereby also improving participation in the search for solutions to problems and increasing peer interaction;
- the use of the software programme has greatly facilitated learning by doing, allowing the children to behave naturally and spontaneously during activities which provided direct experience, with the effect of encouraging feelings of

confidence, shared responsibility, and consolidating skills while, at the same time, decreasing performance anxiety.

KidSmart, therefore, makes for a new approach to mathematics, more stimulating than the traditional one as it encourages a polyhedric development of mental abilities and a mode of learning that refers not only to Mathematics but has also socio-cultural connotations. In this way the old prejudice that by sitting in front of a computer screen one must be passive is refuted. Therefore, in the nursery school, by making children aware of these aspects we discourage false expectations regarding technology, and encourage a more realistic and critical use of computers. As Gardner says (April 10, 1997), computers can be used to manipulate people or to liberate them, they can be used to teach people in the same boring rigorous ways as was done for ages, or they can be used to teach in very new ways [19].

References

[1]   Orientamenti per la scuola materna del 3 giugno 1991, Ministero Pubblica Istruzione.
[2]   Legge n°30 del 10 febbraio 2000 and following Decreto Ministeriale n°61/2003
[3]   Decreto Ministeriale n°59/2004
[4]   Provenzano P., Stell M., Bambini e Computer, (eds) Mantovani S. and Ferri P., ETAS, Milano, 2006.
[5]   The didactic software used for this project are: La Casa della Matematica di Mille; La Casa della Scienza di Sammy; La Casa del Tempo e dello Spazio di Trudy e Thinkin'Things Collection 1,2,3 (Riverdeep).
[6]   S. Papert, The Children's Machine: Rethinking School in the Age of the Computer, Basic Books, New York, 1993.
[7]   D. Norman, Things That Make Us Smart, Addison Weasley, Reading (Mass.), 1993.
[8]   D. Norman, Emotional Design. Why We Love (or Hate) Everyday Things, Basic Books, New York, 2003.
[9]   L.S. Vygotskij, Storia dello sviluppo delle funzioni psichiche superiori ed altri saggi, (ed) M.S. Veggetti, Giunti Barbera, Firenze, 1974.
[10] H.Gardner, Frames of Mind: the Theory of Multiple Intelligences, Basic Books, New York, 1983.
[11] H.Gardner, The Unschooled Mind: How Children Think and How Schools Should Teach, Basic Books, New York, 1991.
[12] H.Gardner, Multiple Intelligences: the Theory in Practice, Basic Books, New York, 1993.
[13] J.S. Bruner, Actual Minds, Possible Worlds, Harvard University Press, Cambridge (Mass.), 1986.
[14] J.S. Bruner, "I mondi di Nelson Goodman" in La mente a più dimensioni, Laterza, Roma-Bari, 1988, pp. 115-129
[15] J.S. Bruner, Acts of Meaning, Harvard University Press, Cambridge (Mass.), 1990.
[16] P. Ferri, Bambini e Computer, (eds) Mantovani S.,Ferri P., ETAS, Milano, 2006, p.95
[17] D.H. Jonassen, Computers as Mindtools for Schools: Engaging Critical Thinking, Prentice Hall, New York, 2000.
[18] http://wwwkidsmartearlylearning.org
[19] http://www.mediamente.rai.it/HOME/BIBLIOTE/intervis/g/gardner.htm

Learning with Interactive Stories

Sebastian A. Weiß[1] and Wolfgang Müller[1]
[1]PH Weingarten, University of Education
Media Education and Visualisation Group
Kirchplatz 2, 88250 Weingarten, Germany
{weiss, muellerw}@ph-weingarten.de,
WWW home page: http://www.ph-weingarten.de

Abstract. Several frameworks and platforms are used for learning or for building virtual environments for game-based learning. In games based on virtual worlds an enormous amount of knowledge is exchanged. But we believe compared to games stories provide more explicit knowledge transfer. For that reason we developed an Interactive Digital Storytelling (IDS) Platform called *Scenejo*, which we use to build examples for different learning showcases. We present our first experiences and discuss challenges for the successful building of interactive storytelling applications.

Keywords: Game-based learning, virtual environments, Interactive Digital Storytelling, Scenejo

1. Introduction

Game-based learning describes the application of computer games for learning, or, as Marc Prensky has put it, it "is precisely about fun and engagement, and the coming together of and serious learning and interactive entertainment into a newly emerging and highly exciting medium" [1]. James Paul Gee [2] has analyzed that computer games are new media that let children and adults experience a learning effect while enjoying themselves. Game-based learning is somehow related to the field of edutainment that especially targets to lead children to scientific topics.

There are a lot of different approaches to Game-based learning. Different kinds of games that are used or especially developed for learning purposes exist. Some of these commercial games follow behavioristic approaches like *Mathematikus*,

Please use the following format when citing this chapter:

Weiß, S.A. and Müller, W., 2008, in IFIP International Federation for Information Processing, Volume 281; *Learning to Live in the Knowledge Society*; Michael Kendall and Brian Samways; (Boston: Springer), pp. 321–328.

Physicus, Informaticus, etc. (part of a whole games series), or simulations such as *Making History* or exemplary *SimCity.*

Frequently, teachers and researchers experiment with commercial gaming platforms and virtual worlds for education. An often applied platform is *Neverwinter Nights* [3], a massively multiplayer online role-playing game (MMORPG). An example for adoption is the project *Altered Learning* [4] that has been accomplished at West Nottinghamshire College in Mansfield, England. At a level appropriate to the learner, teachers give access to scenarios where a learner is confronted with tasks and puzzles she should solve. In agreement with Sanford et al. [5] the game has been modified to the specific needs of this project, and teachers do exactly know about tolerance and prospects of the game and how to instruct the students.

Another example for the utilization of commercial games for learning is *Revolution* [6]. *Revolution* is a multi-player role-playing 3D game based on historical events of the American Revolution. Students have an opportunity to experience the daily social, economic, and political lives of the town's inhabitants. The game is designed to be played in a 45-minute classroom session in a networked environment, which means students can interact with other players. Players can collaborate, debate and compete within this historical simulation that maintains historical suspension of disbelief with graphical and behavioral accuracy. Moreover, players can listen to non-player characters (NPC) that talk to one another about the events taking place. This example shows how students could "teach" themselves by exploring the virtual world of ancient America in groups.

Not only game platforms are used to create "playful learning" scenarios. Currently prevailing is the adoption of virtual realities, first of all *SecondLife* (SL).

Virtual realities are computer-based simulations of a three-dimensional environment for multiple users. Users can inhabit this simulated reality via avatars. These avatars interact with each other. MMORPGs are using virtual realities as an environment.

Also specialized frameworks and platforms have already been developed for building a specific virtual learning environment. Based on these commercial products games can be build similar to MMORPGs or virtual realities like SL. But theses games then are specially designed for usage in a particular field of interest.

Fig.1: Example application of *Olive* simulating a case-study for firefighters [7]

One example for such a platform is *Olive* by Forterra [7] (Fig.1). *Olive* is used for building game-based scenarios in the fields of corporate, medical, defense & intelligence.

2. Problems of Game-based Learning Approaches

While the idea of combining learning with play and games is intriguing and many people are currently trying to follow this vision, the realization of successful game-based learning applications is not really simple. There are various examples illustrating the different problems.

Most of today's commercial learning games can hardly convince as successful game-based learning solutions. In general, these applications fall into two classes: those stressing learning, and those putting the focus on the game idea. While applications from the first class usually lack the targeted levels of fun and playfulness, applications from the second class typically fail to integrate learning and learning elements successfully. In general, these applications incorporate learning elements in term of the presentation of glossaries or texts covering subjects that are necessary to solve a problem in the game. However, most often these problems seem artificial, and, thus, these applications often fail to provide the necessary motivation to analyze the additional documents (examples are applications such as *Mathematikus*). In general, such approaches usually fail to take up state-of-the-art educational theories and constructive elements, limiting learning to behavioristic approaches. Jantke comes to similar results in his review [8].

Trying to utilize the tension provided by computer games, McDivitt tried to apply an off-the-shelf computer game from the genre of history and strategy to learning in history classes in school. In his study he could proof that such games were well accepted by students and that a certain increase of knowledge in history on the specific time-frame could be observed. On the other hand, students also acquired wrong understandings for historic facts, resulting in a failure of this experiment [9].

Very recently, the *Arden* project, a large project started to implement a game-based learning endeavor comparable in quality to commercial games, also admitted it's failure to provide the targeted fun and gaming due to a late consideration of real game elements during the development. [10].

In general, the question on how to integrate learning successfully with elements of play and games is unsolved. Gee [2] provided a list of 36 principles relevant to learning with games. However, he did not address the aspects of fun and drama that a game should also provide.

Applications coming a bit closer to those visions of game-based learning are typically those incorporating strong elements of simulation that provide real "choices" to the user [11] where she can observe the effects of decisions directly and, thus, can develop other levels of understanding. Simulations are well accepted as valuable tools to support learning (see for instance Schank [12]). However, a good simulation does not necessarily provide the wanted levels of fun and motivate for further exploration. Also, it is difficult to provide learners adequate support and guidance in such environments, and their development is complex and costly.

3. Interactive Digital Storytelling

The concept of Interactive Storytelling has the potential to become a paradigm for future interactive knowledge media. It couples dramatic narrative with interactions of users, providing highest forms of engagement and immersion. It also stands for the connection of games and stories by utilizing inherent structural elements of both. Artificial characters taking the role of actors within a plot play an important role in the concept of Interactive Storytelling.

Digital storytelling agents can achieve more than simply being single virtual guides and virtual tutors, which are commonplace today in a variety of software products. As in stories, their role could be to interact with each other as a set of characters to present a dramatic storyline; and as in games, they have the potential to serve as all sorts of sparring partners for players to interact with, such as representing the bad guys, or companions who ask for help.

Interactive Storytelling Principles

Independently from the actual content, there are design problems to solve concerning the dynamics of real-time interactive storytelling systems. At the same time, drawing from dramatic storytelling principles gives new possibilities to design the conversations in a way that fits the target group and provides some entertainment and fun. An interactive story that involves several characters has to fulfill the following requirements, thereby confronting the storyteller with open design issues:

- **Characters and story world:** Characters with complex interpersonal relationships interest people. However, it takes a great deal of time to relay these issues through dialogue. For an E-learning application, these relationships still can be of some use in the sense that several characters can take roles (the Smart and the Dumb, the Teacher and the Buddy, etc.). For good storytelling, the combinations of characters induce much of fun and interesting dialogues, and also assign a role for the student. Mostly, good designed characters live in an accordingly designed world that matches their goals and personality, sketching a special not normal situation.
- **Hook:** The audience shall be captivated within the first few moments by something that makes them stay and be interested in the details of the main objective of the story. According to the target group, there can be a theme from folktales or interpersonal relationships. The main design question here is how much fiction is appropriate.
- **Agency:** It is very important that the students perceive themselves immediately as active participants with a direct influence on the dialogue itself. This has to be communicated within the first few moments, by the interface or by the dialogue.
- **Dramatic arcs:** If a hook has been presented, there should be a satisfying story resolution to each student's individual experience. It is an important design issue to manage the different individual time for the interactive parts, while not ending a lesson within a certain timeframe but without a resolution of the story.

- **Usability:** Interaction shall be possible with text-based input, as well as through actions. According to the target group and its age and the context of the task, text input is not always appropriate. Therefore there is a demand to design alternative interface hardware, especially for younger children with no writing capabilities, to replace the input of numbers, given words and sentences. Within our project, these issues are planned but not yet implemented.

The result of the overall work is dependent on all of these and even more aspects. The achievement of any storytelling educational application will depend on a successful integration of these design issues with the mechanics that the runtime platform can provide. The platform for interactive dialogues shall be able to let authors define characters with personality, choose a story model to decide on possible dramatic arcs and turns in learning concepts, and define interactions that are integrated within the written dialogue.

4. Technological Approaches

Successful implementations of intelligent conversations with animated virtual characters are rare, and there is no real success on the entertainment market to date. One of the few examples examining a middle course between the two approaches of linear stories and emergent behavior is M. Mateas' and A. Stern's *Façade* [13]. It is based on a specialized dialogue management system and allows users to participate in a predefined and pre-recorded conversation between virtual characters. However, the system's design is focused on a specific scenario and authoring is currently supported for programmers only. *art-E-fact* [14] and *Scenejo* present similar integrations of simulation and plot. In contrast to *Façade*, an authoring system is central to the way a story is built in *art-E-fact*. Defining digital conversations, Storywriters start with a story graph of explicit dialogue acts, similar to branching. They provide more complex interactions by adding rules and chatbot patterns within nodes of the graph.

Beside this implementations, we want to mention *Fear Not!* [15] by Ana Paiva et al.. This system is based on synthetic and empathic agents. It is being developed to tackle and eventually help to reduce bullying problems in schools. This is one of the first interactive storytelling applications used in an educational context.

Scenejo

Scenejo [16] is our technological approach to develop a framework for interactive storytelling applications for learning. *Scenejo* enables such playful simulations of dialogues between several conversational agents and multiple users. As mentioned above, *Scenejo* employs animated virtual characters and current chatbot technology as the basis for text-based interactions. The result is an emerging dialogue, influenced by the users' inputs and the bots' databases of possible lines matching a text pattern coming from either a user or another bot. The bots also take into account parametric settings and scene descriptions provided by an author.

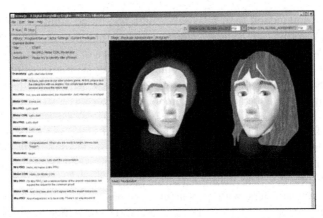

Fig. 2: Main application window of *Scenejo* showing the dialog history and two actors

With *Scenejo*, we follow a similar goal as in *art-E-fact*, but start at the opposite end. From the start, we use chatbot text patterns to provide free conversational interaction with users, and in a bottom-up way, we introduce a story graph allowing writers to line up conversational scenes and their parameters.

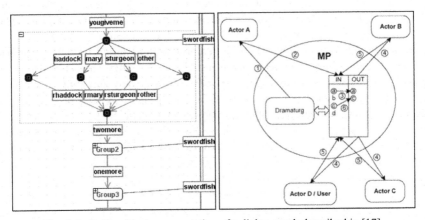

Fig. 3: Left: Graphical representation of a dialog graph described in [17].
Right: Schematic drawing of the communication concept of implemented components:
Meeting Point with Dramatic Advisor and Actors

5. Discussion

Does *Scenejo* meet the challenges of playful learning? To date, only partially, there are still a lot of open tasks. One of the open questions is how to simply control the agents and media at all. At the moment, we are working on a simple to use graphical programming language for describing dialogs, events and, as mentioned, to control applied elements. Identifying elements of digital storytelling leads to another problem. Currently, no common technological standard does exist.

Not only technological questions have to be answered. We also have to stress that Interactive Digital Storytelling is about the development of a new genre. At present, we do not know what good interactive stories are and how multi-branch stories should be designed. However, answers to these questions are preconditions for applying IDS successfully in the field of learning.

First experiments are however promising. The *Killer Phrase game*, a small and simple educational game on rhetoric and communication could be implemented successfully based on the Scenejo framework. So far, it has shown that there is a potential for designing successful games for learning involving virtual actors based on digitally implemented agents [18]. But there is a need for further technical development.

As mentioned above, authoring represents a central problem in today's approaches to IDS. Similar to the developments in Multimedia and the World-Wide-Web, interesting and convincing contents can only be expected in a wider scale if appropriate and easy to use authoring tools are available that allow non-experts in the field and especially non-technician to fully exploit the potential of the medium. In the context of education and learning this means that educators and teachers need to be enabled to express their ideas of interactive learning stories and game-based learning contents. Further application scenarios may develop, when usability of such tools reaches a level where students and children as novice users may utilize such authoring tools. This would allow collaborative learning scenarios in the sense of group storytelling, allowing students to tell their own stories, exchange and integrate them with others, take different roles and play a scene, and reflect on the different aspects expressed in such interactive endeavors. Experiences in this direction are very limited. Nevertheless, rethinking subject topics and processes in terms of interactive stories has already proven to be a valuable concept in learning [19].

Still, a high degree of usability will not be the only problem to solve. The already mentioned aspects of a very new genre make it difficult to foresee all requirements for authoring tools for IDS. We certainly may assume that new metaphors for describing and visualizing such contents need to be found. From experience we know that progress in such new contexts can best be achieved based on small development steps and frequent evaluation of concepts and prototypes. Scenejo may well be understood as one of the first steps in this direction.

6. Conclusion

We discussed the differences between game-based learning and Interactive Storytelling and have shown some disadvantages of the game-based approach. Also we have described how Interactive Storytelling could be a valuable approach for learning. In conclusion the question comes up, whether Interactive Digital Storytelling should be preferred to the game-based learning approach.

Also, we introduced *Scenejo* as a first step towards an implementation of Interactive Storytelling concepts and presented our first experiences. Current problems have been identified and discussed, too.

References

1. Prensky, M. (2001). Digital Game-Based Learning; McGraw-Hill, New York
2. Gee, J.P. (2003). What Video Games Have To Teach Us about Learning and Literacy; Palgrave Macmillan, New York
3. BioWare (2002). Neverwinter Nights. http://nwn.bioware.com/ (last visited 02.06.2007)
4. Altered Learning (since 2005). West Nottinghamshire College (Mansfield England); http://www.alteredlearning.com and http://www.westnotts.ac.uk/ (last visited 02.06.2007)
5. Sanford, R., Ulicsak, M., Facer, K. and Rudd, T. (2006). Teaching with Games, Using Commercial Off-the-Shelf Computer Games in Formal Education; Bristol: Future-lab. http://www.futurelab.org.uk/research/lit_reviews.htm
6. The Education Arcade (since 2004): Revolution; http://www.educationarcade.org/revolution (last visited: 02.06.2007)
7. OLIVE - On-Line Interactive Virtual Environment; Forterra Systems Inc. http://www.forterrainc.com (last visited January 2008)
8. Jantke, Klaus P. (2006). Games That do not Exist - Communication Design Beyond the Current Limits; Proceedings of the 24th annual ACM international conference on Design of communication
9. McDivitt, David: Do Gamers Score Better in School? http://seriousgamessource.com/features/feature_051606.php (last visited 08.01.2008)
10. Naone, Erica (2008). Grandios gescheitert. Technology Review, January 2008. http://www.heise.de/tr/artikel/100944
11. Crawford, C. (2005). Chris Crawford on Interactive Storytelling; New Riders, Berkeley
12. Schank, R.C.; Cleary, Ch. (1995). Engines for Education; Laurence Erlbaum Pub
13. Mateas, M. and Stern, A. (2003): Integrating Plot, Character and Natural Language Processing in the Interactive Drama Façade. In: Proceedings of TIDSE 2003, Darmstadt, pp. 139-151.
14. Spierling, U., Iurgel, I. (2003): „Just Talking About Art"– Creating Virtual Storytelling Experiences in Mixed Reality. In: Virtual Storytelling, Using Virtual Reality Technologies for Storytelling, Proceedings of ICVS 2003, Toulouse, France: Springer LNCS volume 2897, pp. 179-188.
15. Paiva, A., Dias, J., Sobral, D., Aylett, R., Sobreperez, P., Woods, S., Zoll, C., and Hall, L. (2004). Caring for Agents and Agents that Care: Building Empathic Relations with Synthetic Agents; Proc. AAMAS 2004, New York, July 19-23, pp 194-201.
16. Weiss, S., Müller, W., Spierling, U., and Steimle, F. (2005). Scenejo – An Interactive Storytelling Platform. Demonstration paper in: Virtual Storytelling, Using Virtual Reality Technologies for Storytelling, Third International Conference, Proceedings, Strasbourg, France, pp. 77-80.
17. Spierling, U., Weiß, S.A., Müller, W. (2006). Towards Accessible Authoring Tools for Interactive Storytelling. In: S. Göbel, R. Malkewitz, and I. Iurgel (Eds.): TIDSE 2006, LNCS 4326, pp. 169-180.
18. Spierling, U. (2008). "Killer Phrases": Design steps for a digital game with conversational role playing agents; Post Conference Proceedings of Isaga 2007, edited by I. Mayer and H. Mastik (Eburon publishers. To be published 2008).
19. Spierling, U.; Müller, W.; Vogel, R.; und Iurgel, I. (2004) Digital Conversational Storytelling Elements for Teaching Mathematics in Primary School, ED-MEDIA 2004 - World Conf. on Educational Multimedia, Hypermedia & Telecommunications, Lugano

From e-learning to "co-learning": the role of virtual communities

Luigi Colazzo[1], Andrea Molinari[1] and Nicola Villa[2]

[1] University of Trento - Department of Computer and Management
Sciences
via Inama 5, 38100 Trento, Italy. Tel +390461882144, +390461882344
eMails: colazzo@cs.unitn.it, amolinar@cs.unitn.it
[2] University of Trento - Laboratory of Maieutics
via Inama 5, 38100 Trento, Italy. Tel +390461882327
eMail: nvilla@economia.unitn.it

Abstract. The paper presents the analysis of changes introduced in learning environments through a different approach respect to traditional e-learning. In our experience, the introduction of the metaphor of "virtual community" changed not only the relationship between people involved in educational activities (teachers, students, tutors, administrative staff etc.), but also the technical approach to services supplied by the e-learning platform. Thanks to the "community" approach, all the services of a traditional e-learning system (CBT, LMS, LCMS, etc.) must be re-designed, thus allowing to extend the potentialities of services delivered to the audience. The introduction of the "community" concept allow the e-learning platform a greater flexibility: concepts like "role", "rights", "duties"; "hierarchy", "participant", typical of a community system, allow to use e-learning services in different contexts that help a greater integration between educational services and the information system of the institution. We therefore think that e-learning should evolve (at least) towards "co-learning", meaning not only "collaborative-learning", but (more realistically) "community-learning", i.e., using virtual communities to learn.

1. Introduction

The subject of this work is the conceptual structure of the architecture of e-learning systems when these are employed in complex training activities. We will conduct our research on the basis of our experience in developing an e-learning system that is, at the moment, undergoing for the third time a complete revision with the aim of adjusting it to new tasks and scenarios. Drawn from examples taken from the development of these platforms, we will discuss the effects of metaphors used in e-learning systems, their architecture, the evolution of e-learning processes from a

Please use the following format when citing this chapter:

Colazzo, L., Molinari, A. and Villa, N., 2008, in IFIP International Federation for Information Processing, Volume 281; *Learning to Live in the Knowledge Society*; Michael Kendall and Brian Samways; (Boston: Springer), pp. 329–338.

point of view based on the transfer paradigm (from one teacher to a number of students), shifting to a more realistic paradigm of community-learning [1], that is, upon learning sustained by belonging to a community.

Our research group has been working for years on designing, building, experimenting and managing software platforms in collaborative contexts, at first aimed at learning, and now oriented towards more articulated forms, such as lifelong learning contexts [11] or the integration between the e-learning worlds and the organizational information system. Our first work (*On Line Courses* – 1998) had been created around the metaphor of "course". Each teaching course carried out by a training institution had been coupled to an *"e_course"*. That is to say, the platform enabled us to define abstract structures called just that *"e_courses"*, and to link them to real structures (the courses carried out by a training institution). An *e_course* enabled its three actors (student, tutor and teacher) to access a certain number of communication services (synchronous and asynchronous), creating a virtual space suitable for forms of blended teaching. The three actors had freedom of action in the different and rigid communication services. This system had been for some years the e-learning platform of some of the Institutes of our University and of some of the training environments outside it. The experience gained from *On Line Courses* has shown three aspects that have conditioned the evolution of our present platform.

- An e-Learning system used in a real training context cannot act like an isolated system, on the contrary, it has to be considered part and parcel of the information system of a training institution [2].
- The metaphor of the course used in that first attempt was not capable of covering the needs for communication and cooperation that are carried out in the daily work of a training institution [3].
- The daily interaction of subjects within the community of people who take part in a course, needed higher flexibility in defining roles, rights, duties, permissions, etc., within the environment of this "community" of people.

If we consider "communities" [4, 5, 6, 7, 8] as aggregations of people and participants, it will be clear that in any training (and not only) situation, the aggregation of people in groups is not limited to the frontal training moment and – most of all – does not necessarily have a didactic connotation. A first technological evolution has, therefore, concerned the elimination of this limitation and the introduction of the concept of "community". Both from a conceptual point of view and a technological one, this innovation has lead to a complete rethinking of the e-learning platform, certainly a most arduous and difficult task, seeing that the biggest part of "traditional" e-learning services had already been ready and working for years. This effort has, however, brought about a much bigger range of possibilities and a flexibility of the platform, opening the path to some interesting extensions towards what we call "co-learning", that is, a learning environment based upon the concept of community. This concept, as is evident, crosses over the aspects of pure e-learning in order to face environments of social networking, collaboration, and the user participation in the community, all concepts very dear to new environment of web 2.0.

The work is organised as follows: in section two we will introduce the passage from an e-learning approach to that of co-learning. In section three we will describe briefly the state of the present version of On Line Communities; in section four we will focus our attention on the crucial question of a virtual community environment, that is to say, roles and permissions to be used in the communication services foreseen by the system.

2. E-learning and co-learning

Within the environment of our project of virtual communities the shift from the concept of course to community has shown to be rather natural, as already mentioned in the introduction. The examples of the use of the e-learning platform are various as, for example, the need to be able to invert the teacher – student roles, the possibility to access courses that are not necessarily hinged on academic logics, or the need to aggregate users without passing through the concept of "course". We have avoided to attach external modules to the platform in order to approximate the "community" concept, like some LMS do (i.e., Moodle™). Instead, we have preferred a radical re-write of the platform, in order to natively implement the complex network of concepts involved in the management of a "virtual community", that is in our view just an ordinary aggregation of people, reunited in a virtual place (hence "virtual community") for the most varied reasons and aims. Some examples of virtual communities of our system are:

- Community of a teacher's thesis writers
- Community of the board members of the faculty
- Community of the secretariat of the presidency
- Community of the trade union representatives of the university
- Community of the course "Database Management System" of the Faculty of Engineering
- Community of the course "Database Management System" of the Faculty of Economics
- Community of the recreational circle of the University of Trento

From these examples it can be seen that a platform that supports the activities of the non educational structures, but with other aims, becomes very useful. We wished to equip from the start our e-learning platform with the possibility of integrating it with the various information systems that concentrate around training situations, for example, the information system of personnel, of research, of marketing, etc. Our conviction, reinforced with the passing of time and the experience we are describing here, is indeed that the e-learning system needs to be considered as an important part of the information system of the institution and that as such it is to be fully integrated with the rest of its components. We find it difficult to envisage an non permeability among e-learning platforms and, for example, with the information system of the students secretariat where the greatest part of data concerning users is kept.

The rethinking of our e-learning platform started with these premises in 2002; this meant re-projecting and re-implementing the old system. In the new platform the metaphor of e-course has been abandoned in favour of the more abstract "virtual community"; "*On Line Communities*" (the name of the new system) has substituted the old platform in the teaching at our university, at present in use and subject to

Luigi Colazzo et al.

continuous functional innovations. The substitution with a more abstract metaphor has enabled the system to be used for the need of aggregation and collaboration among a wide range of communities like, for instance, an entire training cycle or a student organisation, thus creating a series of services that support the training activities but which are not necessarily correlated.

The differences between services within a platform of virtual community and a classical one based on the metaphor of course, are noteworthy. To give an example, let us imagine a classical e-learning service such as files upload/download; in this way teachers can make available to the users the Learning Objects associated with a teaching course. In an e-learning system based upon the metaphor of "course", the service is cabled in the architecture of the e-course. In an architectural approach based on "virtual communities" the same service must be separated into (at least) three components:

- The service in the strictest sense that makes the upload and download of a file.
- The operational context in which the service is being used.
- The "collaborative" context in which the service must run, that is to say, the management of the permissions concerning the users (upload, download, change of owner, modification, cancellation, transversal action with other communities, etc.)

The same upload/download service could be used to exchange documents to be discussed within the community of the members of the faculty board. It is not possible to use in this context such roles as "student" and "teacher". The same service should, however, be used for organising for instance a photographic competition of the community of students association, for making available didactic material within the virtual community associated to a course, or for reports between thesis writers and their tutors. This circumstance brings with it problems connected to permissions for the use of the services and the roles of the users who, as already mentioned, cannot at present be any longer limited to traditional "student", "tutor" or "teacher".

In a communitarian logic, the role becomes an identifier ascribed from an administrator (of the community) to a specific user or group of users, with associated permissions (according to the type of community). This is how new concepts come about within the technical terminology of the platform: community, type of community, roles, rights, duties, permissions.

Notice, furthermore, how the experience of "community" is, therefore, transversal in the world of training and it embraces any environment where one wants to aggregate people around a concept of "community" mediated through ICT. This is one of the reasons for which our present platform has recently been chosen by the Autonomous Province of Trento (P.A.T.) for the development of a new technological infrastructure for its Lifelong Learning projects[1]. P.A.T. wishes to set up a platform with a double objective: on the one hand setting up training actions

---

[1] Contract between P.A.T. and University of Trento n, 36672/335

aimed at primary and secondary schools and, on the other, the construction of training projects for employees of the public administration that operates on the territory of the Province. The project has a temporary function of three years with the objective of preparing a software to be tested at least on one pilot project.

At present, the project is in its initial phase, meaning, in the process of defining the requirements of the future Lifelong Learning system (LLLs). Our previous (and still valid) experience urged us to open a serious debate on the impact of virtual communities within a training situation that is very different from an academic one. In this context virtual communities are considered as the extension into the virtual of the underlying social dynamics that is widely articulated.

3. On Line Communities

On Line Communities is an dynamic web application, based on the metaphor of virtual learning communities in a blended approach [9, 10], that guarantees the work organization of cooperative users group named Community.

The topic of Virtual Communities (VC) has been recently explored in the e-learning research field. A virtual community is defined as a communication space that is shared by a certain number of people, for whatever reason not only related to educational aspects. Each community has at least one coordinator, and the participants are not anonymous. It comes spontaneous, in fact, to imagine VC as aggregations of subjects created through ICT tools, as an extension in the virtual of a typically "didactic" environment, like the classroom and the course that is held in it. The system has been designed from scratch, and is able to support whatever user of the system (teacher, student, tutor, lecturer, secretary, external expert, porter, dean, chancellor, consultant etc.) in using real, virtual, face-to-face or distance communication. In this way the construction of virtual communities of different nature becomes possible; i.e. in a community of "Faculty Board" all members (teachers, student representatives, representatives of technical staff) are at the same level, that is to say, they have the same role of participants and only the principal of the faculty takes on a special role.

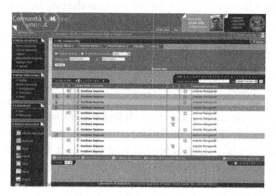

Fig. 1 "On Line Communities", the list of communities

Membership in a community can be obtained automatically, as a right or as a free choice: for example, a student enrolled in the Faculty of Economics and taking the course "Database 2007/2008" is a member of this community by choice and for a limited period of time, while s/he is member of the Faculty community automatically. The participants are non-anonymous and they also have (multiple) roles, each role having specific rights and duties within the community. Thus, the actors of the system participate in several virtual communities at the same time, acting in different roles with different rights and duties.

On Line Communities was released on 2005, but was under the experimentation on a limited number of courses from the end of 2003. The Faculty of Economics started to use the system from September 2005, and now other faculties of our University are experimenting it in many types of courses. The system has about 7.500 registered users, a monthly average of 33.000 accesses, and 700.000 total real accesses with a login on the system in two years; the impact on the whole information system of the University and on the daily life organization of members is not trivial.

"*On Line Communities*" offers different kinds of communication services: whiteboards, forum, chat, calendar, lesson schedule, mail, learning objects download/upload, sticky notes, agenda, syllabus, work areas, etc. All these services are reactive components of the web application and users access them in order to cooperate in organisational and educational processes in various ways.

4. Permission Management within a Virtual Community

The set-up we find ourselves facing is very complex; there is an ever increasing need to provide, in the logic of integrating systems, a single moment of aggregation of the various services in order to enable subjects and systems with different interests (if they are not divergent) to access the same object, acting according to their own competences.

In this section we will present five entities, that make it possible to define in detail the logic on which our system is based for the management of the access to the communities. In the first place, the actor who access the system, called by us *Person*. The person has a *Role* within the *Community*, and the hinge between persons – community – role is manifold: one and the same person can enrol in different communities, in each of which s/he can take on different roles.

The extension of the "course" concept to the more natural one of "community" has completely changed the concept of "user" of an e-learning system (that is, student, tutor, teacher). Not only, if we include a fundamental element in the study of virtual communities, meaning *time*, we will understand how temporal management constitutes an important factor in the basic relationship "person – community – role". A typical example is the evolution of the role of a user from "student" to "thesis writer", to "PhD student" and then perhaps "assistant" or "researcher", while always remaining the same person. Such evolution can be a hard test for the traditional e-learning systems as well as the information system of the students secretariat, requiring the creation of more types of users for the same person, or cancellation of the previous history for the new needs.

As already mentioned, *time* is a factor that radically changes the vision of a co-learning system: the virtual community must guarantee the membership of the subjects and the use of their "community rights/duties" according to the role of that moment, with relative complexity. There is, however, another factor, perhaps even more determining in the passage from e-learning to co-learning and that is "**inheritability**" factor. This factor enormously increases the conceptual, technical and operative complexity of a co-learning system, manifesting itself in at least two central concepts: the roles and the communities. As far as the roles are concerned, it seems evident how the extension of the original system from the metaphor of courses to that of virtual communities, while still remaining in the university teaching environment, has introduced into the system a certain number of new actors with different roles hierarchically related to each other. The hierarchy of roles in a university environment is probably less relevant than in a private or public organisation, but it exists and is important. The further extension to liefelong learning projects makes the group of actors dynamic, that is to say, the system must guarantee the possibility to introduce new actors and, if necessary, change the hierarchy of roles.

This is made necessary by the fact that in liefelong learning experiences the user's contexts of learning can be very different from each other. Some may be based on traditional structures (training courses for the use or a new fiscal regulation), others on very different organisational structures, such as a practising community of professionals who work for the public body in various territorial sectors (like for instance municipal secretaries). Each user has the faculty, after an application process, to accede to a group of *Communities*, every one of which will comprise a series of *Services* aimed at teaching or not. At the moment of registering into a community, each user will be identified with a specific *Role*. Subsequently, all these subjects will need to access the same object through different modalities, called *Permissions*. It becomes clear that to create this manifold way of accessing/roles/permissions would be senseless in a system based on the metaphor of "course", in as much as it is over-dimensioned. Perhaps this is also the reason why many e-learning platforms do not enter into such details. LMS systems, like the excellent Moodle™, while introducing the idea of community do not, however, by nature express the concepts connected with the co-learning metaphor, especially not the effect of propagation which the same presents in case of nesting of the community.

The second concept linked to the problem of inheritability is that of "community"; examples of communities that inherit characteristics from "father" communities are most common in the academic world. Take for instance the "Faculty" community which contains a series of "Degree Course" communities, each of which in turn contains various "courses" within which there can be sub-articulations (for example per alphabetic order of participants when there are many of them in a course). It is clear and, at the same time, natural and hence indispensable, that there should be within the hierarchy mechanisms of propagation of the basic concepts such as "role", "permission", "rights", "duties".

The example of a *Service* could be the register of the lectures where the teacher signs the date, hour and the topic taught in a course; a typical administrative service, useful for counting the hours of a teacher. But if, further to the administrative function, the service also offers the possibility to register the didactic material of each lesson, we will have an interesting mix between support service and didactic service. If we further connect the registry dates with the personal agenda of the teacher, visible (with permissions) to students, we have another integration level, i.e., with the specific "information system" of the community user. At this point, however, inserting such a service into a context of virtual communities, as implemented in our platform, we will need to limit the authority to access such information to a small group of members, for example to teachers. Widening the range, it is possible to imagine guaranteeing the access to the services only to *Persons* who are duly authorised and identified through a specific *Role*. Increasing the complexity of management of virtual *Communities,* each subject or group of subjects will be associated with a *Profile*, that is, a set of *Permissions* that consents to take on a specific *Role* within the community.

The *Service* "register of the lectures" will be viewable by the members of the community according to different angles, be it that of a simple participant, a teacher or a tutor. Indeed, to each *Role* are assigned *Permissions*, for example the role of "teacher" will have assigned permissions for writing, such as changing a line of the lecture register, or associating some type of didactic material to the lectures. In contrast, the student will necessarily have permissions for reading like, for instance, consulting the lecture register. These implications show how a co-learning application like ours will have a degree of intrinsic difficulty much higher than an applicative system that does not need to manage the mechanisms of interaction among members of different communities.

We can sum up the whole debate in the diagram under figure 2, where all previously mentioned entities are represented. At present, in our system there are about fifty different *Roles* that identify each user within each *Community* through the *Permissions* to be used in the various functions offered by each *Service*.

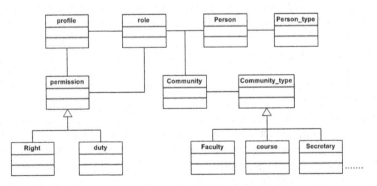

Fig. 2 Relationship between the Entities of On Line Communities

In our system there are, further to a high number of roles, also a series of different *Permissions* that can also be associated in multiple ways to each role and, therefore, the *Person* who accesses the system. One example is the permission for reading the information offered by a service, or that of reading or modifying the information or, again, the possibility for a user to assign in turn permissions to other participants. The latter, obviously is a very critical type of permission, obtainable only by the administrator of the system and the community; a fundamental step within this process is the management of the registered members who participate in our e-learning tools.

The mechanism that we though of using is based on permitting the administrator to validate or not the registration of a user or to block the accesses for the most varied motives, depending even on the faulty use of the system.

5. Conclusions

The paper presents the idea of how the introduction of the concept of virtual community leads to a considerable conceptual change, technical and operative, of an e-learning system, transforming the approach in something that we prefer to call "co-learning". We have specifically highlighted the aspect of community of our approach and how it influences the development and use of a new system no longer oriented towards traditional e-learning but, rather, connected to the concepts of "role", "permit", "rights", duties", "inheritability", "time". Perfectly natural aspects in real life but which have to be formalised somehow in a system oriented at virtual communities and no longer at simple courses.

References

1. Brown A. L., Campione J. C. (1994) Guided discovery in a community of learners, in K. McGilly (a cura di),Classroom lessons: Integrating cognitive theory and classroom practice, Cambridge, MA, MIT Press, 1994, pp. 229-270
2. Colazzo L., Molinari A. (2002), *"From Learning Management Systems To Learning Information Systems: One Possible Evolution Of E-Learning"*, in Proc. Communications, Internet and Information Technology (CIIT) Conference, St. Thomas, USA - November 18-20, 2002
3. Colazzo L., Haller H., Molinari A. (2007) *WAYS – What Are You Studying? A community tool for learners on the move*, Proc. of ED-MEDIA 2007, edit by Craig Montgomerie & Jane Seale,June 25- June 29, 2007; Vancouver BC, Canada
4. Jones S. G., Cybersociety, Sage, London, 1995.
5. Jones S. G., Virtual Culture, Sage, London, 1997.
6. Lévy P., Qu'est-ce que le virtuel?, La Découverte, Paris, 1995 (trad. It. Il virtuale, Raffaello Cortina, Milano, 1997).
7. Rheingold H., The Virtual Community, 1993 (trad. It. Comunità virtuali, Sperling & Kupfer, Milano, 1994).

8.   Turkle S., Life on Screen. Identity in the Age of Internet, New York, Simon & Shuster (trad. It. La vita sullo schermo. Nuove identità e relazioni sociali nell'epoca di Internet, Apogeo, Milano, 1997).

9.   Brunn H. G., Frank C., (2002) *Online Communication: A Success Factor for Blended Learning,* in World Conference on E-Learning in Corp., Govt., Health., & Higher Ed., Vol. 2002, Issue. 1, 2002, pp. 1477-1480

10. Franks P., (2002) *Blended Learning: What is it? How does it impact student retention and performance?* in World Conference on E-Learning in Corp., Govt., Health., & Higher Ed., Vol. 2002,Issue. 1, 2002.

11. Fieldhouse R. (2000) *Lifelong Learning – Apprendimento lungo tutto l'arco della vita,* (Glossario dell'educazione degli adulti in Europa pp 25-26)

Chapter 13

Workshops

Workshop: A Creative Introduction to Programming with Scratch

Ralf Romeike
University of Potsdam
Department of Computer Science
A.-Bebel-Str. 89
14482 Potsdam, Germany
romeike@cs.uni-potsdam.de

Abstract. This workshop introduces a creative way of teaching computer science. Creativity will be regarded as essential for CS and for motivation and interests of students. The relevance of creativity for CS education will be discussed; criteria for creative CS lessons and a creativity teaching framework are presented. Together we will run through an introduction to programming while exploring and being creative with the programming environment. Scratch offers an intuitive way into programming and leaves lots of space for creativity. Participants will leave the workshop with ideas how to design creative lessons and familiarity in the use of Scratch.

Intended audience

Secondary and early post-secondary CS educators who are interested in challenging their students by applying creativity in the CS classroom and/or want to get to know Scratch.

Presenter Biography

Ralf Romeike is a research associate at the University of Potsdam, Germany as well as a teacher for computer science at a high-school in Potsdam. He studied computer science and music and focuses his research interest on the use and encouragement of creativity in computer science education.

The teaching example used in the workshop has been conducted and evaluated by the presenter. Versions of this workshop have been hold previously by the

Please use the following format when citing this chapter:

Romeike, R., 2008, in IFIP International Federation for Information Processing, Volume 281; *Learning to Live in the Knowledge Society*; Michael Kendall and Brian Samways; (Boston: Springer), pp. 341–344.

presenter at two major German conferences for computer science teachers and received good feedback.

Materials provided

Each participant receives both a paper and electronic copy of (1) detailed handouts to be used during the lecture portions of the workshop, (2) descriptions of the creative teaching technique, creativity criteria and the underlying theory (3) A lesson outline for the lesson unit that can be applied in class-room right away, including working sheets (4) an installation routine for Scratch plus material from the Scratch developers (5) ideas, ideas, ideas.

Audio/Visual and Computer requirements

Ideally, participants will have wireless internet access and laptop power at each seat, but the workshop could proceed without these as internet use will not be central to the workshop. The practical part of the workshop will contain exercises and challenges to be solved in Scratch. We will also need a digital projector (for presenters) and a flipchart with pens or blackboard (for collecting ideas). Windows and Mac laptops will be supported.

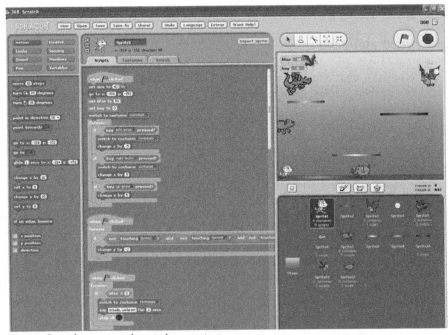

Fig. 1: Scratch programming environment

Laptop

Recommended
Not everybody will need to have a laptop.

Maximum number of participants

Up to 40 participants should be fine. Depending on the facilities even more than that should be possible, just not as cozy.

Other critical information

The teaching unit central to the workshop was awarded the 1st prize of the teachers instruction competition of the German Computer Science Association (GI) 2007.

Brief description of what will be done in the workshop

This workshop introduces a creative way of teaching computer science. Creativity will be regarded as essential for CS and for motivation and interests of students. The relevance of creativity for CS education will be discussed; criteria for creative CS lessons [1] and a creativity teaching framework [2] are presented. Together we will run through an introduction to programming while exploring and being creative with the programming environment. Scratch offers an intuitive way into programming and leaves lots of space for creativity. Participants will leave the workshop with ideas how to design creative lessons and familiarity in the use of Scratch.

Creativity

How shall an educator expect new and original achievements from his students? Boden [3] describes two aspects of creative achievements. Historical creativity (H-creativity) describes ideas which are novel and original in the sense that nobody has had them before. Something that is fundamentally novel to the individual Boden describes as psychologically creative (P-creativity). In an educational context the latter is more interesting and can be aimed for in the classroom. We want to call something creative if it leads to personal new, unique and useful ideas, solutions or insights (cp. [4, 5]). As summarized by [6], in the classroom creativity can enhance learning through improved motivation, alertness, curiosity, concentration and achievement.

Scratch

The visual programming (mini) language Scratch was originally designed for young students to develop 21st century skills [7]. It allows creating animations, games and other programs by "clicki ng together" programming constructs represented as building blocks. Nevertheless, due to its intuitive appearance and usability it is used in computer club houses, high schools and even in introductory programming college courses. We chose Scratch because it emphasizes practical learning of fundamental CS concepts and at the same time supports the idea of fostering creativity in CS classes. Mini languages are said to provide an insight into programming and teach algorithmic thinking for general computer science in an intuitive, simple but powerful way [8]. Thus Scratch meets the needs for the intended purpose.

References

1. Romeike, R. Kriterien kreativen Informatikunterrichts. in 12. GI-Fachtagung Informatik und Schule - INF© 2007." 2007. Siegen, Germany: Kßen.
2. Romeike, R. Applying Creativity in CS High School Education - Criteria, Teaching Example and Evaluation. in the 7th Baltic Sea Conference on Computing Education Research, Koli Calling. 2007.
3. Boden, M.A., The creative mind: myths & mechanisms. 1990, London: Basic Books.
4. Runco, M.A. and I. Chand, Cognition and Creativity. Educational Psychology Review, 1995. 7(3): p. 243-267.
5. Kaufman, J.C. and R.J. Sternberg, Creativity. Change: The Magazine of Higher Learning, 2007. 39(4): p. 55-60.
6. Fasko, D., Education and creativity. Creativity Research Journal, 2000. 13(3-4): p. 317-327.
7. Maloney, B., Kafai, Rusk, Silverman, Resnick (2004): Scratch: A Sneak Preview. IEEE Computer Society, 104-109.
8. Brusilovsky, P., Calabrese, E., Hvorecky, J., Kouchnirenko, A. and Miller, P. (1997): Mini-languages: a way to learn programming principles. Education and Information Technologies, 2, 65-83.

Using Alnuset to construct the notions of equivalence and equality in algebra

Giampaolo Chiappini, Bettina Pedemonte and Elisabetta Robotti
Istituto per le Tecnologie Didattiche – CNR
V. De Marini 6, 16149 Genova, Italy
{chiappini, pedemonte, robotti}@itd.cnr.it
http://www.itd.cnr.it

Abstract. We analyse the role of technology in the development of algebraic crucial knowledge and competences, such as those involved in the comprehension and use of the notions of equivalence and equality. The hypothesis of our research is that technology can be exploited to make available new operative and representative possibilities which structure a new phenomenological space to investigate the algebraic knowledge and to improve the teaching and learning processes of algebra. We analyse the characteristics of the phenomenological space structured by Alnuset, a system developed by the authors within ReMath European project. Through examples taken from experimentations that we have performed with Alnuset, we illustrate and discuss how such characteristics can be exploited to develop competences and knowledge in the algebraic domain and to improve the teaching of algebra.

1   Introduction

What does it mean that two algebraic expressions are equivalent? How can the equal sign between two algebraic expressions be interpreted? Can an algebraic expression be equal to another one without being equivalent to it? What is the role of the universal quantifier and the existential quantifier in characterising different meanings that the equal sign can assume in a proposition? How can the transformation of an algebraic expression and the solution of an equation be interpreted?

Answering these questions might not be easy for students, as well as justifying appropriately their replies or fulfilling tasks that require a good mastery of the notions of equivalence and equality involved in these questions [1,2]. In the current teaching practice, students mainly learn to use algebraic rules properly, but they often show difficulties both in justifying them and in assigning meanings to the previously mentioned notions. In order to develop these competencies changes and new levels of mediation in teaching are necessary. A first essential change might

Please use the following format when citing this chapter:

Chiappini, G., Pedemonte, B. and Robotti, E., 2008, in IFIP International Federation for Information Processing, Volume 281; *Learning to Live in the Knowledge Society*; Michael Kendall and Brian Samways; (Boston: Springer), pp. 345–348.

consist in focusing the students' attention either on the numerical quantities indicated by a literal symbol or expression or on the numerical quantities that can condition the truth value of an equality. We name this kind of algebra as *algebra of quantities*. We observe that currently it could be hard to work out this change because available tools are not quite suitable to mediate the relationship between algebraic expressions and equalities on one hand, and numerical quantities on the other. Moreover, the current approach to algebra teaching based on formal operations should be deeply modified and integrated with algebra of quantities. The main purpose of such change is the modification of current algebraic manipulation teaching, mainly centred on learning and reinforcement of algebraic transformation rules through a drill and practice pedagogical strategy. We think that the change should favour both the solution of cognitive problems involved in the construction of schemes for algebraic transformations and the development of semiosis processes to assign meaning to the performed transformations and to the involved algebraic phenomena. In order to work out these changes and to integrate algebra of quantities with algebra of formal operations, specific teaching mediation tools are necessary. We have designed these tools and we have embedded and integrated them in the Alnuset system. In this workshop we discuss the role of Alnuset in structuring a new phenomenological space to favour the development of algebraic notions of equivalence and equality.

2   The Alnuset system

The Alnuset system (Algebra of NUmerical SETs) has been developed within the ReMath European project (IST-4 -26751) to allow the development of algebra of quantities in school practice and its integration with a deeply innovated teaching of algebra of formal operations. This system is oriented to students of lower and upper secondary school (from 13 to 17 yrs). Alnuset includes three closely integrated components - the Algebraic Line component, the Symbolic Manipulator component and the Cartesian Plan component. In this workshop we refer to the first two components designed to favour the integrated development of algebra of quantities and algebra of formal operations respectively.

The Algebraic Line Component

The Algebraic Line structures a new phenomenological space where processes, relationships and objects of algebraic nature can be investigated through a quantitative approach. Through digital technology the traditional numbers line was characterized with new operative and representative possibilities, namely:
- with three different editors to construct and represent algebraic expressions on the line, specifically with a geometrical editor, a linear editor and a bidimensional editor;
- with the drag of mobile points associated to letters on the line which determines the automatic movement of points of expressions containing the dragged letters on the same line;
- with a graphic and computational model to determine the roots of polynomials;
- with graphical models to define and validate the truth set of algebraic propositions.

The user can directly and dynamically control these new operative and representative possibilities exploiting their visual, spatial and motor experience. These possibilities can be used to explore what expressions and propositions denote within the considered numerical domain.

The Symbolic Manipulator Component

The Symbolic Manipulator structures a new phenomenological space where the norms, the rules and the conventions of algebra can be investigated in order to structure an idea of Algebra as the science of formal operations, namely, as the theory and practice of formal operations that preserve equivalence in the performed transformations. This space is characterized by new operative and representative possibilities such as:

- exploring the hierarchical structure of the expression or proposition that has to be manipulated;
- exploring the rules of transformation of the interface that can be applied on each selected structure;
- exploring the effects that the applications of a rule produce;
- verifying that in the performed transformation the equivalence has been preserved;
- creating a new rule of transformation, once it has been proved using the rules available with the interface;

These new operative and representative possibilities can be exploited to construct general schemes for algebraic transformations and to develop a theoretical approach to algebraic transformation that can be accessible to students.

3   The construction of meanings for the notion of equality and of equivalence in algebra

In order to discuss the usefulness of the phenomenological space structured by the Algebraic Line of Alnuset as referred to the development of the notion of algebraic equality, let us present, as an example, the following task taken from our experimentation.

Consider the two following equalities $2*x+3*x=5*x$ e $2*x+3=5*x$. Write how you can interpret them Represent the expressions $2*x+3$, $2*x+3*x$ e $5*x$ on the algebraic line of Alnuset and use the editor to construct the two equalities. Exploit the representative possibilities of Alnuset to verify the previously given answer and to eventually modify it.

Many students of the 9-10 grade interpret the first equality as correct and the second one as wrong; few students are able to interpret them respectively as identity and as equation. In the activity with the algebraic line of Alnuset some representative phenomena useful to favour the development the understanding of algebraic equality can emerge. The first phenomenon concerns the representation of the expressions on the algebraic line (see Figure 1.1 and Figure 1.2). Every point on the line is characterized by a post-it that contains all the constructed expressions which indicate the value of that point. We observe that the two expressions 2x+3x and 5x correspond to a same point on the algebraic line and they always belong to the same post-it when the mobile point associated to the variable x is dragged along the line (Figure 1.1). The expression 2x+3 belongs to the same post-it of 5*x only when the mobile point of the variable x is dragged on the numeric value 1 of the line (Figure 1.2). The drag of the mobile point associated to the variable x can be a useful way to experience what the expressions indicate, while the post-it can be a useful representation to explore the value of variables that make their result equal.

A second important representative phenomenon emerges when the two equalities 2x+3x=5x and 2x+3=5x are inserted in the Truth Sets window of the algebraic line environment through the algebraic editor (see Figure 1.3 and Figure 1.4)

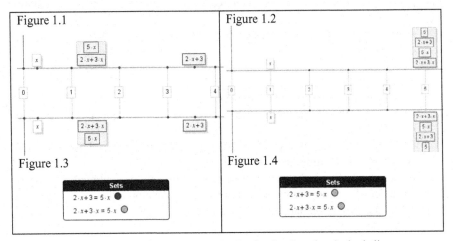

Fig. 1. The representation of the expressions 5x, 2x+3x, 2x+3 on the algebraic line

In the Truth Sets window the two equalities are associated to a ball that turns red or green according to the truth value of these equalities (respectively false and true). The truth value of these equalities and of their corresponding balls can be conditioned by the movement of the variable point x on the algebraic line. In our example, when the mobile point x is dragged on the value 1, both the balls of the two equalities are green (Figure 1.4), while when it is dragged on any another value of the line the ball corresponding to the equation 2x+3=5x is red and the ball corresponding to the identity 2x+3x=5x remains green (Figure 1.3).

4. References

1. Arzarello F., Bazzini L., Chiappini G., (2001), A model for analyzing algebraic process of thinking, in Sutherland R., Rojano T., Bell A. (Eds), *Perspectives on school algebra*, Kluwer Academic Publisher, p. 61-82.
2. Sfard, A., Linchevski, L. (1992) Equations and inequalities: processes without objects? In Geeslin W. & Ferrini-Mundy J. (Ed.), *Proceedings of the Sixteenth Annual Conference of the International Group for the Psychology of Mathematics Education PMEXVI*, 3, Durham, NH: University of New Hampshire, p.136.

PITO: A Children-Friendly Interface for Security Tools

Luigi Catuogno

Dip. di Informatica ed Applicazioni, Università di Salerno
Via Ponte Don Melillo, 84 084 - Fisciano (SA) - ITALY
luicat@dia.unisa.it

Abstract. Current Operating Systems and user applications provide several security tools that are designed to automatically handle a set of well-known events and threats, whereas they inform the user that something potentially dangerous is happening an ask her to take a decision. Since we believe that this learning process could have a relevant educational value for children, we present, in this paper, an interface for Security tools featured by operating systems, user applications or third party security suites. The interface, that has been designed as "Pito": a digital pet , is purposed to allow children that use computer to be softly introduced in security issues that usually occur when navigating the Internet. Alerts notified by the underlying security tools are mapped as some simple events into the Pito's world. These events change the state of Pito and, according to the current state, the young user is asked to do some action in order to keep Pito's sane and happy, that is to keep safe the computer.

1 Introduction

Current operating systems and applications provide a set of security tools like firewalls, virus scanners, spam filters, diagnostic facilities and so on[1] as well as these critical features are provided by many commercial *security suites*[2][3][4] that have been proposed as an "all inclusive" solution to main security threats.

These security tools (ST), are designed to automatically handle a well-known set of events (in-coming of known virus and intrusion patterns) and, moreover, in presence of some borderline events or user action that may be potentially dangerous, the ST inform the user and possibly ask her if the event (or action) that arisen the event can be approved (confirmed) or not (*e.g.*, execution of an application that have just been downloaded, allowing an application to connect somewhere over the

Please use the following format when citing this chapter:

Catuogno, L., 2008, in IFIP International Federation for Information Processing, Volume 281; *Learning to Live in the Knowledge Society*; Michael Kendall and Brian Samways; (Boston: Springer), pp. 349–352.

network, installation of an unsigned device driver and so on). Information produced by STs notifies to the user what is happening in the computer and also educates her about risks and possible consequences of her actions and moreover, it also suggests the proper behavior. ST's notifications are published through different interfaces *e.g.*, message boxes, log file, blinking icons, etc. and are thought to be understood by adult users, that can learn the meaning of messages, that can easily read manuals and are smart enough to reasonably assess the arisen issues.

On the other hand, such some interfaces, are not suitable for young users that often are not able to understand what is happening. Therefore, the usual security infrastructures, even if well configured, are inadequate to protect Children on line. For this reason, the main kind of security measure purposed to young users consists of so-called *Parental Control Systems* (PCS). These products, typically included in the applications used to access the Internet (or even embedded into the operating system)[5], allow parents to monitor or limit what a child can see or do. Parental Control Systems may allow for the blocking of various websites, such as those containing pornography, or other undesired contents. Thus, parents configure the software through a black list, or a through set of rules. Instead of STs, Parental control systems work rather transparently; hence they do neither inform the user nor educate her. In other words, a traditional PCS does not introduce the young user to the problem of security, does not teach him that something of *strange* is happening, that some decision have to be taken and, consequently, which action are suggested to solve the problem.

In this paper we present a "child interface" for security tools that introduces the young users to security issues commonly arisen when somebody uses computers and navigates the internet. Instead of simply rewriting text in ST's message boxes with more simple words, we designed our interface as a Digital Pet[6]. In our project, a small character, named "Pito", lives in his world inside an application window. A configurable subset of security events is mapped to a set of events that happen in the Pito's world and, on the other hand, what Pito does in his world is mapped to a configurable set of security actions in the "real world". Let us to see an example. Suppose that parents agree that their children do not use the computer more than two hours. Thus they configure Pito to look tired when the time is going out. When Pito looks tired, the children simply bring him to bed and, in such a way, they shut down the system. We point out that Pito does not replace a PCS, but integrates it where parents wish to introduce a certain level of *free will* in educating their children to correctly use computers and internet.

In Section 2 we give an overview of the project and describe the architecture of Pito. In Section 3 we discuss some implementation issues of our first *proof-of-concept* prototype. Finally, in Section 4, we outline the work we still have to do.

2   Project Overview

The architecture of Pito is composed of three components: the sensors, the engine and the interface.

A sensor is a stand-alone agent purposed to listen a specific event (*e.g.*, an incoming connection, the arrival of an e-mail message). Whenever the event is arisen, the sensor forward it to the engine. Note that, sensor are designed to be specific for the underlying operating system, security suite or applications and report the event in a general way to the engine. Thus for example, we can have an anti-spam sensor, plugged in our favorite mail-agent, which reports the arrival of a spam messages (that may carry a fishing attack or simply offending contents). Different mail-agents can be handled by means of their own APIs but all respective sensors forwards events to the engine through the same protocol. Moreover, a sensor could parse system logs and reports some relevant events, warning or errors (*e.g.*, disk full, service failure, etc.) as well as a sensor could be plugged in the firewall in order to handle requests about inbound or outbound connections.

When launched, Pito is in its initial state (*quiet*). The events arisen by the sensors and the actions done by the user may change this state. The engine updates the current state according the in-coming events or actions performed by the user. The way in which the Pito's state changes is defined, through a simple set of rules by means of a configuration panel that allows parents to configure the desired behavior of Pito with respect to a certain set of events and actions. Look at the following scenario as an example. Suppose that Parents configured the anti-spam engine to accept messages with a spam score less than a security threshold and silently discard messages with a score over a higher threshold. Whenever a message with an intermediate score is received, the sensor alerts the engine that a *potentially* spam message has arrived. The engine changes the state of Pito to *scared* showing a mail icon. Now, the user has been perceived that a potentially dangerous message is in the mailbox. Hence she can choice either to inspect it or erase it directly by putting the letter into the Pito's trash can. Moreover, whenever the crash of an OS service occurs so that the system becomes instable, the state of Pito is changed to *sick*. Hence the user has to give medicines to Pito, e.g. all open applications are closed and finally, the system reboots.

The interface maps the Pito's state and occurring events through a small application window on the desktop. Each state is mapped to a given expression of the Pito's face as well as, any configured event is showed as something happening into the Pito's world. The interface also provides some controls that feature allowed actions.

3   Implementing PITO

We are working on a prototype for the Windows operating system. We designed Pito as a WMI[7] based application. We are implementing sensors as WMI providers that present themselves to the engine through a CIM[8] classes and events. This choice makes the integration into the operating system and in many native applications transparent and simple. In fact, handlers of relevant system events, together with newly written providers that handle events and data featured by third party application, lay underneath the same general API, making the Pito engine independent to the current system configuration. Moreover, many commercial

Luigi Catuogno

security tools for Windows XP already feature their own WMI provider in order to be compliant to the Windows Security Center, making the implementation and testing of Pito in real-world conditions easy. The outlook of the Pito's window is currently rather poor. A remarkable restyling of the whole interface is currently in progress.

4 Conclusion

In this paper we outline the design of a children-friendly interface to the security tools embedded in applications and operating systems. This interface has been designed as a "Digital Pet". A proof-of-concept implementation of Pito is currently in progress for the Windows Operating system. There are some important aspects of this work that need to be investigated carefully. First, will young users "accept" the presence of Pito and will they use it? Second, will parents agree the approach we suggest? And third, will Pito effectively make conscious the children about security issues? Our first tests with a group of children form the primary school (10 years old) have given encouraging results. We are designing a set of more rigorous experiments with 8-10 years old children (and their parents) in order to validate our approach. These experiments, together with a fully featured prototype will be hopefully discussed in a future work.

References

[1] Microsoft Corporation, 2007, *Windows XP service pack2 (Part 3): The new Security Center*, Technical Article no. 889737, http://msdn.microsoft.com
[2] Symantec Corporation, 2008, *Norton Internet Security*, http://www.symantec.com
[3] Sophos Corporation, 2008, *Sophos Anti-Virus*, http://www.sophos.com
[4] Sophos Corporation, 2008, *Sophos PureMessage*, http://www.sophos.com
[5] Microsoft Corporation, 2006, Microsoft Windows Vista Security Advancements, white paper, http://msdn.microsoft.com
[6] Wikipedia Foundation, 2008, *Digital Pets*, http://en.wikipedia.org/wiki/Digital_Pets
[7] Microsoft Corporation, 2000, *Windows Management Instrumentation*, Technical article number MS-811553, http://msdn.microsoft.com
[8] Distributed Management Task Force, 2007, *CIM schema version 2.15*, http://www.dmtf.org

Chapter 14

Posters

WAPE - a system for distance learning of programming

Victor Kasyanov and Elena Kasyanova

A.P. Ershov Institute of Informatics Systems / Novosibirsk State University
Novosibirsk, 630090, Russia
kvn@iis.nsk.su

Summary

A challenging research goal is the development of advanced Web-based educational applications that can offer some amount of adaptivity and intelligence. In the paper the WAPE project being under development as an intelligent and adaptive environment for supporting distance learning of programming is presented.

The WAPE system supports users of four types: students, instructors, lecturers and administrators. Users access WAPE through a standard Web-browser, which present HTML-document provided by the HTTP server on the server side. After authorization of the user as a student, the appropriate menu shell is opened. The WAPE system supports the following tree levels of learning process:

(1) when a student learns theoretical material in a specific domain with the help of hypertext textbook,

(2) when the system tests student's conceptual knowledge concerning theoretical material learned,

(3) when a student under the control of the system solves the practical educational problems (projects).

The third level is assumed to be the main one in using the system; in order to learn a course supported by WAPE a student has to perform several individual projects: tasks and exercises.

Any course supported by WAPE is based on a knowledge model which consists of a finite set of concepts and some relations on it. For any concept s a model of a student x includes a grade of knowledge that x has on s. We use four grades which divide all students on experts, advanced students, beginners or novices with respect to s. The student model is used to provide the student x with the most suitable individually planned sequence of concepts to learn and the projects to solve. For example, every time when the student x is going to solve a project the system checks whether all prerequisite concepts are sufficiently known by x. If not, the student x cannot begin to solve the project.

Please use the following format when citing this chapter:

Kasyanov, V. and Kasyanova, E., 2008, in IFIP International Federation for Information Processing, Volume 281; *Learning to Live in the Knowledge Society*; Michael Kendall and Brian Samways; (Boston: Springer), pp. 355–356.

Many adaptive systems detect the fact that the student reads some information to update the estimate of his knowledge. Some of them also include reading time or the sequence of read pages to enhance this estimation. While this is a viable approach, it has the disadvantage that it is difficult to measure the knowledge a student gains by "reading" an HTML page. In contrast we decided to take into account neither the information about visited pages nor the student's path through the hypertext books. Instead we use only the projects (tasks and exercises) and the tests for updating the student knowledge model.

The WAPE system uses three problem solving support technologies: intelligent analysis of student solutions, interactive problem solving support, and example-based problem solving support.

For intelligent analysis of student solutions to every task are assigned a set of program tests and a set of inference rules. The program tests are used to decide whether a program constructed by a student is a correct solution of the task or not, find out what exactly is wrong or incomplete. The inference rules are used to possibly identify which missing or incorrect knowledge may be responsible for the error and to update the student model when the program constructed is an incorrect solution of the project.

Instead of waiting for the final solution of a task, the WAPE system can provide a student with intelligent help on each step of problem solving. The level of help can vary: from signaling about a wrong understanding of the statement of the task, to giving the next suitable learning goal.

Tests are questions that the system uses for testing student's conceptual knowledge concerning theoretical material learned. We use tests of three types (single choice, multiple choice and textual tests) and distinguish three types of tests: verbal, quantitative and analytical questions. All tests which are aimed to check the student's knowledge related to the same concept are grouped into so-called test space which is used for random generation of sequence of tests for concept as a path from an input test to an output test.

One of the main issues in development of advance technology learning environment is a gap between pedagogues and technicians. The WAPE project is aimed to overcome the gap. Lecturers without programming skills will be able to create adaptive educational hypermedia courses supported by the WAPE system.

Topic Maps for Learning Design

Giovanni Adorni, Mauro Coccoli, Gianni Vercelli and Giuliano Vivanet
DIST - University of Genoa
Viale Causa 13, 16145 Genova, Italy
{adorni, mauro.coccoli, gianni.vercelli, giuliano.vivanet}@unige.it

Summary

Topic Maps (TM) are an ISO standard whose aim is describing knowledge structures and associating them with information resources. XML Topic Maps (XTM) is an XML-based encoding scheme to represent topic maps and similar knowledge structures. In this poster, TM and XTM are proposed as a knowledge representation system to be exploited in e-learning environments for a suited integration with semantic web technologies. They may be a useful tool to facilitate the design of learning contents and their delivery in different contexts.

The most fundamental elements in the TM paradigm are *Topic*, *Association* and *Occurrence*. According to ISO definition, a topic is a symbol used within a topic map to represent one *subject*, in order to allow *statements* to be made about the subject, that can be "*anything whatsoever, regardless of whether it exists or has any other specific characteristics, about which anything whatsoever may be asserted by any means whatsoever*". In substance a subject is anything about which the creator of a topic map chooses to discourse; for instance an object, an event, a place, a name, a concept, etc. An association represents a relationship between two or more topics. An occurrence is a representation of a relationship between a subject and an information resource.

Therefore, as it can be observed in the poster, two layers can be identified into this paradigm: a *knowledge layer* that represents topics and their relationships and an *information layer* that describes information resources. The existence of two different layers is one of the most interesting features of this model; in fact the same topic map could be used to represent different sets of information resources, or different topic maps could be used to represent the same resource repository.

Each topic can be featured by any number of *names* (and *variants* for each name); by any number of occurrences and by its *association role*, that is a representation of the involvement of a subject in a relationship represented by an association. All these

Please use the following format when citing this chapter:

Adorni, G., Coccoli, M., Vercelli, G. and Vivanet, G., 2008, in IFIP International Federation for Information Processing, Volume 281; *Learning to Live in the Knowledge Society*; Michael Kendall and Brian Samways; (Boston: Springer), pp. 357–358.

features are statements and have a *scope* that represents the context within which a statement is valid. Using scopes it is possible to remove ambiguity about topics; to provide different points of view on the same topic (based on users' profile) and/or to modify each statement depending on users' language, etc. Topics, topic names, occurrences, associations and associations' roles require a *type* element (becoming instances of classes). These classes are also topics, which might, again, be instances of other classes. Therefore, to solve ambiguity issues, each subject, represented by a topic, is identified by a *subject identifier* (usually a URI, similarly to RDF). This unambiguous identification of subjects is also used in TM to *merge* topics that, through these identifiers, are known to have the same subject. This feature could be used in order to share the knowledge and to solve redundancy issues.

The proposed scenario is considering the use of the TM paradigm as a tool for the design of educational paths and contents. This standard could be profitably considered as a mean for describing the table of contents of a course as well as the outline of a lesson according to the logical structure of the course itself. In addition, semantic information is stored within the TM in a well formed form and in a standard language, thus it can be easily exported over the Internet and many systems can re-use and interoperate with the XTM representation of the topic map. Moreover, the layered structure also enables authors to define different maps based on a common repository of resources so that personalized learning paths can be defined while the contents at the occurrence level remain the same and different educational strategies can be implemented.

In the context of education, TM can be used as a means to express knowledge and to organize and retrieve information in a more efficient and meaningful way. According to Koper *"an important question related to the educational semantic web, is how to represent a course in a formal, semantic way so that it can be interpreted and manipulated by computers as well as humans"*. The semantic representation of learning courses opens the possibility to solve parts of some problems such as the interoperability of educational contents; the development of flexible, problem-based, non-linear and personalized web-based courses; the building and sharing catalogues of learning and teaching patterns; the adaptation to learners' profile and the semantic research capabilities.

Systematic Exploration
of Informatics Systems

Peer Stechert

Universität Siegen, FB12 DIE, Hölderlinstr. 3, 57076, Siegen, Germany,
stechert@die.informatik.uni-siegen.de

Summary

Our research is part of a broader research study towards an education model for understanding of informatics systems at upper secondary level. There are three characteristics specific to informatics systems: their observable behaviour, their internal structure, and implementation aspects. Informatics systems represent networked fundamental ideas of informatics. Thus, networking these concepts within a mental model is essential to understand informatics systems. Observation exercises and systematic exploration have been identified as a means to overcome the cognitive barrier build by complex informatics systems.

Analysis of international curricula and recommendations has shown a lack of strategies to understand the behaviour of informatics systems based on informatics concepts. Thus, we created a sequence of steps to explore an informatics system systematically. Main objective was to make students cope with informatics systems in a conscious way. Hypotheses about intended behaviour of the system avoid trial-and-error approaches. We decided to substantiate the systematic exploration with learning theory on problem orientation, educational experiments, and inclusion of different cognitive processes. The steps of the systematic exploration are:

1. Answer questions about the intended behaviour of a given informatics system (remember; factual knowledge),

2. Outline the procedure for conducting the experiment (understanding; procedural),

3. Document the data observed (apply; factual knowledge),

4. Examine data and identify informatics concepts, e.g., access control (analyze; conceptual knowledge),

5. Establish a set of special cases to be tested and evaluate them (evaluate; conceptual knowledge),

6. Create a series of hypotheses for using the informatics system in a real-world or more complex scenario (create; factual knowledge).

Please use the following format when citing this chapter:

Stechert, P., 2008, in IFIP International Federation for Information Processing, Volume 281; *Learning to Live in the Knowledge Society*; Michael Kendall and Brian Samways; (Boston: Springer), pp. 359–360.

In a first field study we conducted a unit on strategies for understanding of informatics systems. In the informatics course at upper secondary level, 23 students at age 17 have taken part. There have been 13 lessons; three lessons per week. The systematic exploration had to be refined according to a formative evaluation including test, a questionnaire of acceptance by the learner, and an interview with the supervising teacher. One difficulty for students was to combine views on behaviour and internal structure. Searching for the reasons of these difficulties, we see two main aspects: on the one hand, students have no experience with exercises as systematic exploration, so it has to be integrated into the curriculum in more detail and by stating the relevance more precisely. On the other hand, some difficulties could also be caused by typical cognitive barriers and misconceptions of object-oriented modelling. To get more insights, the strategy was investigated applying the Think Aloud method. There are two kinds of results: Firstly, we identified formal problems in the description of the systematic exploration, e.g. terms were unclear, and some focal points of the systematic exploration were not understood. Secondly, we got insights about students' methodologies while they explored an informatics system.

As a last step of the development and refinement cycle, systematic exploration of informatics systems was part of a second curriculum intervention, where the students had to explore two systems given two different schemata: First, the refined, but still abstract steps as described above were given. For a further systematic exploration, a contextualized variation was given. We observed different methodologies: A first group divided the GUI into different parts, which belong together, e.g. belonging to the roles administrator, user, and guest. They described them from the left to the right according to the reading direction. A second group sorted parts of the GUI by programming elements as labels, text fields, and buttons. However, there was anecdotic evidence that the new introduction of the methodology into the classroom, which put more emphasis on the necessity of hypotheses, was successful. During the description of relations between observable elements of the GUI, a student asked: "When can we try out, whether our conjecture holds?" So, the students took making hypotheses more serious, which is necessary for experiments and avoids trial-and-error approaches.

Development of E-Learning Design Criteria with Secure Realization Concepts

Christian J. Eibl and Sigrid E. Schubert
Didactics of Informatics and E-Learning, University of Siegen
Hölderlinstr. 3, D-57076 Siegen, Germany
{eibl | schubert}@die.informatik.uni-siegen.de

Summary

Information security is a major quality factor for informatics systems and essential for enduring web-based offerings like e-learning. The term e-learning is used in practice in many different ways such that in parts even simple web pages with downloadable files like lecture notes are considered as e-learning. To get a definition of well acceptable and facilitating e-learning systems really focusing on the learning process, the underlying research project, first, investigates requirements from affiliated disciplines like educational science. This resulted in demands for equal opportunities (A1), social support by co-operation and communication facilities (A2), activities of students as important steps of the learning process (A3), priority to meet learning objectives (A4), flexible learning with sufficient adaptability to different target groups (A5), and integration of e-learning in an existing learning environment (A6). Since every criterion applied in implementing such a system increases the system's complexity, this undoubtedly leads to further demands for information security investigation to meet newly emerging security issues. Hence, to manage this complexity resp. high complex software creation in general aspects of the research field of software engineering are included in the examination of design criteria for e-learning.

Demands stated by software engineering are mostly focusing on good software quality which can be classified in a structured set of criteria and sub-criteria as follows: functionality (B1), reliability (B2), usability (B3), efficiency (B4), maintainability (B5), and portability (B6). Especially usability and functionality demands are important for not restraining learners in their learning process and provide them with an easy to use interface, such that interactions with the learning system are possible without distracting them by technical issues. Maintainability and portability give options to adapt the system appropriately to different target groups and allow reactions to changing infrastructures.

Please use the following format when citing this chapter:

Eibl, C.J. and Schubert, S.E., 2008, in IFIP International Federation for Information Processing, Volume 281; *Learning to Live in the Knowledge Society*; Michael Kendall and Brian Samways; (Boston: Springer), pp. 361–362.

Considering privacy aspects like learning process and progress as well as personal data like different kinds of relations among learners, it gets obvious that security aspects must be considered accordingly. In this research project we consider e-learning systems to be secure if they guarantee availability (C1), integrity (C2), and confidentiality (C3) for authorized users where all of these aspects are given with respect to sufficient access control mechanisms (C4). These aspects must be managed from a technical point of view, e.g., for an appropriate infrastructure with sufficient control and detection mechanisms, as well as from an organizational point of view where privileges are assigned according to planned activities of different roles in the system.

Based on interdisciplinary requirements of education and informatics we propose a theoretical realization of design criteria of appropriate security architectures and give a prototype for the practical realization of all stated criteria in form of a proxy server for automated security processes in the learning management system "Moodle". This proxy server demonstrates the feasibility of stated concepts and enables outsourcing of security-related tasks, i.e., automate such processes without further user interaction. Although the current prototype shows the feasibility of applying and implementing stated design criteria, further research is necessary to firm up relevant criteria for necessary parts of a learning environment integrating e-learning.

New e-learning environments
for teaching and learning Science

Zdena Lustigova[1] and Frantisek Lustig[2]
[1]Charles University, Faculty of Mathematics and Physics,
Laboratory of Online Learning, Prague, V Holesovickach 4,
CZ-180 00 Praha 8, Czech Republic
lustigo@plk.mff.cuni.cz
[2]Charles University, Faculty of Mathematics and Physics,
Prague, Ke Karlovu 3, CZ-121 16 Praha 2, Czech Republic
fl@plk.mff.cuni.cz

Summary

Online learning is developing along the lines of integrated learning and combining multiple approaches; but until now, it has very rarely included virtual and remote experimental environments to form a unified body of information and knowledge.

With progress in information technologies, the chance to handle real objects by application of remote and virtual experiments across the Internet has emerged. This chapter will describe how a scientifically exact and problem-solving-oriented remote and virtual science experimental environment might help to build a new strategy for blended science education. The main features of the new strategy are (1) the observations and control of real world phenomena, possibly materialized in data and their processing and evaluation, (2) verification of hypotheses combined with the development of critical thinking, supported by (3) highly sophisticated relevant information search, classification and storing tools and (4) cooperative teamwork, public presentations and the defense of achieved results, all either in real presence or in telepresence. Only then can real understanding of the mathematical formalism of generalized science laws and their consequences be developed.

This blended learning environment, developed by Charles University in Prague, used since 2003, has been offered mainly 1/ to in-service science teachers within the frame of "State Information Policy in Education Program" (2002-2005, app. 500 in service teachers), and to science and ICT teachers within the frame of "New Ways to Science Education" Project (2006-2008, app. 350 teachers).

Please use the following format when citing this chapter:

Lustigova, Z. and Lustig, F., 2008, in IFIP International Federation for Information Processing, Volume 281; *Learning to Live in the Knowledge Society*; Michael Kendall and Brian Samways; (Boston: Springer), pp. 363–364.

Although remote and open laboratory use is frequently put forward as a new way of working, the management of complexity, uncertainty, and communication in science education and research, and integrating selected parts of ROL - the remote data acquisition, data processing and process control theme across the curriculum- is not a completely seamless process. That is why the Remote and Open laboratory is offered to students in a parallel way to traditional labs. Mostly students with part or full time jobs, distance students, in-service teachers and both faculty members and students involved in professional training and life long learning use these facilities. Some numbers are presented in Table No. 1.

Table No. 1

Total Number of completed experiments data downloads – selected examples (since February 2004 till February 2008)						
Water level control	Meteor-ology station	Elmg induction	Natural and driven oscillations	Solar energy conversion	Diffraction on microobjects	Σ
3573	2401	2748	1282	1515	862	12 381

Building Virtual Communities
and Virtual Teams of Science teachers
– the case of Telmae

Zdena Lustigova
Charles University, Faculty of Mathematics and Physics,
Laboratory of Online Learning,
Prague, V Holesovickach 4,
CZ-180 00 Praha 8, Czech Republic
lustigo@plk.mff.cuni.cz

Summary

As an example of national and international effort on this field, and concrete model of solution, the author presents TELMAE Virtual Community Environment (VCE) and Learning Object Repository (LOR), developed at Faculty of Mathematics and Physics, Charles University in Prague, for interactive online support of science education and educators. The virtual community of teachers was built mainly within the frame of "State Information Policy in Education Program" (2002-2005) when app. 500 physic teachers participated, and within "New Ways to Science Education" project (2006-2008, app. 350 participants).

In the meaning time Telmae LOR and virtual learning environment serves to large number of in-service teachers (physics, science) as both, formal and informal, supportive environment for their professional development.

The Telmae virtual learning environment and community space (http://telmae.eu) consists of (1) gateway to Telmae online courses and other online interactive educational sources, (2) learning object repository LOR EDUPORT and (3) SCORM based "unified gateway" to the large variety of learning objects at all Czech universities, participating in the project. The learning environment is surrounded by (4) virtual community of active subscribers and consultants, discussion forums and special interest groups, easy accessible by synchronous and asynchronous communications tools. We also offer (5) special consultancy services, called "Active teachers' online support" (ATOS) and (6) interactive environment, including remote and virtual laboratories, for physics teachers (Telmae Remote and Open Laboratory – ROL).

Please use the following format when citing this chapter:

Lustigova, Z., 2008, in IFIP International Federation for Information Processing, Volume 281; *Learning to Live in the Knowledge Society*; Michael Kendall and Brian Samways; (Boston: Springer), pp. 365–366.

As part of the development we are constantly evaluating it and are including users feedback into its improvements. Generally, users' responses are positive and are improving over the years as the technology becomes more available and the teachers get more experienced in using it. Although students are quite often aware of the limitations of the remote access to learning resources like remote labs and online courses they also value their advantages in case of Telmae:1/ validity, 2/ reliability 3/easy access, 4/ simple and comfortable operating and control and 5/readiness for school practice. From social and psychological point of view they appreciate mostly virtual consultancy support and the potential for building virtual teams (to lose the feeling of the "loneliness in the cyber space").

The key advantages and limitations of this solution for the support of interdisciplinary approach to science education, team work, problem and inquiry based learning activities, and the real benefit for virtual learning community of teachers, arising from the creative background of Telmae supportive learning environment, are discussed in many research studies, authors and developers published in last 5 years.

Data Communications Laboratory as a Core Element for Modern Education

Tomáš Zeman, Jaromír Hrad, Jakub Slíva and Jiří Hájek
Czech Technical University in Prague, Faculty of Electrical Engineering,
Department of Telecommunication Engineering
Technická 2, CZ-166 27 Praha 6, Czech Republic
{zeman,hrad,slivaj1,hajekj3}@fel.cvut.cz, http://www.comtel.cz

Summary

The present education in the area of data communications brings one substantial pedagogical dilemma. The given area is purely technical one. Its education inherently includes the contact with teachers during lectures, theoretical seminars, simulations of various processes, real measurements and analyses in a laboratory. Therefore the popular e-learning approaches cannot be fully utilized since that could possibly prevent students' access to laboratory measurements. On the other hand, preserving of fully contact education would be a drawback, perceived negatively by students as well as their teachers.

We were looking for a way to prepare a modern curriculum for education in data communications and we decided for a procedure based on a project of a new Data Communications Laboratory that should become a core element in the modernized pedagogical process.

Modern education clearly requires the following formal components in order to satisfy the needs of all involved parties: data warehouse for storage of lectures (pre-recorded audiovisual materials) for flexible use at any time, consulting lectures to clarify difficult parts of the pre-recorded materials, simulations of procedures in data communications supporting remote access and control, workplace for configuration of data communications devices supporting remote access and control, laboratory equipment and workplaces with flexibly scheduled access, set of laboratory tasks, portal for processing of laboratory reports (results, simulations) and testing, including a suitable communication interface, electronic library of supporting materials (textbooks, articles, slides, etc.), control workplace for teachers, research unit for the further development of the respective area.

Please use the following format when citing this chapter:

Zeman, T., Hrad, J., Slíva, J. and Hájek, J., 2008, in IFIP International Federation for Information Processing, Volume 281; *Learning to Live in the Knowledge Society*; Michael Kendall and Brian Samways; (Boston: Springer), pp. 367–368.

Our team has proposed a methodology for education that takes into consideration the implementation of all the above-listed components, forming a compact system. Its technological core is the newly designed Data Communications Laboratory.

The essential requirement for education at a modern university is the independence of the students from any specific time for lessons. This condition determines the need to use a wide spectrum of various distance education forms, especially e-learning ones. This is, however, complicated by the necessity to provide practical education that must be performed in a laboratory. Nevertheless, even such type of education can be optimized for the students in the terms of its proper time scheduling. The solution consists in flexible selection of free time slots in the laboratory that are reserved by the students well in advance or just before the respective measurement.

In the optimized curriculum, the lectures will be pre-recorded and available to students as streamed media from the data warehouse. This way will be used for routine chapters that do not require extensive explanation. More complex topics will be discussed at the scheduled special seminars and/or lectures.

The principal advantage of this solution is that the respective activities are not strictly bound with one specific time (except the advanced lectures). There are defined relatively wide time windows (providing sufficient reserve for a subject covered by two hours of lectures and two hours of exercises weekly) respecting the individual pace of study as well as time possibilities of all students.

It is important to mention the laboratory exercises. While the configuration and simulation tasks (as well as the processing of the project) are performed individually, the laboratory work is a team one. The measuring team consists of three students at most so that the individuality is not suppressed. The composition of the teams may change for every measurement tasks out of the four (in the case of our example) – students choose a suitable (and available) time window, without knowing the partners or having a chance to influence their choice. Thanks to this principle, students learn to collaborate within a heterogeneous group.

The present project shows that the modern concept of education cannot be simplified just to e-learning; our attention must be paid to all different aspects of education.

Towards an intelligent tool based on Concept Maps for an Automated Meaningful Learning

Lorenzo Moreno[1], Evelio J. González[1], Beatrice Popescu[1], José D. Piñeiro[1]
and Claudia L. Oliveira Groenwald[2]
[1] Dpto. Ingeniería de Sistemas y Automática y Arquitectura y Tecnología
de Computadores. Universidad de La Laguna, CP 38207.
Tenerife, Spain, lmoreno@ull.es
[2] Faculdade de Matemática, Universidade Luterana do Brasil

Summary

The goal of this work is the development of an intelligent tool that would help teachers and students in order to improve the learning process, making use of a variation of the concept map paradigm. The authors propose a novelty in their use for determining the actual student status, that is, what a student currently knows, which concepts a student needs to revise, etc.

The proposed tool describes the subject to learn from an evolution of conceptual maps, called Pedagogical Concept Instructional Graph (PCIG), generated by the teacher. A PCIG does not order the concepts following arbitrary relationships among them as in the case of a general concept map, but the concepts are placed depending on the logical order in which they are presented to the student. After that, the expert system makes use of an adaptive test, generating several questions that deal with those concepts included in the PCIG.

From each student's answers, it can be obtained a personalized PCIG describing what the student knows a priori about the subject to learn. Comparing both models the expert system will determine a learning path, based in cases and personalized for groups of students presenting similar characteristics.

There are two points of view in order to implement the proposed tool: the learner that must pass the tests and view the contents related to some concepts and the teacher that creates the concepts, the test questions, the contents, defines works and assigns them to the learners.

- The entry point is a PCIG describing the relations between the concepts. An edge [concept1, concept2] denotes that concept1

Please use the following format when citing this chapter:

Moreno, L., González, E.J., Popescu, B., Piñeiro, J.D. and Groenwald, C.L.O., 2008, in IFIP International Federation for Information Processing, Volume 281; *Learning to Live in the Knowledge Society;* Michael Kendall and Brian Samways; (Boston: Springer), pp. 369–370.

depends on concept2, thus a learner couldn't know concept1 without knowing concept2.

- The teacher should create the questions specifying those parameters found in each Bayesian-type networks, since the adaptive tests have been implemented following that approach.

- Definition of the *initial concepts* that the learner should already know from previous completed works and the *objective concepts* (those that the learner should take and pass a test in order to complete the task).

- Tracking the state of each learner by the teacher.

- Create contents related to each concept.

- A student can only choose those concepts that he has not already passed, and do not depend on not-passed concepts.

The proposed tool has been implemented as a web-based application written in Java tested for Tomcat application server and using a MySQL database. A test algorithm is defined and implementations for the following actions are provided. First, the way the next question is chosen from the list of available questions. The available questions are questions related to the currently testing concept and that is not related to concepts that the learner hasn't passed yet. The way the points obtained modify if he responded correctly or not at the previous question when the test stops. Currently this is implemented using an ANTLR parser and in code using the Bayesian algorithm and it is being validated with real users, in particular, in the field of Maths in secondary education. This validation will allow the teachers to carry out a realistic and personalized teaching planning, based on meaningful learning. For the inclusion of mathematical formulae, the tool includes DragMath Editor for MathML.

References

1. Novak, J.D. Clarify with concept maps: A tool for students and teachers alike. The Science Teacher. 1991, 58(7), 45-49.
2. Michael J. In pursuit of meaningful learning. Adv. Physiol. Educ. 2001, 25: 145–158.

Multilanguage e-Learning Course for Industrial Automation

Jaromír Hrad, Tomáš Zeman and Jiří Hájek
Czech Technical University in Prague, Faculty of Electrical Engineering,
Department of Telecommunication Engineering
Technická 2, CZ-166 27 Praha 6, Czech Republic
{hrad,zeman,hajekj3}@fel.cvut.cz, http://www.comtel.cz

Summary

Compared to traditional forms of education, we can find many advantages for increasing the qualification with the help of interactive e-learning courses. Let us mention for example lower training costs, almost unlimited capacities (concerning the number of students taking the course simultaneously) and the possibility to return (even repeatedly) to already studied topics. The e-learning methods also bring opportunity to choose the most appropriate pace of training.

The Leonardo da Vinci project ELefANTS (E-Learning for Acquiring New Types of Skills) that was concluded in the autumn 2007 had the main objective to help various groups of people (also the handicapped ones) to enter the labor market and increase their opportunities to be integrated into the work process.

The main contribution of the project consists in the development and evaluation of e-learning tools – two independent courses – that support the placement of people from the target groups in the job market. The first course, within its nine modules, provides an overview of working with a personal computer from the very beginning, explaining the fundamental concepts of networking, teleworking and Customer Relationship Management (CRM); the second one introduces the contemporary automation technology and its relation to teleinformatics. Let us briefly introduce the latter.

Besides the topic, the most important detail is that the entire course is available in 7 different languages (English, French, German, Czech, Slovak, Polish and Slovenian), which (together with the multilingual multimedia dictionary that is also available online) dramatically increases its usability and opens a new dimension that helps to overcome barriers in the united Europe; the trainees get access to a reference material containing large volume of special terminology, facilitating not only their professional growth, but also the improvement of their language skills.

Please use the following format when citing this chapter:

Hrad, J., Zeman, T. and Hájek, J., 2008, in IFIP International Federation for Information Processing, Volume 281; *Learning to Live in the Knowledge Society*; Michael Kendall and Brian Samways; (Boston: Springer), pp. 371–372.

The course can be visited online at "http://elefants.cvut.cz/", currently still free of charge. The necessary equipment of the prospective users is as simple as a common personal computer with Internet browser (and network connection, of course). The visitor can register for the course and choose a login name and password. After receiving the confirmation of registration by e-mail the study may begin.

The course is divided into the following modules covering the areas of industrial automation and teleinformatics: Automation, its Scope and Importance; Control Systems; Digital Telecommunication Networks, Radio and Satellite Communications, GSM, NGN; Fundamentals of Design Using PLC; Logical Systems; Digital Systems, Controllers and Filters; Simulation and Modelling of Real Processes; Rudiments of Fuzzy Logic Summary; Artificial Intelligence in Automation; Reliability in Technical Systems; Recent Trends and Expectations in Control Systems. The thematic relations among the individual modules are relatively loose, which means that no specific order of study is required.

We have also prepared a project for further development of the courses. Specifically, we plan to increase the number of available languages, emphasizing the European dimension, and to employ more interactive elements, such as animations, simulations and self-evaluation tests. We hope that such changes will greatly improve the usability and attractiveness of the products for their final recipients. The results should be available in the autumn 2009.